God's Plan

-Simplified

Group Discussion Guide Included

From the author:

I have worked on this book for the past 5 years because I was called to fill a need. I have never been to seminary school, and I have no formal Bible education. I do, however, have a deep enthusiasm for learning, and my gift has always been teaching. My emphasis in education has always been to both learn and teach the whole truth, even if it stretches beyond the comfort zone. My goal is not to indoctrinate you into a particular denomination or standardized belief system – it is to help you understand why you believe what you believe, just as I have learned why I believe what I now believe. I expect you may have some surprises reading this book, and like me, you may have to face some mental and spiritual reckonings. If you are reading this, I believe God has put it before you for a reason. He has work for all of us to do, and He will supply what you need to do the job He calls you to do. I have repeatedly witnessed His hand guiding this work.

In this book, the truths He has given to us are presented in a progressive Q&A format following a spiral learning structure in which each answer builds on knowledge gained from earlier answers. This structure was dictated by the nature of the Bible itself, with its complexly interwoven reports, stories, and letters. Because of this, the book should be read in order for maximum clarity. Please consult original language Scripture and various reliable translations on your own and decide for yourself what you believe. Always take the time to thoroughly study a position before claiming it as your own, and never assume that a teaching is true simply because you've been hearing it for many years. You will see as you read that God's sincere hope is, if we disagree on a particular teaching, we do not let our interpretations divide us. Not one of us has all the answers, but we can all learn and teach together.

Stormy Stouder

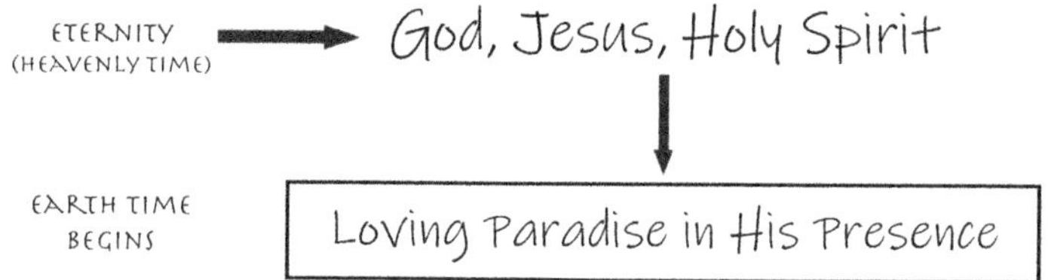

Satan's jealous act - The Betrayal - Need for restoration

Noah passes thru door & cleansing water to new life

Abram/Abraham chosen to begin the Israelite nation

Egypt enslaves growing Israelite nation

Moses leads Israelites thru door & cleansing water to new life

Feast days given by God

Jonah, a sign for the Door, passes thru cleansing water to new life

Jesus' First Coming - Door and cleansing water open to all

Apostles begin work to lead all to Door and cleansing water

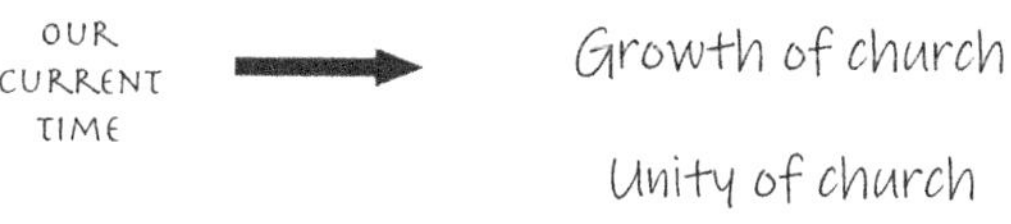

Unity of church

Jesus' Second Coming - Door closes

Full restoration is accomplished

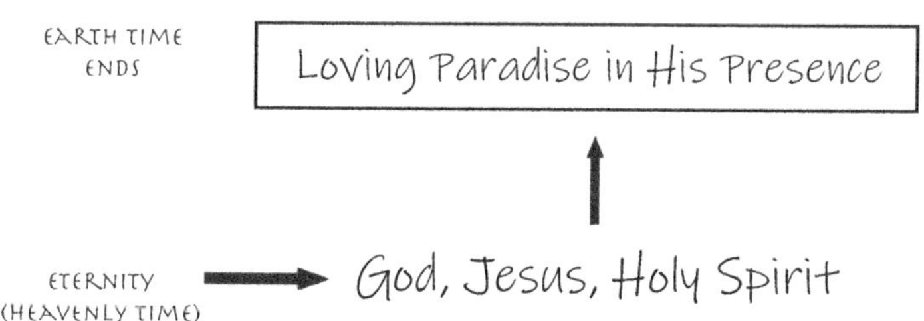

God's Plan Simplified
eBook ISBN: 978-1-7371779-0-6
Paperback ISBN: 978-1-7371779-1-3
Printed in the United States of America

First published on May the Fourth,
for those who know and have A New Hope
May God's Force Be With You

Published by StouderHouse Books
a division of StouderHouse LLC
www.StouderHouse.com
www.StouderHouseBooks.com
www.GodsPlanSimplified.com

God's Plan

-Simplified

As for me and my house, we will serve the LORD.
Joshua 24:15b KJV

The meaning of life is to find your gift.

The purpose of life is to give it away.

-Pablo Picasso

Semper quaeritis

Latin for "Always seeking"

Our journeys to understand all God wants us to know should never stop. The reward for our faithfulness to Him will exceed any fantasy our limited human minds can imagine. We cannot understand everything, but if we keep seeking, God will continue to give us answers. He never ignores those who sincerely call on Him.

. . .Now we see God as if we are looking at a reflection in a mirror. But then, in the future,
we will see him right before our eyes. Now I know only a part, but at that time
I will know fully, as God has known me.

1 Corinthians 13:12b

Our earthly experiences have taught us:
Weakness is undesirable, only the strong survive.
When you're dead, you're gone – it's all over.
When you give something away, you no longer have it.
When you surrender, you lose.

When we look at God's Word through this mirror of earthly experience,
His truths seem at odds with what we think we know:
Weakness is reflected as strength.
Death is reflected as life.
Giving is reflected as receiving.
Surrender is reflected as victory.
These reflections will make sense when we can see them through His eyes.

"Continue to ask, and God will give to you. Continue to search, and you will find.
Continue to knock, and the door will open for you."

Matthew 7:7

All verses are quoted from the Easy to Read Version of the Bible, unless otherwise noted.
A Group Discussion Guide is included beginning on page 423.
A Reference Timeline is located at the beginning and the end.

God's Plan

- Simplified

For those who believe...

There is so much we can learn about God, so much to read and study. You may find the pursuit of Biblical knowledge rewarding, or you may find that trying to absorb all the information in the Bible is overwhelming, or confusing, or even unnecessary. You may prefer shorter, devotional-type books that break Bible topics down into smaller bites that are easier to apply to your everyday life. This book is something like that, with logically sequenced questions and answers intended to quickly and simply bring you to a much better understanding of His plan. Hopefully, it will make your path clearer by showing how some of the plentiful information in the Bible fits together and explains what God is doing. In the interest of simplicity, only some of the Bible stories will be used, but all of the many, many parts of His Story add to the evidence of God's plan.

For the unsure...

You've heard of God. You may even believe that He is out there somewhere. You just don't know how to go about understanding Him – how He works, what He thinks, what He wants from you. You may think that you aren't good enough for God, or you may be intimidated by the very idea of attending a church because "church people" seem to know what they're doing when it comes to God. On the other hand, you may have known church people who didn't seem like they were on the right path, and you may think churches are full of people who preach one standard but live by another. What you need to know is that at all of the churches, all of the people are imperfect – and deep down most of them know it, whether they are willing to admit it or not. Some of the people attending church are just going through the motions – doing it out of habit or guilt, or doing it to improve their image

– and not really growing in their knowledge or faith, but many of the people attending church are sincerely trying to learn more about God, His plan, and what He wants for them and from them.

For the disenchanted...

You may have been discouraged by the conflicts between modern science and the Bible – conflicts that modern science seems to have won, based on the content of our schools and media. Perhaps you've been confused and disappointed by what seem to be contradictory statements in the Bible. Maybe you've been ridiculed to the point of shame for believing in God's Word by someone who is influential in your life, or maybe someone you've long believed to be a godly person suddenly veered off the path and left you feeling betrayed and disillusioned. Some of you may have felt uneasy when you realized you were a part of a church family that views themselves as superior to members of other churches. If you feel your relationship with God and His Word has been wounded, our discussion aims to lead you to the Balm that can heal all wounds.

For all those who seek God...

Everyone who is seeking God is on the same journey – it's just that we're all at different places on that journey. Each of us will take our own paths on that journey, so no two trips look the same even though we're all trying to reach the same destination – The Happy End. Moving forward in our own journeys is good and right. We know this because God is always moving forward, working toward the completion of His plan. He does not turn back in His journey, so you should not turn back in yours. Keep moving forward.

Keep seeking Him.

****

Understanding God's plan is simple.
He has one theme – Love.
He has one desire – Family.
He has one plan – Freedom.
If you are being tossed about on the sea of loneliness,
the sea of confusion, the sea of depression, the sea of defeat,
the sea of searching, the sea of waiting –
wherever you are, He has thrown you a lifesaver –
a circle of love, family, and freedom.
If you will accept it and hold fast to it,
He will tow you to safety.

He will take you to the place where there is no more sea.
He will take you to The Happy End.

****

In the Bible, the sea represents chaos. God has dominion over the sea,
as He demonstrates throughout the Bible.

When He demonstrates this, He is showing us that He has the power
to turn the chaos and stress of this imperfect world into perfect order and peace.

Before we begin, what is the framework for this discussion?

If you first need some proof that God exists, consider the following:

Do you believe the universe exists?

Do you trust the proven laws of science (as opposed to the unproven theories)?

- Hubble's Law tells us that **the universe** is expanding – meaning it was smaller in the past – it **had a beginning point** (this is where the Big Bang Theory originated).

Something existed before our universe.

- The first law of thermodynamics is the law of conservation of energy:
  Energy cannot be created or destroyed.
  In other words, **something cannot come from nothing**.

Something was the source for our universe.

What is the something that existed before our universe and was the source for our universe? Certainly, it must be a life force infinitely more developed than humans. Considering the extreme vastness combined with the intensely microscopic detail of our universe, surely it was created for a reason. Proof, in a courtroom today, is 'beyond reasonable doubt.' How much evidence is enough for you?

While recognizing and appreciating that everyone who participates in this discussion comes to the table with his/her own unique background, the purpose of this book is not to prove the existence of God.

Our discussion will proceed on the basis that God existed before our universe, and that He created our universe with purpose. Because of this, we are also going to proceed on the principle that the Bible only exists because God exists.

Review: God existed before our universe. He created our world with a plan. His Bible tells us His plan.

How can we know for sure that God has a plan?

The format of the Bible doesn't provide a clear, Roman numeral outline of God's plan, but the answer to this question will become more apparent as our discussion progresses and we take a look deep into the past. Before we get started, let's imagine a present-day commentary on the Jewish religion vs. the Christian faith from one possible Christian point of view for just a moment. This may begin to help us understand why we have such different perspectives today and why so many of us don't fully recognize His plan.

If you have no idea what is meant by some of these words, please be patient. We will explain them all in the course of our discussion.

Jews and Christians all believe in the same God, but the Jewish religion seems very different from the Christian faith. The Jewish people only believe in the Old Testament portion of the Bible with the "old God" and all of His many rules. They observe numerous religious customs, and every year they celebrate solemn feast days with ancient Hebrew names. They remember Pesach in the spring and eat matzah for Chag HaMatzot – which includes Yom HaBikkurim. In summer, they celebrate Shavuot. Then there are the fall feast days of Yom Teruah and Yom Kippur followed by Sukkot. Each feast has particular traditions, ceremonies, and requirements. There are many rules a faithful Jew must follow.

A modern Christian might shake his head and wonder, "Don't the Jews know that all of their Old Testament customs and feast days are pointless? Don't they know that Jesus has come and none of that really matters anymore? Christians have it so much easier! We basically just have Easter and Christmas, and those are fun, upbeat holidays, what with all the egg hunts and presents. We don't need all of the rules and harsh judgments of the Old Testament anymore. All of that is finished. Jesus is the loving, forgiving Lord of the New Testament portion of the Bible, and He has made it all so easy for us."

You may have heard comments similar to these before. You may agree with this point of view, or at least part of it. Now, let's look at why this perspective needs to change. . .

Those strange-sounding feast days the Jewish people carried on with such determination through centuries of hardships are the very reason both the Jews and the Christians can be absolutely certain God has a plan. Those special feast days God instructed the Jews to keep in His Old Testament list of rules are the foundation on which His New Testament house of love and forgiveness is built. God's plan begins on page one of the Old Testament and extends through to the last page of the New Testament – in other words, the whole Bible, from the very beginning to the very end, tells us about God's plan. Once we understand and accept this, we can see that the depictions of the judgmental Old Testament God and the forgiving New Testament Jesus aren't exactly correct.

Now a short rebuttal from the Jewish side. . .

A Jewish person might say, "Jesus may have been a great man, but He wasn't the Savior, the Messiah, we were waiting for. We are still waiting." (In other words, the Old Testament list of rules is still in effect, and the New Testament section of the Bible isn't valid.)

Jewish people are waiting for the Savior God promised to send. Christians believe Jesus Christ was that Savior.

The Jewish religion and the Christian faith of today are very different from what they were 2,000 years ago in Jesus' time. Looking at the **original** feast days – not simply how they appear today, or even how they were celebrated 2,000 years ago – will show that the Savior did, in fact, come, and that even the oldest intelligence provided for us in the Bible is still important in explaining God's plan.

And, finally, a Christian dismissal of the oldest parts of the Bible. . .

"Well," a Christian might say, "those old stories and celebrations don't really matter. I already believe in Jesus, and my faith is rock-solid."

If your faith is a rock, Satan, who is our enemy because he is the enemy of God, has a hammer and chisel. He is constantly trying to chip away at your faith and break it down.

1 Corinthians 10:12

So anyone who thinks they are standing strong should be careful that they don't fall.

The only hope you have of keeping your rock of faith strong is to feed it. By adding to your knowledge about God and His plan, you add to your faith. You strengthen your rock so that it dulls Satan's chisel.

This is a battle you do not want to lose.

You might hear someone say, "God has a plan for everything." You may even agree. A Christian might add, "Jesus is the plan," or, "Jesus is all we need." You may agree with this, too. But how can you be sure you know WHY you agree with these statements? By knowing what Jesus has to do with those ancient Jewish feast days, by knowing how the Bible stories work together to explain God's plan, and by knowing what you need to do to be right with God, you can be absolutely certain you know what God's plan is and why Jesus is all you need.

Trying to sum up His plan in a few hundred pages may very well be a crazy idea. What would be the point of cramming all of the details into this book – if it were even possible? If you want to know all of the details, read the Bible, right? Agreed. This book is more like a summary that reviews but also examines some stories you may already be familiar with to show how they link to those Jewish feast days (and why we should care), and to explain how we can know what we need to do today as members of God's assembly, as members of His church, as believers in Him. If we can begin to see how everything God created and planned ties together, we can be more in tune with what God wants us to do and have a better idea of what He has in store for us.

Today's Jews and Christians can help each other understand God's plan. When we truly understand God's plan, we can see that all of the Jews and all of the Christians should be one united group of believers. Only in our unity do we fully reflect the truth, honor, and glory that we are made in His image.

Romans 15:5-9a

All patience and encouragement come from God. And I pray that God will help you all agree with each other, as Christ Jesus wants. Then you will all be joined together. And all together you will give glory to God the Father of our Lord Jesus Christ. Christ accepted you, so you should accept each other. This will bring honor to God. I tell you that Christ became a servant of the Jews to show that God has done what he promised their great ancestors. Christ also did this so that the non-Jewish people could praise God for the mercy he gives to them.

Review: Open your heart and mind to the idea of unity in God.
The more we gather in unity, the more we reflect the image of God.
In unity, we can more clearly see His plan.
The whole Bible tells the whole Truth.

Where should we begin?

We are all familiar with the idea of placing events in history on a timeline to help us better understand the unfolding of the story. If we start at the beginning and follow the events in the order of time, the story will make more sense. Looking at a particular segment of history, the timeline seems to be a straight line. This is because we are zoomed in on a short period of time. When we zoom out and look at the entire history of humankind, we discover it isn't a long line stretched out from left to right. The history of humankind is going in a big circle that begins and ends with – and is guided along by – God and His plan for us.

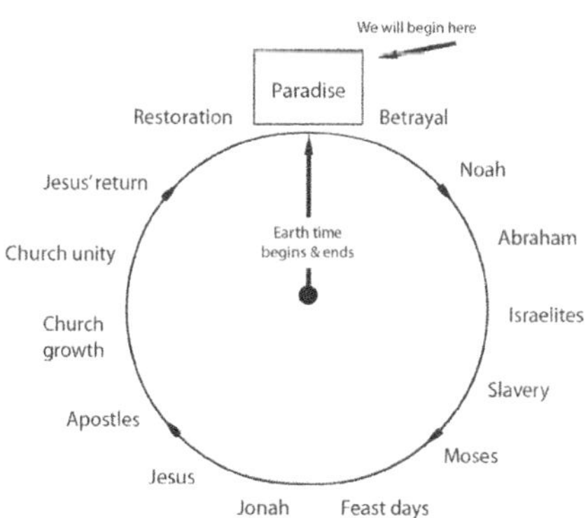

Our discussion will start at the beginning of the timeline (even though it is a circle, there is a beginning point) and follow through some of the major events recorded in the Bible. There are a number of questions that will take a good bit of discussion to answer because some parts of His Bible are only truly accessible if you are willing to search out the original languages, but the goal of this book is to show just how simple God's plan is when we focus solely on His plan as He told it to us. God's facts, His truths, are clear and logical – His stories are easy to understand. We will begin at the beginning and lay our foundation well, because God is bringing us back around for a second beginning. That new beginning is the best part, and it begins when we reach The Happy End of this journey.

Revelation 22:13

"I am the Alpha and the Omega, the First and the Last, the Beginning and the End."

Isaiah 46:10a

"In the beginning, I told you what would happen in the end. A long time ago, I told you things that have not happened yet. When I plan something, it happens."

Review: God's Bible tells us His plan from beginning to end.
The end is a new, and better, beginning.

What's the first step to understanding God?

Believe that He exists. Knowledge and confidence that God is in control and that what He tells us in His Bible is true is a comfort and joy He has asked us to share with everyone. We are sharing security, love, and happiness, and we are strengthening each other and building each other up with hope for a bright future. God has proven over and over again He is real and His words are true.

Psalm 19:7a

The LORD's teachings are perfect.

Proverbs 30:5

You can trust this: Every word that God speaks is true. God is a safe place for those who go to him.

Some people believe the oldest stories in the Bible are just that – stories – that they aren't true. Some historians have even put forth the idea that the oldest Bible stories weren't written by the people we think they were, that the authors of those stories got their ideas from older myths, such as the stories of the Egyptian gods or the wanderings of Odysseus. These skeptical historians and others who agree with them would like to convince us that the Bible stories are just like all the other old myths – that they aren't true.

Some churches today will not even discuss the earliest stories of the Bible due to this historicity controversy combined with the modern scientific teachings of evolution and carbon dating. We will address the argument of science vs. the Bible briefly in the extra Q&A's at the end of the book, but that debate is not our primary purpose. We can summarize the results of it here, though, because the entire discussion boils down to two basic schools of thought: either you believe that our world is the result of an accident (Big Bang theory and/or random evolution/mutation theory), or you believe there was an intelligent Creator with a purpose. Sift that down a bit further – you choose to believe in chaos, or you choose to believe in order. The purpose of our discussion is to begin to show just how much order God has provided for us.

1 Corinthians 2:14
People who do not have God's Spirit do not accept the things that come from his Spirit. They think these things are foolish. They cannot understand them, because they can only be understood with the Spirit's help.

Many ancient myths have been carefully preserved in museums. Sometimes there is one copy of a myth, legend, or tale, and sometimes there are several. Historians get very excited when they find more than one copy of an ancient tale, because the clues provided by each copy, the differences between the copies, or the details about where each copy was found help them learn more about the writer or writers of the story and the circumstances of the time or place in which the writer lived. Finding more than one copy adds to the credibility of the story as well as its author.

In the case of the Bible, there are literally thousands of copies of ancient Scripture written over a period of 1,500 or more years on three different continents that have been preserved – and there are no measurable differences between the various copies. Many of the more modern verses in the Bible quote from and confirm the accuracy of the more ancient verses. The reason these stories all agree in such specific detail is that, although humans did the physical writing, God is the author of them all. He has made sure His people have more than enough information to be certain He is real, His stories are real, and He can be trusted.

2 Peter 1:20-21

Most important of all, you must understand this: No prophecy in the Scriptures comes from the prophet's own understanding. No prophecy ever came from what some person wanted to say. But people were led by the Holy Spirit and spoke words from God.

Scientists, archaeologists, and historians have discovered many facts over the years, but not one of these discoveries has ever proved that anything in the Bible is false. On the contrary, many of the discoveries they have made – and continue to make – actually prove the facts, locations, people, and events in the Bible to be true. Some Biblical scholars as well as average Christians speak or write about these findings to defend their faith. This practice is called Apologetics, from the Greek word **apologia**, which means to give reasons, justification, or defense for your ideas, beliefs, or actions. Here are some examples:

FACT: If you remember your grade-school history, you know that in the late 1400's, Christopher Columbus was revolutionary in thinking the earth was round. His sailors were afraid they were going to sail off the edge of the flat earth. One very old verse in the Bible told us thousands of years beforehand that the earth is indeed round.

Isaiah 40:21b-22

Surely you understand who made the earth. It is the Lord who sits above the circle of the earth.

LOCATION: Over time, some cities or places disappear or change names, but archaeologists make discoveries all the time that confirm what the Bible tells us. In the 1800's, archaeologists found a pool described in the Bible as a site where Jesus healed a lame man. The site was further excavated in the mid-1900's. Prior to its discovery, there had been no archaeological evidence that the pool described in the Bible ever existed.

John 5:1-2

Later, Jesus went to Jerusalem for a special Jewish festival [feast day]. In Jerusalem there is a pool with five covered porches. In Aramaic it is called Bethzatha (Also called Bethsaida or Bethesda, a pool of water north of the Temple in Jerusalem). This pool is near the Sheep Gate.

PEOPLE: In the early 1990's, an ancient slab with engraving dated to approximately 900 BC was found in Tel Dan, Israel. The engraving tells the story of a war victory and mentions the king of Israel and the king of the house of David, verifying, among other facts, the Bible's report of a line of kings beginning with David that would rule forever.

2 Samuel 7:12b-14a (God speaking to King David through the prophet Nathan about David's descendant, Jesus)
I will make one of your own children become the king. He will build a house for my name, and I will make his kingdom strong forever. I will be his father, and he will be my son.

EVENT: An archaeological find in the late 1930's consisted of pottery with writing carved on it that told of the last days of the Jewish people's struggle before they were conquered by Babylon. This was the first evidence found of what the Bible tells us about the Jewish nation being carried off to Babylon as captives of war.

2 Kings 24:10,14
At that time the officers of King Nebuchadnezzar of Babylon came to Jerusalem and surrounded it. Nebuchadnezzar captured all the people of Jerusalem, including the leaders and other wealthy people. He took 10,000 people and made them prisoners. He took all the skilled workers and craftsmen. No one was left, except the poorest of the common people.

The Bible is a collection of individual books that are divided into two main sections called testaments. The books are full of stories, directions, reports, histories, prophecies, and advice that all tie neatly together. For each quote used to support an answer in our discussion, the Bible book and where it can be found in that book are listed. In Bible lingo, each quote is cited with book (name), chapter (number), and verse (number).

These are just a few examples of the countless scientific, archaeological, and historical findings that lend credibility to the Bible stories and give apologists material for their arguments. You can find more using internet searches – see the Discussion Guide at the end of the book for suggestions. In addition to all of the facts, locations, people, and events that have been verified by studies outside of the Bible, there are also hundreds of predictions made in the Bible that have come true. We will discuss several of those in the following pages, but those fulfilled prophecies provide enough material to write another whole book.

Some people object to believing in the old Bible stories that sound like make-believe children's stories. As humans, if we are trying to convince a crowd to believe what we tell them, we really sell it. We might back our story up with a variety of facts and data. We might have very educated people speak to crowds or endorse our story to increase its validity and acceptance. We aren't subtle – we are loud and flashy. We package our story in the most appealing and/or sophisticated way we possibly can. God doesn't work that way. He purposefully chooses the simple, the plain, the ordinary to do His work – and sometimes He makes His work look foolish. He tells us why in His Word:

1 Corinthians 1:27-29

But God chose the foolish things of the world to shame the wise. He chose the weak things of the world to shame the strong. And God chose what the world thinks is not important – what the world hates and thinks is nothing. He chose these to destroy what the world thinks is important. God did this so that no one can stand before him and boast about anything.

1 Corinthians 1:25

Even the foolishness of God is wiser than human wisdom. Even the weakness of God is stronger than human strength.

1 Corinthians 1:19-21

As the Scriptures say, "I will destroy the wisdom of the wise. I will confuse the understanding of the intelligent." So what does this say about the philosopher, the law expert, or anyone in this world who is skilled in making clever arguments? God has made the wisdom of the world look foolish. This is what God in his wisdom decided: Since the world did not find him through its own wisdom, he used the message that sounds foolish to save those who believe it.

If you select any one of those "simple" stories and study to see how it fits into the overall picture of the Bible, you will find that those childish-sounding stories hold vast spiritual truths that are woven together with truths from other Bible stories in a deeply intricate, multi-dimensional design.

God has given us proof after proof. We just have to decide to accept it and believe in Him. Once we believe He is real, He will help us learn what we need to know. Believing in a God you cannot see requires trust – it requires faith, but He has provided plenty of evidence that He exists in the things we <u>can</u> see.

Romans 1:20a

There are things about God that people cannot see – his eternal power and all that makes him God. But since the beginning of the world, those things have been easy for people to understand. They are made clear in what God has made.

Jesus, whose truth will also be discussed in the following pages, was born thousands of years after the earliest stories in the Bible, and He repeatedly confirmed the accuracy of those ancient stories. Both the Jews and the Christians accept the existence of Jesus as a man, and, until modern times, both accepted those ancient Bible stories as truths. After Jesus' death, some of His followers were spreading His story. They were stopped and brought before a Jewish religious council to be questioned. One of the councilmen, a well-respected man named Gamaliel, wisely advised the other councilmen:

"Men of Israel, be careful of what you are planning to do to these men.
Remember when Theudas appeared?
He said he was an important man, and about 400 men joined him.
But he was killed, and all who followed him were scattered and ran away.
They were not able to do anything. Later, during the time of the census,
a man named Judas came from Galilee. Many people joined his group,
but he was also killed, and all his followers were scattered.
And so now I tell you, stay away from these men. Leave them alone.
If their plan is something they thought up, it will fail.
But if it is from God, you will not be able to stop them.

You might even be fighting against God himself!"

Acts 5:35b-39a

The stories of the Bible have persisted since the beginning of human history because they are true and they are from God Himself. The stories are how God speaks to us, and if He is speaking, we should be listening. Thinking that any of the Bible stories are untrue can seriously limit our understanding of God's plan. Imagine that each of the stories is a puzzle piece. . .we can get some understanding of what the puzzle's picture is without all the pieces, but the more pieces we have in place, the clearer the picture.

The Bible says there is nothing new in this life here on earth. The things that happen today are the same types of things that have happened since the beginning of time. Humans behave in the same ways they always have, and we can use that knowledge to learn from those stories of old. Because our basic human nature hasn't changed, we can understand how we fit into God's plan – what our purpose is – and how we can achieve our purpose by studying these old stories.

Ecclesiastes 1:9

All things continue the way they have been since the beginning. The same things will be done that have always been done. There is nothing new in this life.

Romans 15:4 (Notice the first word - everything - not part, but all)

Everything that was written in the past was written to teach us. Those things were written so that we could have hope. That hope comes from the patience and encouragement that the Scriptures give us.

He has made it easy for us to understand the things we need to know, and this should bring us comfort and peace as we put more pieces of the puzzle in place and grow in understanding. That growth of understanding is what our God-seeking journeys are all about – we are trying to learn how God works in our lives, and what He wants from us. When we begin looking for Him, He helps us find a way to reach Him.

Matthew 11:28-30 (For those who trust, it is easy)

"Come to me all of you who are tired from the heavy burden you have been forced to carry. I will give you rest. Accept my teaching. Learn from me. I am gentle and humble in spirit. And you will be able to get some rest. Yes, the teaching that I ask you to accept is easy. The load I give you to carry is light."

The Bible has hundreds of stories. Many of those stories show us how things on earth are related to things in heaven. It says the things of earth are a shadow of the things in heaven – they are similar to and help give us an idea of what is to come – which means we can understand the simple truths of God because He has given us truths in this earthly life that relate to truths in heaven. Knowing this will help us understand God's plan.

Hebrews 9:23a

These things are copies of the real things that are in heaven.

One basic earthly truth we can all understand is there should be a special relationship between a parent and a child. Children instinctively trust good parents who provide them with food, protection, love, and guidance. Good parents also make decisions for their children that are in the children's best interest and cheer their children on when they face difficult tasks. They help their children learn by correcting them when they make mistakes. Good parents expect their children to obey their commands. They love their children at all times – even when the children have disobeyed.

Although we may not all have personally experienced such a wonderful, loving relationship here on earth with our parents, we can still understand that this is the ideal. God gave us this knowledge so that we can understand our relationship to Him. Just like a good parent, God will meet our needs – but we must invite Him into our lives and, like a child, trust He will provide for us and guide us in the way we should go. We must learn to listen to Him and accept what He is teaching us.

2 Timothy 3:15b-16a

These Scriptures are able to make you wise. And that wisdom leads to salvation through faith in Christ Jesus. All Scripture is given by God. And all Scripture is useful for teaching. . .

1 Thessalonians 5:20-22
Don't treat prophecy like something that is not important. But test everything. Keep what is good, and stay away from everything that is evil.

John 8:32
"You will know the truth, and the truth will make you free."

Review: The Bible exists because of God.
All the words of the Bible are true and useful for people of every time.
There is nothing new in this earthly life. The simple truths of God are easy to understand because they relate to truths in this life that we can understand.
Turn toward God, and He will help you find a path to Him. Let Him guide you.

Who is God?

He is our parent. He created us. According to His Bible, we are made in His image. We bear a likeness to God just as we bear a likeness to our earthly parents. He provides life, security, and love, in the same way a good father and mother would for their children.

2 Corinthians 6:18 (from 2 Samuel 7:14, 7:8)
"I will be your father, and you will be my sons and daughters, says the Lord All-Powerful."

Matthew 6:8b
"Your Father knows what you need before you ask him."

Isaiah 66:13a
"I will comfort you like a mother comforting her child."

In Chapter 34 of the Bible book called Exodus, God describes Himself in five ways that are all desirable in a good parent. Translated from the original Hebrew in which they were written, those describing words are compassionate, merciful, slow to anger, and abundantly loving and trustworthy. Throughout the Bible, God refers to Himself often as our Father, but He also displays numerous motherly attributes. In fact, the Hebrew word that is translated as compassionate – which is the very first word God used to describe Himself in the Exodus verse above – comes from the same root word as womb. This word, **rachum**, is only used in the Bible when describing the compassion of God.

Truly, He is the ultimate parent. God acts as both a mother and a father to us. If we, as male and female, are made in His image, then He has all the traits of both.

People today often say an expectant mother is "nesting" when she begins to prepare the house for a new arrival. This earthly preparation is a shadow of what God did to prepare a home for the humans He created.

In the very beginning, when God created the heavens and the earth and all that is in them, He prepared a special place on the earth called the Garden of Eden as a home for His children. Eden was perfect – it was an earthly Paradise. The temperature was never too hot or too cold. Food, in the form of fruit, grew in plenty on a variety of trees God made to grow in the Garden. Wild animals would not attack or do harm. There were no storms or weather dangers. When He saw that everything was ready, He made the first two people – a man and a woman – Adam and Eve. God visited with them in their home. He walked with them and talked with them. Life was wonderful.

Genesis 1:27

So God created humans in his own image. He created them to be like himself. He created them male and female.

Genesis 2:8

Then the LORD God planted a garden in the East, in a place named Eden. He put the man he made in that garden.

Genesis 1:31a

God looked at everything he had made. And he saw that everything was very good.

God's original creation is very similar to the description of the place He is preparing for us to live in the future. He has told us He plans for us to live in Paradise. He has told us He plans to restore a close relationship with humans and be with His children in a much more physical way once again. He has told us some people are already in Paradise. While there is some minor debate about what, exactly, Paradise is (we will discuss that later), we do know for sure that it is in the presence of God. He wants us to personally know Him and to love Him as much as He loves us. God tells us He is kind, He is full of love for us, and He can be trusted. His desire to be with us is why He is still working toward the completion of His plan.

Malachi 2:10a

We all have the same father. The same God made every one of us.

Psalm 16:11

You will teach me the right way to live. Just being with you will bring complete happiness. Being at your right side will make me happy forever.

Revelation 2:7b

"To those who win the victory I will give the right to eat the fruit from the tree of life, which is in God's paradise."

Luke 23:43

Then Jesus said to him, "I promise you, today you will be with me in paradise."

Exodus 34:6b

"YAHWEH, the LORD, is a kind and merciful God. He is slow to become angry. He is full of great love. He can be trusted."

Review: God is the perfect parent. He created us in love.

He wants to have a close, loving relationship with us.
We can trust Him completely. He will take care of His children.

We don't live in Eden now. . .what happened?

God placed Adam and Eve in the Garden of Eden where they had everything they could ever need, and life was perfect. Perfect because all of the plants and animals and both of the humans – all the earthly creatures He had made – lived and thrived – as God intended – in His presence. Adam and Eve ate the grain from the plants and the fruit of the trees, and animals ate the plants and grass, not each other. All of God's earthly creations lived in peace and harmony with one another – united under His direct care.

Genesis 1:29-30

God said, "I am giving you all the grain bearing plants and all the fruit trees. These trees make fruit with seeds in it. This grain and fruit will be your food. And I am giving all the green plants to the animals. These green plants will be their food. Every animal on earth, every bird in the air, and all the little things that crawl on the earth will eat that food." And all these things happened.

God gave Adam one rule to follow. Humans were to eat from any of the many desirable trees in the Garden, but there were two trees that God specifically placed in the middle of the Garden that were significant. One was the tree of life, from which God wanted His people to eat, and from which He says we will eat again in Paradise. The other was the tree whose fruit would give them knowledge about good and evil. God told them that on the day they ate from that tree, they would die. So, there was a tree of life, and what was essentially a tree of death.

Genesis 2:9

Then the LORD God caused all the beautiful trees that were good for food to grow in the garden. In the middle of the garden, he put the tree of life and the tree that gives knowledge about good and evil.

Genesis 2:15-17

The LORD God put the man in the Garden of Eden to work the soil and take care of the garden. The LORD God gave him this command: "You may eat from any tree in the garden. But you must not eat from the tree that gives knowledge about good and evil. If you eat fruit from that tree, on that day you will certainly die!"

Why did God put that terrible tree of death in the Garden of Eden if He didn't want His people to eat from it? From the very beginning of our world, people have had to make a conscious decision to choose life – to choose to obey God. He longs for us to choose to listen to Him, to believe Him, to follow Him, to trust Him, to love Him. **God gives us freedom to choose because true love and trust cannot exist without freedom.** He wants our relationship with Him to be based on true love and trust. He IS faithfulness, He has set that example for us, and He desires faithfulness from us.

Everything was fine in the Garden of Eden for a time, but another of God's creations, an angel, became jealous and full of pride (the angels also have freedom to choose). That misbehaving angel, often called the Devil, or Satan, rose up against God. He lashed out at God by attacking the innocence of God's children and spoiling the perfection of His creation.

Satan tempted Eve by telling her a lie. He told her she would not die and she would become more like God if she ate the fruit God had told her not to eat. Satan tricked her into eating the forbidden fruit, then she convinced Adam to eat some as well. They each had a choice, and they each chose the wrong path. In breaking God's only rule, Adam and Eve violated God's trust in them – they betrayed Him – they sinned against Him.

John 8:44b (Jesus talking about Satan)

"He was a murderer from the beginning. He was always against the truth. There is no truth in him. He is like the lies he tells. Yes, the devil is a liar. He is the father of lies."

Genesis 3:4-5 (Satan posed as a snake when tempting Eve)

But the snake said to the woman, "You will not die. God knows that if you eat the fruit from that tree you will learn about good and evil, and then you will be like God!"

As it turned out, they didn't fall down dead after eating it, so what did God mean when He said they would die if they ate that fruit? Why did Jesus call Satan a murderer? Humans have a physical body as well as a soul and a spirit. The Bible tells us that the knowledge that one has sinned causes a spiritual death. Adam and Eve immediately knew they had sinned, so their spirits immediately died. Death did not exist in the Garden until sin was known by humans. Sin and death go hand in hand.

Romans 7:9-10a (Paul describing his own spiritual death once he understood sin)

Before I knew the law [before I had the knowledge to know what sin was], I was alive. But when I heard the law's command, sin began to live, and I died spiritually.

Romans 6:23a (Sin is defined as a crime against God)

When people sin, they earn what sin pays – death.

God loved His children, and He had wanted them to live their physical and spiritual lives forever in a state of true love and trust – close to Him. But Adam and Eve chose to break that trust by doing something God had specifically told them not to do, and they were no longer the innocent and pure people God had created. Satan had corrupted them, and God did not want them to remain in the Garden of Eden where they could eat fruit from the tree of life and live forever, so He sent them out into the world – away from their safe and comfortable home in Eden – without all the perfect provisions God had prepared. Sin separates us from God, and the punishment for sin is death – spiritually and physically. Outside of God's Paradise – without God's fruit from the tree of life – their physical bodies would begin the process of decay that ends in death, but God is merciful. He would allow them to live for a time. In their remaining time on earth, they would have a chance to come back to Him and be born again spiritually.

God explained spiritual death and rebirth to us in a Bible story that tells of a son who left his father's house and went out into the world and lived a sinful life (specifically, he wasted his entire inheritance by making reckless decisions that catered to his physical whims). Eventually, the son was sorry for what he had done and returned home to his father, completely humbled himself, and apologized sincerely. The father was overjoyed and said,

"My son was dead, but now he is alive again!" (Luke 15:24a). The son obviously wasn't physically dead. The father was talking about the son's spirit. Likewise, God never wanted His children to leave their home with Him (their inheritance), physically or spiritually, and He is overjoyed when they return to Him.

When God confronted Adam and Eve with their sins, they did not humble themselves and accept responsibility for their own choices like the son in the story above. Adam blamed Eve, and Eve blamed Satan. They stubbornly chose to remain spiritually dead. But Satan was the root of the problem – he tempted the people to sin. What happened to him? Satan is still loose in the world, and he has other angels who choose to follow his lead. As a group, they are referred to as fallen angels because they were cast down out of heaven for rebelling against God. Since that time, Satan and his fallen angels have been fighting against God's holy angels by trying to tempt all of humankind to turn away from God and join their side. We are witnessing – in fact, we are living right in the middle of – a HUGE war between good and evil, and we must choose a side.

Romans 11:1a

So I ask, "Did God force his people to leave him?" Of course not.

Deuteronomy 30:19-20a

"Today I am giving you a choice of two ways. And I ask heaven and earth to be witnesses of your choice. You can choose life or death. The first choice will bring a blessing. The other choice will bring a curse. So choose life! Then you and your children will live. You must love the LORD your God and obey him. Never leave him, because he is your life."

As an obedient child of God, you will inherit life. Choosing not to honor and trust God will ultimately lead to punishment and death.

Jude 6a

And remember the angels who lost their authority to rule. . .

The verses below from the Bible book of Ezekiel are interwoven with verses about an ancient king of Tyre and the punishment God would bring on him for his wicked ways.

Ezekiel 28:13part, 14a, 15, 16b

"You were in Eden, the garden of God. . .God made you strong. You were one of the chosen Cherubs who spread your wings over my throne. I put you on the holy mountain of God. . .You were good and honest when I created you, but then you became evil. . .and you sinned. So I treated you like something unclean and threw you off the mountain of God."

The following verse refers in part to a Babylonian king, whom God would also punish. A thorough study of the Bible shows that Babylon is representative of all earthly evil, from the very beginning of the Bible to the very end.

Isaiah 14:12a

"You were like the morning star, but you have fallen from the sky."

These verses are all similar to those found in the book of Revelation that tell of Michael, an archangel (chief angel, or angel of high rank), fighting against Satan and throwing him out of heaven and down to the earth. Because of these and other verses, we know that angels are warriors.

Revelation 12:7-9

Then there was a war in heaven. Michael and his angels fought against the dragon. The dragon and its angels fought back, but they were not strong enough. The dragon and its angels lost their place in heaven. It was thrown down out of heaven. (This giant dragon is that old snake, the one called the devil or Satan, who leads the whole world into the wrong way.) The dragon and its angels were thrown to the earth.

Some teach that the verses above are not about Satan – they are simply about the kings of Tyre and Babylon. Note that in the Ezekiel verses, the offender was in Eden and was thrown from the mountain of God for his rebellion, and we know that Satan was in Eden but the king was not. In the Bible, stars can represent angels, as seen in the Isaiah verse. Satan is specifically named in the Revelation verses, and we are clearly told his punishment for rebellion was to be thrown down to the earth.

It is reasonable to interpret that these verses in the books of Ezekiel, Isaiah, and Revelation are speaking to us about Satan, who is the fallen, evil spirit behind not only these kings but all earthly wickedness.

Luke 10:18-19a

Jesus said to them, "I saw Satan falling like lightning from the sky. He is the enemy, but know that I have given you more power than he has."

Revelation 12:12

"So rejoice, you heavens and all who live there! But it will be terrible for the earth and sea, because the devil has gone down to you. He is filled with anger. He knows he doesn't have much time."

In this physical, earthly world he has been limited to, Satan's most dangerous power is urging humans to act against God. Satan worked through these kings to accomplish his own wicked deeds. Each of us has free will, which means we have the power to stop him. Even if we fail like Adam, Eve, and these kings did, God will put a complete stop to all of the evil – it's in His plan.

Job 1:7
The LORD said to Satan, "Where have you been?" Satan answered the LORD, "I have been roaming around the earth, going from place to place."

1 Peter 5:8
Control yourselves and be careful! The devil is your enemy, and he goes around like a roaring lion looking for someone to attack and eat.

Review: Satan is jealous of God and His love for us. He is trying to ruin our relationship with God by tempting us to be unfaithful to Him. He works through people to achieve his evil goals.

Where does this leave us?

God is all good, and He always wants good – for all of us. He is the root of good, He is goodness itself, and all good things come from Him alone. Because God is perfectly good, He is also a perfectly fair judge. He is just. For a human to be just, s/he must always be guided by truth and by what is right. God is the root of that truth and righteousness. He IS truth. He IS righteousness. He rewards good, He punishes evil. He is ever and always perfectly good and perfectly just – even if it doesn't seem like it at the time or from our point of view. This is because we cannot see the whole picture and judge as fairly as He does.

James 1:17a

Everything good comes from God. Every perfect gift is from him.

Psalm 7:9b-12a

God, you are fair. You know what people are thinking. God helps people who want to do right, so he will protect me. God is a good judge. He always condemns evil. If the wicked will not change, then God is ready to punish them.

If we stay true to God, He will help us through all the trouble and temptations Satan sends our way. God will never tempt us to sin. It is against His nature. Satan is the root of ALL the evil we experience, and ALL of his temptations are lies. There is no truth in him. If we believe Satan's lies and turn from God, we are asking God to leave us alone. God is a good parent – He is the best parent – so, we know that because of His love for us, He will not completely leave us while there is still time to save us. He continues to call us, but we must listen and answer His call before our earthly time ends and it is too late.

God's placement of the deadly tree in the Garden was not an effort to tempt Adam and Eve. When Satan tempts you, he tries very hard to get you to do something you know you should not do. The placement of the tree was a test of their character (their soul – the part of them that makes them who they are), and God told them very explicitly how to pass the test.

The imperfect life we live today began with Adam and Eve's sin. They were sent away from what had been the perfect paradise of the Garden of Eden – before Satan entered it and corrupted them. To be very clear, Satan was only able to corrupt them because they allowed themselves to be led astray. They each, individually, had a choice, and they each made the wrong decision. God punished them individually for their unfaithfulness to Him. Bearing children would be difficult for Eve – for all women after her. Finding food – providing for his family – would be difficult for Adam – for all men after him. (We still have these problems today because all sin has consequences, and those consequences will continue until God's plan is complete.) Because He is a loving Father, God comforted them in their punishment. He gave them a promise of a future without Satan, He gave them clothing, and He gave them time to spiritually return to Him.

Genesis 3:16part (part of Eve's punishment)

"I will cause you to have much trouble when you are pregnant. And when you give birth to

children, you will have much pain."

Genesis 3: 19part (part of Adam's punishment)

"You will work hard for your food, until your face is covered with sweat. You will work hard until the day you die, and then you will become dust again."

Genesis 3:21

The LORD God used animal skins and made some clothes for the man and his wife. Then he put the clothes on them.

Genesis 3:15b (God promised Satan that he would be punished, too)

"You will bite her child's foot, but he will crush your head."

After God judged them, He sent Adam, Eve, and Satan out of Eden and secured the entrance. Adam and Eve would no longer have access to the tree of life.

Genesis 3:22-23a ("us" in these verses is God, Jesus, and the Holy Spirit – we will discuss their relationship later)

The LORD God said, "Look, the man has become like us – he knows about good and evil. And now the man might take the fruit from the tree of life. If the man eats that fruit, he will live forever." So the LORD God forced the man out of the Garden of Eden. . .

Satan promised Eve she would be more like God if she ate the forbidden fruit, and, in a way, she was. She gained the knowledge of good and evil, but all she really gained was sin. Sin begins with the knowledge of it. She knew she had been misled. She said, "The snake tricked me, so I ate the fruit" (Genesis 3:13b). If she had accepted responsibility for her own poor choice, she might have said, "I'm sorry I didn't trust You. I allowed the snake to trick me, and I ate the fruit."

In the course of time, Adam and Eve had children, those children had children, and so on through the ages. Satan and his followers roamed freely among the believers and the unbelievers, and they continue to do so today.

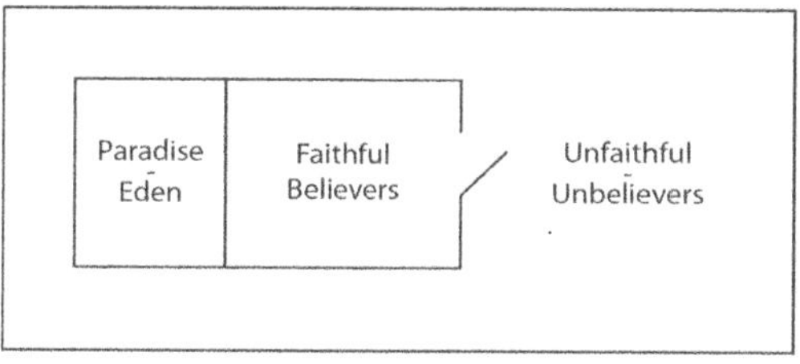

After the Fall of Humankind

And so, we inherited this less-than-perfect world. We know its imperfection in physical ways, because we know the pain of giving birth. We know its imperfection in environmental ways, because we have to protect ourselves from the weather and wild animals, and we know that food can be difficult to afford, to grow, to catch, or to find. We know the world's imperfection in psychological and emotional ways, because we know the pain and frustration of trying to get along with imperfect people. We know our world is imperfect in other ways, because Satan is constantly offering us temptations that we know are not what God wants for us.

James 1:13

Whenever you feel tempted to do something bad, you should not say, "God is tempting me." Evil cannot tempt God, and God himself does not tempt anyone.

Titus 1:2b

. . .God does not lie.

God, because He is good, has given us the joy that blurs the memory of childbirth pain, although it does not block it out completely. He has given us provisions for shelter, protection, and food, but they are not perfect like they were in the Garden. He has left us with directions on how to get along with one another, but Satan, working through people, has made it difficult. God has given us power and weapons to fight off Satan, but we cannot do it alone. He will help us get through painful times, He will help us obtain the things we need, He will help us be kind to one another, and He will help us resist Satan, but we have to ask Him first. The Bible says He is standing at the door knocking. We must open the door and invite Him into our lives. Then we have to trust that He can and will give us the help we need. His help may come in a form we did not expect, or it may come at a time we did not expect – but we can't see the whole picture, and we must trust that God knows what He is doing. This is the beginning of faith.

Jeremiah 29:12-13

Then you will call my name. You will come to me and pray to me, and I will listen to you. You will search for me, and when you search for me with all your heart, you will find me.

Revelation 3:20

"Here I am! I stand at the door and knock. If you hear my voice and open the door, I will come in and eat with you. And you will eat with me."

Deuteronomy 31:6

Be strong and be brave. Don't be afraid. . .because the LORD your God is with you. He will not fail you or leave you.

And our faith can grow over time. The Bible says God is light – there is no darkness in Him – and Satan is darkness – there is no light in him. Complete darkness is scary. Have you ever experienced a power outage in the middle of the night when there is absolutely no light to guide you in any way? That stumbling, groping, searching, insecure, scared feeling is what life is like without God. Many of us will not admit how insecure we feel without God until we're facing serious troubles or even death, but if we turn to Him, we begin to have a little bit of hope. If there is a little bit of light, we begin to feel better. Even with just a little bit of God, the darkness is beginning to be driven out of our lives. If there is some light, then it is no longer truly dark. Grow that relationship with God, and the light will grow brighter and brighter, driving away more and more of the darkness.

John 1:5

The light shines in the darkness, and the darkness has not defeated it.

Job 12:22b

He sends light into places that are as dark as death.

Daniel 2:22b

Light lives with him, so he knows what is in the dark and secret places.

John 12:46 (Jesus talking about Himself)

I came into this world as a light. I came so that everyone who believes in me will not stay in darkness.

Satan has corrupted this world, but God will deliver us from this corrupt world, He will punish Satan, and He will give us another perfect world and perfect life which Satan cannot corrupt and which will never be taken from us, but we cannot have that life unless we have His protection. We must ask Him to be with us. God wants to have a close, personal relationship with each and every one of His children.

2 Thessalonians 2:14, 16-17

God chose you to have that salvation. He chose you by using the Good News that we told you. You were chosen so that you can share in the glory of our Lord Jesus Christ. We pray that the Lord Jesus Christ and God our Father will comfort you and strengthen you in every good thing you do and say. God loved us and gave us through his grace a wonderful hope and comfort that has no end.

James 1:18b

He wanted us to be the most important of all that he created.

God will restore everything. We must follow His directions and be patient.

1 Peter 1:9

Your faith has a goal, and you are reaching that goal – your salvation.

Revelation 21:1a, 5part

Then I saw a new heaven and a new earth. . ."Look, I am making everything new!"

Review: God will always be there for us if we let Him.
We should follow His Guiding Light and avoid the dark traps of Satan.

Why doesn't God just get rid of Satan?

As His Book says, God is God of everything, so why doesn't He just get rid of Satan? Why hasn't He done so already? The Bible tells us God can do what He wants, when He wants. Here are some characteristics of God we should know:

God is omnipotent – all powerful – God has power everywhere over everyone and everything.

Isaiah 44:24

The one who rescued you is the LORD, the one who formed you in your mother's womb. He says, "I, the LORD, made everything. I put the skies there myself. I spread out the earth before me."

God is omnipresent – all present – God is present everywhere at all times.

Revelation 1:8

The Lord God says, "I am the Alpha and the Omega (the first and last letters in the Greek alphabet, meaning the beginning and the end). I am the one who is, who always was, and who is coming. I am the All-Powerful."

God is omniscient – all knowing – God knows everything, even secret things.

Psalm 147:5

Our Lord is great and powerful. There is no limit to what he knows.

God is omnibenevolent – all good – God is always good and always wants good.

Psalm 100:5

The LORD is good! There is no end to his faithful love. We can trust him forever and ever!

We say God can do everything, but there is something God cannot do: He cannot lie – which means He cannot be inconsistent, He cannot be unfaithful. God has power over these things – He has the power to judge lies/inconsistencies/unfaithfulness – but God will not commit these crimes Himself because they are an abomination to Him. He is omnibenevolent – He is always good and always wants good. Lying and speaking inconsistencies (saying one thing is true, then saying an opposite thing is true) or acting hypocritically (saying one thing but doing the opposite) – demonstrate unfaithfulness – they are bad character traits. God is all good, and He has only good characteristics.

Hebrews 6:18

These two things cannot change: God cannot lie when he says something, and he cannot lie when he makes an oath. So these two things are a great help to us who have come to God for safety. They encourage us to hold on to the hope that is ours.

The Bible clearly shows us God has a detailed plan to restore humankind to our rightful place. His plan includes the complete exile of Satan, his cohorts, and his followers to a place of eternal torturous punishment at the time of the end of this world. God has already set His plan in motion, and He is sticking to His plan – because He IS faithfulness.

Job 42:2-3 (A man named Job apologizing to God for his complaints)

"I know you can do everything. You make plans, and nothing can change or stop them. You asked, 'Who is this ignorant person saying these foolish things?' I talked about things I did not understand. I talked about things too amazing for me to know."

Ecclesiastes 3:1

There is a right time for everything, and everything on earth will happen at the right time.

Ecclesiastes 3:11b

. . .he does everything at just the right time.

Galatians 4:4

But when the right time came, God sent his Son, who was born from a woman and lived under the law.

1 Timothy 6:14-15a

Do what you were commanded to do without fault or blame until the time when our Lord Jesus Christ comes again. God will make that happen at the right time.

Ephesians 1:10

God's goal was to finish his plan when the right time came. He planned that all things in heaven and on earth be joined together with Christ as the head.

We know when we have a project and we plan out what needs to be done, getting those things done will take time. It may seem to us that He is taking a long time to fix everything, but God's perspective of time is different from ours. God is eternal – He has always been and always will be. We are only capable of operating on earthly time, while God operates on heavenly time. We can't fully understand the complexity of heavenly time yet, but He has given us a hint of its multi-dimensional features – the Bible tells us that a day to God is like a thousand years and a thousand years is like a day. The Bible also tells us over and over that certain events happen after a specific amount of time has passed – God favors the orderliness of certain numbers, and His numbers have meanings. Big events occur only after specific details are all put in order. God works through people to get many of these details just right. Working through people requires His patience, because we can be slow to understand or to accept what He wants us to do. He is waiting for us. He gives us freedom to choose, but we sometimes take a long time to make our decision. He is patient and kind. He is giving us time to come to Him.

Psalm 90:4

To you, a thousand years is like yesterday, like a few hours in the night.

2 Peter 3:8-9

But don't forget this one thing, dear friends: To the Lord a day is like a thousand years, and a thousand years is like a day. The Lord is not being slow in doing what he promised – the way some people understand slowness. But God is being patient with you. He doesn't want anyone to be lost. He wants everyone to change their ways and stop sinning.

Comparing two unlike things using the word "like" or "as" is a figure of speech called a **simile**. God's words in the Bible are deliberate – and He is not changing the definition of a day, here. God did not say in these verses that a thousand years IS a day. He said a thousand years is LIKE a day, or AS a day. He is explaining to us that in terms of eternity – which is the infinite amount of time God has – a few hours, a day, and a thousand years are all insignificant amounts of time.

We cannot know all the details that must be taken care of, but we can understand to a certain degree based on our own life experiences. Good parents act in their children's best interest, but they do not necessarily discuss all of the details with their children. We are God's children, and He has told us all we need to know. If there is a detail we don't fully understand, we have to trust that God knows what He is doing. The Bible tells us we will have a full understanding one day. Everything will be made clear to us. We do not have the ability to understand everything yet. We are like young children who cannot fully grasp why they must eat vegetables when dessert tastes so much better. Full understanding requires maturity, and maturity takes time.

Numbers 23:19

God is not a man; he will not lie. God is not a human being; his decisions will not change. If he says he will do something, then he will do it. If he makes a promise, then he will do what he promised.

1 Corinthians 13:11, 12part

When I was a child, I talked like a child, I thought like a child, and I made plans like a child. When I became a man, I stopped those childish ways. It is the same. . .Now I know only a part, but at that time I will know fully. . .

Other things in this life take time. Education takes time, building a home takes time, baking bread from scratch takes time – but all of these good things are well worth the effort and time we spend on them. Because we know this, we know the fix for our relationship with God that He is working on will take His effort (His patience with us) and some time (as He waits for us to mature), but it will be really, really good. The Bible tells us that God has promised He will make everything right and that God keeps ALL of His promises. Faith in His promises will guide us through this imperfect life until we can see and understand everything clearly.

Revelation 17:14

"They will make war against the Lamb. But the Lamb will defeat them, because he is Lord of lords and King of kings. And with him will be his chosen and faithful followers – the people he has called to be his."

Review: God knows He will defeat Satan, but it will take time to complete His plan.

What has God done in His war with Satan?

War is defined as a series of battles. A war is not just one fight, it is many. The Battle of the Bulge was only one of thousands of battles fought during World War II. The Battle of Shiloh was one of about 50 major battles of the American Civil War, and there were many hundreds of minor battles fought as well. These earthly wars are a shadow of what is happening in God's war with Satan. We can read about the ancient battles recorded in the Bible, we can read about later battles in history books, we know we are currently living in a world full of battles, and we can read what the Bible tells us about a final conflict in which Satan and his followers will be completely defeated.

One major battle in the great war of good vs. evil is described in the Bible book called "Genesis," which means "The Beginning." This battle occurred in the time of Noah, a preacher. Noah loved God and trusted Him – he did everything God asked him to do. The other people of Noah's time were following the greatest deceiver, Satan. The Bible says that, aside from Noah, everywhere God looked, He saw only evil.

Genesis 6:11-12

When God looked at the earth, he saw that people had ruined it. Violence was everywhere, and it had ruined their life on earth.

We know that God is fair, and we know that God is patient, and we will discuss that more in the pages to come. Noah's story tells us what the root of the problem was:

Genesis 6:1-2

The number of people on earth continued to increase. When these people had daughters, the sons of God saw how beautiful they were. So they chose the women they wanted. They married them, and the women had their children.

Genesis 6:4

During this time and also later, the Nephilim people lived in the land. They have been famous as powerful soldiers since ancient times.

Let's examine one widespread understanding of these verses. Many teach that 'sons of God' refers to angels. The belief is that these angels left their proper place in God's creation, took human women as wives, and reproduced with them. Their angel/human offspring were powerful giants called Nephilim. Because the word Nephilim appears again much later in the Bible, the belief is that these hybrid giants existed both before and after this battle, meaning that God did not accomplish what He set out to do in this battle. While this understanding of the verses has persisted for a very long time, it is not consistent with the rest of the Bible and should be examined more closely.

The phrase 'sons of God' occurs a handful of times in both the Old and New Testaments – the two major sections of the Bible. Originally, the Old Testament was mostly written in Hebrew, while the New Testament was mostly written in Greek. The Hebrew phrase **benei Elohim**, and the Greek phrase **huios theos** are literally and easily translated as sons of God, or children of God. In the New Testament, **huios theos** is always translated as sons/children of God and always refers to humans.

There is no reason to assume that the Bible is referring to angels when it says, 'sons of God' in the Old Testament. In fact, when the Old Testament is telling us about angels, the phrase **mal'achi Elohim**, literally, messengers of God, or just **mal'achi**, messengers, is used. We know for a fact that God uses angels as messengers throughout the Bible, so it's relatively safe to assume that when He means angels, He says messengers, not sons. If the angels are clearly messengers, then who are the sons/children of God? The entire Bible tells us repeatedly that humans are children of God when they have faith in God as their Father who will provide.

Then, why is **benei Elohim** translated as angels in this verse? The reasoning seems to lie exclusively with the translation of **benei Elohim** as angels found three times in the Old Testament book of Job. The book begins by stating that Job regularly made appearances before God to seek forgiveness for any sins his adult children may have committed, so we know immediately that Job is a righteous man who loves God and wants to please Him. The first sentence in each of the first two verses below is extremely important in giving us context.

Job 1:6

*Then the day came for the [**benei Elohim** - sons/children of God] to meet with the LORD. Even Satan was there with them.*

Job 2:1

*Then another day came for the [**benei Elohim** – sons/children of God] to meet with the LORD. Satan joined them for this meeting with the LORD.*

Job 1:7

The LORD said to Satan, "Where have you been?" Satan answered the LORD, "I have been roaming around the earth, going from place to place."

Who are the children of God who have regularly scheduled meetings with Him? We will learn more as we progress, but God required His faithful children to present themselves before Him three times each year on specific feast days – the same feast days the Jews celebrate. We know that Satan was cast down to earth, and we know his goal is and always has been to upset the relationship between God and His children, so it is reasonable to expect Satan to try to interfere with their meetings.

The final reference to **benei Elohim** in the book of Job occurs when God is scolding Job and asking where he was when God created the heavens and the earth, and His creations celebrated His work.

Job 38:4a, 7

*"Where were you when I made the earth. . .when the morning stars sang together and the [**benei Elohim**] shouted with joy?"*

Many Bible translations insert angels for **benei Elohim** in this verse. If that is correct, then who are the morning stars that sang together? In the verse below, Jesus, the Son of God, explains a vision seen by a faithful follower named John. Jesus says that the seven stars John sees represent angels.

Revelation 1:20b

The seven stars are the angels of the seven churches.

Given this information, let's examine the possible interpretations. Some say that the morning stars (which represent angels) and the **benei Elohim** (translated as angels) celebrated the greatness of God. . .that is, the angels sang and the angels shouted in celebration of His work.

That might be a plausible interpretation, but doesn't it make more sense, fit well scripturally, and agree with the original language better if we translate morning stars as angels and **benei Elohim** as children of God? Then Job 38:7 would mean, the angels sang and God's children shouted in celebration of God's work.

Another interpretation says that the morning stars (the Pleiades, perhaps) represent life due to their appearance in the sky at times of planting and harvesting. This flows nicely with Jesus identifying Himself as the Bright Morning Star who gives life to all, as we will see later. Following this line of thought, the verse would state: Those who had life sang together and the children of God shouted with joy. Of course, those who have life (specifically, the promise of a joyous, everlasting life) are those who are faithful, whether they are angels or humans. This is also sensible and fits with the rest of the Bible teachings.

Revelation 22:16

*"I, Jesus, have sent my angel [Greek: **aggelos** - messenger] to tell you these things for the churches.*

I am the descendant from the family of David. I am the bright morning star."

Revelation 2:26, 28

"I will give power over the nations to all those who win the victory and continue until the end to do what I want. . .They will have the same power I received from my Father, and I will give them the morning star."

Additionally, the story of Noah states that God was troubled by the errant behavior of humans while not mentioning the angels (as stars or messengers) at all or referring to a hybrid state of humanity.

Genesis 6:3 (God is limiting human life to 120 years and/or warning that this battle will begin in 120 years)

Then the LORD said, "People are only human. I will not let my Spirit be troubled by them forever. I will let them live only 120 years."

The interpretation of **benei Elohim** as angels in Genesis 6:1-2 goes against every other fact we are told about angels in the Bible. Angels are spirits and do not have human bodies. As far as we know, angels were never told to procreate – in the Bible, only humans and animals were given this directive – and may very well be unable to procreate, as Jesus suggests later. Furthermore, God said repeatedly in the beginning that every species would reproduce after its own kind.

Lastly, but very importantly, the book of Hebrews in the New Testament repeats two Old Testament scriptures explaining very explicitly that Jesus, the human form of God, is His Son, and the angels are not.

Hebrews 1:5 (from Psalm 2:7 and 2 Samuel 7:14)

God never said this to any of the angels [messengers]: "You are my Son. Today I have become your Father." God also never said about an angel [messenger], "I will be his Father, and he will be my son."

Because the book of Hebrews was written specifically to the Jewish people (who were the keepers of God's Word in ancient times), and because there are other examples in the Bible of Jesus correcting errant Jewish thinking, perhaps this was a direct response to their misinterpretation of sons of God as angels in the ancient Scriptures.

When you hear a teaching that isn't consistent with your knowledge of the Bible, take the time to examine the relevant verses in their original languages. While various translations of the Bible are largely accurate, sometimes a word is translated using the wrong definition. Each word should be examined in its context to determine the correct definition. For example, suppose you need to translate just the English word *run* into another language. How will you know which definition to indicate? Does *run* mean *sprint*, *excursion*, *control*, *spread*, or *compete*? Knowledge of the context of the sentence or story it's used in is required in order to choose the correct definition.

Which brings us to the next translation issue: **nephilim** is a Hebrew word that can mean *fallen* but can also mean *distinguished*, so it is conservatively understood as *people who have fallen away from God and raised themselves up to dominate and rule over others*. We have already seen how Eve fell away from God's teaching and tried to build herself up to a God-like level. Later stories in the Bible tell us of others who make similar attempts. God never looks favorably upon this behavior – the common behavior of the fallen, the prideful, who try to build themselves up to be greater than others, including God.

Proverbs 16:18

Pride is the first step toward destruction. Proud thoughts will lead you to defeat.

Proverbs 21:4

Proud looks and proud thoughts are sins. They show a person is evil.

There is another problem. Although Hebrew is written using what we would call today a block script, an ancient translator decided to capitalize the word **nephilim**. The capital letter is a very disruptive interpretation, because it suggests that Nephilim is a proper noun rather than simply a descriptive noun.

Examples of proper nouns: Jews, Egyptians, Romans
Examples of descriptive nouns: teachers, students, followers, (the) fallen

In the context of the sentence, capitalizing the first letter suggests that the Nephilim are a nation. The word **nephilim** has also been translated as giants, which has been broadly understood to mean those of very large stature. Now we begin to see why the definition of **nephilim** as a nation of giants has persisted. If we believe that the sons of God are angels who somehow procreated with humans, then their offspring would certainly be unique, right? And so, we are blown off course in our thinking.

This off-course thinking has been rationalized even further: If somehow it is true that angels and humans were marrying, then clearly that is a severe violation of the God-designed human marriage. Furthermore, if the fallen angels were somehow procreating with humans, they were contaminating the human genetic line and would eventually eliminate the possibility of the human that God had already promised would crush Satan. Satan received this promise from God directly, and all the work Satan and his followers do is intended to thwart God's plans. While this would be a very good reason for God to engage in this particular battle, we have already seen some of the serious problems with this interpretation.

Here is another problem: because the Hebrew word Nephilim, capitalized in translation and understood as giants, is used again many years after this battle by scouts sizing up an enemy, those who teach that the Nephilim are the giant offspring of angels and humans are therefore also teaching that God did not complete His mission in this battle – that some of the corrupt, giant, angel/human hybrids survived.

On the subject of giants, the Old Testament refers to people of large stature a number of times. When an actual, physical giant is described in the Bible, his height or size is mentioned.

1 Samuel 17:4 (The story of David and Goliath)
The Philistines had a champion fighter named Goliath, who was from Gath. He was over 9 feet tall.

1 Chronicles 11:23a
And Benaiah killed a big Egyptian soldier. That man was about 7½ feet tall.

Giants, people with giantism, still exist today.

It is certainly also worth noting that the ten men who used the word Nephilim all those years later to describe an enemy they were too fearful to fight were struck dead by God for their testimony.

Numbers 14:37b (They had no faith that God would help them do the job He was sending them to do)
So the LORD caused a sickness to kill all those men.

Two other men were witnesses of the enemy as well but did not give the same testimony. Those two men, Joshua and Caleb, not only lived, but went on to take that enemy's land (Joshua became the leader of God's people after Moses died). If God struck the ten men dead for their testimony that showed a complete lack of faith in God and His promises, is it more sensible to trust them or God's consistent pattern of behavior?

Everything God sets out to do is done – completely under His control and in His good time. He has let the war with evil continue because He has a plan that will be perfectly accomplished exactly when He planned it would be.

After careful consideration of the issues surrounding the translation of **benei Elohim** and **nephilim** and rereading the verses from Genesis 6, a conservative interpretation follows:

> Sons of God, men who had previously been faithful, began to fall away from God (through the negative influence of Satan and his band of fallen angels) and marry women who were the daughters of people who had already fallen away from God, and the world was becoming full of unfaithful people.
>
> These fallen people and/or their children, like others of their time and those who came later, were gaining reputations/distinguishing themselves as powerful warriors – giants among men – and dominating others with their might. (They were violent, war-like people.)
>
> Some people, both before and after this battle, were of large stature – what

we would call giants.

Throughout the Bible, God repeatedly warns His followers not to marry the unbelievers/ unfaithful, because this union can be hazardous to one's faith. The unfaithful influence can cause a follower to fall away from God.

Joshua 23:12part, 13part

"They are not a part of Israel [those who love God]. Don't marry any of their people. . . They will become like a trap for you."

Exodus 34:15-16

"Be careful not to make any agreements with the people who live in that land. If you do this, you might join them when they worship their gods. They will invite you to join them, and you will eat their sacrifices. You might choose some of their daughters as wives for your sons. Those daughters serve false gods. They might lead your sons to do the same thing."

Notice God says, "might," not "will." Later, we will see an example of a woman who was raised as an unbeliever but married into a faithful nation and became faithful herself. Read about her in the book that has been given her name, Ruth. While there are always some exceptions, God knows it can be very difficult for us to stand up to bad influences. He tells us it is in our best interest to not expose ourselves to them.

Regardless of how we interpret **benei Elohim**, the root of the problem was a large turning away from God (today, we call this **apostasy**), and the result was rampant wickedness. The people had turned sharply away from God and, aside from Noah's family, there was nothing but evil everywhere God looked.

Genesis 6:5-6

The LORD saw that the people on the earth were very evil. He saw that they thought only about evil things all the time. The LORD was sorry that he had made people on the earth. It made him very sad in his heart.

Some people teach that God cannot be in the presence of sin (or, evil), and that is why Adam and Eve were removed from Eden, and that is why God punished the wicked people of Noah's age, but we can already see that is not sound Biblical teaching. Adam and Eve were removed from Eden to keep them from eating from the tree of life – God said so. He also directly addressed Satan in the Garden of Eden, so He must be able to be in his presence.

Genesis 3:15b (In Eden, God promised Satan that he would be punished by a descendant of Eve – a human)
"You will bite her child's foot, but he will crush your head."

Satan can work subtly among humans, as he did with Eve, but he can be brazenly bold before God. Recall how he presented himself along with the children of God in the Job verses mentioned earlier.

When God's creations betray Him and do things that go against Him (when they are unfaithful to Him, when they disregard their proper relationship with Him), and if they will not turn to Him and stop doing bad things, they will be punished for their sins. God doesn't give out rules arbitrarily. He has good reasons for what He tells us to do or not do – even if we cannot understand them at the time.

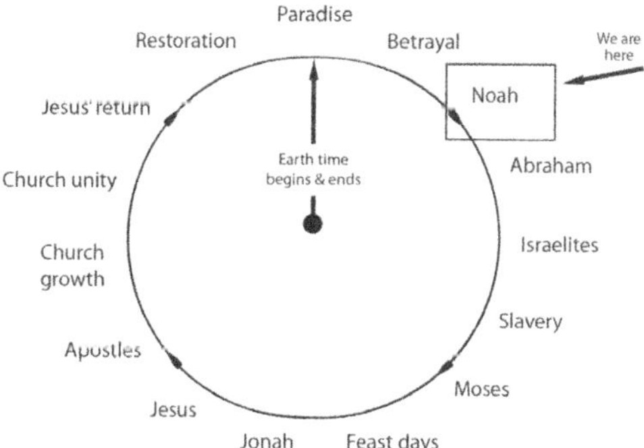

After all these explanations, we finally come to what God decided to do about the almost complete apostasy of Noah's day. God made a decision to punish those people who had fallen for the temptations of the evil one and had almost exhaustively corrupted God's people. The whole earth would suffer in this punishment.

Genesis 6:7

So the LORD said, "I will destroy all the people I created on the earth. I will destroy every person and every animal and everything that crawls on the earth. And I will destroy all the birds in the air, because I am sorry that I have made them."

Because God is love and God is fair, He saved those who were not guilty. He did not punish any of His true followers. He made a covenant with Noah to keep him and his family safe from the judgment – the punishment – He would send on the earth. God told Noah to build a huge boat that would hold Noah's family of eight people, enough of God's animals to reproduce later, and food and supplies for all on board. An object that holds something inside of it and keeps it safe is called an ark, so this story is often called "Noah's Ark."

Genesis 6:9

This is the history of Noah's family. He was a good man all his life, and he always followed God.

Genesis 6:14a

"Use cypress wood and build a boat for yourself."

Genesis 6:18

"I will make a special agreement with you. You, your wife, your sons, and their wives will all go into the boat."

Noah did everything God commanded him to do. It took a long time for Noah to build this boat – he had no power tools or heavy equipment, and he had no lumber yards or hardware stores. People could see him building this massive boat (approximately 450 feet long x 75 feet wide x 45 feet high), and perhaps some of them asked questions. God waited patiently, but obviously, no one was convinced by Noah's words or by his actions.

Genesis 6:22

Noah did everything God commanded him.

2 Peter 2:5b

Noah was a man who told people about living right.

1 Peter 3:20part

God was waiting patiently for people while Noah was building the big boat.

When Noah was finished, God told him to take the animals He sent and his family and get on board the ark. God was going to wash the whole earth with a huge flood – He planned to completely cover it with water – to remove the wickedness that had ruined it and allow life to begin anew. God would send a cleansing flood.

Genesis 7:1,4

Then the LORD said to Noah, "I have seen that you are a good man, even among the evil people of this time. So gather your family, and all of you go into the boat. . .Seven days from now, I will send much rain on the earth. It will rain for 40 days and 40 nights, and I will wipe everything off the face of the earth. I will destroy everything I made."

Genesis 7:5

Noah did everything the LORD told him to do.

Once the animals, Noah and his wife, their three sons, and their three daughters-in-law were all safe on board, God closed the door of the ark and then caused the springs of water to come up from deep in the earth. This cracking of the earth's crust into separate pieces (now, we call them plates) and sudden gushing of water was very powerful, and new geographical landscapes were formed all over the world. Then the windows of heaven were opened and it began to rain like it had never before rained. The water rose higher than the highest mountains. All the people and animals that were not in the ark died. Their bodies and all of the trees and plants were tossed around by the waters and buried by the swirling sand and silt.

Genesis 7:16b

Then the LORD closed the door behind Noah.

Genesis 7:11part

The springs under the earth broke through the ground, and water flowed out everywhere. The sky also opened like windows and rain poured down.

2 Peter 2:5a, 9a

And God punished the evil people who lived long ago. He brought a flood to the world that was full of people who were against God. But he saved Noah and seven other people with him. . .So you see that the Lord God knows how to save those who are devoted to him.

After the waters had begun to recede, Noah came out of the ark and showed God his respect by building an altar to honor Him. God was pleased with Noah, and He promised to never again send a flood to destroy every living thing on earth. God made the rainbow a symbol and reminder of His promise. God used the Flood to remove the evil that Satan and his fallen angels had spread and to wash His earth clean – but this cleansing by water was only temporary.

Genesis 9:18-19

Noah's sons came out of the boat with him. Their names were Shem, Ham, and Japheth. . . These three men were Noah's sons. And all the people on earth came from these three sons.

Genesis 8:20a, 21part

Then Noah built an altar to honor the LORD. . .and it pleased him.

Genesis 9:11, 17

"This is my promise to you: All life on the earth was destroyed by the flood. But that will never happen again. A flood will never again destroy all life on the earth." So God said to Noah, "This rainbow is proof of the agreement that I made with all living things on earth."

As time went on, Noah's sons began to have children with their wives. Everyone on earth still spoke the same language. After a time, as the population grew, humankind began to drift away from God's direction once again. The people were strong in number and cooperative with each other and could see that they had the ability to accomplish great things working together. Unfortunately, instead of continuing to respect God and wanting to work with a love for Him in their hearts as Noah had done – instead of honoring Him as the source of their abilities, they began to think very highly of themselves – they were full of pride. They had an idea to build a great city with a great tower to show how great they thought they were. This prideful idea of power, which had tempted Eve and the **nephilim** (fallen ones) before the Flood, was again tempting God's people.

God tells us in the Bible that we should be humble – we should honor Him as our all-knowing parent and source of life, just as small children would. God, like a good parent, came down to redirect His children's behavior. He showed them that people cannot build themselves up to God – God comes down to people. It was at this time that He separated the people into their family groups, gave them different languages, and sent them away from each other to the different parts of the earth where those family groups became nations.

Genesis 11:4a

Then the people said, "Let's build ourselves a city and a tower that will reach to the sky [heaven]. Then we will be famous."

The name of the place where the people were building came to be called (depending on their language) Babel, meaning confusion, Babilu, meaning gate of God, or Babylon. Babel, Babilu, Babylon are all spelled "bbl" in Hebrew (actually, "lbb," since Hebrew, a language which uses no vowels, is written from right to left). Remember, Babylon in the Bible is not only a physical, historical location and nation, it also represents all earthly evil.

Throughout the Bible, God collectively refers to His faithful people as a bride, while unfaithful people are referred to as prostitutes. In the book of Revelation, the unfaithful are represented by a woman who is drunk on the blood of God's people. She is described as having a title on her forehead that reads: "THE GREAT BABYLON – MOTHER OF PROSTITUTES AND THE EVIL THINGS OF THE EARTH" (Revelation 17:5part).

Genesis 11:8-9

So people stopped building the city, and the LORD scattered them all over the earth. That is the place where the LORD confused the language of the whole world. That is why it is called Babel. And it was from there that the LORD caused the people to spread out to all the other places on earth.

A more literal translation of verse 9 (underlined) from the original Hebrew would read: *And so He proclaimed her name Babylon. . .*

Genesis 10:25a

Eber was the father of two sons. One son was name Peleg [which means 'division']. He was given this name because the earth was divided during his life.

We've seen how God punished the people who were sinning against Him, but what about Satan and the other fallen angels who had cast away their God-given role and followed their own selfish interests and led God's people astray? While no extra or specific punishment for them is mentioned in this story, we already know that Satan and all the fallen angels who decide to follow his example are punished for their sins by being limited in their abilities and excluded from God's care until He judges them.

2 Peter 2:4

When the angels sinned, God did not let them go free without punishment. He sent them to hell. He put those angels in caves of darkness, where they are being held until the time when God will judge them.

Jude 6

And remember the angels who lost their authority to rule. They left their proper home. So the Lord has kept them in darkness, bound with everlasting chains, to be judged on the great day.

What was the God-given role for angels? Angels were created to inhabit the spiritual realm and serve as messengers for God, to be protectors for and ministers to humans, to be warriors for God, and to be worshippers of God.

Psalm 91:11

He will command his angels [messengers] to protect you wherever you go.

Hebrews 1:14

All the angels are spirits who serve God and are sent to help those who will receive salvation.

God's faithful angels are very powerful spiritual beings – they are more powerful than humans – but the fallen angels have less power than humans. The fallen angels aren't literally bound with chains in caves of darkness – this is descriptive language much like the woman depicting Babylon. We can understand "bound with chains" to mean that God reduced their power when they sinned against Him, and "in caves of darkness" to mean that they do not have the light of God's presence and love. Hell is anyplace that doesn't have God or the light of God's love, and so we refer to their home as hell.

Why didn't they die as the humans did for sinning against God? Angels don't die the way people do. When God's good angels fight the fallen angels on our behalf they only thwart the fallen angels' efforts to tempt us away from God – they do not kill them. So, the fallen angels (also called demons) are roaming the earth, trying to lead us astray, but God has limited their powers – He is restraining them until the great day of judgment that will occur near the very end of His plan. If we walk in His light, He will help us defend ourselves against the temptations of the dark side.

1 John 4:4b

The one [God] who is in you is greater than the one [Satan] who is in the world.

The Bible is full of stories in which God has defeated Satan – these are battles in the great war. When we look at the world today, sometimes it seems as though Satan is winning, but God will prevail. Good will conquer evil because that is God's plan, God is in control, and He will complete His plan.

Isaiah 42:13

The LORD will go out like a strong soldier. Like a man going into battle, he will be full of excitement.

He will shout with a loud cry, and he will defeat his enemies.

Remember: There is nothing new in this life. Countless books, plays, movies, shows, and games are based on the theme of good vs. evil. In these stories, the villain is seldom defeated in just one battle. The true, but sometimes unrealized, inspiration for all of these stories is the original and ultimate story of good vs. evil – the Bible.

Review: The Bible is full of God's battles against Satan. It is the ultimate good vs. evil story.

If God is at war, if He is fighting, why do people say God is Love?

The Bible is also the greatest love story ever told.

1 John 4:8

Anyone who does not love does not know God, because God is love.

The Bible (a name that literally means, The Book) is a big book made up of many smaller books written by many different people (all under the influence of God) at different times in history (His Story). The Book is how He tells us His Story. He wants to tell us His Story because He loves us. The Bible is His love story to us – something like a family album or scrapbook. Like a good parent, He wants us to know where we came from, but He also wants us to know where we are going.

2 Timothy 3:16a

All Scripture [the words that make up the Bible] is given by God.

The first book in the Bible tells us that the marriage of Adam and Eve completed Creation (the birth of our world and humankind). The Bible tells us this story so that we can understand how God works. God was with Adam and Eve in the Garden of Eden because He loved them, but they were unfaithful to Him. They lost their faith, their trust, in God. He did not leave them, they left Him. Without our trust, without our faith, we cannot have a true relationship with God. He will call to us, but He will not accept us unless we come to Him with faith. He loves us more than we can ever know, and He wants us to be with Him, but we must love Him and trust Him – in all things.

1 Corinthians 13:4-8a

Love is patient and kind. Love is not jealous, it does not brag, and it is not proud. Love is not rude, it is not selfish, and it cannot be made angry easily. Love does not remember wrongs done against it. Love is never happy when others do wrong, but it is always happy with the truth. Love never gives up on people. It never stops trusting, never loses hope, and never quits. Love will never end.

The Bible says God is love, love is not jealous, and God is jealous. How can this be? A loving relationship should not have the negative energy generated by jealousy over one another's successes – each should be happy for and rejoice with the other. When God speaks of His jealousy, He is not jealous of what His beloved has accomplished, rather He is righteously protecting the monogamy of the relationship. This jealousy should invoke positive feelings in His beloved, because He is demonstrating His concern for their exclusive bond. For example, a godly husband and wife belong to one another. When an outsider tries to interfere with that bond, or when one partner allows an intrusion, is it not righteous jealousy that is felt by the betrayed partner? God created us. We are made in His image. We are His. Of course, He is jealous when we do not protect our relationship with Him and we allow Satan to interfere.

Exodus 34:14 (God's jealousy is referenced when He warns His people against worshiping false gods)

Don't worship any other god. I am YAHWEH KANAH – the jealous LORD. That is my name. I hate for my people to worship other gods.

2 Corinthians 11:2-3 (Paul speaking to new believers who were beginning to follow false teachers)

I am jealous for you with a jealousy that comes from God. I promised to give you to Christ. He must be your only husband. I want to give you to Christ to be his pure bride. But I am afraid that your minds will be led away from your true and pure following of Christ. This could happen just as Eve was tricked by that snake with his clever lies.

For those of you who like to peek at the last page of a book to see how it ends, here's a summary of the end: The last book in the Bible tells us about the final conquering of Satan and his band of followers as well as the happy marriage of Jesus (the Son of God, the last man God made) to the church (all of His faithful people – not an actual church building or a particular religion). These events will complete God's plan. It will be a celebration – a perfectly planned, perfectly executed, and perfectly happy wedding celebration in which our Father (God) will gaze proudly at His Son (Jesus) and Jesus' bride (the faithful believers). A perfect love.

Deuteronomy 7:9b

"He shows his love and kindness to all people who love him and obey his commands. He continues to show his love and kindness through a thousand generations. . ."

1 John 3:1a

The Father has loved us so much! This shows how much he loved us: We are called children of God. . .

What's in all those books in between? Many wonderful, frightful, sad, and happy stories that all play a part in His Story. Understanding the Bible can be difficult without an overall picture of what God is trying to tell us. The many stories inside it mean so much more if we can understand the big picture. All well-written stories have a theme, a topic of discussion that holds everything together. The theme of the Bible is love. The battle stories help us understand how much God loves us – He is willing to do whatever it takes to save us from Satan's evil grasp. We just have to allow Him to save us.

John 10:10 (Jesus speaking)

A thief comes to steal, kill, and destroy. But I came to give life – life that is full and good.

The whole Bible tells of a marriage between God and His people. In this marriage, His people have been unfaithful, but He is kind and good and forgiving. He has offered to restore all of us to our original relationship as though we had never left Him. All we have to do is accept His proposal for a new marriage with Him. He loves us, and He wants us to love Him above all else. What is love? Faithfulness and commitment that we truly want to demonstrate to another are how we show true love. When we decide in our hearts that we truly want to be faithful and committed to someone, we have decided to truly love that person. This is how God shows His true love to us, and it is how we show true love to God and to each other.

God has always been faithful and committed to us. A return of that love is all He asks of us.

Daniel 9:4a

I prayed to the LORD my God and told him about all my sins. I said, "Lord, you are a great and awesome God. You keep your agreement of love and kindness with people who love you."

2 Chronicles 6:14b

You keep the agreement that you made with your people. You are kind and loyal to those who follow you with all their heart.

Lamentations 3:22-24

We are still alive because the LORD's faithful love never ends. Every morning he shows it in new ways! You are so very true and loyal! I say to myself, "The LORD is my God, and I trust him."

We often read in the news about scientists who have discovered some new insect or star or planet or some new theory about how the world or the mind or the body works. Scientists may find something that no one before has found, or they may figure out something that no one before has figured out, but nothing that scientists discover is actually new. God made it all – He knows it all – He is The Creator. His Book has facts or hints about a wide variety of subjects. It has only been in the last 50 years or so that scientists have discovered the following, but God has known it all along and He put it in His Book for us to understand:

The most basic need of every single human being ever born on the face of the earth is love. Love is ALL we need. Why? Because love will feed us, love will protect us, love will teach us, love will encourage us, love will help us, love will save us.

1 Corinthians 13:2b

. . .if I don't have love, I am nothing.

Review: We all need love, and God loves us all.
God is fighting Satan because He loves us and wants a better life for us.

How can we love God if we cannot see or hear Him?

Adam and Eve had distanced themselves from God, and this presented a problem. Because of this distance, God could not be close to His people in the same way He had been in the Garden when He had walked with them and talked with them, so how was He to communicate with them?

As the population multiplied, God selected certain men and women to speak to His people for Him. These people are called His prophets. The Bible says that God will not do something until He has told His prophets first, so they can tell His people – His plan is not a secret. Noah, Moses, Isaiah, Jeremiah, Daniel, and Deborah are some of the prophets found in the Old Testament section of the Bible.

The Bible can be divided into two main groups of books:

- The Old Testament tells His Story from Creation until about 400 years before Jesus was born.

- The New Testament tells us about Jesus and His followers and gives us a peek into the future.

Amos 3:7

When the Lord GOD decides to do something, he will first tell his servants, the prophets.

The prophets of the Old Testament had a very tough job. They spoke for God, telling the people of His love for them, telling the people to follow Him, telling the people that

God would send someone to close the gap in their relationship. Some of the prophets were chosen to write down His words so they could be read later. The five books Moses wrote (Genesis, Exodus, Leviticus, Numbers, Deuteronomy) became known as The Law – they're also called the Torah, or the Pentateuch (a Greek word meaning five books), but neither of these names is used in the Bible. The books written by other prophets became known as The Books of the Prophets. The prophets who wrote the shortest books are known as the Minor Prophets, and those who wrote the longest books are known as the Major Prophets.

Jeremiah 7:25b

My servants are the prophets. I sent them to you again and again.

Jeremiah 7:27a, 28a

"Jeremiah, you will tell these things to the people. . .you must tell them these things. . ."

Malachi 1:1

This is a message from the LORD to Israel. God used Malachi to tell this message to the people.

The words these prophets spoke and wrote down for us are God's love letters to us. He sent these faithful, willing servants to deliver His messages to His people. God was wooing His bride. To "woo" means to seek the love of someone with an intent to marry that person – to be with that person forever. Here is a message – really, it's the core message God is always sending – that Moses delivered for God:

"Remember my laws and commands, and obey them. . .
I will not turn away from you.
I will walk with you and be your God.
And you will be my people."

Leviticus 26:3,11b-12

Let's review the word marriage. A marriage is a formal contract between two people in which each person contributes something to the union. Another way to describe marriage is to call it a covenant relationship. A covenant is an agreement in which both parties agree to do something for each other. In a marriage, the bride and groom agree to love and honor one another in sickness and in health, for richer or for poorer, and so on. In other words, they will love and look after one another in good times and in bad times – no matter what. That is their covenant – what they agree to do for each other. God wants a covenant relationship with His people. In the verses above, God promises to take care of those who will obey His commandments. Why will He take care of you? Because He loves you. Why would you obey His commandments? Because you love and trust Him. What are His commandments? In short form, He wants you to be faithful to Him above all else and to treat other people with love and respect because He loves them, too, and doesn't want to see them treated poorly.

God sent His prophets to deliver this core message to the people, but all of the people did not listen. Satan was persuasive, and some did not always resist the wicked temptations Satan set before them. Again, and again, God sent prophets to them. God was faithful to the people. He did everything He said He would. He never broke any of His promises. The people knew all of this, but still some resisted. They sent away some of the prophets – worse, they beat up some of His prophets. Saddest of all, the people even killed some of God's prophets – and all these faithful people had done was try to deliver a message from God to His beloved.

2 Chronicles 24:19

God sent prophets to the people to bring them back to the LORD. The prophets warned them, but they refused to listen.

Luke 11:49b

"I will send prophets and apostles to them. Some of my prophets and apostles will be killed by evil men. Others will be treated badly."

Acts 7:52a

They persecuted every prophet who ever lived. They even killed those who long ago said that the Righteous One would come.

Nehemiah 9:26

And then they turned against you. They threw away your teachings. They killed your prophets. Those prophets warned the people. They tried to bring them back to you. But our ancestors said terrible things against you.

How was God ever going to get through to them? But wait. . .God is all-powerful, right? He can do anything, right? Yes, He is, and He can. So, why didn't He just force the people to do what He wanted?

Because that isn't love. **Love must be freely given.**

You make decisions to be loyal, to be faithful, to be present and involved with certain people. When this faithfulness is rendered with a sincere, positive feeling in your heart, it is love. When you are faithful to someone but you resent "having" to be loyal to that person, your faithfulness is hypocritical – it is insincere, it is false love. In order to truly love someone, you must be faithful to that person because you truly want to be faithful to him/her.

In order to have a true, fulfilling, loving relationship with God (or another person), you must both be sincere.

Romans 12:9a

Your love must be real [sincere].

God has given us free will. In ANY matter that concerns our hearts, we have control. We are completely free to do as we like when it comes to God. We can decide to ignore God, or we can decide to love Him completely. It's an all-or-nothing deal. He has given us this gift of free will so that we have the opportunity to experience true love. True love is a love you willingly give with your whole being – all of who you are – your heart, your soul, your mind, and your strength (will). This is how God loves us, and it is the love He wants to receive from us. He has very clearly described how our relationship with Him should be. We must come to Him of our own free will. Every person must come on his/her own. No one can speak for you – no one can answer for you. Every person has his/her own voice and choice with God.

2 Chronicles 20:20b

"Have faith in the LORD your God, and you will stand strong! Have faith in his prophets, and you will succeed!"

Isaiah 44:26a

The Lord sends his servants to tell his messages to the people, and he makes those messages come true. He sends messengers to tell the people what they should do, and he proves that the advice is good.

Joshua 24:14a, 15part

Then Joshua said to the people, "Now you have heard the Lord's words. So you must respect the LORD and sincerely serve him. . .But maybe you don't want to serve the LORD. You must choose for yourselves today. Today you must decide who you will serve. . .as for me and my family, we will serve the LORD."

Ok, but if I don't choose God, I die? That isn't much of a choice! Yes, that is a valid point. You could give in to Satan's temptations and do whatever looks desirable to you in this earthly life. That's your only other choice. Just remember that ALL of the devil's temptations are lies. Satan makes his traps look, feel, or sound desirable to lure you into them – without these lures, you would never choose to follow him. Every choice in this life comes at a cost. Anytime we make a choice, we are choosing one thing at the expense of another. Economists call this opportunity cost. Is it worth giving up eternal happiness for temporary physical/emotional/mental pleasure?

Titus 3:3a

In the past we were foolish too. We did not obey, we were wrong, and we were slaves to the many things our bodies wanted and enjoyed.

This is about good vs. evil. It's a matter of opposites: good and bad, light and dark, life and death, paid up and in debt, found and lost, freedom and slavery, heaven and hell (remember, hell is anyplace that doesn't have God). What God is offering you FOR ETERNITY is ALL GOOD – it's freedom from slavery. It will bring you peace in your heart. It will fill you up with the truest of loves until you are overflowing. Why wouldn't you choose Him?

You will harvest what you plant.

*(Some people call this **karma**, which is a cause and effect teaching in Hinduism and Buddhism.)*

If you live to satisfy your sinful self, the harvest you will get from that will be eternal death.

But if you live to please the Spirit, your harvest from the Spirit will be eternal life.

Galatians 6:7b-8

You can follow sin, or you can obey God.

Following sin brings spiritual death, but obeying God makes you right with him.

Romans 6:16b

In the Bible, there are many stories about God's people and how they treated Him. If we zoom out for the big picture, we can see that God's people would honor Him and follow Him for a while, and then they would fall away from Him for a while. Much like a roller coaster ride, the people would find themselves down low, in the dark. Then they would turn to God, and He would raise them up. He would help them turn away from the wickedness that was dragging them down, look up to His light and love, and restore their end of the covenant. They would rejoice in His care and remain close to Him for a time, but fear or doubt or temptation would sneak in (Satan is always lurking about, making bad suggestions), and they would come thundering back down to the low, dark places again. Remember, God does not turn away from His people – they turn away from Him.

Perhaps they found it too difficult to maintain their end of the long-distance relationship. In the years before Jesus, the people did not have direct access to God. Only God-selected people, the prophets (and later, priests), could appeal to God directly. The other people had to have one of these people to act as a go-between – a mediator. God knew this time would be difficult, so through the prophets, He sent many messages to His people to try to maintain contact.

Review: God sent His prophets to deliver many messages to His people. It was a long-distance relationship.

How does Jesus fit in as a prophet?

God wants to have a close relationship with each one of His people. He wants to be close to us, and He wants us to be close to Him. He wants all of us to be with Him forever. Even when we do wrong, He still loves us. God wants the best for us, and the best for us is to be with Him all the time.

God tried and tried to get the people to listen to Him, but He does not want only some of the people or even most of the people. He isn't happy to have 99 out of every 100 people. Because He loves all of us, He wants 100 of every 100. There is a story Jesus tells in the Bible that is commonly known as "The Shepherd and the Lost Sheep" or "The Parable of the Lost Sheep."

"If a man has 100 sheep, but one of the sheep is lost, what will he do? He will leave the other 99 sheep on the hill and go look for the lost sheep. Right? And if he finds the lost sheep, he is happier about that one sheep than about the 99 sheep that were never lost. I can assure you, in the same way your Father in heaven does not want any of these little children to be lost."

Matthew 18:12-14

We are His children. Jesus' words are God's words to us.

Jesus told this story to help people understand just how much God loves each and every one of us – even those of us who have wandered away from Him. In this story, Jesus is the Shepherd and we are the sheep. He related the joy in heaven over a lost soul returning to God to the joy of a shepherd finding a lost sheep, because most people at that time either raised sheep or were very familiar with raising sheep (or other animals). Jesus told many stories in this way. These stories that relate a heavenly truth to an earthly truth are called parables.

1 Timothy 2:4-6a

God wants everyone to be saved and to fully understand the truth. There is only one God, and there is only one way that people can reach God. That way is through Christ Jesus, who as a man gave himself to pay for everyone to be free.

Hebrews 1:1-2a

In the past God spoke to our people through the prophets. He spoke to them many times and in many different ways. And now in these last days, God has spoken to us again through his Son.

Deuteronomy 18:18-19a

"I will send them a prophet. . . This prophet will be one of their own people. I will tell him what he must say, and he will tell the people everything I command. This prophet will speak for me. . . "

John 10:14-15 (Jesus speaking about Himself)

"I am the shepherd who cares for the sheep. I know my sheep just as the Father knows me. And my sheep know me just as I know the Father. I give my life for these sheep."

When Jesus began telling the people His Message, about 400 years had passed since God had sent the last Old Testament prophet. Many of the people who heard His stories wondered if Jesus might be the special prophet who had been written about in the Old Testament. They wondered if Jesus was the One the prophets of old had said would come. God's people knew the Scriptures well (books, pens, and paper were not common household items then, so most of them had memorized large portions of Scripture), and they knew that God had promised to send someone who would restore their relationship. They had been eagerly awaiting this special prophet, also called the Messiah, or Savior.

John 6:14

The people saw this miraculous sign that Jesus did and said, "He must be the Prophet who is coming into the world."

John 7:16

Jesus answered, "What I teach is not my own. My teaching comes from the one who sent me."

John 8:28

So he said to them, "You will lift up the Son of Man. Then you will know that I AM. You will know that whatever I do is not by my own authority. You will know that I say only what the Father has taught me."

Jesus came to tell the people to follow God, just like the prophets of old had done, but those old prophets had only brought messages. How was Jesus' Message different? Remember those special meetings God called with His faithful children (**benei Elohim**) – the meetings mentioned in the book of Job that Satan showed up to, uninvited? Those special meetings were religious feast days that God had instructed His faithful people to observe at specific times. Jesus' arrival and the completion of His first mission fulfilled the first four of the seven Jewish feasts, as we will see. His completion of those feasts proved to all of God's people who were willing to accept it that He was the Messiah they had been expecting. He ended the long-distance era of humanity's relationship with God and brought His people back into His presence. Jesus' work made it possible for everyone to be with God. God sent Jesus to do this work. God wants to save everyone from Satan's evil traps. He wants to find all those who are lost and bring them home.

John 14:2-3

"There are many rooms in my Father's house. I would not tell you this if it were not true. I am going there to prepare a place for you. After I go and prepare a place for you, I will come back. Then I will take you with me, so that you can be where I am."

Jews of today are mostly descended from people who saw or heard about Jesus during His time on earth but did not believe that He was the Messiah, the Savior, God had promised. These Jews are still waiting for the "real" Messiah.

Review: Our Lord (Jesus – the Prophet – the Great Shepherd – the Son of God) will call to and search for EVERY lost soul and try to bring it home to His Father's (God's) house.

How can we be with God if we have sin?

Here on earth, a judge issues a punishment to a criminal to justify a crime – the sentence served by the criminal is supposed to make amends for his/her crime. When the sentence has been served, the criminal is free to return to life. This idea of justice is not new. Humans did not invent justice – God did. He is the ultimate and final judge.

In spite of our sins, we can have a close relationship with Him because God is good, God is love, God is our Father, and God has a plan. He set up the biggest and best debt-forgiveness program the world has ever known. With His plan, He could erase all the debt (disobedience, sin, wrongdoing) that His people had accumulated. The punishment for their wrongs could be served, and He could completely forgive them. With God's plan, the people could start fresh and have a direct relationship with Him.

The first step in His plan was to teach the people how serious sin is. God needed the people to understand that sin would not only create a great distance between them, but that the distance would be very difficult to close – so difficult that they could not do it without His help, His mercy, His forgiveness. Without His help, they would not only die an immediate spiritual death, but they would also – if they remained spiritually dead – suffer a permanent physical death.

God also needed the people to understand that He is a fair judge – He rewards good, He punishes evil. The punishment for sin is death. If a person sinned, the punishment should be suffered by that person. God is fair.

But God is good and merciful, too, and He wanted His people to know that.

Ecclesiastes 3:17b

God has planned a time for everything, and he has planned a time to judge everything people do. He will judge good people and bad people.

Psalm 7:11a

God is a good judge.

In order to teach them all these things, God set up a system of sacrifice. He allowed sinners to offer an animal (one that had value and would be a physical and/or financial cost for the person) for punishment in their place. The guilty person could offer this animal sacrifice to atone for (or cover) his/her sin. The people understood that life is in the blood, and that the life blood of the sacrificed animal was atonement for their sin. Because of this, they began to understand that blood is tied to the soul, to sin, and to holiness. They understood that in place of the loss of their own spiritual lives, God was merciful and willing to accept the physical life blood of the animal. They understood that sin brings death. They understood that to be truly fair and righteous – and God is the fairest, most righteous judge of all – punishment must be served for sin.

Remember that after Adam and Eve sinned, God gave them animal skins as clothing. Could this have been the first animal sacrifice to atone for human sin? The Bible doesn't specifically say, but that interpretation is definitely in harmony with the overall structure of Scripture.

Parents know that punishment is an unpleasant but necessary part of teaching children and guiding them in the way they should go. Often the punishment is harder on the parents than it is on the child who has done wrong.

God does not enjoy punishing His people. One of the Old Testament prophets, Hosea, tells us in his book that God does not want sacrifices from His people – He just wants our faithful love. But the sacrifices must be offered, because sins have been committed and punishment must be served. A truly righteous judge (a judge who always and completely seeks the good and right) does not sweep crimes under the rug and ignore them. We could not respect or trust Him if He did. God judges everyone fairly.

Hosea 6:6

"This is because I want faithful love, not sacrifice. I want people to know God, not to bring burnt offerings."

Psalm 51:16-17

You don't really want sacrifices, or I would give them to you. The sacrifice that God wants is a humble spirit. God, you will not turn away someone who comes with a humble heart and is willing to obey you.

The messages from the prophets and the sacrifices to pay for the people's sins went on for a long time with varying degrees of success as God prepared His people for the next step in His plan. He was preparing the people for someone they would surely listen to – someone higher than the prophets, someone with more authority than a servant.

When the time was right, God sent His most precious representative in heaven to deliver His most intimate and earnest request yet to His beloved people.

Isaiah 9:6b-7

God will give us a son who will be responsible for leading the people. His name will be "Wonderful Counselor, Powerful God, Father Who Lives Forever, Prince of Peace." His power will continue to grow, and there will be peace without end. This will establish him as the king sitting on David's throne and ruling his kingdom. He will rule with goodness and justice forever and ever. The strong love that the LORD All-Powerful has for his people will make this happen!

Malachi 3:1b

Yes, the messenger you are waiting for, the one who will tell about my agreement, is really coming!

God sent His Son, Jesus, in the form of a baby. This special baby was miraculously conceived by God's Spirit in Mary, a young woman, a virgin, whom God decided should be the mother of His Son. Jesus grew up like other children of that day and time, with the same human problems and concerns we all still experience. Like other Jewish boys, He studied the Torah (the first five books of the Bible – all the books of The Law that God had told His prophet Moses to write) and the other Jewish writings (the other prophets' books, the poetry books, and the history books). Together, those writings were known as the Scriptures (Words of God), and today we call them the Hebrew Bible or the Old Testament. As Jesus grew, He learned the trade of His earthly father (Mary's husband, Joseph), who was a builder. Jesus worked and did not marry. Jesus did not begin to tell the people God's message until He was about 30 years old. Then for three years, He traveled around from town to town explaining God's Message to the people using demonstrations and stories they could understand and miracles to prove that He was who He said He was.

Matthew 1:23
"The virgin will be pregnant and will give birth to a son. They will name him Immanuel." (Immanuel means "God with us.")

Luke 1:35
The angel said to Mary, "The Holy Spirit will come to you, and the power of the Most High God will cover you. The baby will be holy and will be called the Son of God."

Matthew 1:20b-21
The angel said, "Joseph, son of David, don't be afraid to accept Mary to be your wife. The baby inside her is from the Holy Spirit. She will give birth to a son. You will name him Jesus. Give him that name because he will save his people from their sins."

Luke 3:23a
When Jesus began to teach, he was about 30 years old.

Because God loves us so much, He sent His Son to deliver His message for Him. Jesus' coming to earth as a man was the most earnest proposal God could make to His people.

Romans 6:23
When people sin, they earn what sin pays – death. But God gives his people a free gift – eternal life in Christ Jesus our Lord.

Many people listened, but many did not.

Some not only didn't listen and obey they revolted against Him. Some even wanted Jesus dead. The people guilty of this thought were the very people who claimed to love and serve God the most. These religious leaders were jealous. They believed that Jesus would turn the people away from their religious leadership – and they were right. Jesus was trying to turn the people away from the religious leadership of men and back to God. These leaders had strayed from God, but they did not realize that they had – or they were unwilling to admit that they had. These religious leaders decided that the only way to get rid of the threat Jesus was causing to their important positions in religion and society was to kill Him. But God knew they would do this.

Matthew 26:3a, 4a

Then the leading priests and the older Jewish leaders had a meeting at the palace where the high priest lived. . . In the meeting they tried to find a way to arrest and kill Jesus without anyone knowing what they were doing.

Romans, a book in the New Testament, tells us that God can make even the worst thing turn out for the good for those who love and serve Him.

We know that in everything God works for the good of those who love him.

Romans 8:28a

God's plan was to use this terrible deed for great good – for all of us who are willing to accept it. In fact, He made what would seem like the absolute worst thing turn into the absolute best thing that could ever happen. This event, for which God had carefully prepared His people using the feast days He had instituted, is the central part of His plan to restore a close relationship with us, His children, and to conquer Satan.

John 12:24 (Jesus talking about His mission to save us all)

"It is a fact that a grain of wheat must fall to the ground and die before it can grow and produce much more wheat. If it never dies, it will never be more than a single seed."

Ephesians 5:27

Christ died so that he could give the church to himself like a bride in all her beauty. He died so that the church could be holy and without fault, with no evil or sin or any other thing wrong in it.

John 10:11,18

"I am the good shepherd, and the good shepherd gives his life for the sheep. . .No one takes my life away from me. I give my own life freely. I have the right to give my life, and I have the right to get it back again. This is what the Father told me."

Jeremiah 33:8

They sinned against me, but I will wash away that sin. They fought against me, but I will forgive them.

Isaiah 25:7-8

But now there is a veil covering all nations and people. This veil is called "death." But death will be destroyed forever. And the Lord GOD will wipe away every tear from every face. In the past, all of his people were sad, but God will take away that sadness from the earth. All of this will happen because the LORD said it would.

Acts 2:22-23

"My fellow Israelites, listen to these words: Jesus from Nazareth was a very special man. God clearly showed this to you. He proved it by the miracles, wonders, and miraculous signs he did through Jesus. You all saw these things, so you know this is true. Jesus was handed over to you, and you killed him. With the help of evil men, you nailed him to a cross. But God knew all this would happen. It was his plan – a plan he made long ago."

Review: God developed the ultimate debt-forgiveness plan that Jesus came to set up.

When did God come up with this plan?

God has had His plan since the beginning – a Savior was always the plan, because God knew humans would betray Him and some of them would regret their choice. He spoke about a Savior first to Adam, Eve, and Satan right after Adam and Eve had sinned. Later, He sent His prophets with messages promising that a Messiah would come to save His people. God began sending these prophets at least 2,000 years before Jesus' time on earth. He set up the system of sacrifice to help the people understand what Jesus would do for them, and He gave the people seven specific feast days so they would know without a doubt that Jesus was the Messiah for whom they had been waiting.

1 Peter 1:20a
Christ was chosen before the world was made. . .

Matthew 25:32a, 34 (Jesus telling us what will happen when He comes again)
"All the people of the world will be gathered before him. Then he will separate everyone into two groups. . . Then the king will say to the godly people on his right, 'Come, my Father has great blessings for you. The kingdom he promised is now yours. It has been prepared for you since the world was made.'"

To see how Jesus fulfilled those messages, sacrifices, and feast days – how He made God's promises come true – you must know about the promise God made to a very early prophet who came to be known as Father Abraham. Here's a summary of His Story that is found in the Bible. The whole story covers thousands of years as God carried out the steps of His plan.

Flashback to the Creation (at least 5,500 years ago):

Remember, Adam and Eve were the first people, and we are all descended from them. Also remember Noah, the ark builder who, with God's protection, survived the major, world-wide flood. We are all descendants of Noah through one of his three sons.

Acts 17:26
God began by making one man, and from him he made all the different people who live everywhere in the world. He decided exactly when and where they would live.

Genesis 10:32 (This begins what is now called the Table of Nations - a listing of the family nations)
This is the list of the families from Noah's sons. They are arranged according to their nations. From these families came all the people who spread across the earth after the flood.

Acts 10:34-35

Peter began to speak: "I really understand now that God does not consider some people to be better than others. He accepts anyone who worships him and does what is right. It is not important what nation they come from."

Many years after the Flood, God spoke to a man named Abram and told him to leave the place where he was living. God told Abram to travel to a land that He would show him, and **God would bless all the people on earth through him**.

Jeremiah 29:11

"I say this because I know the plans that I have for you." This message is from the LORD. "I have good plans for you. I don't plan to hurt you. I plan to give you hope and a good future."

After a time, when Abram and his wife, Sarai, were living in the land of Canaan that God had shown him, God told Abram, "All this land that you see I will give to you and your people who live after you" (Genesis 13:15a). Sometime later, God spoke to Abram again and said, "Look at the sky. See the many stars. There are so many you cannot count them. Your family will be like that" (Genesis 15:5b). Some years later, God told Abram that his name would be changed to Abraham, which means *the father of many nations*, and Sarai's new name would be Sarah, which means *princess*, because "kings of nations will come from her" (Genesis 17:5, 15-16). At this time, God restated His covenant with Abraham: if Abraham obeyed God, he would become the father of many nations, God would be their God, and God would bless all the nations through Abraham. Abraham was required to show that he agreed to the covenant by circumcising himself and all the male members of his household and all their descendants. This would be the sign of his agreement with God. Abraham did as God asked.

Abraham believed God's promise that he would have many descendants even though he and his wife were quite old and did not have any children. After a time, when Abraham and Sarah were very old and well past child-bearing years, they had a son and named him Isaac. As Isaac grew, God tested (not tempted) Abraham's trust in Him. God told Abraham to sacrifice his son. Abraham, his faith in God strong, made the preparations to do as God asked. He reasoned to himself that God could raise the dead, because God had told him he would have as many descendants as there are stars in the sky. Just before Abraham killed Isaac, God stopped him and said, "I see that you are ready to kill your son, your only son, for me" (Genesis 22:12b). Then God gave Abraham a ram (an adult male sheep) for sacrifice in Isaac's place. God was pleased that Abraham believed He could keep His promise that he would have many descendants even if Isaac died. God was pleased that Abraham had enough faith in Him to offer his only son as a sacrifice. This story foreshadows the beginning of the feast days and the most important event in His Story.

Isaac grew up and married. He had twin sons named Esau and Jacob. When Jacob grew up and married, he had 12 sons, and God changed Jacob's name to Israel. His descendants later became known as Israelites. . . the nation of Israel. Israel's sons became the fathers of the 12 tribes (family clans) of Israel. When Israel's sons were grown, the entire family moved to Egypt because there was not enough food in their homeland and because they would be cared for in Egypt by one of Israel's sons, Joseph, whom God had placed in a position of authority in the Egyptian royal household.

Because they were jealous of him, Joseph's brothers had secretly sold him into slavery some years before and lied to their father, Israel, about it by allowing him to think Joseph had been killed by a wild animal. God had taken this terrible deed and turned it around by raising Joseph up and putting his brothers at his mercy.

Exodus 6:8a

"I made a great promise to Abraham, Isaac, and Jacob. . ."

After many years, a time came when God allowed Abraham's descendants, the Israelites, to be made slaves in this foreign land, Egypt. Then, after a long time of slavery, the Israelites, who had neglected their relationship with God, began to remember the God of their forefathers – the God of Abraham, Isaac, and Jacob. The people began to call on God for help. God heard their calls (He is always listening) and sent a man named Moses to help them escape slavery and travel back to the land God had promised Abraham. Moses delivered God's messages to the people. God told Moses what to say, what to do, and what to write down – Moses was a prophet.

Deuteronomy 6:4

"Listen, people of Israel! The LORD is our God. The LORD is the only God."

Proverbs 16:4a

The LORD has a plan for everything.

Exodus 3:10 (God speaking to Moses)

"So now I am sending you to Pharaoh. Go! Lead my people, the Israelites, out of Egypt."

Exodus 3:15a

And God said, "Tell the Israelites that you were sent by YAHWEH, the God of your ancestors – the God of Abraham, the God of Isaac, the God of Jacob."

Exodus 6:5-6

"Now, I have heard their painful cries. I know that they are slaves in Egypt. And I remember my agreement. So tell the Israelites that I say to them, I am the LORD. I will save you. You will no longer be slaves of the Egyptians. I will use my great power to make you free, and I will bring terrible punishment to the Egyptians."

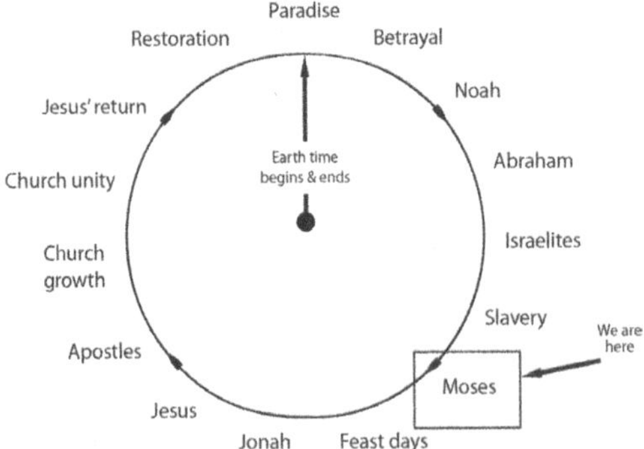

God told Moses to talk to the king. The king of Egypt in those days was called Pharaoh. Moses asked Pharaoh to let God's people leave. Pharaoh said no. Moses warned him that God would send terrible troubles to the land of Egypt if Pharaoh did not let the people leave. The king said he would not let them leave. So, God sent ten terrible troubles to the people of Egypt, but He protected His people from most of these sufferings. God continued to offer Pharaoh a way out of the punishments. Before each terrible trouble (the Bible calls them plagues, but they weren't all illnesses), He sent Moses to speak with the Egyptian king to find out if his heart had softened and he was ready to let God's people leave. Pharaoh was very stubborn, so God continued to send punishment.

The Bible does say that God hardened Pharaoh's heart, but it also says that Pharaoh hardened his own heart. The two statements are not contradictory. Pharaoh acted out of his own stubbornness for the first five plagues. As it is recorded throughout the Bible with those who see the glory and power of God but refuse to accept it, their hearts become even harder because of God's mighty display. This did not happen to Pharaoh until the sixth plague. God gave Pharaoh many chances to repent. When some of Pharaoh's officials believed Moses' warning and acted on it, they were spared (Exodus 9:20-21). God was punishing an extremely wicked and unrepentant king and nation, but He was also using them to ultimately show His great mercy for all people, as we will see.

The ten troubles God sent were not just bad things that happened. Each one had a special meaning. The Egyptian people worshipped many gods. They had made up stories about gods of the sun, a god of the harvest, gods of the water, etc. The first nine of these ten terrible troubles, or plagues, directly defeated, or proved false, one or more of the made-up Egyptian gods by showing the ONE TRUE GOD to be more powerful than any of the false Egyptian gods. For example, to defeat the "powerful" Egyptian god of the sun, God made it dark during the day. In other words, if the false Egyptian god could cause the sun to shine every day, the ONE TRUE GOD could cause the sun to shine, or He could keep the sun from shining during the day.

The last plague God sent was to show that there was indeed no other God like Him. This plague, called "Death of the Firstborn" in the Bible, proved to the Egyptians and to any Israelites who had doubts, that the ONE TRUE GOD was the ONLY true God. The LORD would come to Egypt one night to take the lives of the firstborn of each household, including the prince of Egypt.

If you are thinking that God seems unnecessarily cruel to the Egyptians, read Exodus Chapter 1. The Egyptian people had cruelly enslaved the Israelites for some time, trying to reduce their numbers. God was watching over the Israelites, and their population count continued to prosper. Pharaoh, annoyed by this, ordered all the Israelite baby boys to be killed at birth. Read Chapter 2 to find out how God used two women and a girl to save baby Moses from this edict.

God told Moses to tell His people how to protect themselves from this last punishment, this plague, this judgment of death for sin. This protective action officially began the feast days – but the Israelites did not yet know that. First, let's review what they were told to do. In order to understand this story fully, you must know, as the ancient Israelites did, that there is life in blood – if you have no blood, you cannot live.

God instructed His people to prepare a lamb for dinner at every house. The lamb could have no defects of any kind – the lamb that was sacrificed must be a perfect lamb. In those days, people prepared their own food. First, they had to kill the lamb, then they had to cook it. When the lamb was killed, the people were to collect the blood. This blood from the lamb would save their lives. God's people were to take the lamb's blood and paint some on the top and sides of the door frame around their front doors. It sounds gruesome, but God had a purpose. He always does.

God's people were to go into their houses – pass through the doorway that was painted with the blood of the perfect lamb – before dark and stay inside until the next morning. Doing this would save God's people from the judgment of death. This time in His Story became known as the Passover, because the LORD would see the blood of the lamb on the doorways and pass over the houses of His faithful people. All of the people who obeyed God would be saved from death by the blood of the lamb. This night was the very first Passover feast, and God instructed His people to celebrate it every year after that, so they would remember how God had saved them using the blood of the lamb. If God's people remembered the Passover, it would help them to understand God's plan when the next phase began. It was after this terrible night that the Pharaoh let God's people leave Egypt – they were finally freed from slavery. They were beginning a new life closer to God, and they were going to the Promised Land – the land God had promised many years before to give to Abraham and his descendants.

Exodus 9:16 (God to Pharaoh)

"But I have put you here for a reason. I have put you here so that I could show you my power. Then people all over the world will learn about me!"

Exodus 12:12b-13a

"I will judge all the gods of Egypt and show that I am the LORD. But the blood on your houses will

be a special sign. When I see the blood, I will pass over your house."

Exodus 7:4b-5a

"And I will lead my army, my people, out of that land. I will punish the people of Egypt, and they will learn that I am the LORD."

In His words and actions during this time, God began to grow the trust of His people once again. He had never left them, but they had failed to turn to Him, so their trust – their faith – was weak. God can only grow our faith when we allow Him to work in us. God made the Israelites' faith grow by making statements about what He was going to do and following through with those promises. God can still grow our faith today, but we have to allow Him to do it. First, we have to accept what He has already promised and delivered, and then God can build our faith on that foundation.

Exodus 14:31

The Israelites saw the great power of the LORD when he defeated the Egyptians. So the people feared and respected the LORD, and they began to trust the LORD and his servant Moses.

Exodus 12:26-27a

"When your children ask you, 'Why are we doing this ceremony?' you will say, 'This Passover is to honor the LORD, because when we were in Egypt, he passed over the houses of Israel. He killed the Egyptians, but he saved the people in our houses.'"

Review: God has had this plan for His people since the beginning:
THE BLOOD OF THE LAMB WOULD SAVE THEIR LIVES.

Do we have to sacrifice a lamb every year so that God will protect us?

No, the sacrifice of a lamb at Passover was God's way of preparing His people for what would happen many years later. God was preparing them for Jesus and His message.

John 1:29b

"Look, the Lamb of God. He takes away the sins of the world!"

Hebrews 10:18

And after everything is forgiven, there is no more need for a sacrifice to pay for sins.

Review: The Passover lamb of the Old Testament was a teaching tool God used to help His people understand Jesus and His mission.

Flash-forward again to the time of Jesus (about 2,000 years ago):

During His ministry, some of the people believed what Jesus was telling them about God and began to follow His teachings. This group of followers included many people whose ancestors had been God's people in the Passover story. At the time of the first Passover, God's people were called Israelites. By Jesus' time, they were known as Jews (a name given to them by foreign captors many years before (see the book of Esther), possibly because their land was called Judah at that time). The group of people who followed Jesus' teachings also included other people who were not Jewish (the Jews called anyone who was not Jewish, a Gentile). So, Jesus had Jewish and Gentile followers who were listening to His Message and turning to God.

Other towns had buildings called synagogues where the Jewish people met to worship God, but the main Jewish place of worship was in the city of Jerusalem and was called the Temple. Remember those special meetings that the children of God had with Him? Great masses of faithful Jews traveled to the Temple in Jerusalem to celebrate at least three of the feasts every year – these were the special meetings. The Temple leaders in Jerusalem felt threatened by Jesus, because some of the Jews were beginning to follow Him instead of them. Power is very tempting and very addictive. Remember that Satan also tempted Eve with power – he told her she would be God-like if she had the knowledge of good and evil.

The Temple leaders were also the political leaders of the nation of Israel – there was no separation of church and state. These Jewish leaders secretly arrested Jesus (after paying off one of His disciples (students) for information on His whereabouts) and arranged a false trial in the middle of the night in which they, of course, found Jesus guilty of sinning against God. By saying that He was the Son of God, Jesus was giving the impression that He thought He was equal to God. The Jewish leaders considered this behavior blasphemy. Blasphemy is the sin of saying bad things about God or of saying that you are God-like. The Jews considered blasphemy to be punishable by death. They declared Jesus a criminal and put Him on death row. The religious leaders were not allowed to execute Him themselves, because their homeland was controlled by the Roman Empire at that time, and the Roman government didn't allow the Jews to execute criminals. So, the Jewish religious leaders brought Jesus to the Roman governor, Pontius Pilate, and asked that He be executed. The Roman governor questioned Jesus but could not find Him guilty of any crime under Roman law. The Jewish leaders insisted that Jesus had violated Jewish law and must be executed. Then the leaders riled up the crowd that had come to watch, and the crowd began to shout that Jesus should be put to death. To prevent a revolt – to keep the crowd under control – Jesus would be killed.

The trial and execution of Jesus showed a complete lack of justice in every respect, because the humans demanding justice and acting as judges in these events were corrupted by Satan. This is a stark contrast to the ultimate display of perfect justice that will be seen when God issues His final judgment on all of His Creation.

Jesus demonstrated a humble earthly life from beginning to end. He, like a lamb, was born in a sheltered place where animals were housed – likely a cave in the rocky hillsides of that area. His parents had no rank or status. He learned a trade. He didn't own a home. He traveled from place to place on foot. He often camped. While on trial, He did not have a lawyer or anyone to speak for Him. His friends deserted Him. He was alone. He did not try to defend Himself. He was beaten severely. The people made fun of Him. Someone made a "crown" for Him out of a thorny vine and put it on His head. They NAILED His hands and feet to a wooden cross and set it upright, so He could hang from it – suffering and struggling for breath until He died. That is the awful and bitter truth of what Satan can accomplish in this world if he can find willing servants to do his evil work.

Luke 22:2

The leading priests and teachers of the law wanted to kill Jesus. But they were trying to find a quiet way to do it, because they were afraid of what the people would do.

Matthew 26:2 (Jesus speaking to His followers)

"You know that the day after tomorrow is Passover. On that day the Son of Man will be handed over to his enemies to be killed on a cross."

Isaiah 25:1b

The words you said long ago are completely true; everything happened exactly as you said it would.

Mark 15:10

Pilate knew that the leading priests had handed Jesus over to him because they were jealous of him.

Mark 15:13

The people shouted, "Kill him on a cross!"

Acts 2:23b

God knew all of this would happen. It was his plan – a plan he made long ago.

Review: God's plan has always been Jesus.
Jesus, the Son of God, came to earth as a man to deliver God's message to us and to fulfill God's promise to Abraham, but He was rejected by some of His own people and executed like a criminal.

How does Jesus fit into God's debt-forgiveness plan?

In the Old Testament sacrifice system, the people learned that blood is life. They understood that God accepted the blood of the animals in place of their own. Today, we also know that, from a medical point of view, life is in the blood. A physically injured or ill person who doesn't have enough blood will die, but they can be given blood by a donor. A donor is someone who freely gives up something of his/her own for the benefit of someone else, especially someone in need. Blood from a donor has the power to give life – it has the power to free a person from death.

Leviticus 17:11

This is because the life of the body is in the blood. I have told you that you must pour the blood on the altar to purify yourselves. It is the blood that makes a person pure.

Jesus gave up His place in heaven to come to earth, then He gave up His life, His blood, in place of our own to save us all from death. He is the perfect donor because He is completely without sin, and His sacrifice was offered with a pure and perfect love for God and for all of God's children. We have all sinned against God, and we all deserve punishment. The Bible says the punishment for sin is death. It is through Adam's sin that we all suffer a physical death, because we no longer have access to the tree of life. The punishment for our own sin is a spiritual death. We deserve that spiritual death, but our loving Lord Jesus suffered the punishment for our sins for us.

Colossians 2:13-14

You were spiritually dead because of your sins and because you were not free from the power of your sinful self. But God gave you new life together with Christ. He forgave all our sins. Because we broke God's laws, we owed a debt – a debt that listed all the rules we failed to follow. But God forgave us of that debt. He took it away and nailed it to the cross.

In giving up His blood, giving up His life, He once and for all time completed the sacrifice step in God's plan. Jesus' sacrifice was so pure and so perfect a demonstration of love that God has forgiven us all for all of our sins. There is no greater offer of apology, no greater punishment we could serve that would balance out and bring total forgiveness for all of our sins. The scales of justice have been permanently tipped in our favor. There is no greater love than His love for us.

God made the trial that was so hateful, selfish, and unjust become the most loving and generous court ruling humans will ever know. Because of His sacrifice, both our spirits and our bodies can live again.

Colossians 1:20

And through him [Jesus], God was happy to bring all things back to himself again – things on earth and things in heaven. God made peace by using the blood sacrifice of his Son on the cross.

Jesus also fulfilled God's promise to Abraham, that God would bless all the nations of the earth through him, because **Jesus was born in the family line of Abraham**. The Bible outlines His earthly family tree. Jesus was born into the family clan, or tribe, of Judah, one of the 12 sons of Jacob (remember, God renamed him Israel). Jacob's (Israel's) grandfather was Abraham.

Galatians 3:14

Because of what Jesus Christ did, the blessing God promised to Abraham was given to all people. Christ died so that by believing in him we could have the Spirit that God promised.

Galatians 3:28-29

Now, in Christ, it doesn't matter if you are a Jew or a Greek, a slave or free, male or female. You are all the same in Christ Jesus. You belong to Christ, so you are Abraham's descendants. You get all of God's blessings because of the promise that God made to Abraham.

We are all in need of His blood to cleanse/heal/cure our sin, so that God can completely forgive us, so that the distance in our personal relationship with God can be removed. Although humans created the distance by not trusting Him, and we all continue to doubt God from time to time, God Himself provided the cure to heal our relationship with Him. He allowed His Son to suffer the punishment for us all. He allowed Jesus' death as a substitute for our own. It is a gift from our God who is kind and good and full of mercy. All we have to do is accept His gift. Without Jesus' blood, we cannot be saved.

2 Timothy 1:9 (God's gift was available to people before earthly time began)

God saved us and chose us to be his holy people, but not because of anything we ourselves did. God saved us and made us his people because that was what he wanted and because of his grace. That grace was given to us through Christ Jesus before time began.

John 10:10b-11

". . .I came to give life – life that is full and good. I am the good shepherd, and the good shepherd

gives his life for the sheep."

John 10:2, 3b, 4part

". . .the man who takes care of the sheep. . .is the shepherd. . .And the sheep listen to the voice of the shepherd. He calls his own sheep, using their names, and he leads them out. . .Then he goes ahead of them and leads them."

John 10:9

"I am the gate. Whoever enters through me will be saved. They will be able to come in and go out. They will find everything they need."

Revelation 3:8part

"I have put before you an open door that no one can close."

Review: Only the blood of a perfect donor can remove sin from our souls and erase the debt that we owe to God. If the sin is not removed, we cannot be with God. Jesus removed our sins, but we must accept that gift.

What if I was born bad? What if I have done too many bad things? What if I have done things that are too wrong to be forgiven?

There is no such thing. Sin is not something we are born with. . . it is something we choose to do. God has given us free will, and we have the power to choose. The Bible says that Satan tempts us to do wrong, and he makes it seem so desirable that sometimes we find it very difficult to resist. God never tempts us to do wrong. Ever. And He will always help us turn away from sin if we ask Him. God has given us power over Satan. Satan is very tricky, but we have more power than he does.

James 1:13-15

Whenever you feel tempted to do something bad, you should not say, "God is tempting me." Evil cannot tempt God, and God himself does not tempt anyone. You are tempted by the evil things you want. Your own desire leads you away and traps you. Your desire grows inside you until it results in sin. Then the sin grows bigger and bigger and finally ends in death.

1 Corinthians 10:13 (You are not alone)

The only temptations that you have are the same temptations that all people have. But you can trust God. He will not let you be tempted more than you can bear. But when you are tempted, God will also give you a way to escape that temptation. Then you will be able to endure it.

Matthew 6:13 (Jesus said to pray for help)

"Don't let us be tempted, but save us from the Evil One."

Mark 8:33b (We have the power to tell Satan to leave)

"Get away from me Satan! You don't care about the same things God does. You care only about things that people think are important."

Ephesians 4:27 (We can control ourselves)

Don't give the devil a way to defeat you.

God does not have a limit on the number or type of sins He will forgive. He will forgive you if you have done something very bad. He will forgive you if you have done something bad many times. He will forgive you if you have done many bad things many times for many years. He will forgive you no matter what you have done or how many times you have done it – IF you are sincerely sorry for what you have done and you turn your life over to Him and what He has planned for you.

Isaiah 1:18

"I, the LORD, am the one speaking to you. Come, let's discuss this. Even if your sins are as dark as red dye, that stain can be removed and you will be as pure as wool that is as white as snow."

Joel 2:1b, 12part, 13part

The LORD's special day is coming; it is near. . .This is the LORD's message: "Now come back to me with all your heart. . .Show that you are sad for doing wrong." Come back to the LORD your God. He is kind and merciful.

Romans 2:4

God has been kind to you. He has been very patient, waiting for you to change. But you think nothing of his kindness. Maybe you don't understand that God is kind to you so that you will decide to change your lives.

Acts 3:19

So you must change your hearts and lives. Come back to God, and he will forgive your sins.

Jesus tells a story to teach this very lesson to a man named Simon, who was one of the Jewish religious leaders.

Luke 7:36-50

One of the Pharisees [religious leaders] asked Jesus to eat with him. Jesus went into the Pharisee's house and took a place at the table. There was a sinful woman in that town. She knew that Jesus was eating at the Pharisee's house. So the woman brought some expensive perfume in an alabaster jar. She stood at Jesus' feet, crying. Then she began to wash his feet with her tears. She dried his feet with her hair. She kissed his feet many times and rubbed them with the perfume.

When the Pharisee who asked Jesus to come to his house saw this, he thought to himself, "If this man were a prophet, he would know that the woman who is touching him is a sinner!"

[Jesus knew the man's thoughts.]
In response, Jesus said to the Pharisee, "Simon, I have something to say to you."

Simon said, "Let me hear it, Teacher."

Jesus said, "There were two men. Both men owed money to the same banker. One man owed him 500 silver coins. The other man owed him 50 silver coins. The men had no money, so they could not pay their debt. But the banker told the men that they did not have to pay him. Which one of those two men will love him more?"
Simon answered, "I think it would be the one who owed him the most money."

Jesus said to him, "You are right."

Then he turned to the woman and said to Simon, "Do you see this woman? When I came into your house, you gave me no water for my feet. [The streets were very dusty, and it was customary to wash your feet upon entering a house.] But she washed my feet with her tears and dried my feet with her hair. You did not greet me with a kiss, but she has been kissing my feet since I came in. You did not honor me with oil for my head, but she rubbed my feet with her sweet-smelling oil. I tell you that her many sins are forgiven. This is clear, because she showed great love. People who are forgiven only a little will love only a little."

Then Jesus said to her, "Your sins are forgiven."

The people sitting at the table began to think to themselves, "Who does this man think he is? How can he forgive sins?"

Jesus said to the woman, "Because you believed, you are saved from your sins. Go in peace."

If we have faith in Him and His plan and we follow His path, God forgives sins of any number or type. Be careful to understand that this does not mean you can live a life doing whatever you please and then skid into God's home plate at the last minute to repent of your errant ways. If you have made that decision, then you are already guilty, because you already know that what you are doing is wrong. Pay attention to your heart. If your heart is telling you that you are doing something wrong, that is God correcting you. Listen to Him!

It is never too late to repent – to turn away from the wrong path and choose to follow God instead. God is very patient with us because He loves us, but in the verse above, the prophet Joel warns us that the day of Jesus' return is coming. We don't know exactly how long we have until that time, but he says it is near. We should repent, and worship God sincerely now, before it's too late.

Not only do we have the power to turn away from wrong, but God can also completely remove ALL of the wrong things we have ever done. The Bible tells us that our sins aren't just forgiven, they can be **completely erased**. They will no longer exist. He can put our sins – every single wrong thing we have ever done no matter how bad it was – as far away from us as the east is from the west. Can you measure that? He can drown our sins at the bottom of the deep sea. They can never come back.

If God can let them go, we certainly can.

Romans 4:7-8 (from Psalm 32:1-2)

"It is a great blessing when people are forgiven for the wrongs they have done, when their sins are erased! It is a great blessing when the Lord accepts people as if they are without sin!"

Hebrews 10:17 (from Jeremiah 31:34)

Then he says, "I will forget their sins and never again remember the evil they have done."

Psalm 103:12

And he has taken our sins as far away from us as the east is from the west.

Micah 7:19b

He will throw all our sins into the deep sea.

Isaiah 44:22a

Your sins were like a big cloud, but I wiped them all away. Your sins are gone, like a cloud that disappeared into thin air.

1 Timothy 1:13part

But God gave me mercy because I did not know what I was doing.

Colossians 2:10a, 11part

And because you belong to Christ you are complete, having everything you need. . . In Christ. . . you were made free from the power of your sinful self.

Review: No one is born bad. We can all be completely forgiven.
Sincerity is what counts with God – be sorry and really mean it.
God can completely forgive us, so we should forgive ourselves and each other.

What happened after Jesus died?

After Jesus died, His body was wrapped in a burial cloth by two of His friends and put into a cave-like tomb that had been dug into a wall of rock. The jealous Jewish leaders remembered that Jesus had said He would rise from death. They didn't want any of His followers to steal the body and claim that Jesus had conquered death, so they asked Governor Pilate to place a guard at the tomb. Pilate agreed, so Jewish leaders and Roman soldiers went to the tomb. The tomb was sealed shut with a large stone, and the Roman soldiers stood guard.

Luke 23:52-54
He [Joseph of Arimathea] went to Pilate and asked for the body of Jesus. He took the body down from the cross and wrapped it in cloth. Then he put it in a tomb that was dug in a wall of rock. This tomb had never been used before. It was late on Preparation day. When the sun went down, the [special] Sabbath day would begin.

Matthew 27:65-66
Pilate said, "Take some soldiers and go guard the tomb the best way you know." So they all went to the tomb and made it safe from thieves. They did this by sealing the stone in the entrance and putting soldiers there to guard it.

Jesus' followers had very quickly buried His body. They had prepared His body for burial but perhaps did not spend the usual amount of time doing so, nor did they have a funeral for Him. Here's why:

The Jewish people measured a day from nightfall to nightfall, not midnight to midnight as we do today – so, each new day began after the sun had set. Jesus died at 3 o'clock in the afternoon. By the time His friend, Joseph, asked and received permission from the Roman authorities to take His body down, and then actually removed His body from the cross on which He was killed, it was getting late in the day. This particular nightfall was the beginning of a special Sabbath, a holy day, for the Jews – a day on which God had told them not to do work of any kind, including burying a body – it was the Feast of Unleavened Bread. Because of this, Jesus' friends were in a great hurry to bury the body and clean themselves up before the evening ceremonies and meal that would introduce the holy day at nightfall. Working in any way on a holy day was a sin against God, and no one wanted to be found guilty. It wasn't until the next non-holy day that Jesus' body would be given further attention. As He had said He would be, He was in His tomb for three nights and three days. Very early Sunday morning, some women went to the tomb with herbs and spices hoping to receive permission to further prepare His body. Even though He had told them He would rise from death, those women were astounded to find that Jesus was gone.

Matthew 28:2-4 (Before dawn Sunday)

Suddenly an angel of the Lord came from the sky, and there was a huge earthquake. The angel went to the tomb and rolled the stone away from the entrance. Then he sat on top of the stone. The angel was shining as bright as lightning. His clothes were as white as snow. The soldiers guarding the tomb were very afraid of the angel. They shook with fear and then became like dead men [most likely, they fainted].

Luke 24:1-3

Very early Sunday morning, the women came to the tomb where Jesus' body was laid. They brought the sweet-smelling spices they had prepared. They saw that the heavy stone that covered the entrance had been rolled away. They went in, but they did not find the body of the Lord Jesus.

In His sacrifice, in the sacrifice of His blood, Jesus had not just covered sin like the animal sacrifices of old that had to be performed year after year to cover the sins of the people. His offering was so great a sacrifice that it removed all sins for all time. Even today, my sins and your sins are forgiven by God. He does not hold our sins against us if we say we are sorry and truly mean what we say. We show we mean it by being baptized and then following God's path for us. He has offered us forgiveness, but we must accept that forgiveness and choose to have a relationship with Him.

As if defeating sin wasn't amazing enough, Jesus also conquered death. This does not mean that our bodies won't die, it means that we will live because Jesus lives. His act of rising from the dead, His revival, is called His Resurrection. Jesus said:

"I am the resurrection. I am life. Everyone who believes in me will have life, even if they die. And everyone who lives and believes in me will never really die."

John 11:25part

One of God's messengers, an angel, came to the women at the tomb and told them Jesus was alive again. The women hurried to tell Jesus' other friends and word spread. In the six weeks following His death, He was seen to be very much alive by hundreds of people.

Matthew 28:5-7

The angel said to the women, "Don't be afraid. I know you are looking for Jesus, the one who was killed on the cross. But he is not here. He has risen from death, as he said he would. Come and see the place where his body was. And go quickly and tell his followers, 'Jesus has risen from death. He is going into Galilee and will be there before you. You will see him there.'" Then the angel said, "Now I have told you."

Matthew 28:8-9

So the women left the tomb quickly. They were afraid, but they were also very happy. They ran to tell his followers what happened. Suddenly, Jesus was there in front of them. He said, "Hello!" The women went to him and, holding on to his feet, worshiped him.

Hebrews 2:14-15a (He knows your pain and struggles)

These children are people with physical bodies. So Jesus himself became like them and had the same experiences they have. Jesus did this so that, by dying, he could destroy the one who has the power of death – the devil. Jesus became like these people and died so that he could free them.

Psalm 16:10b (David to God about Jesus) (quoted by Peter in Acts 2:27)

You will not let your faithful one rot in the grave.

Acts 2:24

Jesus suffered the pain of death, but God made him free. He raised him from death. There was no way for death to hold him.

1 Corinthians 15:3b-6a

I told you the most important truths: that Christ died for our sins, as the Scriptures say; that he was buried and was raised to life on the third day, as the Scriptures say; and that he appeared to Peter and then to the twelve apostles. After that Christ appeared to more than 500 other believers at the same time.

Forty days after His Resurrection, Jesus said goodbye to the small group of men He had selected as His apostles – they were called His apostles because He had specifically trained them to deliver His Message – and He rose into the clouds to return to heaven as they stood watching. His act of rising to heaven is called His Ascension. Before ascending, He told His apostles two very important things: (1) they would take His Message to everyone, and (2) they were to wait in Jerusalem until the Holy Spirit came to them. The Holy Spirit would keep them company and comfort them until Jesus returns to earth to claim His bride (all of His faithful followers). We learn in the New Testament book of Acts that the Holy Spirit will come to anyone who accepts Jesus as his/her Savior. If you sincerely commit yourself to God, His Holy Spirit comes to live in you. Your body becomes a house of God.

Hebrews 4:14

We have a great high priest who has gone to live with God in heaven. He is Jesus the Son of God. So let us continue to express our faith in him.

1 Peter 3:18

Christ himself suffered when he died for you, and with that one death he paid for your sins. He was not guilty, but he died for people who are guilty. He did this to bring all of you to God. In his physical form he was killed, but he was made alive by the Spirit.

Romans 8:23b

We have the Spirit as the first part of God's promise. So we are waiting for God to finish making us his own children. I mean we are waiting for our bodies to be made free.

Luke 24:46-49

Jesus said to them, "It is written that the Messiah would be killed and rise from death on the third day. You saw these things happen – you are witnesses. You must go and tell people that they must change and turn to God, which will bring them his forgiveness. You must start from Jerusalem and tell this message in my name to the people of all nations. Remember that I will send you the one my Father promised. Stay in the city until you are given that power from heaven."

Acts 1:4b-5

He said, "Wait here until you receive what the Father promised to send. Remember, I told you about it before. John baptized people with water, but in a few days you will be baptized with the Holy Spirit."

Matthew 28:19

"So go and make followers of all people in the world. Baptize them in the name of the Father and the Son and the Holy Spirit."

Acts 1:9

After Jesus said this, he was lifted up into the sky. While they were watching, he went into a cloud, and they could not see him.

Philippians 1:6

I am sure that the good work God began in you will continue until he completes it on the day when Jesus Christ comes again.

Acts 3:21

"But Jesus must stay in heaven until the time when all things will be made right again. God told about this time when he spoke long ago through his holy prophets."

Review: Through His sacrifice at Passover and His Resurrection, Jesus made it

possible for all of us to escape sin and everlasting death.
His Holy Spirit will stay with us until He returns.

How does Jesus' sacrifice complete Passover?

Remember the Passover lamb from the Israelites' time of slavery in Egypt? God's people were to kill the lamb and paint the doorposts and lintel (sides and top of the door frame) with its blood. They were then to go through the doorway and stay inside the house. When the LORD came, the houses with blood on the doorposts and lintel would be passed over and everyone in that house would be spared God's punishment. This sacrifice became known as the Passover, and God's people were to celebrate this feast every year. There were many similarities between the Passover feast that was ordered by God to save His people from the punishment of the Egyptians and what happened when Jesus came to save people from eternal punishment for their sins. The purpose of the Passover feast was to help God's people recognize their Savior when He came.

- A lamb without physical flaws (a perfect lamb) was selected by each family and examined for several days before the sacrifice to make sure it was worthy.
  Jesus, a man without character flaws (a perfect man), arrived at the Temple several days before the sacrifice for everyone to see that He was worthy.

- A lamb makes no protest before the slaughter. It goes willingly to its death.
  Jesus did not resist arrest or defend Himself during his trial. He went willingly with the authorities even though He knew they would kill Him.

- A lamb's blood was painted on the top and sides of the door. The blood would have dripped from those places and landed on the threshold of the door. God's people were to pass through these blood-stained doorways and stay inside the house in order to be saved from God's punishment of the Egyptians.

Jesus' blood on the sides, top, and bottom of the cross represents the blood-stained doorway through which we must pass to be saved from the punishment God will send on Satan and the people who choose to follow him. Jesus is the Door and, if we pass through, we will one day live forever with God.

God is a God of Order. He made our world to function in an orderly way. The seasons, the ocean tides, the stars and planets, the reproduction of plants and animals and people, the laws of science (motion, gravity, etc.), even our numbers show an intricate level of detail in the order of God's world. Likewise following an orderly pattern, the major events of Jesus' direct interaction on our behalf line up perfectly with the seven festivals, or feasts, God gave the Israelites to celebrate each year. He did this in order to teach them and to prepare them for Jesus. He wanted His people to be able to recognize His plan as it progressed through the stages. God's people were to celebrate these special days in particular ways, following the directions He gave them. The first feast God's people were to celebrate each year was Passover. This celebration of freedom from a life of slavery was such an important day, that God made Passover mark the beginning of their religious year.

The Bible says that Jesus IS The Passover Lamb. Why is He?

From the time of the first Passover in Egypt until Jesus' time, the community of God's people was identified by a lamb. God had used the blood of a lamb to save them in Egypt, and they remembered and celebrated that rescue with the blood of a lamb every year at the same time. You might call it a sort of Jewish Independence Day – Passover and the Feast of Unleavened Bread are remembrances/celebrations of the freedom the Israelites received directly from God. Just as a lamb was sacrificed to protect them from the punishment of death and to rescue them from enslavement to the sinful Egyptians, so Jesus was sacrificed to protect us from the punishment of eternal death and to rescue us from the slavery of sin. Without Him, we cannot live. Jesus is our Passover Lamb, as God clearly planned from the beginning:

– In the Bible book of Genesis, Abraham says to Isaac, "God himself is providing the lamb for the sacrifice. . ." (Genesis 22:8part). Abraham's ultimate act of love and devotion to God in his willingness to offer his son as a sacrifice foreshadowed God's ultimate act of love and devotion to us. "Yes, God loved the world so much that he gave his only Son. . ." (John 3:16a).

God provided Jesus to be our sacrificial Lamb.

– In the next book, Exodus, the prophet Moses says that the Passover lamb that will be sacrificed "must be completely healthy" (Exodus 12:5part). It must be perfect. Only God as a man could be perfect. Jesus is also called Immanuel, which means *God with us*. Talking about Jesus, the apostle Peter said, "He was a pure and perfect sacrificial Lamb" (1 Peter 1:19b).

Jesus was a perfect man because He was a man completely without sin.

– God tells His people through Moses, "when I see the blood, I will pass over your house" (Exodus 12:13part). God provided His Son "so that everyone who believes in him would not be lost but have eternal life" (John 3:16b).

If we believe that Jesus died for us – to erase our sins and permanently close the gap in our relationship with God – and we enter into a relationship with God through the blood-stained Door that is Jesus, then we are saved from sin. If we believe that Jesus rose from the dead and conquered death, then we are saved from eternal death. We will live forever in the presence of God.

We will see in a few pages that there is an answer for those who never knew Jesus.

God – the one who made all things and for whose glory all things exist –

wanted many people to be his children and share his glory.

So he did what he needed to do.

He made perfect the one who leads those people to salvation.

He made Jesus a perfect Savior through his suffering.

Hebrews 2:10

Besides all of these signs and clues given about Jesus to help us understand that He was the ultimate Passover Lamb who forever fulfilled the sacrifices required to make us holy before God, God gave us other signs as well. God knows we can be doubtful, and He is very patient with us.

Before the sacrifice of Jesus, only the High Priest could enter the holiest place in the Temple – the Holy of Holies or the Most Holy Place – God's personal area in the Temple. The priest had to perform elaborate cleansing rituals, including a ceremonial, purifying bath in which his entire body was washed, before he could enter this area, and he could only enter it once each year on the feast known as the Day of Atonement.

The men who served as priests in the Temple were all from the family line of Levi, one of the 12 sons of Jacob (Israel). When God brought the Israelites out of Egypt, He assigned the Levites to religious duty.

Ezekiel 44:11
The Levites were chosen to serve in my holy place. They guarded the gates of the Temple. They served in the Temple. They killed the animals for the sacrifices and burnt offerings for the people. They were chosen to help the people and to serve them.

1 Chronicles 23:28-31a
The Levites had the job of helping Aaron's [Moses' brother] descendants in the service of the LORD's Temple. They also cared for the Temple courtyard and the side rooms in the Temple. And they made sure all the holy things were kept pure. It was their job to serve in God's Temple. They were responsible for putting the special bread on the table in the Temple and for the flour, the grain offerings, and the bread made without yeast. They were also responsible for the baking pans and the mixed offerings. They did all the measuring. The Levites stood every morning and gave thanks and praise to the LORD. They also did this every evening. The Levites prepared all the burnt offerings to the LORD on the Sabbath days, during New Moon celebrations, and on the other special meeting days [feast days]. They served before the LORD every day.

Malachi 2:7 (Not all Levites were priests, but all priests were Levites)
A priest should know God's teachings. People should be able to go to a priest and learn God's teachings. A priest should be the LORD's messenger to the people.

At the very moment Jesus died, there was an earthquake and the big curtain (also called the veil – like a bride wears) that separated the Most Holy Place from the rest of the Temple was torn in half from top to bottom. This was a very large and high curtain – think of a stage curtain. Tearing it in half from the top down and exposing the Most Holy Place to all was a message from God. The curtain represented our separation from God. This time of separation – the long-distance part of humankind's relationship with God – ended when Jesus died for us.

We all now have direct access to God through the power of Jesus' sacrifice. Because a sacrifice to cleanse all sin forever had been made, God opened the holiest place in the Temple (His personal space) to everyone. We no longer need to have a priest who will pray to God for us. Each of us can appeal directly to God, and He will listen! We no longer need to have a priest make sacrifices for our sins. Jesus was the ultimate and final sacrifice. Jesus closed the gap between God and humans that had existed since the time Adam and Eve sinned.

Exodus 12:3b, 6-7a (The Passover lamb was the only sacrificial animal the people were directed to watch over)
"On the tenth day of this month each man must get one lamb for the people in his house. . .You should watch over the animal until the 14th day of the month. On that day all the people of the community of Israel must kill these animals just before dark. You must collect the blood from these animals and put it on the top and sides of the doorframe of every house. . ."

Hebrews 9:25
The high priest enters the Most Holy Place once every year. He takes with him blood to offer. But he does not offer his own blood like Christ did. Christ went into heaven, but not to offer himself many times like the high priest offers blood again and again.

Hebrews 8:5a, 6a
The work that these priests do is really only a copy and a shadow of what is in heaven. . . But the work that has been given to Jesus is much greater than the work that was given to those priests.

Hebrews 10:12
But Christ offered only one sacrifice for sins, and that sacrifice is good for all time. Then he sat

down at the right side of God.

Hebrews 10:14a

With one sacrifice Christ made his people perfect forever.

1 Corinthians 5:7b

. . .Christ our Passover Lamb has already been killed.

1 Peter 1:19

You were bought with the precious blood of Christ's death. He was a pure and perfect sacrificial Lamb.

Hebrews 10:9b-10

So God ends that first system of sacrifices and starts his new way. Jesus Christ did the things God wanted him to do. And because of that, we are made holy through the sacrifice of Christ's body. Christ made that sacrifice one time – enough for all time.

John 3:16

Yes, God loved the world so much that he gave his only Son, so that everyone who believes in him would not be lost but have eternal life.

Matthew 27:51

When Jesus died, the curtain in the Temple was torn into two pieces. The tear started at the top and tore all the way to the bottom. Also, the earth shook and rocks were broken.

Hebrews 10:19-20

And so, brothers and sisters, we are completely free to enter the Most Holy Place. We can do this without fear because of the blood sacrifice of Jesus. We enter through a new way that Jesus opened for us. It is a living way that leads through the curtain – Christ's body.

Ephesians 2:13, 18

Yes, at one time you were far away from God, but now in Christ Jesus, you are brought near to him. You are brought near to God through the blood sacrifice of Christ. Yes, through Christ we all have the right to come to the Father in one Spirit.

Ephesians 3:12a

In Christ we come before God with freedom and without fear.

Review: Jesus is THE Passover Lamb, and because of His blood we all have direct access to God and the promise of everlasting life.

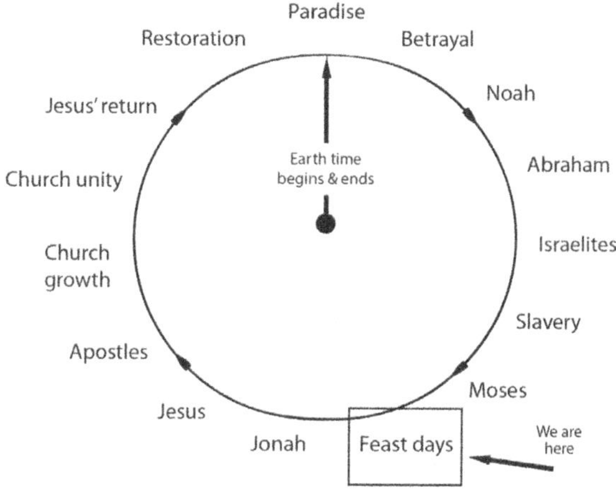

What other feasts did God tell the Israelites to celebrate?

Festivals or feasts of God can be understood to mean appointed times of God. These appointed times were given to Moses after the Israelites left Egypt. God's people were to observe these special times in particular ways. God's whole plan for closing the gap in our relationship with Him and restoring humans to the perfect life He intended for us centers around these feasts. Each one marked an appointed time when God would complete another step in His plan. You can read about the feasts in the Old Testament book of Leviticus, Chapter 23.

God told His people to celebrate seven feasts every single year to help them recognize what He was going to do for them. God used (and is still using) these special times as a teaching tool to help His children understand His plan.

Passover – The people celebrated their Salvation at Passover. Salvation means rescue. The LORD passed over His people's houses in Egypt (those marked by the blood of the lamb) and did not punish them when He punished all those who refused to obey. Passover, which Jews call **Pesach**, was celebrated in spring in what God declared would be the first month of the religious year. On His calendar, the Passover meal was eaten on the evening of the 14th day of the first month – so, the lambs were sacrificed earlier that same day. The 14th was also called Preparation day, because it was a day before a special Sabbath – the Passover meal was part of a week-long feast celebrating freedom.

The 14th day of the first month, Passover, is **not** a special Sabbath.

Completed: Passover, which marked the beginning of God's old covenant with His people when He took them out of Egypt (delivered them from sin), also marks the beginning of our new covenant, our new relationship, with God. Jesus' sacrifice at Passover began that new covenant. Through Jesus, God delivered the people who obey Him from sin.

Leviticus 23:5

"The LORD's Passover is on the 14th day of the first month just before dark."

Joshua 5:10

The Israelites celebrated Passover while they were camped at Gilgal on the plains of Jericho. This was on the evening of the 14th day of the month.

Jeremiah 31:31-32a (Telling about the new agreement that began with Jesus' sacrifice)

This is what the LORD said, "The time is coming when I will make a new agreement with the family of Israel and with the family of Judah. It will not be like the agreement I made with their ancestors. I made that agreement when I took them by the hand and brought them out of Egypt."

John 19:14-16

It was now almost noon on Preparation day of Passover week. Pilate said to the Jews, "Here is your king!" They shouted, "Take him away! Take him away! Kill him on a cross!" Pilate asked them, "Do you want me to kill your king on a cross?" The leading priests answered, "The only king we have is Caesar!" So Pilate handed Jesus over to them to be killed on a cross.

John 1:29

"Look, the Lamb of God. He takes away the sins of the world!"

John 19:30b-31a

He said, "It is finished." Then he bowed his head and died. This day was Preparation day. The next day was a special Sabbath day [the next feast, the Feast of Unleavened Bread].

Mark 15:42-43a

This day was called Preparation day. (That means the day before the Sabbath day.) It was becoming dark. A man named Joseph from Arimathea was brave enough to go to Pilate and ask for Jesus' body.

Luke 23:54

It was late on Preparation day. When the sun went down, the [special] Sabbath day would begin.

Hebrews 8:6b

The new agreement that Jesus brought from God to his people is much greater than the old one. And the new agreement is based on better promises.

Hebrews 8:10, 12 (from Jeremiah 31:33, 34b) (Reminding the Jews about the Old Testament prophecy)

"This is the new agreement I will give the people of Israel. I will give this agreement in the future, says the Lord: I will put my laws in their minds, and I will write my laws on their hearts. I will be their God, and they will be my people. . . And I will forgive the wrongs they have done, and I will not remember their sins."

God instructed His people that the first and last days of the next feast, the Feast of Unleavened Bread, were important holy days – God actually called them holy convocations (or, special meetings, as we saw in the Job verses), but they came to be known as special Sabbaths. These special Sabbaths were to be celebrated in addition to the weekly day of rest, which is also known as the Sabbath, that God instructed His people to celebrate every Saturday. Saturday is the seventh day of the week, and the day on which God rested from His work during Creation. God instructed His children to observe the seventh day as a holy day of rest and to not do any work. The word Sabbath began to be used to describe these special meetings because these days as well as the weekly holy days were ordered by God to be days of rest but using the same word for both has created some confusion.

Genesis 2:2-3

God finished the work he was doing, so on the seventh day he rested from his work. God blessed the seventh day and made it a holy day. He made it special because on that day he rested from all the work he did while creating the world.

Leviticus 23:3

"Work for six days, but the seventh day, the Sabbath, will be a special day of rest, a holy meeting. You must not do any work. It is a day of rest to honor the LORD in all your homes."

Feast of Unleavened Bread – During the Feast of Unleavened Bread, the people celebrated walking with God and being free from sin. Sin is symbolized by yeast in this celebration, so God's people ate bread that had no yeast for a week. Jewish people today call this unleavened bread, **matzah**, and the Hebrew name for this feast is **Chag HaMatzot**. The Feast of Unleavened Bread marked the Israelites' first complete week of freedom from slavery for the sinful Egyptians, which began the day they walked out of Egypt in victory and headed for the Promised Land. God's people – His army – had defeated the enemy by standing aside and letting God fight for them. They had special meetings on the first and last days of the feast. The evening of Passover – when night had fallen and it was the 15th of the first month – began this week-long feast. The 15th was a special meeting day, a special Sabbath. In order to be ready to properly observe a Sabbath – to do no work – one must spend the day before preparing, thus the name Preparation day. So, again, the day of Passover (the 14th) is a Preparation day for the special Sabbath (the special meeting) that begins on the 15th (at nightfall after the day of the 14th).

Completed: Jesus was laid in His grave just before this feast began at nightfall. This is when His body was dead – His death having freed us from the slavery of sin.

Exodus 12:15

"For this festival you will eat bread made without yeast for seven days. On the first day, you will remove all the yeast from your houses. No one should eat any yeast for the full seven days of this festival. Anyone who eats yeast must be separated from the rest of Israel."

Exodus 13:3, 18b

Moses said to the people, "Remember this day. You were slaves in Egypt, but on this day the LORD used his great power and made you free. You must not eat bread with yeast." . . .The Israelites were dressed for war [ranked in a military formation] when they left Egypt.

Numbers 33:3

On the 15th day of the first month, they left Rameses. That morning after Passover, the Israelites marched out of Egypt with their arms raised in victory.

When your arms are raised in victory, they are extended toward heaven. In the practice of yoga, this position is called the victory pose or the praise pose. Outside the practice of yoga, the gesture is used and understood to mean victory or praise by people all over the world from toddlerhood to old age. If you are a true follower, when you stand in this pose, you are thanking God for the blessings He is showering down on you. Your body is like a vessel, a goblet, that He is filling. When you are as happy about your blessings as the Israelites were about escaping slavery, your cup is overflowing. Challenge: when you are feeling defeated, stand in this pose for 30 full seconds and let it help you change your momentum. God has set you free!

Leviticus 23:6 (This feast has two special Sabbaths)

"The LORD's Festival of Unleavened Bread is on the 15th day of the same month. You will eat unleavened bread for seven days. On the first day of this festival, you will have a special meeting. You must not do any work on that day. For seven days, you will bring sacrifices offered as gifts to the LORD. Then there will be another special meeting on the seventh day. You must not do any work on that day."

Exodus 13:9

"This festival will help you remember; it will be like a string tied on your hand. It will be like a sign before your eyes. This festival will help you remember the LORD's teachings. It will help you

remember that the LORD used his great power to take you out of Egypt."

1 Corinthians 5:7-8

Take out all the old yeast, so that you will be a new batch of dough. You really are bread without yeast – Passover bread. Yes, Christ our Passover Lamb has already been killed. So let us eat our Passover meal, but not with the bread that has the old yeast, the yeast of sin and wrongdoing. But let us eat the bread that has no yeast. This is the bread of goodness and truth.

John 8:34-36

Jesus said, "The truth is, everyone who sins is a slave – a slave to sin. A slave does not stay with a family forever. But a son belongs to the family forever. So if the Son makes you free, you are really free."

The idea of spring cleaning is not new. God instituted it when He instructed the Israelites to clean all the yeast from their homes in preparation for this springtime feast. The Jews took this very seriously, searching for and removing even the smallest crumbs of bread from their homes and burning the yeast-infested grain in the fire. Removing the yeast was a symbolic act to help the Israelites understand Jesus' true removal of sin.

Jesus, who gave us the new covenant of freedom, demonstrated the physical way of removing sin from one's house. In the days before His sacrifice, Jesus went to the Temple and threw out the sinful people who were conducting dishonest trade in the courtyard. He also dismissed the one disciple (student) in His tightly knit group of 12 men who was following the temptations of Satan.

Exodus 12:18-20

"So on the evening of the 14th day of the first month, you will begin eating bread without yeast. You will eat this bread until the evening of the 21st day of the same month. For seven days, there must not be any yeast in your houses. Anyone, either a citizen of Israel or a foreigner living among you, who eats yeast at this time must be separated from the rest of Israel. During this festival you must not eat any yeast. You must eat bread without yeast wherever you live."

Did you notice how many times God repeated Himself? The instructions go on for six full verses in Exodus 12:15-20 and are repeated in other verses as well. The Passover meal was also to be eaten with unleavened bread. No wonder the Jews took the removal of yeast so seriously.

Feast of First Fruits – This feast occurred on the first Sunday after Passover during the week of the Feast of Unleavened Bread. The people brought offerings for God from the very first gatherings of their barley crops (the first grain crop of the year) to show their thankfulness for what God had provided, and to show their faith that God would provide the full harvest. The Jewish people call this feast **Yom HaBikkurim**. This celebration began when the Israelites finally entered the land promised to Abraham and were able to partake of its bounty. God had provided them with food (sweet bread called manna) while they were traveling in the desert, but the manna stopped when they reached the Promised Land.

Joshua 5:10-12a

The Israelites celebrated Passover while they were camped at Gilgal on the plains of Jericho. This was on the evening of the 14th day of the month. The day after Passover, [which was the first day of the Feast of Unleavened Bread] the people ate food that grew in that land. They ate bread made without yeast and roasted grain. The next morning, the manna from heaven stopped coming. This happened the first day after the people ate the food that grew in the land of Canaan.

The Sunday after Passover, the Feast of First Fruits, is **not** a special Sabbath.

> **Completed:** This is the Sunday morning when Jesus rose from the dead. Jesus is the First Fruits from the dead. God will gather the full harvest later.

Leviticus 23:9-11

The LORD said to Moses, "Tell the Israelites: You will enter the land that I will give you and reap its harvest. At that time you must bring in the first sheaf of your harvest to the priest. The priest will lift the sheaf to show it was offered before the LORD. Then you will be accepted. The priest will present the sheaf on Sunday morning."

Proverbs 3:9-10

Honor the LORD with your wealth and the first part of your harvest. Then your barns will be full of grain, and your barrels will be overflowing with wine.

Revelation 1:5part

Jesus is the faithful witness. He is first among all who will be raised from death.

1 Corinthians 15:20, 23

But Christ really has been raised from death – the first one of all those who will be raised. But everyone will be raised to life in the right order. Christ was first to be raised. Then, when Christ comes again, those who belong to him will be raised to life.

Review: The first three feasts occur in a very short period of time. Passover and the Feast of First Fruits are not special Sabbaths, while the Feast of Unleavened Bread has two special Sabbaths.

What has happened over the years as believers try to honor Jesus' completion of these three feast days?

Early in church history, decisions were made to deliberately distance the Christian calendar from the Jewish calendar. Unbelieving Jewish leaders likewise made changes to distance Jesus and His works from the feast days because the details are too convincing and other Jews might begin to believe, too. Over time and for various reasons, other people have added religious practices and seasons to the year to suit what they believe is a good way to acknowledge what Jesus has done for us.

After Jesus' death, burial, resurrection, and ascension, the early Christians debated how to mark these occasions. Some wanted to celebrate them on Passover, regardless of the day of the week on which it landed in any given year, and some wanted to celebrate them on the Feast of First Fruits, the Sunday after Passover. For nearly 300 years, various groups of believers celebrated as they wished. In the year AD 325, a leading Christian religious council met in Nicaea and officially declared the first Sunday after the first full moon of spring would always be the day to celebrate Jesus' resurrection. This day came to be known as Easter, or Resurrection Sunday, but neither name is found in the Bible. The date chosen is not a date of any significance in the Bible, although it sometimes coincides with the Feast of First Fruits. The name Easter probably comes from a pagan goddess of fertility, Ishtar.

Some Christians, as a preparation for Easter, celebrate the season of Lent, a period of repentance that includes 40 days before Easter. From Ash Wednesday, when people present themselves at church to repent (express sincere regret about their sins and turn away from them) and receive a cross of ashes on their foreheads as a symbol of their repentance, until Easter, people fast on certain days, abstain from certain foods or activities, and participate in church ceremonies. The day before Ash Wednesday is the last day that participants have to enjoy those foods or activities from which they will abstain during Lent, so the Tuesday before has come to be a day of celebration and revelry called Shrove Tuesday, or Mardi Gras (French for Fat Tuesday). Mardi Gras is the last day of another season, called Carnival or Shrovetide, that was added between Epiphany (January 6th, when some believe the wise men visited the baby Jesus and/or when some believe Jesus was baptized) and Ash Wednesday. Epiphany has grown to include Twelfth Night (Epiphany Eve). The list goes on, but let's stop here. **None of this is in the Bible.**

Some Christians today celebrate Palm Sunday as the day Jesus entered Jerusalem before His sacrifice. The day was given the name Palm Sunday because of the palm leaves that the crowds of people (who were in Jerusalem for the Passover) brought when they went out to meet Jesus as He entered the city, our humble and peaceful High Priest, riding on a donkey. As He rode into the city, the crowd shouted, "Hosanna!", which means, "Save us!" They were also reciting Scriptures that praise God for saving them. Interestingly, those Scriptures go on to speak about a sacrifice. The verses are prophecy because they foretold Jesus hundreds of years before His birth.

John 12:13 (from Psalm 118:25-26 below)

They took branches of palm trees and went out to meet Jesus. They shouted, "'Praise Him!' 'Welcome! God bless the one who comes in the name of the Lord!' God bless the King of Israel!"

These are praises traditionally shouted to a homecoming king who has won a battle. Jesus is our King, but He is also our High Priest. In His first visit, He came as our High Priest. When He returns, it will be as the King of kings.

Psalm 110:4 (David's prophecy about Jesus)
The LORD has made a promise with an oath and will not change his mind: "You are a priest forever - the kind of priest Melchizedek was."

Hebrews 6.20

Jesus has already entered there [the Most Holy Place] and opened the way for us. He has become the high priest forever, just like Melchizedek.

Genesis 14:18a (Melchizedek was both priest and king)
Melchizedek, the king of Salem and a priest of God Most High. . .

Psalm 118:25-29
The people say, "Praise the LORD! The LORD saved us! Welcome to the one who comes in the name of the LORD." The priests answer, "We welcome you to the LORD's house! The LORD is God, and he accepts us. Tie up the lamb for the sacrifice and carry it to the horns of the altar." Lord, you are my God, and I thank you. My God, I praise you! Praise the LORD because he is good. His faithful love will last forever.

Zechariah 9:9b, 10b-11a
People of Jerusalem, shout with joy! Look, your king is coming to you! He is the good king who won the victory, but he is humble. He is riding on a donkey, on a young donkey born from a work animal. . .Your king will bring news of peace to the nations. He will rule from sea to sea, from the Euphrates River to the ends of the earth. Jerusalem, we used blood to seal your agreement.

Some people hoped that He was the political leader who would save them from Roman rule. They threw the palm branches as well as their cloaks down in His path, possibly as a symbol of tribute to the man they hoped would be their new king. Another angle from which to view these actions is that palm branches are used in the seventh feast during which the people celebrate living under God's direct care. Whichever meaning is assigned to their actions (one could easily argue that both are correct), the book of John reports that the people didn't fully realize the significance of what they were doing.

John 12:16
The followers of Jesus did not understand at that time what was happening. But after he was raised to glory, they understood that this was written about him. Then they remembered that they had done these things for him.

Although the Bible comes very, very close, it does not specifically state that Jesus rode into Jerusalem on a Sunday. We do know He was the Passover Lamb, and as such He likely would have presented Himself at the Temple on the 10th day of the first month, which, in that year, based on the knowledge we do have, must have been a Sunday, four days before the sacrifice. The 10th day of the first month had come to be known by the Jews as Lamb Selection Day, because in the directions God gave for the feast of Passover, He said:

> *"This command is for the whole community of Israel: On the tenth day of this month each man must get one lamb for the people in his house. . .You should watch over the animal until the 14th day of the month. . ."*
>
> *Exodus 12:3, 6a*

Just like the Passover lambs, Jesus was among the people, available for public examination from the time He presented Himself at the Temple until His sacrifice. He selected Himself as the Passover Lamb.

Review: While they may have been instituted out of good intentions, not a single one of the "holidays" that people began celebrating after Jesus' sacrifice was ordered by God in the Bible.
Not one.
We should look carefully to see exactly what the Bible does say.

How can we attempt to put Jesus' last week onto a calendar?

Scholars have generated a massive amount of information on this subject. What follows is a summary of points that help shape the events of that all-important week. Perhaps one of the most important points to understand is the fact that the Jewish nation was not a wholly united nation at that time.

The nation of Israel had divided itself into two parts after the death of King Solomon (King David's son) around 930 BC. Judea was the southern part of the nation and included the rather metropolitan city of Jerusalem, which was the home of the Temple and, therefore, the center of Jewish worship. The religious authorities who had Jesus executed were Judean Jews. Judea was cooperative with the Roman invaders. Galilee, the northern part of the nation where Jesus was raised, was considered by southerners to be quite rural and unsophisticated. Although the Galileans were fiercely patriotic Jews (fanatical groups, called Zealots, routinely staged revolts against Roman control of their homeland), Judeans generally viewed Galileans as less serious about their religious practices – about following the exact letter of the Law as recorded by Moses and obeying the teachings of the influential Jewish rabbis. Between them was Samaria, a country populated by people who were perhaps part Jewish but who were looked down on by both Judean and Galilean Jews. You can read about Samaria's history in 2 Kings 17:24-41. The Jewish nation had been divided politically, culturally, geographically, and somewhat religiously for a long, long time. The friction between the various Jewish groups is illustrated in a number of verses:

2 Kings 17:33a

They [the Samaritans] respected the LORD but also served their own gods.

John 12:42

But many people believed in Jesus. Even many of the Jewish leaders believed in him, but they were afraid of the Pharisees [one party of religious leaders], so they did not say openly that they believed. They were afraid they would be ordered to stay out of the synagogue.

John 4:3-4, 7, 9

So he left Judea and went back to Galilee. On the way to Galilee, he had to go through the country of Samaria. A Samaritan woman came to the well to get some water, and Jesus said to her, "Please give me a drink." The woman answered, "I am surprised that you ask me for a drink! You are a Jew and I am a Samaritan woman!" (Jews have nothing to do with Samaritans.)

John 7:1

After this, Jesus traveled around the country of Galilee. He did not want to travel in Judea, because the Jewish leaders there wanted to kill him.

Luke 23:5-7, 11b-12a (Testimony by Jewish leaders at Jesus' trial)

But they kept on saying, "His teaching is causing trouble all over Judea. He began in Galilee, and

now he is here!" Pilate heard this and asked if Jesus was from Galilee. He learned that Jesus was under Herod's authority [Herod had jurisdiction over Galilee, while Pilate was the governor of Judea]. Herod was in Jerusalem at that time, so Pilate sent Jesus to him. . .Then Herod sent him back to Pilate. In the past Pilate and Herod had always been enemies.

1 Thessalonians 2:14b-15a

I mean that you were treated badly by your own people, just as those believers in Christ Jesus were treated badly by other Jews – the same Jews who killed the Lord Jesus and the prophets.

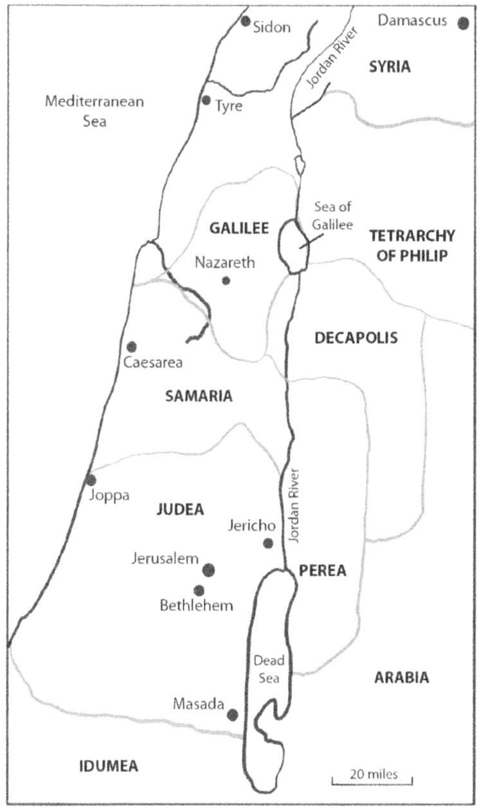

Map of Israel in Jesus' Time

When you read the word Jews in the New Testament, most likely it is referring to the Judean Jews, or, more specifically, to the Judean religious authorities (or, even more specifically, to the party of Temple leaders) who were against Jesus. Jews might also refer to people who supported those Temple leaders. The disciple who betrayed Jesus and turned Him in to the religious leaders was the only possible Judean Jew among the twelve – all the others were Galileans.

The population of Jerusalem would swell tremendously during the days leading up to Passover. Galileans, Judeans, and Jews from other countries would travel to the city for the first feast of the new year, because it was one of the three annual feasts for which God commanded their appearance at His Temple (remember the sons of God in the book of Job who had special meetings with the LORD). All through the city, preparations would be made for this very important feast day and the week-long feast that it began. People would clean the yeast from their homes and select lambs for the sacrifice. People would shop for food and goods to prepare for the special Sabbath as well as the weekly Sabbath. There was much to do, as this week would have two days in which no work could be done.

Review: Before we can attempt to put His last human days on a calendar,
we need to understand the atmosphere of His times.
The Jewish world was very conflicted.

Doesn't the Bible give all the details about that important week?

Debate about the calendar of Jesus' last week has circulated for many years, because, when taken at a glance, the Bible does not make it perfectly clear which details occurred on which day. In fact, some of the verses seem to contradict one another. With close examination, we can clear up most of those misunderstandings. Some people today call that week Passion Week, from the Greek word **pascho**, which refers to the suffering He endured.

The four books of the Bible that tell the most about Jesus' life on earth are the first four books of the New Testament. Three of those books are very similar, telling many of the same stories in almost exactly the same words and order – they give a synopsis, or summary of the events of His earthly life, and so they are called synoptic, or the synoptic Gospels (Gospel means the Good News of Jesus). Because these three are so similar, they can almost count as one testimony. The fourth book, John, is a very different type of testimony that explains more about who Jesus is rather than giving a synopsis of what Jesus did.

Gospel of Matthew
Gospel of Mark } Synoptic Gospels
Gospel of Luke

Gospel of John

Let's look carefully at a few of the statements in question. The synoptic books report that Jesus' disciples were concerned about their group's plans for the Passover celebration and wanted to begin making preparations.

Jesus had already told them that He would be killed on Passover, but His followers failed to fully understand His words.

Matthew 26:1-2 (Remember, a day (date) begins at nightfall - He was arrested and killed on the same date)
After Jesus finished saying all these things, he said to his followers, "You know that the day after tomorrow is Passover. On that day the Son of Man will be handed over to his enemies to be killed on a cross."

The religious leaders knew they could not arrest Him during the Feast of Unleavened Bread, which coincides with Passover.

Mark 14:1-2
It was now only two days before the Passover and the Festival of Unleavened Bread. The leading priests and teachers of the law were trying to find a way to arrest Jesus without the people seeing it. Then they could kill him. They said, "But we cannot arrest Jesus during the festival. We don't want the people to be angry and cause a riot."

Then we read that the disciples apparently wanted to begin preparing for Passover on the first day of the Feast of Unleavened Bread. How can this be? Remember, the first day of the Feast of Unleavened Bread is a special Sabbath, and it begins at nightfall after the day of Passover.

Matthew 26:17

"On the first day of the Festival of Unleavened Bread, the followers came to Jesus. They said, "We will prepare everything for you to eat the Passover meal. Where do you want us to have the meal?"

Verses we have read, including those in Mark, Luke, and John, clearly record that Jesus was sacrificed on the day leading up to the evening Passover meal, which is Preparation day – the day of Passover – the day before the Feast of Unleavened Bread.

John 19:13b-14a, 31, 42

It was now almost noon on Preparation day of Passover week. . .This day was Preparation day. The next day was a special Sabbath day [the first day of the Feast of Unleavened Bread]. . .The men put Jesus in that tomb because it was near, and the Jews were preparing to start their Sabbath day.

We know that the first day of the Feast of Unleavened Bread was a special Sabbath on which no work could be done, so the disciples were obviously not making preparations on that day. We also know the Passover meal occurs on the evening that the special Sabbath begins. If it were the DAY of the special Sabbath, then the Passover meal would have already occurred. So, why does the Bible have this contradiction?

In Matthew 26:17 above, the words **day** and **feast/festival of** were not present in the original Greek writing but were added years later during translation – some Bibles have these words in italics to show they have been added. If we remove them, we are left with **"On the first unleavened bread..."** The word **first** was translated from the Greek word **protos** which actually indicates the beginning of an order of events or **before** an order of events, so the verse would be better translated as, **"Before the unleavened bread..."** the followers wanted to make preparations. The Passover meal was also eaten with unleavened bread, so this statement can easily refer to the time before any of the spring feasts began.

Matthew 26:17 is so contradictory to itself that it is readily apparent there must be an error in translation. No Jewish person would prepare for a feast day AFTER the feast day was over AND on a Sabbath. Verses with this much error in translation are rare in the Bible. If you ever have any questions about the validity of a translation, look it up in the original Hebrew (Old Testament) or Greek (New Testament). This usually clears up any confusion. The Bible isn't wrong – it doesn't contradict itself – erroneous translations are the problem.

Think about the phrase, "Lost in translation," and what it means in terms of understanding the Bible, understanding other cultures, understanding historical settings – understanding God. We cannot possibly understand everything about God – it's lost in the translation between the spiritual and the physical. We are imperfect physical beings right now, and this is what we can understand. God gives us many physical examples to explain the spiritual, and they're very good examples, but we won't understand the full spiritual meanings of everything until God completes His plan and fully perfects us both spiritually and physically.

There was also a tradition among some Jews (and many Jews today still celebrate it) that firstborn children would fast on the day leading up to the Passover meal – it's called the Fast of the Firstborn (**Ta'anit Bechorot** in Hebrew). Remember, it was the firstborn of each house that was in danger during the last Egyptian plague. Those participating in the fast would have a Last Supper (**Seudah Maphsehket**) on the evening before, called Passover Eve (**Erev Pesach**). This meal would kick off the series of Passover celebrations. Jesus and His followers may very well have been doing this in the synoptic Gospel accounts, because historical Jewish literature (the **Mishnah**) records the Last Supper as a Passover tradition among Galilean Jews.

The **Mishnah** in Jesus' time was an oral record of Jewish tradition, an oral Torah that accompanied the written Torah (the first five books of the Bible written by Moses that record the Law). These oral traditions were not written down until after the Temple was destroyed by the Romans in AD 70. Today, you can find information about the Fast of the Firstborn in the written **Mishnah**, which is a section of the **Talmud**, in Tractate Soferim 21:3.

The Last Supper, the Fast of the Firstborn, Passover, the Feast of Unleavened Bread (a week which begins and ends with a special Sabbath), and the Feast of First Fruits all occur in a nine-day time frame. The name Passover is often used to refer to the entire season of celebrations rather than just the specific day. Much like Christians today would say, "What are your plans for Christmas?" – the question would not be a narrow focus on just Christmas Day – the question would refer to any activities or plans during the entire Christmas season. Much like Christmas, there is a bustling of activity in the weeks and days leading up to the events that make up the Passover season. We can apply our own experience with this when we read that Jesus calls the meal Passover in the synoptic gospels.

Luke 22:15

Jesus said to them, "I wanted very much to eat this Passover meal with you before I die."

The word Passover in this verse comes from the Greek **pascha**, which can refer to the day, the meal, the week-long feast, the sacrifice – essentially anything to do with that season – even the Last Supper and Fast of the Firstborn. In the English language, using a part of something to refer to the whole is a figure of speech called a **synecdoche**. If you do independent research on these feasts, be aware that MANY articles you will encounter refer to the 15th as Passover, when, in fact, it is the first day of the Feast of Unleavened Bread.

Because Jesus refers to the meal as Passover in the synoptic gospels, some scholars argue that there is an indication that Galilean Jews may have celebrated Passover a day earlier than Judean Jews due to calendar differences – that the Last Supper Jesus shared with His disciples was actually the Passover feast. If so, this would have allowed Jesus to participate in a Passover celebration AND be the sacrifice for a Passover celebration. However, if He participated in a Galilean Passover meal with His disciples and was arrested afterward, the authorities would actually be arresting Him on a Galilean special Sabbath, the first day of the Feast of Unleavened Bread. The Judean Jews were the ones who executed Him, and they would have been doing so on their Passover, which is not a Sabbath. This would definitely be a handy way to explain the differing reports, but consider this: while there was definite disagreement between Galilean and Judean Jews, would the Judeans have blatantly disregarded the Galilean Sabbath by conducting a trial and execution? Maybe, but if so, wouldn't there be some record of the Galileans protesting this?

There is another significant note of doubt that the last meal Jesus shared with His disciples was the actual Passover feast. During the meal, Jesus sent the disciple Judas away without saying why. The apostle John, who was present at the meal, records that the disciples assumed Judas was being sent to shop for the feast (the Passover meal), indicating they must not have been eating the actual Passover feast.

John 13:29a

"Since Judas was the one in charge of the money, some of them thought that Jesus meant for him to go and buy some of the things they needed for the feast."

They did not yet realize that Jesus was likely removing the yeast (sin) from their "house" to prepare for the feast. Judas was the disciple who told the Judean religious authorities where they could find and arrest Jesus that night. He was paid for disclosing this information. Jesus knew Judas was guilty. Remember, cleaning out the yeast in preparation for Passover is taken very seriously. The Passover feast is to be eaten with unleavened bread, and there is to be no leavened (yeast) bread in the house for the following week.

Matthew 26:14-16

Then one of the twelve followers went to talk to the leading priests. This was the follower named Judas Iscariot. He said, "I will hand Jesus over to you. What will you pay me for doing this?" The priests gave him 30 silver coins. After that Judas waited for the best time to hand Jesus over to them.

The payment of 30 pieces of silver may also have significant meaning. It was the set reimbursement price paid to a master for his loss of a servant who was killed. God told Moses to include this in the Law after the Israelites left Egypt.

Exodus 21:32a
But if the bull kills a slave [servant], the owner of the animal must pay the master 30 pieces of silver.

Only God is the Master of Jesus, but the Bible says Judas was paid. Let's look a little closer to clear up the confusion. This same amount of money was written about many years before by the prophet Zechariah when God was disgusted with people who refused to honor their agreement with Him and dismissed His chosen prophet.

Zechariah 11:12-13
Then I said, "If you want to pay me, pay me. If not, don't!" So they paid me 30 pieces of silver. Then the LORD told me, "So that's how much they think I'm worth. Throw that large amount of money [God is being sarcastic here – it's a small amount of money – the people are insulting Him with this payment] into the Temple treasury." So I took the 30 pieces of silver and threw them into the treasury [the offering box] at the LORD's Temple.

This foreshadowing, this prophecy, is very specifically fulfilled when Judas realizes what he has done.

Matthew 27:3b-5a
When he [Judas] saw what happened [that the authorities were going to kill Jesus], he was very sorry for what he had done. So he took the 30 silver coins back to the leading priests and the older leaders. Judas said, "I sinned. I handed over to you an innocent man to be killed." The Jewish leaders answered, "We don't care! That's a problem for you, not us." So Judas threw the money into the Temple.

God, as Master, was indeed paid the 30 pieces of silver for the death of His Servant when Judas threw the blood money into His house.

Equally compelling, 30 pieces of silver is the price to redeem a woman of marrying age who has been promised as a servant for the LORD (to serve in the Temple).

Leviticus 27:1-2, 4part
The LORD said to Moses, "Tell the Israelites: You might promise to give someone to the LORD as a servant. The priest must set a price for that person [to be redeemed] . . .the price for a woman . . .is 30 shekels [pieces of silver]."

Jesus came to redeem His bride, and the payment thrown into the Temple was 30 pieces of silver, the bride price. God follows the rules He set down.

Furthermore, the only foods mentioned at this Last Supper that Jesus shared with his disciples are bread and wine, which were components of any Jewish supper. None of the Bible accounts of this preparation or event mention any of the participants going to the Temple to get a lamb or attending the sacrifice of the lambs (by this time, the sacrifice of the lambs took place in the Temple court). Jesus, in His discussion of the food, does not make mention of the lamb or of the bitter herbs that God ordered them to eat on the Passover. Some discussion of the original Passover would be an expected part of the Passover meal, but this is not the conversation that is recorded for us. The conversation and demonstrations of Jesus that are recorded for us are instructional about our future.

Because it seems like the most logical explanation, let's assume that Jesus and His disciples are beginning the Passover season by celebrating a Last Supper before some of them (Jesus was the firstborn son of Mary) would fast on the day leading up to the evening Passover meal (Fast of the First Born). Jesus used the opportunity this Last Supper provided to give His disciples their final instructions on humility and serving others and on remembering that He was humble and served us. He stated that He would fast from the Passover feast until God's kingdom had physically come.

Luke 22:16

"I will never eat another Passover meal until it is given its full meaning in God's kingdom."

Jesus repeatedly told His disciples and followers that He would be killed on Passover, but they failed to understand His words and actions much like they failed to understand the significance of the people's words and actions when He entered Jerusalem riding on a donkey.

Review: Some portions of the synoptic Gospel accounts of the last week of Jesus seem to contradict the account in John's Gospel, but we can easily explain the conflict.
Incorrect additions to the original Greek, even though some Bibles put the added words in italics or brackets, have led to false assumptions, as well as unbelievers' accusations of contradictory statements in the Bible.
Some Greek words have more than one possible meaning.
A common practice among the Jews of referring to the first three feasts and the events surrounding them collectively as Passover leads to some confusion.

Jesus is the Door

Based on what we've discussed, what would a calendar showing the last week of Jesus' life probably look like?

On one of these days, Jesus cleaned the yeast (sin) from God's house (Temple) by removing those who were cheating others. He is recorded cleansing the Temple from sin twice - once very early in His ministry and again at the end. John records that Jesus celebrated three Passover feasts during His three-year ministry. Luke tells us He was in the habit of going to the Temple every Passover. These inspections and cleansings bear an interesting resemblance to God's instructions in Leviticus 14:33-45 for cleansing a house that has been contaminated. When the owner (God) of a house (Temple) suspects contamination, the owner must notify the priest (Jesus). The priest will come to the house and inspect it. If, after the third inspection by the priest, the house is still deemed unclean, the house is to be destroyed. The Temple was destroyed in AD 70. Not one stone was left in place.

Sunday - 10th
- Lamb Selection Day
- Jesus arrives at the Temple

Monday - 11th

Tuesday - 12th

Wednesday - 13th
- Last Supper
- Judas sent away

Arrest and Trial overnight

Thursday - 14th
- Fast of Firstborn
- Preparation Day
- Jesus and lambs sacrificed
- Jesus in tomb before nightfall ----- Day
- Passover meal

----- Night

Friday - 15th
- Special Sabbath for first day of Feast of Unleavened Bread ----- Day

----- Night

Saturday - 16th
- Weekly Sabbath ----- Day

----- Night

Sunday - 17th
- Jesus is Risen
- Feast of First Fruits

Jesus in tomb
Day
Night
Day
Night
Day
Night

Passovers during Jesus' ministry: John 2:13, 6:4, 13:1

Luke 2:41-42

Every year Jesus' parents went to Jerusalem for the Passover festival. When Jesus was twelve years old, they went to the festival as usual.

In this series of events, He selected Himself as the Passover Lamb and presented Himself for inspection on the 10th day of the first month, just as Moses told the people to select a lamb on the 10th and watch over it until the 14th day when it would be sacrificed. Jews called the 10th Lamb Selection Day.

On that day or one of the next two days (it is difficult to be certain), Jesus cleansed His Father's house of sin in preparation for the upcoming Passover. This cleansing may have been symbolic in other ways, as noted in the chart.

He celebrated a Last Supper on Passover Eve with His followers and then declared He would fast (Fast of the Firstborn, perhaps, which is not in the Bible but is a Jewish tradition) from the Passover meal until He partakes of it again when the kingdom is physically established. He cleansed their "house" (the place they were staying and/or their group) of sin by dismissing Judas.

That same night, He was arrested. By morning, He had been tried by the Jewish authorities. By noon, He had been tried and sentenced by the Romans and was crucified. So, He was sacrificed with the lambs on the 14th (Preparation Day), just as He said He would be, and just as God had ordered the Israelites to do.

He was put in the tomb that same day just before evening when the Passover meal would be eaten and nightfall when the Feast of Unleavened Bread (and, therefore, a special Sabbath) would begin.

He was in the grave all of Friday and Saturday – both of which were Sabbaths. He arose sometime after nightfall on Saturday but before sunrise on Sunday (either way, it's Sunday night to a Jewish person) – the next non-Sabbath day.

This series of events would put Him in the grave Thursday night, Friday day, Friday night, Saturday day, Saturday night and Sunday day, by our midnight-to-midnight reckoning – three nights and three days. By Jewish nightfall-to-nightfall reckoning, He would be in the grave Thursday day (before nightfall, so still Thursday), Friday night, Friday day,

Saturday night, Saturday day, and Sunday night (rising before dawn, so before Sunday day) – three days and three nights. Note the verses below in which Jesus says **days** first and **nights** last. The Jewish reckoning matches His words perfectly and is in alignment with the sign of Jonah.

Jonah 1:17
When Jonah fell into the sea, the LORD chose a very big fish to swallow Jonah. He was in the stomach of the fish for three days and three nights.

Matthew 12:39b-40 (Jesus speaking about His burial)
The only sign will be the miracle that happened to the prophet Jonah. Jonah was in the stomach of the big fish for three days and three nights. In the same way, the Son of Man will be in the grave three days and three nights.

John 2:19-21
Jesus answered, "Destroy this temple and I will build it again in three days." They answered, "People worked 46 years to build this Temple! Do you really believe you can build it again in three days?" But the temple Jesus meant was his own body. After he was raised from death, his followers remembered that he had said this. So they believed the Scriptures, and they believed the words Jesus said.

Once again, the people did not realize the significance of what was said or done until after the fact.

John 13:7
Jesus answered, "You don't know what I am doing now. But later you will understand."

Many people have celebrated Good Friday (which is not mentioned in the Bible) as the day of Jesus' crucifixion for many years, but looking at Jesus' own words, it just doesn't add up. Even if we assume the Jewish method of counting days – that any part of a day is a day, so Friday, Saturday, Sunday is three days – that still doesn't allow for three nights, and when the women came to the tomb before sunrise on Sunday, He was already gone – it wasn't even "day" yet. There is simply no way to get the three days and three nights Jesus said He would be in the grave when we count from late Friday afternoon to before dawn on Sunday, whether we're using our current calculations of day and night or following the Jewish method of reckoning time.

Part of the confusion is perhaps due to the fact that for many years, the importance of the Jewish feasts was not fully recognized or understood by Christians. In the very early years of the church, the Jewish religious leaders and the Jesus-believing Jews had some serious clashes of belief, and the early church (which quickly became mostly Gentile) broke completely away from the Jewish religious practices. (Remember the Christian religious council that instituted a new "Christian" date to celebrate the Resurrection.) The Jewish religious leaders went on to draw serious distinctions between themselves and the Jesus-believers. Leading rabbis (Jewish religious teachers) adjusted the Hebrew calendar and began dictating when the feasts should be held to make it religiously illegal for Passover to fall on a Thursday, thereby creating an even bigger division between what they were celebrating and what Christians were celebrating in the spring of each year.

Matthew 28:11-15a

The women went to tell the followers. At the same time, some of the soldiers who were guarding the tomb went into the city. They went to tell the leading priests everything that happened. Then the priests met with the older Jewish leaders and made a plan. They paid the soldiers a lot of money and said to them, "Tell the people that Jesus' followers came during the night and stole the body while you were sleeping. If the governor hears about this, we will talk to him and keep you out of trouble." So the soldiers kept the money and obeyed the priests.

In God's Biblical instructions, He never said that the Passover feast could only be held on certain days of the week. He only said it would be the 14th day of what He said would be the first month of the year. The month begins once the new moon is spotted by two witnesses. The witnesses report the sighting to the priests who then blow trumpets to announce the beginning of the new month. From that time, the people can count 14 days to know when Passover should be celebrated, which is on or very near the first full moon that happens on or after the spring equinox (when the hours of day and night are most equal, but originally noted by weather and plant life signs of spring). All the phases of the moon mark one month's time. This is the amount of time it takes for the moon to travel around the earth one time. Each new moon is like a rebirth – a time of renewal.

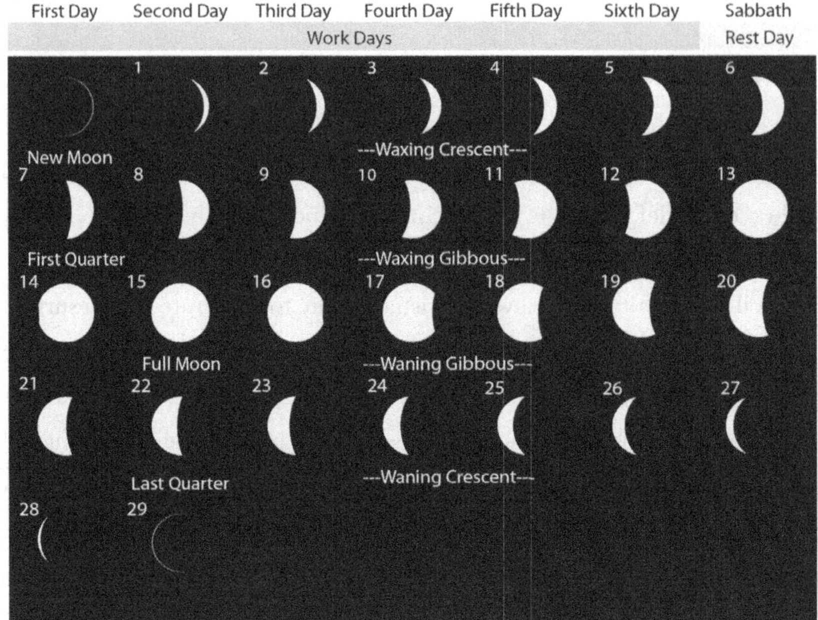

Lunar Month

Another point of confusion may have been that the Bible says nightfall following the day of His death began a Sabbath, and assumptions may have been made that the day must have been the weekly Sabbath on Saturday. We now understand the "special Sabbath" the apostle John spoke of was the first day of the Feast of Unleavened Bread – an additional Sabbath in that week.

John 19:30b-31a

He said, "It is finished." Then he bowed his head and died. This day was Preparation day. The next day was a special Sabbath day.

Review: Lent, Palm Sunday, Good Friday, Easter, Resurrection Sunday. . .
while all of these and others besides have become ways of worshipping

and honoring our Lord and Savior, none of these celebrations
or names are mentioned in the Bible. God gave His people the weekly Sabbath days,
the original seven feast days, and the new moon celebrations.
He has appointed no other holy days, feast days, or other observances.

1 Peter 1:18a

You know that in the past the way you were living was useless. It was a way of life you learned from those who lived before you.

Note that the events of His last week occurred on those weekdays THAT year. They do not fall on the same days of the week every year. Only the Feast of First Fruits always occurs on a Sunday, but it is not always three days after Passover.

****

Discussions and studies to clear up perceived inconsistencies in the Bible is important. Unbelievers and doubters point to these perceived inconsistencies as support for their positions. As Christians, we are told to study and have ready answers.

But keep the Lord Christ holy in your hearts. Always be ready to answer
everyone who asks you to explain about the hope you have.
But answer them in a gentle way with respect. Keep your conscience clear.
Then people will see the good way you live as followers of Christ,
And those who say bad things about you will be ashamed of what they said.
1 Peter 3:15-16

****

This is a carefully studied, conservative guess at the timeline of Jesus' last week. The Bible doesn't provide all the information we need to know for sure, but we can use the information we do have to make educated guesses. Discussions about Jesus' last week should prompt some very interesting conversations, but disagreements should not create divisions in God's people.

The important fact to remember is that Jesus died for all of us, and we are free because of Him.

****

We have said Jesus completed the first four feasts. What was the fourth?

Pentecost – from the Greek, **pentékosté**, meaning fiftieth. This feast occurs on a Sunday exactly 50 days after First Fruits. Pentecost, like the Feast of First Fruits is a harvest festival. First Fruits marks the beginning of the grain harvest, and Pentecost marks the end of the grain harvest. Grain, of course, is used to make bread. Jesus calls Himself the Bread of Life. God told Moses to have the people celebrate Pentecost by making an offering of two loaves of leavened bread – bread with yeast. These loaves were a gift to God from the grain harvest – the first use of their harvested grain. Some scholars suggest that the two loaves represent the Jews and the Gentiles, while the yeast represents the Gospel of Christ that we have spread throughout our respective loaves. Others suggest that one loaf is Christ and the other is His bride (all of His believers), presented to God on this harvest feast day. Pentecost, or **Shavuot** as the Jews today call it, is also called the Feast of Harvest or the Feast of Weeks because it is found by counting to the first Sunday following a week of weeks after First Fruits (7 x 7 = 49 + 1= 50).

Pentecost, or the Feast of Weeks, is a special Sabbath.

Luke 13:20-21

Jesus said again, "What can I compare God's kingdom with? It is like yeast that a woman mixes into a big bowl of flour to make bread. The yeast makes all the dough rise."

We have discussed yeast as a representation of sin, but in the Bible, we learn there is good yeast and bad yeast. Carefully cultivated baker's yeast makes a wholesome and filling bread, much like the Holy Spirit can make us into the purposeful people God wants us to be if we accept Jesus and allow His Spirit to carefully cultivate us. There are also wild yeast spores floating around everywhere in the air looking for a host. When a host is found, the wild yeast will infect, and the unchecked growth of that yeast will eventually lead to the spoilage of the dough. Because of this, we can see that yeast is the physical representation of the spiritual occupation of the human host. Remember, Satan prowls around like a lion looking for someone's weak spirit that he can infiltrate and use for his wicked ends. The contamination by his wickedness can completely infect our spirits and lead to our ultimate decay.

The Bible says that Jesus is the perfectly wholesome loaf that can satisfy our hunger forever. What is that hunger? It is our hunger for love, for justice, for forgiveness, for righteousness, for inclusion, for acceptance, for justification, for pure happiness, for stability, for peace. . . We must allow His Spirit to permeate us completely, so that we can one day become perfect loaves, have all these things, and be united with Him before God.

Just before He ascended to heaven, Jesus told His selected 11 remaining disciples to wait in Jerusalem until they received the Holy Spirit from God, and then take His Message to everyone in the world. Jesus ascended 40 days after He had arisen. We know there are 50 days between the Feast of First Fruits and the Feast of Pentecost, so we know the disciples must have waited 10 days.

On Pentecost, the Holy Spirit came to the disciples and permeated them completely. Now, they were fully equipped to be the apostles (from the Greek **apostolos**, meaning people who are sent) Jesus had trained them to be. Peter went out into the crowded streets of Jerusalem and preached the Gospel to everyone who would listen. This was the first use of His harvested grain – the first use of His Spirit – after God raised Jesus as the First Fruit of His Harvest. Jesus, our Bread, feeds us through the Spirit.

In a sign of the miraculous power of the Holy Spirit, everyone in the crowd heard Peter (and the other apostles) speaking in his/her own language (it was an international crowd, as this was one of the regularly scheduled meetings of God and His sons/children for which the faithful believers would present themselves at the Temple for worship). This miracle of speaking in unknown languages served to increase God's church by about 3,000 members that very day. God was still following His rules about how things work – His miracle isn't contrary to His rules, it simply allows us a peek into the heavenly realm. In heaven, God will speak to His people collectively, and we will all understand, regardless of our physical, earthly language. Some of those in the crowd listening to the apostles were amazed, but others accused the apostles of being drunk. Peter's response was, "These men are not drunk as you think; it's only nine o'clock in the morning" (Acts 2:15). God repeatedly condemns drunkenness (consuming too much wine – not consuming wine), but He does have a sense of humor. He created us with emotions and personalities – He wants to enjoy us.

Completed: This is when the Holy Spirit first came to live in God's people.

We are now the temple of God. His Spirit lives in us. This is the Holy Spirit of promise – our guarantee that Jesus will return for us and take us home to His Father's house.

Leviticus 23:15-17a (How to calculate the day of Pentecost, or Feast of Weeks)

"From that Sunday morning ([the Feast of First Fruits when Jesus arose from the dead], the day you bring the sheaf to be presented to God), count seven weeks. On the Sunday following the seventh week (that is, 50 days later), you will bring a new grain offering to the LORD. On that day bring two loaves of bread from your homes. That bread will be lifted up to show it was offered to God."

John 6:33, 35a

"God's bread is the one who comes down from heaven and gives life to the world." Then Jesus said, "I am the bread that gives life. No one who comes to me will ever be hungry."

Acts 1:3b

The apostles saw Jesus many times during the 40 days after he was raised from death.

Luke 24:49 (Jesus telling His disciples about the Holy Spirit)

"Remember that I will send you the one my Father promised. Stay in the city until you are given that power from heaven."

Acts 2:1, 4a

When the day of Pentecost came, they were all together in one place. . .They were all filled with the Holy Spirit.

Remember that the people didn't always fully understand what was happening. Part of the Holy Spirit's purpose is to help us remember and understand.

John 14:25-26

"I have told you all these things while I am with you. But the Helper will teach you everything and cause you to remember all that I told you. This Helper is the Holy Spirit that the Father will send in my name."

Acts 2:38, 41 (Peter preaching to the crowds in the street on the day of Pentecost after receiving the Spirit)

Peter said to them, "Change your hearts and lives and be baptized, each one of you, in the name of Jesus Christ. Then God will forgive your sins, and you will receive the gift of the Holy Spirit." Then those who accepted what Peter said were baptized. On that day about 3000 people were added to the group of believers.

Review: Jesus perfectly fulfilled the first four feasts that God instructed the Israelites to celebrate. God did not set down His rules and instructions arbitrarily. He has reasons for everything He does.

Now that we know what these feasts are really for, what can we see when we look back to the past?

After He first spoke to Abraham, God patiently waited for many years to allow the Israelite family nation time to grow not only in numbers, but also in the knowledge that they needed His protection and care. When the Israelites as a nation called on Him for help, He further detailed the original agreement He made with Abraham by giving His people the laws that Moses wrote down in the Old Testament. This giving of the Law happened beginning with the first Passover feast (after which the Israelites' left Egypt) and extending until His people were camped at the mountain to which He had led them. There, God wrote the Ten Commandments on two stone tablets for Moses to give to them. This giving of the Law happened during the time period from Passover until Pentecost. When Jesus was crucified at Passover, and the Holy Spirit was received by His people at Pentecost, an Old Testament prophecy was fulfilled:

This is what the LORD said, "The time is coming when I will make a new agreement with the family of Israel and with the family of Judah. It will not be like the agreement I made with their ancestors. I made that agreement when I took them by the hand and brought them out of Egypt. I was their master, but they broke that agreement."
This message is from the LORD.
"In the future I will make this agreement with the people of Israel."
This message is from the LORD.

"I will put my teachings in their minds, and I will write them on their hearts.
I will be their God, and they will be my people."

Jeremiah 31:31-33

God used the same period of time to make the new agreement with His people that He had used to make the old agreement – and it was all marked by the feast days as a sign for us. In the old agreement, God's laws were all written down – it was a physical covenant. In the new agreement, God's laws are written in the hearts and minds of those who believe in Him and trust Him – it is a spiritual covenant. Before Jesus, God's people served Him with physical offerings and sacrifices. After Jesus, God's people are to serve Him with spiritual offerings.

At His first Advent, or coming, Jesus gave full meaning to many of the Old Testament prophets' messages and to the first four of the feast days that God had set aside to teach and prepare His people. He completed the spiritual fulfillment phase of His plan, meaning He has restored our spirits to a relationship with Him. Jesus did not fulfill all of the prophecies or feast days, but He promised that He was coming back (His second Advent). Those unfulfilled prophecies and feast days are signs for us. He will return to satisfy those – and, thus complete the physical fulfillment phase of His plan in which He will restore our bodies to a relationship with Him.

Advent, not a word used in the Bible, is also the name of a season some people have decided to celebrate. Starting four Sundays before Christmas, they count down the days until His birth.

Romans 8:23b

We have the Spirit as the first part of God's promise. So we are waiting for God to finish making us his own children. I mean we are waiting for our bodies to be made free.

Colossians 2:16-17 (The apostle Paul, a Jew, knew the feasts were rehearsals for the real performance by Jesus)

So don't let anyone make rules for you about eating and drinking or about Jewish customs (festivals, New Moon celebrations, or Sabbath days). In the past these things were like a shadow that showed what was coming. But the new things that were coming are found in Christ.

Matthew 5:17-18 (Jesus speaking about His Mission)

"Don't think that I have come to destroy the Law of Moses or the teachings of the prophets. I have come not to destroy their teachings but to give full meaning to them. I assure you that nothing will disappear from the law until heaven and earth are gone. The law will not lose even the smallest letter or the smallest part of a letter until it has all been done."

Matthew 25:31 (Jesus speaking about His return as our King)

"The Son of Man will come again with divine greatness, and all his angels will come with him. He will sit as king on his great and glorious throne."

Romans 15:4a

Everything that was written in the past was written to teach us. Those things were written so that we could have hope.

Review: God was, is, and always will be a God of order, and He follows the plan He made in the beginning. We can see it clearly, if only we look.

****

In God's plan, we are currently between the Feast of Pentecost and the Feast of Trumpets – we are between the four spring/summer feasts and the three fall feasts in which the final harvest is completed. We are supposed to be cultivating the yeast of His Kingdom in others as we wait for the completion of God's plan when Jesus comes to collect the final harvest.

****

John 4:35-36 (Jesus talking to His followers)

"When you plant, you always say, 'Four more months to wait before we gather the grain.' But I tell you, open your eyes, and look at the fields. They are ready for harvesting now. Even now, the people who harvest the crop are being paid. They are gathering crops for eternal life. So now the people who plant can be happy together with those who harvest."

What are the fall feasts, and how will we know when these begin to be fulfilled? Some of the Jews who knew the Scriptures didn't recognize Jesus by the feast signs, so how will I?

Feast of Trumpets – To begin the Feast of Trumpets in ancient times, the priest would blow a horn signaling the people of God (who would have been bringing in the final harvest of the farming year) to come and have a special day of rest and worship. The directions for the feast days do not state any other purpose for this day.

Numbers 10:7part
"But if you want to gather the people together for a special meeting. . .blow a long steady blast on the trumpets."

Jewish people today call this day **Rosh Hashanah**, which means Head of the Year, or New Year's, although we've already learned that God said the month in which Passover occurs is the beginning of the year. It is somewhat confusing, but the number of the month (second, third, fourth, and so on) marks the number of months since Passover, while the month in which the Feast of Trumpets (and two other feasts) occurs, the seventh month, marks the changing of the year. In other words, the month of Passover marks the beginning of the holy/religious/spiritual year, while the seventh month marks the beginning of the civil/governmental year. This parallel method of counting time is based on God's own words.

Exodus 12:1-2 (God's directions for beginning the holy year)
While Moses and Aaron were still in Egypt, the LORD spoke to them. He said, "This month [the month of Passover] will be the first month of the year for you."

Exodus 34:22b (God's directions for beginning the civil year – the last three feasts all occur in the seventh month)
"And in the fall (Literally, at the changing of the year) celebrate the Festival of Shelters."

The proper Hebrew name for this feast is **Yom Teruah** (Day of Shouting/Loud Sounds/Trumpets/Blowing of horns). It is a Sabbath day that God instructed would be celebrated on the first day of the seventh month using the lunisolar calendar given by God. A lunisolar calendar tracks lunar months, and then brings them into agreement with a solar year by making occasional modifications. The Jewish leaders did this by adding a leap month to the end of the 12-month count when necessary in order to make Passover occur in spring. They eventually settled on a schedule of adding a leap month every 2 or 3 years for a total of 7 times every 19 years.

Jewish leaders added a second day to the feast about 2,500 years ago because knowing the correct day to celebrate was sometimes a difficult task, and they wanted to be sure they were observing this special Sabbath on the proper day. A quick astronomy refresher can be helpful for understanding this: the moon travels around the earth as the earth travels around the sun. It takes the moon one month to travel all the way around the earth, and it takes the earth one year to travel all the way around the sun. A new moon occurs when the earth, moon, and sun are all in a straight line in that order. The sun is so bright, that it makes the moon, which is directly in front of it from our perspective, very difficult to see. The new moon is only visible for a few minutes at sunrise and sunset – and if there are clouds, it cannot be seen. Although we now have more sophisticated methods of determining the new moon than spotting it with the naked eye, some Jewish people today still celebrate this feast for two days.

This is the only feast day that occurs on the first day of a month. The correct days for the other festivals were easier for everyone to know because the new moon would have already been announced and the next feast day was determined by counting forward from that day. No one knew for sure when this feast would begin until the religious leaders announced by blowing trumpets that the new moon had been sighted (by two witnesses, as was the Biblical custom), and it was indeed the first day of the month.

Numbers 10:10a

*"Also blow these trumpets for your special meetings [feast days], New Moon [**Rosh Chodesh**] celebrations, and all your happy times together."*

No one knew the exact day in advance – they all had to just wait and observe.

Saying, "No one knows the day," was one way the Jews referred to this feast in Jesus' time. A phrase like this is similar to what we would call an idiom today – like our modern, ***It's raining cats and dogs*** – or – ***Don't beat around the bush.*** These phrases should not be literally translated, because their meanings are misunderstood when taken out of context.

God's people could all be ready for the feast, but they had to wait for God to show the new moon to them to begin the celebration. Faithful people knew that God was very specific about time, and He would show them the new moon when it was His time. The added day to the feast, which was not instructed by God, was done by people out of fear and doubt. God tells us exactly what we need to know.

To be completed: The Bible says that we will not know the day nor the hour when Jesus will come – but it does not say we will not know the season, as we will soon see. We must be ready for Him to announce that this feast – His feast – has begun.

Jesus' return for His final harvest will be signaled by trumpets.

Leviticus 23:24-25

"Tell the Israelites: On the first day of the seventh month, you must have a special day of rest. Blow the trumpet to remind the people that this is a holy meeting. You must not do any work. You must bring an offering as a gift to the LORD."

Numbers 29:1

"There will be a special meeting on the first day of the seventh month. You will not do any work on that day. That is the day for blowing the trumpets."

Matthew 25:13

"So always be ready. You don't know the day or the time when the Son of Man will come."

Matthew 24:36a, Mark 13:32a

"No one knows when that day or time will be."

Acts 1:7

Jesus said to them, "The Father is the only one who has the authority to decide dates and times. They are not for you to know."

1 Thessalonians 5:1-4

Now, brothers and sisters, we don't need to write to you about times and dates. You know very well that the day when the Lord comes again will be a surprise, like a thief who comes at night. People will say, "We have peace and we are safe." At that time destruction will come to them quickly, like the pains of a woman giving birth. And those people will not escape. But you, brothers and sisters, are not living in darkness. And so that day will not surprise you like a thief.

Read the last two sentences again.

Matthew 24:27

"When the Son of Man comes, everyone will see him. It will be like lightning flashing in the sky that can be seen everywhere."

Matthew 24:30-31

"Then there will be something in the sky that shows the Son of Man is coming. All the people of the world will cry. Everyone will see the Son of Man coming on the clouds in the sky. He will come with power and great glory. He will use a loud trumpet to send his angels all around the earth. They will gather his chosen people from every part of the earth."

Everyone on earth will know that Jesus has returned.

1 Corinthians 15:51-52

But listen, I tell you this secret: We will not all die, but we will all be changed. It will only take the time of a second. We will be changed as quickly as an eye blinks. This will happen when the last trumpet blows. The trumpet will blow and those who have died will be raised to live forever. And we will all be changed.

This event of God's faithful followers being translated from their earthly bodies to their heavenly bodies is commonly referred to as the Rapture, although this name is not found in the Bible. There is much debate about exactly when during the time of the end this event will occur. The verse above conclusively gives the answer, and that answer agrees with the account in Revelation, in which John tells us about a series of seven trumpet blasts at the time of the end. The second coming of Christ to rescue His bride will occur "when the last trumpet blows," thereby rescuing His faithful from the bowls of wrath God will pour out on the unfaithful.

1 Thessalonians 4:16-17

The Lord himself will come down from heaven with a loud command, with the voice of the archangel, and with the trumpet call of God. And the people who have died and were in Christ will rise first. After that we who are still alive at that time will be gathered up with those who have died. We will be taken up in the clouds and meet the Lord in the air. And we will be with the Lord forever.

The first time Jesus came, He came quietly and humbly as our Great High Priest, and the month of His ultimate sacrifice at Passover marked the beginning of the holy year for His faithful people. Since the Fall of Humankind, we have been living in a world where Satan is allowed to roam. Because we allow Satan to tempt us into unfaithfulness to (crimes against) God, we need Jesus to be our Great High Priest – to intercede (testify) on our behalf. We cannot earn forgiveness from God, because it is freely available to everyone, but we can show our thankfulness to Him and our dedication to the relationship by continuing to sincerely offer spiritual sacrifices.

When Jesus returns, He will come charging into battle with a trumpet blast as the King, gathering His faithful people and fighting in their defense in His earthly homeland.

Numbers 10:9a

"If you are fighting an enemy in your own land, blow loudly on the trumpets before you go to fight them."

Jesus' victory will physically realize His role as the King of all kings, because all enemy earthly rulers will be utterly defeated. Jesus' earthly return will signal the beginning of a new era in which Jesus will reign as the only King on earth.

Revelation 20:1-3
I saw an angel coming down out of heaven. The angel had the key to the bottomless pit. The angel also held a large chain in his hand. The angel grabbed the dragon, that old snake, also known as the devil or Satan. The angel tied the dragon with the chain for 1000 years. Then the angel threw the dragon into the bottomless pit and closed it. The angel locked it over the dragon. The angel did this so that the dragon could not trick the people of the earth until the 1000 years were ended. After the 1000 years the dragon must be made free for a short time.

Revelation 20:4part
Then I saw some thrones and people sitting on them. These were the ones who had been given the power to judge. . .They came back to life and ruled with Christ for 1000 years.

This new era is often referred to as the Millennial Kingdom. Now we can see why the civil/governmental year count begins with this month. Jesus will return as the victorious King at this time, and the count of His 1,000-year earthly reign will begin.

Review: The blast of the seventh trumpet announces the new moon,
the beginning of the feast day, and Jesus' arrival as our King –
ushering in the Great Day of the Lord, in which He will
utterly defeat all the enemies of His people.
His people will be gathered together for this happy time,
making it an occasion for trumpets to be blown.
His faithful followers will not be taken by surprise.

****

True, not all of the Jews of His earthly time accepted Him.
Was that because the faithful Jews of His time were unable to
recognize Him, or because the unfaithful denied the truth of the
prophecies and the signs they had been given?

Why does God care about time?

As we have discussed, the calendar God gave to the Israelites was simply first month, second month, third month, and so on, with each month beginning with the sighting of the new moon. The Hebrew language uses the same word for month and moon – **chodesh**. God gave the lights in the sky – the sun, moon, and stars – so His people could calculate the passage of time. He planned the feast days from the very beginning.

Earthly time is a mere shadow of the beautiful, multifaceted heavenly time in which He operates. He is eternal – He always has been and He always will be. He is past, present, and future all at once. Our earthly time is a simplified version of heavenly time that we can understand and that He can use to communicate with us.

Genesis 1:14 (God explaining why He made the sun, moon, stars, and planets)

Then God said, "Let there be lights in the sky. These lights will separate the days from the nights. They will be used for signs to show when special meetings [feasts] begin and to show the days and years."

Genesis 1:19 (God teaching us how to calculate a day)

There was evening and then there was morning. This was the fourth day.

Isaiah 40:28 (The omniscience of God)

Surely you know the truth. Surely you have heard. The LORD is the God who lives forever! He created all the faraway places on earth. He does not get tired and weary. You cannot learn all that he knows.

He specifically designed earthly time so that we could know when He was going to do something for us. He set His feast days on a calendar for His people so they could understand and be prepared. God uses time in very specific and intentional ways.

As we have seen, some verses indicate that Jesus Himself does not know the day or the hour of His own wedding (when He comes back to take His bride home).

Mark 13:32b

"The Son and the angels in heaven don't know when that day or time will be. Only the Father knows."

There are several possible explanations for this.

When a young Jewish man of Jesus' day wanted to marry, he typically spent a good deal of time preparing a home for his bride. The man's father had the authority to say when his son was properly prepared. In other words, the father of the groom was the one who dictated when the wedding could proceed. So, perhaps Jesus was deferring to His Father, as any faithful Jewish man of His time would have done, regarding the exact moment of his wedding.

Perhaps as a human, Jesus did not know.

Perhaps, as a humble servant, He was just not allowed to say.

John 12:49

"That is because what I taught was not from myself. The Father who sent me told me what to say and what to teach."

Perhaps He awaits the sign of the new moon (controlled by the Father) that will be verified by two witnesses (chosen by the Father) before He will return to claim His faithful followers – He knows the appointed time (the feast), but not the specific moment. As one of the verses above shows (1 Thessalonians 5:1-4), and we all know from experience, a pregnant woman knows when her time to give birth is near, but she does not know the exact moment her labor will start.

Perhaps He was acknowledging the fact that 6:00pm (just an example time – the Bible doesn't tell us a specific time) on a given day in Jerusalem is a different day on the opposite side of the world.

Many volumes have been written by Bible scholars about these matters, but this fact is undeniable: **God gave the seven feasts as a teaching tool and timeline for all of His children to understand what He planned to do for them. He gave us the celestial bodies and taught us how to use them to track time, both religiously and governmentally.** He has not hidden His intentions or plan from us. We can be confident that our Father loves us and is preparing us for our new life in His presence. He is not trying to trick us or take us by surprise. He tells us repeatedly to be ready.

The book of Revelation, which gives many details about the second coming of Jesus, foretells two witnesses who prophecy just before the blowing of the seventh trumpet when God's bowls of wrath are poured out on the wicked. Their prophecy is a last call for any who will listen and obey. These two witnesses alert us to the beginning of the new era.

The following two parables clearly tell us that those who are living according to God's will when Jesus returns will not be surprised because they are prepared. They have made themselves ready, they have fulfilled their purpose, and they are excited, after a long engagement, to be taken by their Groom to their new, happy home. These stories, told by Jesus and recorded in the book of Matthew, clearly show that those who are prepared and do God's will have nothing to fear. Only those who are not watching and are not ready will be surprised and afraid.

Matthew 25:1-13 (This is about waiting preparedly for the moment the wedding will begin)

"At that time God's kingdom will be like ten girls who went to wait for the bridegroom. They took their lamps with them. Five of the girls were foolish, and five were wise. The foolish girls took their lamps with them, but they did not take extra oil for the lamps. The wise girls took their lamps and more oil in jars. When the bridegroom was very late, the girls could not keep their eyes open, and they fell asleep. At midnight someone announced, 'The bridegroom is coming! Come and meet him!' Then all the girls woke up. They made their lamps ready. But the foolish girls said to the wise girls, 'Give us some of your oil. The oil in our lamps is all gone.' The wise girls answered, 'No! The oil we have might not be enough for all of us. But go to those who sell oil and buy some for yourselves.' So the foolish girls went to buy oil. While they were gone, the bridegroom came. The girls who were ready went in with the bridegroom to the wedding feast. Then the door was closed and locked. Lat-

er, the other girls came. They said, 'Sir, sir! Open the door to let us in.' But the bridegroom answered, 'Certainly not! I don't even know you.' So always be ready. You don't know the day or the time when the Son of Man will come."

Matthew 25:14-30 (This is about our assignment while we wait - we are His representatives until He comes)

"At that time God's kingdom will also be like a man leaving home to travel to another place for a visit. Before he left, he talked with his servants. He told his servants to take care of his things while he was gone. He decided how much each servant would be able to care for. The man gave one servant five bags of money. He gave another servant two bags. And he gave a third servant one bag. Then he left. The servant who got five bags went quickly to invest the money. Those five bags of money earned five more. It was the same with the servant who had two bags. That servant invested the money and earned two more. But the servant who got one bag of money went away and dug a hole in the ground. Then he hid his master's money in the hole. After a long time the master came home. He asked the servants what they did with his money. The servant who got five bags brought that amount and five more bags of money to the master. The servant said, 'Master, you trusted me to care for five bags of money. So I used them to earn five more.' The master answered, 'You did right. You are a good servant who can be trusted. You did well with that small amount of money. So I will let you care for much greater things. Come and share my happiness with me.' Then the servant who got two bags of money came to the master. The servant said, 'Master, you gave me two bags of money to care for. So I used your two bags to earn two more.' The master answered, 'You did right. You are a good servant who can be trusted. You did well with a small amount of money. So I will let you care for much greater things. Come and share my happiness with me.' Then the servant who got one bag of money came to the master. The servant said, 'Master, I knew you were a very hard man. You harvest what you did not plant. You gather crops where you did not put any seed. So I was afraid. I went and hid your money in the ground. Here is the one bag of money you gave me.' The master answered, 'You are a bad and lazy servant! You say you knew that I harvest what I did not plant and that I gather crops where I did not put any seed. So you should have put my money in the bank. Then, when I came home, I would get my money back. And I would also get the interest that my money earned.' So the master told his other servants, 'Take the one bag of money from that servant and give it to the servant who has ten bags. Everyone who uses what they have will get more. They will have much more than they need. But people who do not use what they have will have everything taken away from them.' Then the

master said, 'Throw that useless servant outside into the darkness, where people will cry and grind their teeth with pain.'"

This is why we must use the gifts we have been given by God to help bring others to Him – to increase our Master's household – to fulfill our purpose as stewards of God's estate. We must always be ready for His return, and we must always be serving Him.

John 4:35b-36a

But I tell you, open your eyes, and look at the fields. They are ready for harvesting now. Even now, the people who harvest the crop are being paid. They are gathering crops for eternal life.

Romans 13:11a-13a (Our current darkness will be overcome by perfect day)

Our salvation is nearer now than when we first believed. The night is almost finished. The day is almost here. So we should stop doing whatever belongs to darkness. We should prepare ourselves to fight evil with the weapons that belong to the light. We should live in a right way, like people who belong to the day.

The metaphor about night and day in this verse fits nicely with the definition of a day of the week as darkness first and daylight second that God gave us in Genesis Chapter 1. He is a God of order.

Let's look at time calculations from the Biblical perspective more closely. Based on the earlier time sketch of Jesus' last week, this is what the month would have looked like:

Sunday	Monday	Tuesday	Wednesday	Thursday	Friday	Saturday
First Month						
1st day	2nd day	3rd day	4th day	5th day	6th day	7th day
				New moon sighted at sunset	1 Rosh Codesh - New Moon celebration	2 Sabbath
3	4	5	6	7	8	9 Sabbath
10 Lamb Selection Day	11	12	13 Last Supper	14 Lambs sacrificed - Passover meal after nightfall tonight	15 Special Sabbath -1st day Feast Unleavened Bread	16 Sabbath
17 Feast of First Fruits	18	19	20	21	22 Special Sabbath -last day Feast Unleavened Bread	23 Sabbath
24	25	26	27	28	29	New moon sighted at sunset

Based on this month, here's an estimate of what the annual calendar would have looked like:

First Month						
				New moon	1	2
3	4	5	6	7	8	9
10	11	12	13	14	15	16
17	18	19	20	21	22	23
24	25	26	27	28	29	New moon

Second Month						
1	2	3	4	5	6	7
8	9	10	11	12	13	14
15	16	17	18	19	20	21
22	23	24	25	26	27	28
New moon						

Third Month						
	1	2	3	4	5	6
7	8	9	10	11	12	13
14	15	16	17	18	19	20
21	22	23	24	25	26	27
27	28	29	New moon			

Fourth Month						
				1	2	3
4	5	6	7	8	9	10
11	12	13	14	15	16	17
18	19	20	21	22	23	24
25	26	27	28	New moon		

Fifth Month						
					1	2
3	4	5	6	7	8	9
10	11	12	13	14	15	16
17	18	19	20	21	22	23
24	25	26	27	28	29	New moon

Sixth Month						
1	2	3	4	5	6	7
8	9	10	11	12	13	14
15	16	17	18	19	20	21
22	23	24	25	26	27	28
New moon						

Seventh Month						
	1	2	3	4	5	6
7	8	9	10	11	12	13
14	15	16	17	18	19	20
21	22	23	24	25	26	27
28	29	New moon				

Eighth Month						
			1	2	3	4
5	6	7	8	9	10	11
12	13	14	15	16	17	18
19	20	21	22	23	24	25
26	27	28	New moon			

Ninth Month						
				1	2	3
4	5	6	7	8	9	10
11	12	13	14	15	16	17
18	19	20	21	22	23	24
25	26	27	28	29	New moon	

Tenth Month						
						1
2	3	4	5	6	7	8
9	10	11	12	13	14	15
16	17	18	19	20	21	22
23/New moon	24	25	26	27	28	29

Eleventh Month						
	1	2	3	4	5	6
7	8	9	10	11	12	13
14	15	16	17	18	19	20
21	22	23	24	25	26	27
28	29	New moon				

Twelfth Month						
			1	2	3	4
5	6	7	8	9	10	11
12	13	14	15	16	17	18
19	20	21	22	23	24	25
26	27	28	New moon			

The holy year begins in spring. The calendar is based on the lunar month and the solar year, so each year does not have the correct number of days to keep the beginning of the year in spring over time. This Hebrew calendar year has 354 days to our current calendar's 365. This is why the additional leap month would be added to the end of the year 7 times in every 19 years – to align the year with the earth's rotation around the sun. Darker grey squares indicate weekly Sabbath days and special Sabbath days. Lighter grey squares indicate feast days that are not Sabbaths. Notice the 14th and 17th days of the first month – Passover and the Feast of First Fruits – are light grey, so the day Jesus died and the day He arose were **not** Sabbath days – neither was the day He ascended (that would have been the 26th of the Second Month – 10 days before Pentecost).

Note: In the story of Noah, Biblical years are expressed in terms of 12 months, each consisting of 30 days, so a year is 360 days. The timetable used in this worldwide judgment is important in understanding the timetable of the final worldwide judgment that is still to come. This is God's judicial calendar – some people call it the prophetic calendar.

Notice that all the feasts take place in the first, third, and seventh months. Seven is a Biblical number that indicates completion. It seems reasonable to believe that Jesus will return in the seventh month, at the beginning of the civil year, to make God's plan complete. He will establish His physical earthly kingdom at that time. Also, notice that the Feast of Trumpets is the only feast day occurring on the first day of the month – that is, the day after the new moon has been sighted by two witnesses the night before. Remember, no one knows when that day will be until the new moon has been sighted. We're repeating this, because it's important.

God's plan is so much clearer when viewed on His calendar. Today's calendar separates us from realizing the order and clarity of His appointed times. Most of the modern world functions on the Gregorian calendar, named after Pope Gregory XIII and adopted in 1582. Ten days were skipped when this calendar replaced the Julian calendar (which had been in use since 45 BC and was named after Julius Caesar) in order to realign the celebrations of Christ's resurrection with the spring equinox. Additionally, the terms BC (before Christ) and AD (Latin for **anno Domini** – *In the year of our Lord*) as a means of marking annual time were established in AD 525 by a monk who gave no satisfactory explanations as to the system's logic. Scholars can come close, but it is hard to know for sure what year we are actually in today.

We will discuss the time of the end more, but there will be many clues before Jesus returns.

Review: Earthly time is a tool that God uses for our benefit. By using time,
we can understand God's plan. For every day that passes,
we are one day closer to Jesus' return.
Don't waste the time you have been given to do His work.

What follows the Feast of Trumpets?

Day of Atonement – In ancient times, this was the only day that the high priest could enter into the Holy of Holies (God's private area in the Temple). On this day, the people of God did no work but spent the entire day fasting and confessing their sins, while the high priest spent the day performing purification ceremonies and offering sacrifices to cover (atone for) the sins of the nation of Israel. Jewish people today call this day **Yom Kippur**.

The Day of Atonement is a special Sabbath that follows the Feast of Trumpets by nine days.

To be completed: Jesus has already completed the sacrificial portion of our worship to God, but many still refuse to recognize Him. When Jesus returns, all the world – past and present – believers and non-believers – will recognize and confess that Jesus is indeed our Savior. We will all humble ourselves and bow before the King of kings. Faithful believers have accepted Jesus' offer of atonement for their sins. The unfaithful and unbelievers will have to atone for their own.

Leviticus 23:27-28, 32b

"The Day of Atonement will be on the tenth day of the seventh month. There will be a holy meeting [special Sabbath]. You must not eat food, and you must bring an offering as a gift to the LORD. You must not do any work on that day, because it is the Day of Atonement. On that day the priests will go before the LORD and perform the ceremony that makes you pure. You will start this special day of rest on the evening following the ninth day of the month. This special day of rest continues from that evening until the next evening."

Leviticus 16:30, 34b (This chapter includes a detailed list of instructions for the priest)

"Because on this day, the priest will do this to make you pure and wash away your sins. Then you will be clean to the LORD. . .Once every year you will purify the Israelites from all their sins."

Philippians 2:9-11

So God raised him up to the most important place and gave him the name that is greater than any other name. God did this so that every person will bow down to honor the name of Jesus. Everyone in heaven, on earth, and under the earth will bow. They will all confess, "Jesus Christ is Lord," and this will bring glory to God the Father.

Romans 14:11 (from Isaiah 45:23)
Yes, the Scriptures say, "'As surely as I live', says the Lord, 'Everyone will bow before me; everyone will say that I am God.'"

After the two parables we just read about always being ready and always using our gifts for His good, Jesus went on to describe in more detail what it will be like when He returns – how we will all fully understand His greatness. He also restates our purpose.

Matthew 25:31-46
"The Son of Man will come again with divine greatness, and all his angels will come with him. He will sit as a king on his great and glorious throne. All the people of the world will be gathered before him. Then he will separate everyone into two groups. It will be like a shepherd separating his sheep from his goats. He will put the sheep on his right and the goats on his left. Then the king will say to the godly people on his right, 'Come, my Father has great blessings for you. The kingdom he promised is now yours. It has been prepared for you since the world was made. It is yours because when I was hungry, you gave me food to eat. When I was thirsty, you gave me something to drink. When I had no place to stay, you welcomed me into your home. When I was without clothes, you gave me something to wear. When I was sick, you cared for me. When I was in prison, you came to visit me.' Then the godly people will answer, 'Lord, when did we see you hungry and give you food? When did we see you thirsty and give you something to drink? When did we see you with no place to stay and welcome you into our home? When did we see you without clothes and give you something to wear? When did we see you sick or in prison and care for you?' Then the king will answer, 'The truth is, anything you did for any of my people here, you also did for me.' Then the king will say to the evil people on his left, 'Get away from me. God has already decided that you will be punished. Go into the fire that burns forever – the fire that was prepared for the devil and his angels. You must go away because when I was hungry, you gave me nothing to eat. When I was thirsty, you gave me nothing to drink. When I had no place to stay, you did not welcome me into your home. When I was without clothes, you gave me nothing to wear. When I was sick and in prison, you did not care for me.' Then those people will answer, 'Lord, when did we see you hungry or thirsty? When did we see you without a place to stay? Or when did we see you without clothes or sick or in prison? When did we see any of this and not help you?' The king will answer, 'The truth is, anything you refused to do for any of my people here, you refused to do for me.' Then these evil people will go away to be

punished forever. But the godly people will go and enjoy eternal life."

Once again, none of this will be a surprise to those who know Him and have lived according to His will. The only surprise will be for those who have refused Him. You have the power, as shown in all three of these parables, to decide how you will live.

1 John 2:28-29

Yes, my dear children, live in him. If we do this, we can be without fear on the day when Christ comes again. We will not need to hide and be ashamed when he comes [as Adam and Eve did: The man and the woman heard him, and they hid among the trees in the garden (Genesis 3:8b)]. You know that Christ always did what was right. So you know that all those who do what is right are God's children.

Feast of Booths – In ancient times, God's people celebrated living free from oppression and under God's direct care by re-enacting a time in their history when they traveled and waited in the wilderness (the desert), living in tents (also called booths, shelters, or tabernacles) before they were allowed to enter a land God had set aside for them and have permanent homes. This is the time after they left slavery in Egypt. The people had turned back to God, and He had helped them. He had given them a new life, and He had come to stay with them. The people were traveling to the land that God had promised to the descendants of Abraham. It was a joyous feast of thanksgiving when God dwelt in the Tabernacle among His people. The Tabernacle was a tent used for worship – a portable version of the Temple that would later be built in Jerusalem – by the Israelites while traveling to the Promised Land. Because the people also lived in tents during this time, they were instructed to live in a temporary shelter for a week every year to remember how God had provided for them in their travels. Jewish people today call this celebratory feast **Sukkot**, and it follows the Day of Atonement by five days.

This is one of the three feasts for which Jewish males were required to present themselves at the Temple. Today, we would call these pilgrimage feasts – in Hebrew, they are called **Shalosh HaRegalim**.

Exodus 23:17

"So three times each year all the men will come to the special place to be with the Lord GOD."

For Passover, Pentecost, and the Feast of Booths, the people were called by God to gather themselves together to worship Him. The Jewish people were gathering in Jerusalem for these three feasts during Jesus' time, and so there were large crowds who witnessed the events surrounding Jesus first-hand. Later in Jewish history, the religious leaders made a decision to change which feasts would be holy days and have created a tradition that the Feast of Trumpets and the Day of Atonement are High Holy Days, and the ten days encompassing them are called the Ten Days of Awe or the Ten Days of Repentance, but this is not included in the instructions God gave His people in the Bible.

To be completed: Jesus will return to establish His rule over all the earth. God's people will be free from the troubles and temptations that sin brings. Sin is slavery, sin is oppression, and we will be free from it.

Leviticus 23:34-36

"Tell the Israelites: On the 15th day of the seventh month is the Festival of Shelters. This festival to the LORD will continue for seven days. There will be a holy meeting on the first day. You must not do any work. You will bring offerings as gifts to the LORD for seven days. On the eighth day, you will have another holy meeting. You must not do any work. You will bring an offering as a gift to the LORD."

Hebrews 10:1-2

The law gave us only an unclear picture of the good things coming in the future. The law is not a perfect picture of the real things. The law tells people to offer the same sacrifices every year. Those who come to worship God continue to offer those sacrifices. But the law can never make them perfect.

Hebrews 9:11-12

But Christ has already come to be the high priest. He is the high priest of the good things we now have. But Christ does not serve in a place like the tent that those other priests served in. He serves in a better place. Unlike that tent, this one is perfect. It was not made by anyone here on earth. It does not belong to this world. Christ entered the Most Holy Place only one time – enough for all time. He entered the Most Holy Place by using his own blood, not the blood of goats or young bulls. He entered there and made us free from sin forever.

Zechariah 14:9
And the LORD will be the King of the whole world. At that time all people will worship him as the only LORD with only one name.

Revelation 3:11 (As faithful believers, we are kings - Jesus is the King of kings)
"I am coming soon. Hold on to the faith you have, so that no one can take away your crown."

Review: God gave His people these seven feasts to celebrate each year as a reminder of and preparation for His plan for our redemption (our complete deliverance from sin).

Should we be celebrating these appointed times now?

These feasts were given to God's people long, long before Jesus came to earth. When God gave His people the feasts, He gave them as a part of what is called the Law. The Law's purpose was to help the people lead physically and spiritually healthy lives – to help them understand God and do what He expected of them as His people – and to help them understand the progression of God's plan of salvation when He sent Jesus to begin our restoration.

The Law God gave to Moses included directions about behavior (the moral law). Here are the original Ten Commandments found in the Old Testament book of Exodus 20: 1-17 (some of these are shortened, so read for yourself to see the whole command). God said He would be with His people if they respected Him and each other.

The word **exodus** means the exit of a large group of people – in this case, the exit of the Israelites from Egypt.

The Ten Commandments

How we should behave toward God:	How we should behave toward others:
1. You must not worship any other gods except me. 2. You must not make any idols. 3. You must not use the name of the LORD your God to make empty promises. 4. You must remember to keep the Sabbath a special day.	5. You must honor and respect your father and your mother. 6. You must not murder anyone. 7. You must not commit adultery. 8. You must not steal anything. 9. You must not tell lies about other people. 10. You must not want to take anything that belongs to another person.

In addition to this moral code, the Law God gave also included very specific instructions about ceremonial law, including the animal sacrifices the people were to make on different occasions. When Jesus was sacrificed for us, He was the ultimate and final blood sacrifice. When we make up for a wrong thing we have done, it is said we atone for it. Jesus atoned for all the sins humankind ever did or would commit. His death and resurrection fulfilled the expectations of the sacrificial system for us – He completed the ceremonial law's requirements for us forever. We are no longer required to offer animal sacrifices for our sins.

Hebrews 10:8-9, 14a

Christ first said, "You don't want sacrifices and offerings. You are not pleased with animals killed and burned or with sacrifices to take away sin." (These are all sacrifices that the law commands.) Then he said, "Here I am, God. I have come to do what you want." So God ends that first system of sacrifices and starts his new way. . .With one sacrifice Christ made his people perfect forever.

Further evidence that animal sacrifices are no longer needed lies in the fact that God allowed the Romans to completely destroy the Temple in AD 70, just as Jesus prophesied to His followers approximately 40 years earlier.

Matthew 24:1-2

Jesus left the Temple area and was walking away. But his followers came to him to show him the Temple's buildings. He asked them, "Are you looking at these buildings? The fact is, they will be destroyed. Every stone will be thrown down to the ground. Not one stone will be left on another."

The Western Wall, or Wailing Wall, as it is sometimes called today, is a remnant of a retaining wall built as part of a remodel/expansion undertaken by Herod, a Roman ruler. It was never a part of the Temple.

The Jews, whether they believe Jesus was the Messiah or not, no longer offer sacrifices, because they have no Temple in which to do it.

John 4:21part, 23a

Jesus said, "Believe me. . .The time is coming when you will not have to be in Jerusalem. . .to worship the Father. But the time is coming when the true worshipers will worship the Father in spirit and truth.

In order to accept the forgiveness offered because of Jesus' sacrifice, all we have to do is follow Jesus' teachings. He told us directly and through His parables how we are to behave toward God and how we are to behave toward others.

Jesus gave us only two commandments in Matthew 22:37-39. In verse 40, Jesus says, "All of the law and the writings of the prophets take their meaning from these two commands." So, these are the roots of the original Ten Commandments, as well as all that is written in the Old Testament:

How we should behave toward God:	How we should behave toward others:
1. Love the Lord your God with all your heart, all your soul, and all your mind.	2. Love your neighbor the same as you love yourself.

Notice the Ten Commandments with the dictatorial sounding "you must" and "you must not" rules are not bossy or arbitrary. They are really just rules that teach us how to properly show love for God and for one another. Jesus gave us the simplified commands and set an example for us by how He behaved.

In the very early church, some Jewish believers were pressuring some Gentile believers to follow certain Jewish customs. Paul, an apostle of Jesus and a devout Jew, instructed new believers not to be persuaded to follow human-made rules.

Colossians 2:16-17

So don't let anyone make rules for you about eating and drinking or about Jewish customs (festivals, New Moon celebrations, or Sabbath days). In the past these things were like a shadow that showed what was coming. But the new things that were coming are found in Christ.

Galatians 4:4-5a

But when the right time came, God sent his Son, who was born from a woman and lived under the law. God did this so that he could buy the freedom of those who were under the law.

Galatians 5:1-5

We have freedom now, because Christ made us free. So stand strong in that freedom. Don't go back into slavery [of the Law] again. Listen! I, Paul, tell you that if you start following the law by being circumcised, then Christ cannot help you. Again, I warn everyone: If you allow yourselves to be circumcised, then you must follow the whole law. If you try to be made right with God through the law, your life with Christ is finished – you have left God's grace. I say this because our hope of being right with God comes through faith.

Galatians 5:6b

The important thing is faith – the kind of faith that works through love.

Our worship of God is no longer ceremonial – it is no longer on the outside of our bodies. Even before Jesus was sacrificed, God did not accept ceremonial offerings that were made strictly on the outside. Read the story of Cain and Abel in Genesis Chapter 4. Cain brought a physically acceptable offering, but his heart was not right with God. Offerings must be made with a loving, willing, faithful heart.

Romans 2:29

A true Jew is one who is a Jew inside. True circumcision is done in the heart. It is done by the Spirit, not by the written law. And anyone who is circumcised in the heart by the Spirit gets praise from God, not from people.

Psalm 141:1-2 (Prayer is an offering to God)

LORD, I call to you for help. Listen to me as I pray. Please hurry and help me! Accept my prayer like a gift of burning incense, the words I lift up like an evening sacrifice.

Hebrews 11:1-2

Faith is what makes real the things we hope for. It is proof of what we cannot see. God was pleased with the people who lived a long time ago because they had faith like this.

Read all of Hebrews Chapter 11 for a review of the Old Testament faithful believers and how their love for God and their complete faith in Him pleased God.

Hosea 6:6b

. . .I want faithful love, not sacrifice. I want people to know God, not to bring. . .offerings.

Proverbs 21:3

Do what is right and fair. The LORD loves that more than sacrifices.

Jesus completed the ceremonial law's requirements, but He also told us that His sacrifice has not done away with the Law. We can clearly see that only four of God's seven feasts have been fulfilled, so we can clearly see that His Law is not yet fully executed.

While the ceremonial law of physical offerings has been fulfilled and is no longer necessary, God's moral law, His Commandments as emphasized by Jesus, still stand, and all believers are obligated to them. The offerings we make must still be made from loving, willing faithful hearts, but the offerings are no longer grain, oil, wine, or animals. The only law left is love, and because God's Spirit lives in us, we must demonstrate our love for God by demonstrating that love to others.

Review: Whether or not we celebrate the feast days, we should certainly be mindful of them and remember what they represent.
One thing is certain: the blood sacrifices originally required at a feast are no longer necessary. Hallelujah!

See page 450 of the Group Discussion Guide at the back for suggestions on how to mark these occasions.

What is God's core message to us in the sacrifice of Jesus?

God has made His plan simple for us to understand. Everything we need to know relates to something familiar to us. During the long-distance part of humankind's relationship with Him, God sent the prophets of old with His messages, trying to woo His people back to Him. Some listened, but many did not. After many years and many prophets and messages, God finally sent His Son to deliver the ultimate Message.

John 3:16

Yes, God loved the world so much that he gave his only Son, so that everyone who believes in him would not be lost but have eternal life.

John 14:31a

"But the world must know that I love the Father. So I do exactly what the Father told me to do."

1 Timothy 2:4

God wants everyone to be saved and to fully understand the truth.

John 11:52

Yes, he would die for the Jewish people. But he would also die for God's other children scattered all over the world. He would die to bring them all together and make them one people.

This ultimate Message is a proposal to us – a marriage proposal. He is promising us what it will be like after Jesus comes to claim His bride. Before Jesus ascended to heaven, He told His disciples that His Father's house had many rooms, and He was going to prepare a place for us. Jesus is the groom, preparing a home for His bride – an everlasting home in the presence of God, our Father. Here is a summary of what Jesus says it will be like when He returns for His bride and takes us home to His Father's house: *"Come live in this wonderful home I will make for us. Trust me. I will take care of you. You will never be sad or hurt again. I will never leave you. Your joy will be complete, and no one can ever take it away from you. All of this will be yours if you just choose Me. I love you all."*

John 6:37-40

"The Father gives me my people. Every one of them will come to me. I will always accept them. I came down from heaven to do what God wants, not what I want. I must not lose anyone God has given me. But I must raise them up on the last day. This is what the one who sent me wants me to do. Everyone who sees the Son and believes in him has eternal life. I will raise them up on the last day. This is what my Father wants."

John 16:22b

". . .I will see you again, and you will be happy. You will have a joy that no one can take away."

John 14:1-4

Jesus said, "Don't be troubled. Trust in God, and trust in me. There are many rooms in my Father's house. I would not tell you this if it were not true. I am going there to prepare a place for you. After I go and prepare a place for you, I will come back. Then I will take you with me, so that you can be where I am. You know the way to the place where I am going."

God showed how serious His offer is in the sacrifice of His Son, Jesus. When we accept the proposal delivered by Jesus, we believe God loves us, and we want Him in our lives. This acceptance is like an engagement. In the New Testament book of Ephesians, it says when we believe, when we accept God's proposal (which we prove by admitting we are sinful, by accepting the forgiveness made available to all by Jesus, and by being baptized to show our commitment), we are sealed with the Holy Spirit He promised. We have promised ourselves to God – like an engagement. Because we love God, we will do as He asks. His Holy Spirit comes to live in us as a guarantee of Jesus' promise to take us home one day to our Father's house. His Spirit is like an engagement ring.

Acts 2:38-39a

Peter said to them, "Change your hearts and lives and be baptized, each one of you, in the name of Jesus Christ. Then God will forgive your sins, and you will receive the gift of the Holy Spirit. This promise is for you."

Ephesians 1:13b-14a

When you heard that Good News, you believed in Christ. And in Christ, God put his special mark on you by giving you the Holy Spirit that he promised. The Spirit is the first payment that guarantees we will get all that God has for us.

Colossians 1:5
Your faith and love continue because you know what is waiting for you in heaven – the hope you have had since you first heard the true message, the Good News.

Jesus committed Himself fully to an everlasting marriage to us, His beloved, through His sacrifice. Like in a marriage ceremony, He has already said His vows. It is up to us to accept those vows from Him and give Him our own vows.

Revelation 21:3-4
I heard a loud voice from the throne. It said, "Now God's home is with people. He will live with them. They will be his people. God himself will be with them and will be their God. He will wipe away every tear from their eyes. There will be no more death, sadness, crying, or pain. All the old ways are gone."

We can better understand how our relationship with Jesus is like a marriage if we step back in time about 2,000 years and get a briefing on Jewish culture:

When a marriage agreement (a major concern was the bride price, which both the bride and her father must agree to accept) was reached, the spiritual union of the couple would be sealed/sanctified by a marriage blessing/toast called a **Holy Kiddushin**. Participants would share bread and wine as part of this marriage ceremony. (This ritual (reciting a blessing and sharing bread and wine, which is called a **Kiddush**) is also a standard part of any Sabbath or special Sabbath.) The bride and groom are considered married after the **Kiddushin**, but the consummation of the marriage does not take place until a later, to-be-determined, date.

The bride, with the help of her bridesmaids, would then begin to prepare herself for the next phase (called **nisu'in**), keeping her belongings nearby and her lamp full of oil, because she did not know when her groom would come for her – day or night. She had to wait while the groom prepared a home for them, often on his father's land. When the groom's father gave his approval of the new home the groom had prepared for his bride, the physical marriage, or **nisu'in**, could commence. No physical union of bride and groom could happen until the groom's father said the time was right. When permission was received, the groom and his party would depart to collect the bride. One of the groomsmen would run ahead and blow a horn to alert the bride that her groom was coming.

Now a clear understanding of both the Feast of Trumpets, for which a trumpet will announce the arrival of Jesus, and the Groom coming for His bride are inseparably linked in our expectations for the future. Now we better understand the parable of the ten virgins and the necessity of being ready for the Groom at any time. God, our Father, has accepted the bride price of 30 pieces of silver, funded by the physical death of His Servant, Jesus. You, as the bride of Christ, must agree to the marriage contract, participate in a **Kiddushin**, and prepare for the **nisu'in**.

Review: God wants to have a relationship with us in which
He is committed to us and we are committed to Him – a marriage.
He is preparing a home for us where we will live with Him forever,
if we accept the proposal Jesus delivered and remain faithful and watchful.

What about all the people who never knew Jesus? Can they be saved?

For the Old Testament people, it is a question of faith in God and His promise of a coming Savior, or Messiah (someone who could and would save their spiritual lives by restoring humankind's relationship with God).

Adam and Eve knew God would provide someone to save them because God told them before they left Eden that Eve's child (one of her descendants) would crush Satan. As far as we know, they knew no other details about the Savior that would come, yet they had faith in God's promise. We know they believed because they taught their son, Abel, to believe, and God accepted Abel. In Genesis, we can also read that a younger son, Seth, and his family began calling to God.

Where did Adam and Eve's sons get their wives? Since they were the only humans, they would have had to marry their siblings, and all of their children would be first cousins. After the third generation, the necessity of marriage between closely related people diminishes rapidly. Incest was completely forbidden by God in the Law given to Moses, but it was likely forbidden before that time. Noah's son, Ham, although he had a wife, may have had relations with his mother, producing a son named Canaan (Ham's fourth, and last, son). When Noah became aware of the situation, he cursed the offspring of the union – a curse carried out by God when the Israelites were told to take the land of Canaan (Ham's descendants from that union) for their own after they left Egypt.

Genesis 9:21, 24b-25
One day Noah made some wine. He got drunk, went into his tent, and took off all his clothes. Ham, the father of Canaan, saw that his father was naked and told his brothers who were outside the tent. . .When he [Noah] learned what his youngest son Ham had done to him, he said, "May there be a curse on Canaan! May he be a slave to his brothers."

Leviticus 18:6
"You must never have sexual relations with your close relatives. I am the LORD."

Leviticus 18:8
You must not have sexual relations with your father's wife. . .because that is like having sexual relations with your father. (Literally, "She is the nakedness of your father." Husband and wife are like one person.)

Genesis 1:24
That is why a man leaves his father and mother and is joined to his wife. In this way two people become one.

This interpretation of the story of Noah is just a guess, although it harmonizes well with the rest of Scripture, and better explains the harsh judgment on Canaan. We address it here to show that the incestuous relationship required for the continuation of the human race was only allowed by God temporarily after Creation. When God cleansed the earth in Noah's day, He told Noah to bring his sons and their wives, thereby significantly reducing the need for marriage between close relatives.

Other descendants of Seth must have believed, too, because generations later, Noah believed what he knew of God, and he taught his family to have faith in God. We know Noah and his family believed because God spoke to Noah and told him to build the ark, and he did. God offered Noah and his family salvation, and they accepted it. They passed through the door of the ark, and God kept them safe from the punishment He would send on those who did not obey Him.

Some of Noah's descendants must have believed in God's promise of a Savior, too, because many generations later (and, by the way, there was still no written Scripture at this point, so the promise was delivered by word of mouth from person to person), we know that Abraham believed (Abraham was a descendant of Shem, Noah's oldest son). He left his home and wandered off into the wilderness searching for the land God had told him to find. He did this because he had faith in God's promises. In the first book of the Bible, we can read that Abraham told his son, Isaac, that God would provide a Lamb. Abraham was talking about Jesus – he just didn't have all the details yet. Like others, he didn't realize the significance of his actions and his words, but with the Spirit's help, we can see it now. Abraham was not a perfect man, but a deep love for God was in his heart, and he was called a "friend of God."

James 2:23b

"Abraham believed God, and because of this faith he was accepted as one who is right with God." Abraham was called "God's friend."

Some of Abraham's descendants believed, because Moses, who later wrote down the first Scriptures, also had faith in God. Moses chose to suffer through a difficult life with his people, the Israelites, rather than live the life of luxury he was offered by his adopted Egyptian family because he believed God's promise of a Messiah who would come to save God's people. God used Moses' faith to lead His people out of slavery in Egypt and back to the land He had given Abraham.

Generations later, King David had faith in God. David knew about God's promise of a Savior, too. In addition to all the teachable moments in a person's life that God uses to guide us, David also had the first five books of the Bible that Moses had written down for God, and he had the words and personal guidance of living prophets. He knew very well how good and righteous and holy and fair God is. David was a musician, and he wrote many songs/poems on these topics. Although David was far from perfect, he was called "a man after God's own heart."

There were obviously many people who lived and died before God sent His Son to forgive all their sins. Some of those people lived in a right way, and some lived in a wrong way. God is just – He is fair. Jesus preached to those long ago who were doing wrong.

1 Peter 3:19-21

And by the Spirit he went and preached to the spirits in prison. Those were the spirits who refused to obey God long ago in the time of Noah. God was waiting patiently for people while Noah was building the big boat. And only a few – eight in all – were saved in the boat through the flood-water. And that water is like baptism, which now saves you. Baptism is not the washing of dirt from the body. It is asking God for a clean conscience. It saves you because Jesus Christ was raised from death.

Know that God always looks at the heart – that is, He looks at your willingness to act in a way that pleases Him because you love Him and trust Him to take care of you. This is different from just "being a good person." Do not think that if you are a good person, nothing else you do matters. This is a false teaching. Everything you do matters to God. Our faith in God, our love for Him, and our willingness to do His will must be there in order to be saved. Even though they made mistakes, these people and many others from Old Testament times had faith and a love for God that was strong enough to make them want to do His will. They believed in His promised Savior. The Bible says that Jesus' sacrifice was good for all time. God will take care of ALL of His people.

For the Old Testament people, it is a question of faith in God and His promise of a coming Savior, or Messiah (someone who could and would save their spiritual lives by restoring humankind's relationship with God).

Hebrews 11:1-2

Faith is what makes real the things we hope for. It is proof of what we cannot see. God was pleased with the people who lived a long time ago because they had faith like this.

Genesis 3:15b (God's promise to punish Satan and save His people)

"You will bite her child's foot, but he will crush your head."

Genesis 4:4b

The LORD accepted Abel and his gift.

Hebrews 11:4part

Cain and Abel both offered sacrifices to God. But Abel offered a better sacrifice to God because he had faith. . .And so God called him a good man because he had faith. Abel died, but through his faith he is still speaking.

Genesis 4:26

Seth also had a son. He named him Enosh. At that time people began to pray to [Literally, "to call upon"] the LORD.

Genesis 6:8, 9b, 22

But Noah pleased the LORD. . .He was a good man all his life, and he always followed God. . .Noah did everything God commanded him.

Hebrews 11:7b

With his faith, Noah showed that the world was wrong. And he became one of those who are made right with God through faith.

Genesis 22:8

Abraham answered, "God himself is providing the lamb for the sacrifice, my son."

Hebrews 11:17b-19

Abraham obeyed because he had faith. He already had the promises from God. And God had already said to him, "It is through Isaac that your descendants will come." But Abraham was ready to offer his only son. He did this because he had faith. He believed that God could raise people from death. And really, when God stopped Abraham from killing Isaac, it was as if he got him back from death.

James 2:22

So you see that Abraham's faith and what he did worked together. His faith was made perfect by what he did.

Exodus 14:13a

But Moses answered, "Don't be afraid! Don't run away! Stand where you are and watch the LORD save you today."

Hebrews 11:27part

Moses left Egypt because he had faith. . .He continued strong as if he could see the God no one can see.

1 Samuel 13:14part (Samuel, the prophet, about King David)

The LORD was looking for a man who wants to obey him. He has found that man – and the LORD has chosen him to be the new leader of his people. . .

Hebrews 11:13, 16b

All these great people continued living with faith until they died. They did not get the things God promised his people. But they were happy just to see those promises coming far in the future. They accepted the fact that they were like visitors and strangers here on earth. . .So God is not ashamed to be called their God. And he has prepared a city for them.

Romans 4:5a

But people cannot do any work that will make them right with God. So they must trust in him. Then he accepts their faith, and that makes them right with him.

Hebrews 11:6

Without faith no one can please God. Whoever comes to God must believe that he is real and that he rewards those who sincerely try to find him.

Ephesians 2:8-9

I mean that you have been saved by grace because you believed. You did not save yourselves; it was a gift from God. You are not saved by the things you have done, so there is nothing to boast about.

James 2:18b, 20part

. . . you can't show me your faith if you don't do anything. But I will show you my faith by the good I do. . .Faith that does nothing is worth nothing.

Hebrews 10:10

Jesus Christ did the things God wanted him to do. And because of that, we are made holy through the sacrifice of Christ's body. Christ made that sacrifice one time – enough for all time.

For the other people who were on earth in Old Testament times but weren't a part of God's chosen people (the Israelites), there was still hope. God sent prophets not only to Israel, but also to other nations. These other nations received calls from God directly from His messengers. The story of the prophet, Jonah, who was sent to Nineveh, the capital city of Assyria, is a great example. His words convinced the people in Nineveh – even the king – to repent and change their ways. Jesus said the Ninevites, when the great day of judgment comes, will be witnesses against the people who did not listen to Him.

In addition to these direct messages, other nations or clans heard, probably from traveling merchants or returning soldiers, about the Israelites and their One True God. Even nations that were very far away heard about God and what He could do. A number of those people believed, and some of them even came to live with and become a part of the nation of Israel. We know this because in the book of Leviticus, God gives instructions to the Israelites as well as the non-Israelites who live in their community. Four of these non-Israelites were women whose stories are told in the Old Testament and who, remarkably, became a part of the family line of Jesus and are recorded in the first chapter of Matthew in His earthly family tree.

Another woman who heard about the Israelites and the wise king their God had given them was the Queen of Sheba, in Africa. From her home in Africa, she heard these stories, and was so interested in learning more that she made a long and dangerous journey of about 1,000 miles to speak to King Solomon. When she had answers to her many questions, she praised God and His everlasting love for His people. Jesus says that she will be a witness on the great day of judgment. God does not turn away people who truly have a heart to seek Him.

For the other people who were on earth in Old Testament times but weren't a part of God's chosen people (the Israelites), there was still hope.

Jonah 1:2 (God speaking to Jonah)

"Nineveh is a big city. I have heard about the many evil things the people are doing there. So go there and tell them to stop doing such evil things."

Luke 11:32 (Jesus teaching a crowd that included those who wanted to test Him)

"On the judgment day, you people who live now will also be compared with the people from Nineveh, and they will be witnesses who show how guilty you are. I say this because when Jonah preached to those people, they changed their hearts and lives. And you are listening to someone greater than Jonah, but you refuse to change!"

Ruth 1:16 (Ruth, who was not an Israelite, speaking to her Israelite mother-in-law after Ruth's husband died)

But Ruth said, "Don't force me to leave you! Don't force me to go back to my own people. Let me go with you. Wherever you go, I will go. Wherever you sleep, I will sleep. Your people will be my people. Your God will be my God."

Hebrews 11:31 (Rahab was a woman who lived in Jericho, a sinful city God wanted the Israelites to conquer)

And Rahab, the prostitute, welcomed the Israelite spies like friends. And because of her faith, she was not killed with the ones who refused to obey.

Matthew 1:1, 3a, 5-6 (These verses record the family tree of Jesus and mention the non-Israelite women)

This is the family history of Jesus the Messiah. He came from the family of David, who was from the family of Abraham. . . Judah was the father of Perez and Zerah. (Their mother was Tamar.) . . . Salmon was the father of Boaz. (His mother was Rahab.) Boaz was the father of Obed. (His mother was Ruth.) Obed was the father of Jesse. Jesse was the father of King David. David was the father of Solomon. (His mother had been Uriah's wife.)

1 Kings 10:9 (the Queen of Sheba, Africa, speaking to King Solomon)

"Praise the LORD your God! He was pleased to make you king of Israel. Because of the LORD's unending love for Israel, he has made you king to rule with justice and fairness."

Matthew 12:42 (Jesus speaking to the Jewish religious leaders)

"On the judgment day, you people who live now will also be compared with the queen of the South,

and she will be a witness who shows how guilty you are. I say this because she traveled from far, far away to listen to Solomon's wise teaching. And I tell you that someone greater than Solomon is right here, but you won't listen!"

Acts 10:34-35

Peter began to speak: "I really understand now that God does not consider some people to be better than others. He accepts anyone who worships him and does what is right. It is not important what nation they come from."

The Bible calls the Jewish people a chosen nation, but we need to be careful not to misunderstand what that means. God did not look down from heaven and pick out a group of people that was somehow better than everybody else. He picked out one man – a man who was not perfect but who was willing to do what God wanted. God chose Abraham and then grew a nation from that one man to do His work. He wanted the descendants of Abraham to know that they had a very important job to do for Him. They were a servant nation, working in God's service to record His Story in order that we might all come to know His love. Jesus was born into the Jewish nation and, as a man, acted as a servant of God. God was not excluding non-Jews – He was using the Jews to bring everyone back to Him. If we look at God's work on earth as a whole, the image of a chosen group working to keep God's people close to Him becomes clearer. When the Israelites (the 12 tribes of Israel) left Egypt to form their own country, God told them how to organize their society. He chose one of the 12 tribes to do His work in the Temple and keep all of the tribes close to Him. In the same way, God worked through the Jewish nation to do His work of restoring His people from all the nations of the world to His intended place for us – near Him.

The LORD says, "You people are my witnesses and the servant I chose.
I chose you so that you would help people believe me.
I chose you so that you would understand that 'I Am He' – I am the true God.
There was no God before me, and there will be no God after me.
I myself am the LORD, and there is no other Savior."

Isaiah 43:10-11

For the people who never heard about God during their lives, the Bible says that everyone instinctively knows something about God. Looking at history, we can clearly see that different groups of people all over the world believed in a higher power. Like a bird knows how to fly south in the winter, or a bear knows how to fish, or a beaver knows how to build a dam, people have an instinct to seek food and water and shelter. We also have an instinct to keep ourselves from physical harm as well as spiritual harm. The Bible tells us that we all have some sort of compass in our hearts pointing us to God. The instinct to seek Him is a gift that God has given us. He has also given us a conscience to know when we have done right or wrong. We know when we have hurt someone or when we have made them happy. Jesus told us that doing something for or against others is the same as doing something for or against Him.

True, the people who never heard about God may not have known His Name or been able to identify sin against Him, but Jesus tells us in the book of John that people cannot be guilty of sin if they have no idea what sin is. God is fair, and He will judge each person based on what they knew. These people did instinctively know there was a higher power, and they knew when they had hurt or pleased others. God will look at their hearts. He will judge them fairly. Like children, we must trust that our Father will take proper care of everyone. Remember, He wants EVERYONE to be with Him.

For the people who never heard about God during their lives, the Bible says that everyone instinctively knows something about God.

Romans 2:15, 16part

They show that in their hearts they know what is right and wrong, the same as the law commands, and their consciences agree. Sometimes their thoughts tell them that they have done wrong, and this makes them guilty. And sometimes their thoughts tell them that they have done right, and this makes them not guilty. . .God will judge people's secret thoughts. . .

Romans 1:20

There are things about God that people cannot see – his eternal power and all that makes him God. But since the beginning of the world, those things have been easy for people to understand. They

are made clear in what God has made. So people have no excuse for the evil they do.

James 4:17

If you fail to do what you know is right, you are sinning.

John 15:22

"If I had not come and spoken to the people of the world, they would not be guilty of sin. But now I have spoken to them. So they have no excuse for their sin."

1 Timothy 1:13part

But God gave me mercy because I did not know what I was doing.

Luke 12:48b

"Whoever has been given much will be responsible for much. Much more will be expected from the one who has been given more."

1 Timothy 2:4

God wants everyone to be saved and to fully understand the truth.

Hebrews 4:12

God's word is alive and working. It is sharper than the sharpest sword and cuts all the way into us. It cuts deep to the place where the soul and the spirit are joined. God's word cuts to the center of our joints and our bones. It judges the thoughts and feelings in our hearts.

Here's what Jesus had to say about all those who went before His time on earth:

"I assure you, anyone who hears what I say and believes in the one who sent me has eternal life. They will not be judged guilty. They have already left death and have entered into life. Believe me, an important time is coming. That time is already here. People who are dead will hear the voice of the Son of God. And those who listen will live. Life comes from the Father himself. So the Father has also allowed the Son to give life. And the Father has given him the power to judge all people because he is the Son of Man. Don't be surprised at this. A time is coming when all people who are

dead and in their graves will hear his voice. Then they will come out of their graves. Those who did good in this life will rise and have eternal life. But those who did evil will rise to be judged guilty. I can do nothing alone. I judge only the way I am told. And my judgment is right, because I am not trying to please myself. I want only to please the one who sent me."

John 5:24-30

For the people of today who do not know God, we are the key. He relies completely on us to spread His Word. The news about Jesus and His Message has always been spread from person to person. Today, the Gospel is shared through personal conversation, conferences, radio, social media, blogs, websites, magazines, books, podcasts, phone calls, songs, billboards, movies, shows, bumper stickers, tracts, classes, worship services, Bibles, and much more. People are behind all of this sharing. They are doing the work of God. God does not hide from those who seek Him. If you have a desire to find Him, He will place someone in your path to lead you in the way you should go.

For the people of today who do not know God, we are the key.

Romans 10:12b, 14

The same Lord is the Lord of all people. And he richly blesses everyone who looks to him for help. . .But before people can pray to the Lord for help, they must believe in him. And before they can believe in the Lord, they must hear about him. And for anyone to hear about the Lord, someone must tell them.

2 Corinthians 5:18b, 19b, 20

And God gave us the work of bringing people into peace with him. . .And he gave us this message of peace to tell people. So we have been sent to speak for Christ. It is like God is calling to people through us. We speak for Christ when we beg you to be at peace with God.

Acts 8:4

They [the believers] were scattered everywhere, and in every place they went, they told people the Good News [of Jesus].

Acts 2:39

This promise is for you. It is also for your children and for the people who are far away. It is for everyone the Lord our God calls to himself.

Review: God is always fair and righteous in His judgments.
He knows the people who seek Him.
He depends on us to spread His Message today.

How can we remember, or honor, what Jesus did for us?

Let's look more closely at the last meal Jesus enjoyed with His closest friends and followers just before He was arrested. Christians today (people who have accepted Jesus as their Savior) call it the Last Supper, which, you will recall from our Passover discussion, is the same name Jews who observe the Fast of the Firstborn use. The term Last Supper, although it appears in many translations, is not in the original text of the Bible.

Jesus had chosen 12 men to travel with Him and to learn from Him during the three years of His ministry. He was training them to go everywhere and teach people His Message after His return to heaven. At this last meal, Jesus broke and passed out to them pieces of bread. This bread was probably unleavened bread – bread that has no yeast, so it doesn't rise and become fluffy when it's baked – since at the time of the meal, everyone was preparing for Passover and the Feast of Unleavened Bread by removing all the yeast from their homes. However, according to the calendar we discussed earlier, the command forbidding yeast was 24 hours away from being in effect. Additionally, the original Greek word used to record this event is **artos** which is a general name for bread or food (something provided by God that sustains us), rather than the more specific **zume** which means leavened bread or **azumos** which means unleavened bread.

Jesus gave a piece of the bread (sustaining food) to each of the men and said to eat it and to remember that His body was about to be given for them. Jesus had already told them that He was the Bread of Life – He is our Sustenance. Then Jesus passed around a cup and told them all to drink some and to remember that His blood was about to begin a new agreement from God. He said that we should continue to take the bread and the cup so that we will remember His proposal. This celebration is similar in purpose to the feast days given to the Jewish nation in that we celebrate to help us remember that God is our Salvation. When we celebrate something in order to remember it, we call it a memorial.

This blessing of the cup (wine) and bread is also similar to the Jewish **Kiddush** and **Ha-Motzi** – memorial blessings recited by the leader of a group over the wine and bread (the bread must be whole, then broken) before a Sabbath meal. This tradition was passed down orally by the Jews and recorded after the destruction of the Temple. Although Jews today recite the blessing over the wine before the blessing over the bread (the opposite of Jesus' actions), they acknowledge the bread's superior importance by covering it with a cloth to avoid embarrassing it by blessing the wine first. The **HaMotzi**, the blessing over the bread, translated into English is: "Blessed are You Lord, our God, Ruler/King of the universe, who brings forth bread from the earth." The blessing has its roots in the bread called manna that God supplied for the Israelites after they left Egypt. He provided manna to feed His people for the entire 40 years they were in the desert before they were allowed to enter the Promised Land. So, Passover and the blessing over the bread both have their roots in the Exodus from Egypt in which Moses, a Christ-like figure, led God's people to salvation through water (the Israelites crossed the Red Sea safely, but the pursing Egyptian army was drowned). Jesus is our Bread, and we will soon discuss how He leads us through water.

While the Bible does not specifically say how often you should do so, you should remember the proposal – the promise – God has made to you in the sacrifice of Jesus and remember your acceptance of His proposal by taking part in what many churches now call Communion. Communion is the act in which, together, as a community of believers, we eat of the bread and drink of the cup to remember what He did for us and to recognize our common faith in God and His promises.

1 Corinthians 11:23-26

The teaching I gave you is the same that I received from the Lord: On the night when the Lord Jesus was handed over to be killed, he took bread and gave thanks for it. Then he divided the bread and

said, "This is my body; it is for you. Eat this to remember me." In the same way, after they ate, Jesus took the cup of wine. He said, "This cup represents the new agreement from God, which begins with my blood sacrifice. When you drink this, do it to remember me." This means that every time you eat this bread and drink this cup, you are telling others about the Lord's death until he comes again.

Different churches do it differently and call it by different names (because no name was given for it in the Bible), but they all share the same purpose – to remember Jesus. In a church building, bread will be served. Most churches use unleavened bread such as a cracker or wafer, but some use bread with yeast – and in some places where bread is not available, some other staple food may be used (remember, the original Greek called it **artos**, a sustaining food). After the bread, Jesus passed around what was probably wine, but many American churches use grape juice – at any rate, it's all fruit of the vine (the original Greek calls it a "product of the grapevine"). We share this "meal" with others. It's a symbolic act to help us remember God's kindness toward us in allowing the punishment for our sins to be suffered by Jesus.

Acts 20:7a (The original Greek says, to break bread – "klasai arton" – to eat sustaining food, not "Lord's Supper")
On [the first day of the week] we all met together to eat the Lord's Supper (Literally, "to break bread").

Some believers take it a step further by celebrating an entire meal together – just like Jesus and His disciples did when He began the ritual – and pausing during the meal to share the bread and the cup and to remember Him. The early Christians also shared meals, as shown in the verse above, and would likely have made a practice of blessing and sharing the bread and the wine when they did so – particularly the Jewish believers, who were already in the habit of performing the **mitzvahs** of **Kiddush** and **HaMotzi**.

A **mitzvah** is an obligation, a tradition, or a command related to religious service.

There are some who believe that the bread and the wine, rather than being a memorial, actually become the flesh and blood of Jesus during the ceremony. This belief is called transubstantiation, although this word is not found in the Bible, and this belief is not directly supported by the Bible. Some believe in consubstantiation, which means the bread and the wine co-exist with the body and blood of Christ, although this is not directly supported by the Bible, either. Remember that the Last Supper was one of the Passover meals, and we know that the Passover Feast was a memorial feast – a feast of remembrance. Jesus fulfilled the Passover Feast completely when He was sacrificed for our sins. The Last Supper was instituted by Jesus as a remembrance of His love – His love that replaced the old covenant (the physical covenant) with the new covenant (the spiritual covenant). This is a spiritual remembrance. The bread and the wine are not actually his body and his blood, just as He is not actually a lamb or a door. They are symbolic and meant to help us remember God's grace.

Luke 22:19-20

Then he took some bread and thanked God for it. He broke off some pieces, gave them to the apostles and said, "This bread is my body that I am giving for you. Eat this to remember me." In the same way, after supper, Jesus took the cup of wine and said, "This wine represents the new agreement from God to his people. It will begin when my blood is poured out for you."

*John 6:35 (In the original Greek, Jesus calls himself "**artos**" – sustaining food)*

Then Jesus said, "I am the bread that gives life. No one who comes to me will ever be hungry. No one who believes in me will ever be thirsty."

Review: With other believers, celebrate Jesus' proposal to you regularly. Some churches call it the Lord's Supper, some call it Communion, some call it the Eucharist – it's the same thing – it's a remembrance of God's grace, His forgiveness.

Who should celebrate Communion?

Those who love God and have been baptized to show that they believe in Him and have accepted His proposal through Jesus and want to live a new life based on that love should celebrate Communion. In this new life, you are promising to love God above all else and to treat others with the love and kindness He has shown to you. This is your vow to Him. Repeating it regularly is a good reminder of what you have promised.

A critical element regarding how you celebrate this memorial feast – this remembrance of what God has promised you – what He sent Jesus to offer you – is your attitude. You don't have to be a perfect person to come before Him, but you must be sincere. Be sincere in making your vows to Him just as He was sincere in making His vows to you.

Reading through the Bible, you will see that God values sincerity above everything else. If you do something good, but you didn't truly want to, it isn't valid and won't be accepted because it's counterfeit, fraud, phony, deceitful. We can see this truth in the story of Adam and Eve's sons, Cain and Abel.

Genesis 4:3-7

At harvest time, Cain brought a gift to the LORD. He brought some of the food that he grew from the ground, but Abel brought some animals from his flock. He chose some of his best sheep and brought the best parts from them. The LORD accepted Abel and his gift. But he did not accept Cain and his offering. Cain was sad because of this, and he became very angry. The LORD asked Cain, "Why are you angry? Why does your face look sad? You know that if you do what is right, I will accept you. But if you don't, sin is ready to attack you. That sin will want to control you, but you must control it."

Hebrews 11:4a

Cain and Abel both offered sacrifices to God. But Abel offered a better sacrifice to God because he had faith. God said he was pleased with what Abel offered. And so God called him a good man because he had faith.

We must come before God with a sincere love in our hearts. When we have faith in Him and truly want to honor Him, we will happily do as He asks.

2 Corinthians 13:5

Look closely at yourselves. Test yourselves to see if you are living in the faith. Don't you realize that Christ Jesus is in you? Of course, if you fail the test, he is not in you.

Honestly examine your own feelings. Come before Him with sincere faith in His excellent offer to you. Be baptized to show your new life in Him. Take part in Communion with your brothers and sisters in Christ to celebrate your common membership in His family.

1 Corinthians 10:16-17

The cup of blessing that we give thanks for is a sharing in the blood sacrifice of Christ, isn't it? And the bread that we break is a sharing in the body of Christ, isn't it? There is one loaf of bread, so we who are many are one body, because we all share in that one loaf.

Review: All baptized believers should celebrate Communion.

What is baptism, exactly? And how can you know that you're ready to be baptized?

When we are baptized, we are showing our commitment to serve God and love Him above all else by symbolically washing away all our sin. In the presence of a witness, we are committing to begin a new phase of our life in which we follow His path for us. We are asking God for a clean slate, a chance to start over – we are asking Him to remove our past guilt of sin and grant us a clear conscience moving forward in our new life.

Another way of saying it is, baptism shows the death of our old, sinful self and the birth of our new, saved self. In baptism, we are born again. Just as Jesus was laid in the grave, so you are laid in the water symbolizing the death and burial of your old sinful self. And just as Jesus rose up from His grave, so you rise up from the water symbolizing a resurrection to a new life. Baptism is symbolic of Jesus' death when He conquered sin and His resurrection when He conquered death. Baptism allows us to take part in Jesus' victory over Satan. The only thing Satan can threaten you with is temptation. When you become a part of Jesus' victory over Satan, all you have to do when tempted is tell Satan to go away (and mean what you say – remember, sincerity is very important).

Jesus was about 30 years old when He went to the Jordan River to be baptized. Jesus did not need to be baptized to show His commitment to God and wash away His sins, because He is God and He had committed no sins. He is The Lamb without blemish or fault – He is perfect. Nonetheless, when the time came for Jesus to begin His ministry (teaching the Message of God), this was His first act. He was beginning a new phase of His life – and this is the example He set for us to mark that new phase.

Let's examine the common practice of baptizing babies:

Some Christians practice the baptism of infants and have several arguments for doing so. One argument made is that, based on an Old Testament example, the faith of the parents is enough to baptize a baby. Recall the covenant God made with Abraham – if Abraham obeyed God, he would become the father of many nations, God would be their God, and God would bless all the nations through Abraham. Abraham was required to show that he agreed to the covenant by circumcising himself and all the male members of his household and all their descendants. This would be the sign of his agreement with God. Going forward from that date, God instructed them to circumcise all males born into the covenant when they are eight days old.

Genesis 17:10b, 12a, 13a

This is the agreement between me and you and all your descendants. Every male must be circumcised. . .When the baby boy is eight days old, you will circumcise him. . .So every baby boy in your nation will be circumcised.

Note that saying the faith of the parents is enough to baptize a baby and using this example as support is saying that baptism replaces circumcision as a sign of our vows under the new covenant. We will come back to this in a moment.

As another argument in favor of infant baptism, it is evident from several examples given in the New Testament that the practice of baptizing households was common in the early church. The apostle Paul mentions in 1 Corinthians 1:16 that he baptized the family of Stephanas. Peter oversees the baptism of a Roman officer named Cornelius and his friends and family in Acts 10:48. Paul teaches a woman named Lydia, and she and all the people staying in her house are baptized in Acts 16:15. Then, in verse 33, Paul and Silas baptize a jailer and his people.

Looking at the paragraph above, it appears that whole families were baptized. That combined with the idea that baptism replaces circumcision as a sign of our vows allows us to easily see how some are convinced that the example of infant or child baptism is found in the Bible, but let's dig a little deeper and look at the whole story.

Babies are incapable of belief and have no say in whether they are circumcised or not. Circumcision of the flesh under God's covenant with Abraham marked a man as a Jew. It was a very personal and lifelong reminder to each man that he was a member of God's servant nation – that he had a holy purpose. It was each Jewish man's personal physical sign of the covenant God made with his forefather, Abraham, but God made it very clear that the outward sign of circumcision wasn't what was required to be a true believer in Him.

In the Old Testament, both Moses and the prophet Jeremiah told the people that the true circumcision is the circumcision of the heart. The first sentence below that Moses wrote makes it sound as though God will force the Israelites to follow Him, but verse 10 assures us that the people had free will to choose. God puts a desire, an instinct, to search for Him in our hearts, but we can choose whether we pursue it or not. Once we have decided to follow God, He helps us grow closer and closer to Him. Paul repeats the message for them in the New Testament.

Deuteronomy 30:6, 10 part

The LORD your God will make you and your descendants want to obey him (Literally, "circumcise the hearts of you and your seed"). Then you will love the LORD your God with all your heart. And you will live! But [first] you must do what the LORD your God tells you to do. . .You must obey the LORD your God with all your heart and with all your soul.

Jeremiah 4:4a

Become the LORD's people. Change your hearts. (Literally, "Be circumcised to the LORD. Cut away the foreskin of your hearts." Jeremiah is saying that real circumcision must be from inside a person's heart (mind).)

Romans 2:25-29

If you follow the law, then your circumcision has meaning. But if you break the law, then it is as if you were never circumcised. Those who are not Jews are not circumcised. But if they do what the law says, it is as if they were circumcised. You have the written law and circumcision, but you break the law. So those who are not circumcised in their bodies, but still obey the law, will show that you are guilty. You are not a true Jew if you are only a Jew in your physical body. True circumcision is not only on the outside of the body. A true Jew is one who is a Jew inside. True circumcision is done in the heart. It is done by the Spirit, not by the written law. And anyone who is circumcised in the heart by the Spirit gets praise from God, not from people.

Like physical circumcision, baptism is an outward sign of an agreement, but the true belief is found in the heart. There is no benefit to either circumcision or baptism if the person is not convinced in his/her heart of the One True God and His plan for our salvation through the Messiah.

Circumcision of the heart is done by Christ and the Spirit. His sacrifice and our decision to accept His offer allows the Spirit to come into our hearts. This is what removes (cuts off, circumcises) the sin from our souls. We make a decision in our hearts, we use our free will, to follow God with everything we've got. If we are full of the Spirit, we will pursue God with all of our heart, soul, mind, and strength.

So, what is circumcised – your heart or your soul? All of what makes you YOU is circumcised when you are full of the Holy Spirit of God. What makes you YOU is not your face, your body, or even your physical heart. What makes you YOU is your essence – all that is in your heart (feelings), soul (the part of you that is sincerely and uniquely you), mind (thoughts), and strength (will). These are what is circumcised. The only way these can be circumcised is through faith in what Jesus did for us, and we can only believe what He did if we can understand what He did.

Colossians 2:11

In Christ you had a different kind of circumcision, one that was not done by human hands. That is, you were made free from the power of your sinful self. That is the kind of circumcision Christ does.

Mark 12:29-30 *(This is a choice)*

Jesus answered, "The most important command is this: 'People of Israel, listen! The Lord our God is the only Lord. Love the Lord your God with all your heart, all your soul, all your mind, and all your strength.'"

Once our hearts have been circumcised – once our sinful self has been crucified – we will produce the fruits of the Holy Spirit.

Galatians 5:22-25

But the fruit that the Spirit produces in a person's life is love, joy, peace, patience, kindness, goodness, faithfulness, gentleness, and self-control. There is no law against these kinds of things. Those who belong to Christ Jesus have crucified their sinful self. They have given up their old selfish feelings and the evil things they wanted to do. We get our new life from the Spirit, so we should follow the Spirit.

Circumcised heart = Crucified sinful self

Remember from our discussion of the feasts, when Jesus was crucified at Passover and the Holy Spirit was received by His people at Pentecost, an Old Testament prophecy was fulfilled:

This is what the LORD said, "The time is coming when I will make a new agreement
with the family of Israel and with the family of Judah. It will not be like the agreement I made
with their ancestors. I made that agreement when I took them by the hand and brought
them out of Egypt. I was their master, but they broke that agreement."
This message is from the LORD.
"In the future I will make this agreement with the people of Israel."
This message is from the LORD.
"I will put my teachings in their minds, and I will write them on their hearts.
I will be their God, and they will be my people."

Jeremiah 31:31-33

God used the same period of time to make the new agreement with His people that He had used to make the old agreement – and it was all marked by the feast days as a sign for us. In the old agreement, God's laws were all written down – it was a physical covenant. In the new agreement, God's laws are written in the hearts and minds of those who believe in Him and trust Him – it is a spiritual covenant. Before Jesus, God's people served Him with physical offerings and sacrifices. After Jesus, God's people are to serve Him with spiritual offerings.

So, we can see that baptism is not the New Testament replacement for the Old Testament circumcision, because circumcision was a sign of God's covenant with Abraham to grow the Jewish nation from him and use that nation to bless all the nations of the world. Circumcision was a sign that you were a male member of that Jewish nation.

Our new covenant with God began with Jesus' sacrifice at Passover. The old covenant that it fulfilled was the covenant God made with His people through Moses. We can see this through the fulfillment of the feast days that Jesus accomplished. Moses was given the Law many years after Abraham and God made their covenant. God's covenant through Abraham, to bless all the nations of the earth through him, is still active. As believers, we are all Abraham's children, and we are all still in charge of living His Word so that all the world may know the One True God. The circumcision of our hearts takes the place of the physical, fleshly circumcision. The Law, in terms of animal sacrifice, has been fulfilled, and our offering of spiritual sacrifices from our circumcised hearts is the replacement.

If baptism is not a replacement for circumcision, then using this reason as an argument that the faith of the parents is enough to baptize the child is invalid.

Summary: God's covenant with Abraham was the beginning of the servant Jewish nation and their role in teaching the world about the salvation of the Messiah.
It was God's covenant through Moses that paralleled the sacrifice of Jesus for our salvation.

Now let us examine the household baptism verses to see if they truly endorse infant baptism. Looking more closely at the four examples of household baptism given as support for infant baptism, not one of them mentions children of any age.

Paul says that he baptized Stephanas and his family in the first chapter of Corinthians as noted above, but then he goes on to tell us in the 16th chapter that the family of Stephanas were believers and that they worked in the service of the Lord. If Paul, an apostle of Jesus, counted them as believers and workers for the Lord, they must have been old enough not only to understand, but also to share the Gospel.

1 Corinthians 16:15-16

You know that Stephanas and his family were the first believers in Achaia. They have given themselves to the service of God's people. I ask you, brothers and sisters, to follow the leading of people like these and others who work hard and serve together with them.

Cornelius' story is quite long and detailed – very interesting and worthy of a close study to make sure you have all the information – but just adding the verses below to the verse cited above shows us what we need to know about family baptisms. We find that all the people who were living in Cornelius' house were already worshipers of the one true God, and that Cornelius gathered them all together to listen to what Peter had to teach them.

Acts 10:2a, 24b, 33b

He [Cornelius] was a religious man. He and all the others who lived in his house were worshipers of the true God. . .[Cornelius sent for the apostle Peter to come and teach them.] Cornelius was waiting for them and had already gathered his relatives and close friends at his house. . ."Now we are all here before God to hear everything the Lord has commanded you to tell us."

Acts 10:43 (Part of Peter's lesson)

"Everyone who believes in Jesus will have their sins forgiven through his name. All the prophets agree that this is true."

Acts 10:48a (This is the verse cited in support of infant baptism, but it comes at the end of a long story)

So Peter told them [the Jewish Christians traveling with him] to baptize Cornelius and his relatives and friends in the name of Jesus Christ.

If you read the whole story (all of Acts Chapter 10), you will find that its purpose is not to endorse infant baptism, but rather to explain that Jesus' sacrifice wasn't just for the Jews. It is a story that defines who can be a true believer. Anyone, Jew or Gentile, who hears the Message and accepts Jesus in his/her heart is a true believer. The Holy Spirit came to Cornelius and his crowd, who were all Gentiles, in front of the apostle Peter and his fellow Jews so the Jews could understand that Jesus was sacrificed for everyone who is a true believer.

Lydia was a businesswoman from Thyatira who had traveled, or possibly moved, to Philippi, a city of economic significance. She was with a group of women on the Sabbath day when she met Paul and his companions who had come outside the city gate to the riverside to find a place to pray. The Bible says that Lydia worshiped God, so it is possible that Lydia and the other women had also come to the river for prayer. The Jews situated their places of worship and prayer near water (or, situated water near their places of worship and prayer), so that it could be used for ritual washings, which we will discuss in more detail.

Acts 16:13, 14-15a

On the Sabbath day we went out the city gate to the river. There we thought we might find a special place for prayer. Some women had gathered there, so we sat down and talked with them. There was a woman there named Lydia from the city of Thyatira. Her job was selling purple cloth. She was a worshiper of the true God. Lydia was listening to Paul, and the Lord opened her heart to accept what Paul was saying. She and all the people living in her house were baptized. Then she invited us into her home. She said, "If you think I am a true believer in the Lord Jesus, come stay in my house."

The people in Lydia's house – the place where she was staying/living while in Philippi – may or may not have been her family. It is possible that the text is referring to the women with her by the river, who may have been business partners, coworkers, fellow businesswomen, employees, clients, servants, relatives, or friends. The Bible does not say whether she was married or had children.

The next story in Acts 16:16-40, is the story of the jailer. The apostle Paul and his helper, Silas, were prisoners under his guard when several remarkable events occurred. Following these events, the jailer asked them to teach him what he needed to know.

Acts 16:32-34

So Paul and Silas told the message of the Lord to the jailer and all the people who lived in his house. It was late at night, but the jailer took Paul and Silas and washed their wounds. Then the jailer and all his people were baptized. After this the jailer took Paul and Silas home and gave them some food. All the people were very happy because they now believed in God.

The jailer and all his people were clearly taught by Paul and Silas. The Bible says the teaching took place after midnight (see verse 25), then the jailer took Paul and Silas somewhere to wash their wounds. Following that, the people were baptized. After the baptisms, the jailer took them to his home and fed them. They were <u>all</u> happy because they were now believers.

A person simply cannot believe something unless they are taught and understand it. In each and every one of these examples (and others besides), people are first taught and people then believe. Baptism shows their belief.

Those who teach infant baptism use only portions of Bible stories to support their beliefs. We should always be careful to read our Bibles and discover whole truths for ourselves.

Summary: There are no examples in the Bible of infants or children being baptized.

What does the Bible say about children?

Babies and young children are often baptized by believing parents who want to make sure their children belong to God. If parents truly want to make sure their children know God and grow to have a personal relationship with Him, they would do better to begin teaching their children in age-appropriate stories and songs about Jesus and His wonderful love for all of us. The faith of parents is best used as a tool for teaching children that same faith and for praying that God will touch those children's hearts and lead them to a personal relationship with Him. Baptizing a child as an infant is not going to make him/her a believer. Proper teaching and prayer will help a child grow to be a believer.

Proverbs 22:6

Teach children in a way that fits their needs, and even when they are old, they will not leave the right path.

Children will grow up and ultimately decide for themselves whether or not they will obey God. We have seen that it is our willingness to do what God wants that is most important. The Bible tells us, and we all know from experience that a child has to learn to choose good and refuse evil, and that it takes time before a child has matured enough to make that choice.

Isaiah 7:15 (about a young child)

He will eat milk curds and honey [common food for younger children] as he learns to choose good and refuse evil.

The apostle Paul very clearly tells us that his spirit was alive until he understood what sin was – until he gained the knowledge of good vs. evil.

Romans 7:9-10a (Paul describing his own spiritual death)

Before I knew the law [before I had the knowledge to know what sin was], I was alive. But when I heard the law's command, sin began to live, and I died spiritually.

We must be mature enough to understand both our choices and the consequences of those choices before we can truly make the decision to accept His offer. When we do accept His offer, we should believe and trust just like young children do. Our trust in Him should be simple and complete. Jesus tells us to trust like a child, because God is our Father.

2 Corinthians 12:9part

"My grace is all you need. Only when you are weak can everything be done completely by my power."

In trusting God like a little child would trust a good parent, we are also humbling ourselves to Him. In Jesus' time, children were of very low social status. Jesus elevated children by saying that we should all be humble in the same way children are. He always lifted up those who had been humbled by others. He told us what rewards God has in store for people who are humble: a person who is humble in this world will be great in the kingdom of heaven.

Those rewards will be given with great love. A child receives gifts from good parents and fully absorbs all the love with which those gifts are given. A young child, with no means of income, does not feel the guilt that we, as adults, feel when we are given a gift but have nothing to give in return. The child is happy and joyful and delights in the gifts.

Be a child and joyfully accept God as your Father. Look forward to your reward.

We should not worry that God will not protect our little ones just because they haven't been baptized. Jesus holds children up as examples for us all and instructs us to be aware. He tells us how very special, important, valued, and loved the little children are. He tells us that they have angels who are always in God's presence. Children are precious to Him!

Mark 10:15

"The truth is, you must accept God's kingdom like a little child accepts things, or you will never enter it."

Matthew 18:3-4

Then [Jesus] said, "The truth is, you must change your thinking and become like little children. If you don't do this, you will never enter God's kingdom. The greatest person in God's kingdom is the one who makes himself humble like this child."

Matthew 18:10

"Be careful. Don't think these little children are not important. I tell you that these children have angels in heaven. And those angels are always with my Father in heaven."

Summary: Children are very special to God.
He has given them to us as an example, and He is watching over them.
We must be careful to treat them with the love and care God wants us to
– **we must watch over them the same way we want Him to watch over us** –
and we must teach them to seek Him.

Some have said we each have a guardian angel. While the Bible does not explicitly state this, it does tell us that God sends His angels to minister to His faithful believers when they need help and they turn to Him.

How can you know when you're ready to be baptized? When you are ready to submit to God's will for your life. When Jesus was ready to begin His ministry and commit all of His works to God, He went to the Jordan River to be baptized by His cousin, John. He was humbling Himself and submitting to the will of God.

Matthew 3:15 -16a (John, who recognized Jesus as the Messiah, protested that he was not worthy to baptize Jesus)

Jesus answered, "Let it be this way for now. We should do whatever God says is right." Then John agreed. So Jesus was baptized.

When Jesus rose up out of the water, the Holy Spirit came to Him. Everything He did in His earthly ministry was accomplished through the power of the Holy Spirit.

Mark 1:9b-11

John baptized Jesus in the Jordan River. As Jesus was coming up out of the water, he saw the sky torn open. The Spirit came down on him like a dove. A voice came from heaven and said, "You are my Son, the one I love. I am very pleased with you."

Luke 4:18-19 (Jesus reciting from Isaiah 61:1-2 and 58:6, showing how He will fulfill the promises of God)

"The Spirit of the Lord is on me. He has chosen me to tell good news to the poor. He sent me to tell prisoners that they are free and to tell the blind that they can see again. He sent me to free those

who have been treated badly and to announce that the time has come for the Lord to show his kindness."

Just before He died on the cross, Jesus declared that His work was finished, and He committed His Spirit back to God. Through Jesus' own example, when you have committed yourself, your life, to Him, and you are baptized, the Holy Spirit comes to live in you. If you humble yourself and submit to the will of God, He can accomplish great things through you by the Holy Spirit. If you are faithful to the end, your spirit returns to God when your body dies.

Luke 23:46 (from Psalm 31:5)
Jesus shouted, "Father, I put my life [my spirit] in your hands!"

Being baptized shows to others that you have accepted Our Lord's offer to you. Every person must accept His offer for him- or herself. Others can lead you, but no one can decide for you. The Bible says that we will each stand and answer for ourselves and be punished or rewarded accordingly.

Hebrews 4:13
Nothing in all the world can be hidden from God. He can clearly see all things. Everything is open before him. And to him we must explain the way we have lived.

Romans 14:12
So each of us will have to explain to God about the things we do.

James 4:7
So give yourselves to God. Stand against the devil, and he will run away from you.

Summary: Baptism is an important step that shows you have accepted God's offer of salvation and a never-ending life with Him.
You are promising yourself to Him.
You are putting what God wants for you first in your life.

Some will argue that the act of baptism is what washes sins away. Just remember, our sins were forgiven at the cross – that's what His sacrifice was intended to do.

1 Peter 1:2b

God wanted you to obey him and be made clean by the blood sacrifice of Jesus Christ.

We simply have to accept this truth and have faith in it – our faith in His forgiveness makes us holy before God.

1 Peter 1:22a

You have made yourselves pure by obeying the truth.

We show our commitment to this faith, this new life, with our baptism.

1 Peter 3:18

Christ himself suffered when he died for you, and with that one death he paid for your sins. He was not guilty, but he died for people who are guilty. He did this to bring all of you to God. In his physical form he was killed, but he was made alive by the Spirit.

Acts 2:38

Peter said to them, "Change your hearts and lives and be baptized, each one of you, in the name of Jesus Christ. Then God will forgive your sins, and you will receive the gift of the Holy Spirit."

1 Peter 1:23

You have been born again. This new life did not come from something that dies. It came from something that cannot die. You were born again through God's life-giving message that lasts forever.

Colossians 2:12

When you were baptized, you were buried with Christ, and you were raised up with him because of your faith in God's power. God's power was shown when he raised Christ from death.

Romans 6:3, 4b

Did you forget that all of us became part of Christ Jesus when we were baptized? In our baptism we shared in his death. And just as Christ was raised from death by the wonderful power of the Father, so we can now live a new life.

Colossians 3:1

You were raised from death with Christ. So live for what is in heaven, where Christ is sitting at the right hand of God.

1 Peter 3:21b

Baptism. . .is asking God for a clean conscience. It saves you because Jesus Christ was raised from death.

Acts 22:16

Now, don't wait any longer. Get up, be baptized and wash away your sins, trusting in Jesus to save you.

Ephesians 4:4-6

There is one body and one Spirit, and God chose you to have one hope. There is one Lord, one faith, and one baptism. There is one God and Father of us all, who rules over everyone. He works through all of us and in all of us.

Review: If you know that you need to be forgiven, you are ready to humble yourself and submit to God's will for you, and you believe these things:

- that Jesus is the Son of God – that He is God, and He is of God
- that Jesus came to earth as a mortal human – that He was fully human
- that Jesus was sacrificed to save us all from our sins – that He is THE Lamb
- that Jesus conquered death and rose from the dead – that He is alive again
- that Jesus ascended to heaven and is at the right hand of God – that He is our Priest
- that Jesus will return to take us home to our Father's house – that He is coming again

then you should be baptized to show you believe in Him and
you are committed to Him and what He wants for you.

How do I get baptized?

Let's review for just a moment. . . The Jewish religious leaders asked Jesus for a sign that He was the Messiah. Jesus, knowing their hearts, told them they would receive no other sign than the one they had already received in the miracle that happened to Jonah, a prophet of old. God had told Jonah to go preach to a foreign nation. Jonah didn't want to do that, so he tried to run away from God by getting on a ship headed away from there. This, of course, was unsuccessful (because it wasn't God's will), and Jonah ended up volunteering to be thrown overboard by the crew in order to calm God's wrath and save the men in the ship. He offered himself as a sacrifice to save others. God sent a very big fish – we aren't told what kind – to swallow Jonah whole. God left him in the belly of the great fish for three days and three nights, then God made the fish spit Jonah out onto dry land. The miraculous sign Jesus reminded the religious leaders of with this story was the fact that Jonah was essentially a dead man for the three days and three nights he was in the belly of the fish. In a similar way, Jesus would be a dead man for three days and three nights in the belly of the earth. Jonah had essentially been brought back from the dead after that time, and Jesus actually would be.

Matthew 12:39b-40 (Jesus to the religious leaders)
"The only sign will be the miracle that happened to the prophet Jonah. Jonah was in the stomach of the big fish for three days and three nights. In the same way, the Son of Man will be in the grave three days and three nights."

Water is an important element in the Bible. Noah and his family survived the Flood. Moses led God's people through the Red Sea. Jonah was rescued from certain death in the sea. In each of these cases, the people God wanted to save were brought through large amounts of water that, without God's help, would have killed them, and they were given a new life.

2 Peter 2:5b

He brought a flood to the world that was full of people who were against God. But he saved Noah and seven other people with him.

Exodus 14:21-23, 26, 28b

Moses raised his hand over the Red Sea, and the LORD caused a strong wind to blow from the east. The wind blew all night long. The sea split, and the wind made the ground dry. The Israelites went through the sea on dry land. The water was like a wall on their right and on their left. Then all of Pharaoh's chariots and horse soldiers followed them into the sea. . .Then the LORD told Moses, "Raise your hand over the sea to make the water fall and cover the Egyptian chariots and horse soldiers". . . Pharaoh's army had been chasing the Israelites, but that army was destroyed. None of them survived!

Jonah 2:1-2, 5a, 6part, 10

While Jonah was in the stomach of the fish, he prayed to the LORD his God. He said, "I was in very bad trouble. I called to the LORD for help, and he answered me. I was deep in the grave. I cried to you, and you heard my voice. . .The seawater closed over me. The water covered my mouth, and I could not breathe. . .I was at the bottom of the sea. . .but the LORD my God took me out of my grave. God, you gave me life again! Then the LORD spoke to the fish, and it vomited Jonah out of its stomach onto the dry land.

2 Peter 2:9a

So you see that the Lord God knows how to save those who are devoted to him.

These examples of rebirth through water show one reason why people are baptized in "bodies" of water in which they can be submerged. Going under the water simulates the certain death we would experience if we continued on our errant paths – indeed, while we are under water, we are effectively in our graves – and being able to rise up out of the water simulates God's saving grace that allows us to live and to walk in the path He has laid for us. When we have risen from the water (grave), we are beginning a new life. This is now called "immersion baptism" because you are immersed (plunged or sunk) in the water. The Bible only calls it baptism, but it is now described as "immersion baptism" because there have been major divisions in God's church over disagreements about how baptism should be performed.

Some say that actually going under water is unnecessary and prefer to sprinkle water on someone who wishes to be baptized, much like the priests in the Old Testament sprinkled blood on the altar when making the sacrifices. As another example in favor of sprinkling, some point out that Moses mixed the sacrificial blood and water and sprinkled it on the people to begin the old covenant of the Law.

Hebrews 9:19-20

First, Moses told the people every command in the law. Then he took the blood of young bulls and mixed it with water. He used red wool and a branch of hyssop to sprinkle the blood and water on the book of the law and on all the people. Then he said, "This is the blood that makes the agreement good – the agreement that God commanded you to follow."

Yes, Moses sprinkled blood and water, but Jesus gushed it out for us.

John 19:34

But one of the soldiers stuck his spear into Jesus' side. Immediately blood and water came out.

The original method of forgiveness is finished.

Hebrews 10:9b-10a

So God ends that first system of sacrifices and starts his new way. Jesus Christ did the things God wanted him to do. And because of that, we are made holy through the sacrifice of Christ's body.

The following verses, written to the Jews, show that in the new agreement, it is our hearts that are sprinkled, while our bodies are washed.

Hebrews 10:21-22a

And we have a great priest who rules the house of God. Sprinkled with the blood of Christ, our hearts have been made free from a guilty conscience, and our bodies have been washed with pure water.

Others teach pouring water on a person's forehead for baptism, because there are phrases in the Bible that mention the pouring out of the Holy Spirit that comes to us with baptism.

Acts 2:16-17a (from Joel 2:28)

But Joel the prophet wrote about what you see happening here today. This is what he wrote: 'God says: In the last days I will pour out my Spirit on all people.'

After Jesus was sacrificed – after the blood and water gushed out of Him – He went up to heaven and presented Himself to God – like the priests of the Old Testament presented offerings at the altar. Then, on the day of Pentecost, the Holy Spirit was given to the believers. The verses above from Acts record Peter explaining to the crowd at Pentecost how the coming of the Holy Spirit fulfilled Old Testament prophecies. Notice, in these verses, it is God doing the pouring, not man – and He is pouring out His Spirit for us. In baptism, we are speaking to God. In pouring out the Holy Spirit, God is speaking to us.

Romans, Chapter 6 very clearly explains how our baptism imitates Jesus' death and resurrection. When you come up out of the water, your new life begins.

Romans 6:4-7

So when we were baptized, we were buried with Christ and took part in his death. And just as Christ was raised from death by the wonderful power of the Father, so we can now live a new life. Christ died, and we have been joined with him by dying too. So we will also be joined with him by rising from death as he did. We know that our old life was put to death on the cross with Christ. This happened so that our sinful selves would have no power over us. Then we would not be slaves to sin. Anyone who has died is made free from sin's control.

While the sprinkling and pouring methods can be very handy when people who are very ill or who are physically or psychologically incapable of getting into a body of water want to be baptized, the method of being completely underwater most closely imitates being in the grave like Jesus. If you are at all able, do as Jesus did.

If you are, or if you know someone who is, a very ill or otherwise challenged person who desires to be baptized in a body of water just as Jesus was, listen to the Unashamed podcast, Episode 118. Where there's a will, there's a way.

In the Bible, we find examples of people being baptized, or ceremonially washed. John (John the Baptist, not John the Apostle) baptized Jesus – and many others – in the Jordan River. It is unlikely that Jesus stood on the bank of the river and John brought water up to sprinkle Him with, or that John had a pitcher that he was filling with water from the river to pour on all the people who were coming to him, because the Bible specifically records in Matthew and Mark that **Jesus came up out of the water**. One cannot come up out of the water unless one first goes down into the water. It seems far more likely that these people went down into the water with John, and he completely submerged them. Before we go any further with this argument, let's recognize that, in this paragraph, we are analyzing the event from a Gentile perspective that is many years removed from the actual time and culture in which it occurred. Let's look at it from a more timely, Jewish perspective.

The Bible tells us that John the Baptist was directly descended from Aaron, Moses' brother, who was the first high priest of the Israelites. Beginning with Aaron and down through the ages, God ordered that a man must ceremonially wash his whole body when he was preparing to serve in his priestly duties at the Tabernacle, and later, the Temple. The priests were to perform this ritual to make themselves clean before God – not clean from dirt but purified in mind and spirit – ready to focus solely on God's work. The priests took this command so seriously, that the washing (ceremonial cleansing) generally involved a witness to make sure that the priest was completely submerged, including all of his hair, and was therefore washing his WHOLE body. The Bible says that Jesus is our Great High Priest. When He went to John to be baptized, He was officially beginning His work in that role. When He went to John to be baptized, He was preparing to serve God. Jesus, our Great High Priest, went to John, who was essentially the last earthly high priest ever needed to serve the Jewish nation, so that he could witness Jesus' ceremonial cleansing – His baptism – that marked this change in His life – the beginning of His service to God.

John the Baptist was needed as a priest/prophet
to call the Jewish nation to repentance to prepare them for
the coming of the Messiah, the priest/prophet/king.

Malachi 3:1 (Prophecy about John approximately 400 years before his time)

The LORD All-Powerful says, "I am sending my messenger to prepare the way for me. Then suddenly, the Lord you are looking for will come to his temple. Yes, the messenger you are waiting for, the one who will tell about my agreement, is really coming!"

Matthew 3:1-3 (from Isaiah 40:3)

When it was the right time, John the Baptizer began telling people a message from God. This was out in the desert area of Judea. John said, "Change your hearts and lives, because God's kingdom is now very near." John is the one Isaiah the prophet was talking about when he said, "There is someone shouting in the desert: 'Prepare the way for the Lord. Make the road straight for him.'"

Matthew 3:16

So Jesus was baptized. As soon as he came up out of the water, the sky opened, and he saw God's Spirit coming down on him like a dove.

Mark 1:9b-10

John baptized Jesus in the Jordan River. As Jesus was coming up out of the water, he saw the sky torn open. The Spirit came down on him like a dove.

Jews – not just the priests, but all of the people – men and women – were no strangers to baptism, or ceremonial cleansing. They all performed this same ritual washing ceremony regularly in order to make themselves clean from certain impurities before they participated in worship or to mark a change in their lives. God had given them a list of occasions that required cleansing: before weddings, after childbirth, before feast days, and so on. Additionally, Gentiles who became a part of the Jewish community and converted to Judaism (the Old Testament worship of the One True God) completed a cleansing, or baptism, to mark their new way of life. Because this baptism ritual was so frequently needed, if a place of worship was not located near natural water such as a river or lake, the Jewish people constructed pools for washing. The city of Jerusalem, where the Temple was located atop a hill, has no natural body of water, so the Jews constructed pools, called **mikvehs**, around the city and especially near the Temple. Archaeologists have uncovered hundreds of them throughout Israel, and visitors to Jerusalem today can walk the

Mikveh Trail and see many of them. This practice of ceremonial cleansing, or baptism, in a **mikveh** – going completely under water in order to wash one's whole body – with a witness to make sure every hair is submerged – is still carried on today by Jewish men and women all over the world.

Leviticus 16:4a (God's instructions for the high priest in preparation for the annual Day of Atonement - Yom Kippur)
Aaron will wash his whole body with water and put on the special clothes.

Acts 21:26a (Paul proving his Jewishness by preparing for worship with four other Jewish men)
So Paul took the four men with him. The next day he shared in their cleansing ceremony. Then he went into the Temple area. . .

John 18:28-29 (The Jewish leaders wouldn't jeopardize their Passover ritual cleansing while Jesus was on trial)
Then the guards took Jesus from Caiaphas' (the Roman-appointed high priest) house to the Roman governor's palace. It was early in the morning. The Jews there would not go inside the palace (of a Gentile). They did not want to make themselves unclean (Going into a non-Jewish place would ruin the special cleansing [ceremonial washing] the Jews did to make themselves fit for worship) because they wanted to eat the Passover meal. So Pilate went outside to them and asked, "What do you say this man has done wrong?"

After Jesus' ascension to heaven, we know that His apostles waited in Jerusalem for ten days until the Holy Spirit came to them on the day of Pentecost. Full of the Spirit, Peter, one of the apostles, went into the street and preached to a large crowd. Many Jews had come to Jerusalem to celebrate the Feast of Pentecost, so Peter had a large audience. A great number of those listening believed Peter's words about Jesus, and that same day, 3,000 people were baptized and therefore added to the church – the group of believers. These people may have already performed their ceremonial cleansing in one of the many mikvehs in the city so that they could worship God at the Temple for Pentecost, but this was a different cleansing. This was a baptism into the salvation provided by Jesus, a baptism into the Holy Spirit. This was the last baptism they would ever need – just like Jesus' sacrifice was the last sacrifice they would ever need. Jesus makes us ceremonially clean before God – He washes our souls as white as snow with the sacrifice of His blood for our sins.

Colossians 2:12

When you were baptized, you were buried with Christ, and you were raised up with him because of your faith in God's power. God's power was shown when he raised Christ from death.

Acts 2:41

Then those who accepted what Peter said were baptized. On that day about 3000 people were added to the group of believers.

Some of you may have been baptized by your parents as young children and you may be wondering if you need to do it again. Some of you may have agreed to be baptized at a young age and you realize now that you didn't fully understand what you were doing at the time. You're wondering, too, if you need to do it again. If, in your heart, you feel the need to begin anew based on your new knowledge of Jesus and His sacrifice and all that it means, then you should do so. God is looking at your heart, your soul, and He values sincere offerings.

Many people had been baptized in the Jordan River by John (he was baptizing – ceremonially cleansing – people who wanted to repent of their sins and prepare themselves to worship the Messiah when He came), but the Jordan River is 21 miles to the east of Jerusalem – a long way to walk. So, how was the baptism of the 3,000 people who heard and believed Peter's sermon accomplished? This would never have been a question or a problem for the Jews of that day. The Bible doesn't tell us specifically, but there are compelling reasons to believe the apostles and new believers used what was practical and readily available. Archaeologists have found 200 mikvehs in the city of Jerusalem, and baptisms were a normal part of Jewish religious life. It seems reasonable that they would naturally have turned to these pools for baptism, with the apostles watching over the new believers as they fully immersed themselves to make sure everyone's whole body was cleansed.

Acts 2:38part

". . .be baptized, each one of you, in the name of Jesus Christ."

When you are ready to be cleansed of your sins and begin your new way of life, there is no need to wait. The people listening to Peter's sermon did not wait – they were all baptized that very day. Another time, when the apostle Philip was teaching a foreign government official about Jesus as they rode along in a chariot, the official understood the teaching and wanted to commit himself to God's new agreement as soon as possible. The two men looked up from their studies and saw a body of water. The official ordered his driver to stop, and he and Philip went down into the water immediately, so the official could be baptized.

Acts 8:36-38

While they were traveling down the road, they came to some water. The official said, "Look, here is water! What is stopping me from being baptized? Then the official ordered the chariot to stop. Both Philip and the official went down into the water, and Philip baptized him.

Acts 22:16

'Now, don't wait any longer. Get up, be baptized and wash away your sins, trusting in Jesus to save you.'

Although it was the priests in the Old Testament who performed the sacrifices and purification ceremonies in the Temple, Jesus is our High Priest now, and we have no need of any other priest to make sacrifices for us or to purify us. We simply need someone to teach us about Jesus – and we are all given that job. Anyone can baptize you. The person who does this for you is merely the attendant for and witness of your ceremonial cleansing. If you would like to ask a family member or a special friend to baptize you instead of asking a recognized church leader, that is acceptable because it follows the examples in the Bible. Although John was of priestly heritage, he wasn't serving in the Temple. He was also Jesus' second cousin (their mothers were first cousins). Jesus' apostles were all ordinary men, not priests, but they baptized people, too.

John 4:2

(But really, Jesus himself did not baptize anyone; his followers baptized people for him.)

Hebrews 4:16

With Jesus as our high priest, we can feel free to come before God's throne where there is grace. There we receive mercy and kindness to help us when we need it.

Matthew 28:19 (Jesus speaking to His apostles)
"So go and make followers of all people in the world. Baptize them in the name of the Father and the Son and the Holy Spirit."

Review: Do as Jesus did. If you are serious about your commitment to follow God and you are ready to begin your new life of serving Him, sincerely confess to someone (say, and mean what you say):

- that Jesus is the Son of God – that He is God, and He is of God
- that Jesus came to earth as a mortal human – that He was fully human
- that Jesus was sacrificed to save us all from our sins – that He is THE Lamb
- that Jesus conquered death and rose from the dead – that He is alive again
- that Jesus ascended to heaven and is at the right hand of God – that He is our Priest
- that Jesus will return to take us home to our Father's house – that He is coming again

and ask someone to baptize you (witness your baptism)
in a convenient body of water.

Overall review of Communion and Baptism:

Communion is a joyously solemn occasion (like a wedding) during which we should
remember this: He loved us first, and He fully committed Himself to us.
The bread and wine should be received happily and eagerly, yet seriously,
as His wedding vows to us.
Our acceptance of His vows is our promise to Him.
We are saying, "I do (promise to love Him above all else)."
We show our commitment by being baptized.
Baptism is a ceremony in which we symbolically show
the death of our old sinful self and the birth of our new sanctified self
that is ready to live a life for and with Him.

God, Jesus, the Holy Spirit. . .which one do we worship?

Bible scholars around the world have spent many hours debating the details of the relationship between God, Jesus, and the Holy Spirit. These three are also called the Holy Trinity, although this term is not found in the Bible. The word *trinity* consists of two parts: *tri*, which means three, and *unity*, which means one. The Bible tells how God, Jesus, and the Holy Spirit have visited humans on earth in separate ways and with distinct purposes, yet they are all the same essential, everlasting being.

Some teach that the three are actually all parts of a whole, while some teach that the three are three individual beings. This is a spiritual matter and we are all physical beings, so a full understanding is impossible for us right now. But God tells us what we need to know in ways that we can understand – He always gives us physical, earthly things to explain spiritual, heavenly things.

We have already seen that God is a God of order and that His actions are logical and sound. He has created nothing more logical than mathematics, so let's look at it from that perspective.

If God, Jesus, and the Holy Spirit were all parts of the same essence, we would use fractions because the phrase **part of** in math tells us to divide into portions. So, an equation describing their relationship would look like this:

$$\frac{1}{3} + \frac{1}{3} + \frac{1}{3} = 1$$

The Bible tells us that God is all-powerful and there is none like Him – He is complete in Himself. The Bible also tells us that Jesus, the Son of God, the Son of man, acted as an individual and obeyed God to complete His Father's plan. It also says that the Holy Spirit is currently living in us, while Jesus waits at the right hand of God for His time to return to us. The Bible makes it clear that they are each whole – not 1/3 of a single being. If each of them is a separate being, each with his own nature, they should each have separate essences. In this case, we would add the three individual beings together. In words, the equation would be one and one and one, which is three. The word **and** tells us to add, so the numerical equation would be:

$$1 + 1 + 1 = 3$$

Three beings, in our understanding, would each act in his own interest; however, the Bible makes it very clear that God, Jesus, and the Holy Spirit each act in the same interest – they are all following the same divine plan, they all have the same purpose. They are intimately connected to one another in ways that we can only begin to imagine. Because they act as one, a sum of three doesn't accurately describe their relationship. God, Jesus, and the Holy Spirit are each whole, complete beings, but they are of the same essence, they have the same purpose, they follow the same plan, and they act together as one. Even though they are three whole beings, they are all of the same essence or nature – so, in words, we would say each of them is one of a set of one, which equals one. In math, the phrase **sets of** tells us we need to multiply, so the most logical equation to describe their relationship is:

$$1 \times 1 \times 1 = 1$$

Or, more accurately, as we will see, the design is something like this:

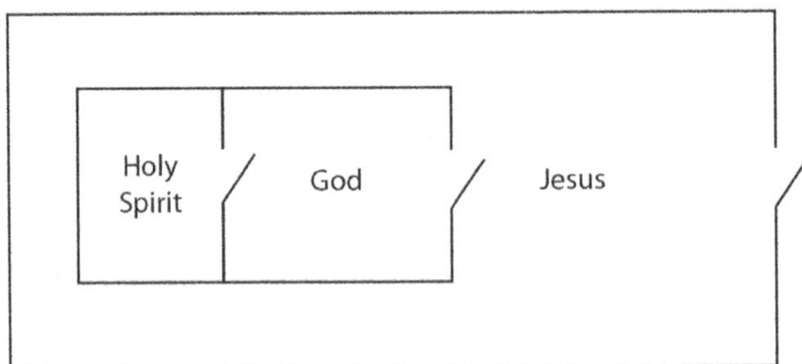

In the book of John, looking at the His words in the original Greek language, we can see that Jesus called the Holy Spirit **allos**, which means 'another of the same kind,' not **heteros**, which means 'another of a different kind.' The Spirit is "another" and yet, "the same."

John 14:16, 26b

"I will ask the Father, and he will give you another [allos] Helper to be with you forever. . .
This Helper is the Holy Spirit that the Father will send in my name."

We must go through Jesus to have a relationship with God and the Holy Spirit. Through the personal knowledge infused in us by the Spirit, we gain an understanding of truth and we receive eternal life in the presence of God.

John 14:6

Jesus answered, "I am the way, the truth, and the life. The only way to the Father is through me. If you really knew me, you would know my Father too. But now you know the Father. You have seen him."

John 14:10b-11a

"The things I have told you don't come from me. The Father lives in me, and he is doing his own work. Believe me when I say that I am in the Father and the Father is in me."

In the beginning, when God made everything, He made humans in His own image.

Genesis 1:26a

Then God said, "Now let's make humans who will be like us."

God has three forms of life:

Jesus – the body of God
Immanuel, meaning God with us
God in the flesh

God – the heart/soul of God
God says He is the "I AM"
this is what makes Him who He is
He is the Living Soul that gives life to the body [Jesus]

Holy Spirit – the Spirit of God

Because we are made in His image, we, as humans, also have three forms of life. Each of our forms can act independently, and each form's actions affect the other forms. Our bodies, souls, and spirits are intimately intertwined.

1 Thessalonians 5:23

We pray that God himself, the God of peace, will make you pure – belonging only to him. We pray that your whole self – spirit, soul, and body – will be kept safe and be blameless when our Lord Jesus Christ comes.

Body – our physical covering, our flesh, our "tent" (temporary house) that will be perfected when Jesus returns

Soul – our spiritual heart – what gives life to our bodies and makes us who we are

Spirit – our innermost part that communes with God's Spirit

Again, a more accurate design looks like this:

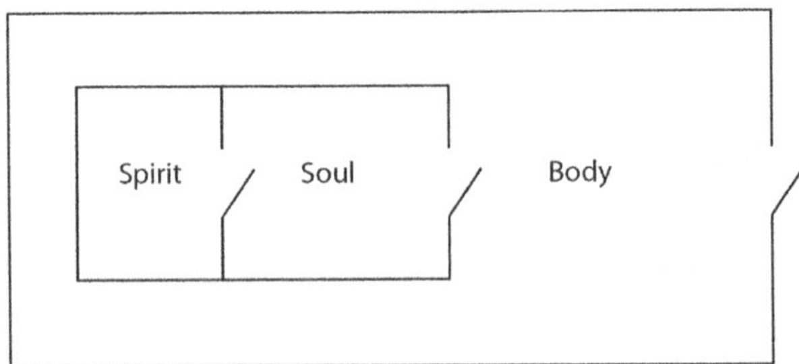

God formed man's body from the dust of the ground. The body came from dust and to dust it will return. The God-breathed soul gives the body life.

Genesis 2:7

Then the LORD God took dust from the ground and made a man. He breathed the breath of life into the man's nose, and the man became a living thing [a living soul – from the Hebrew, ***nephesh****].*

Our physical heart pumps the oxygenated blood that gives life to the flesh. We know that medically, a person can be technically alive but have no animation – they aren't really themselves – just the flesh is alive. This physical, earthly fact is a shadow of and helps us understand the spiritual fact. The spiritual heart, the soul, gives life to the body – it animates the body with the mannerisms and body language that are unique to that person – it gives the flesh a personality. Your soul is what makes you YOU. The blood is the vehicle for the soul. Animals also have a soul because they have oxygenated blood. God said that animals have the breath of life when He said what they would eat for food in the Garden of Eden. What animals lack is the spirit.

Genesis 1:30b

Every animal on earth, every bird in the air, and all the little things that crawl on the earth [everything that has the breath of life – ***nephesh****] will eat that food [the green plants].*

God, the Creator, the Living Soul, made everything, and we can learn things about God through observing His creations. He made the stars and the clouds, the land and the seas, the plants and the trees. He made all the animals. Some of the things God made are living, but they have no soul – they do not have the breath of life. These are the plants and the trees. Some of His creations are living things that also have souls. These are the animals. Some of His creations are living things with souls and spirits. These are the humans.

God's creation is like a window through which we can "see" Him. When you look at an artist's work, you see something of that person in each of his/her creations. God created many things, and through the observation of those things, we can understand Him in some way. The best way to understand Him is through His self-portraits – humans. The only creations God made in His image are humans, so He only gave humans a spirit. God works in us through our spirits.

Hebrews 12:9b

So it is even more important that we accept discipline from the Father of our spirits. If we do this, we will have life.

Jesus tells us that our forms of life are each independent:

John 3:6

"The only life people get from their human parents is physical. But the new life that the Spirit gives a person is spiritual."

Matthew 10:28

"Don't be afraid of people. They can kill the body, but they cannot kill the soul. The only one you should fear is God, the one who can send the body and soul to be destroyed in hell."

Our forms of life bear a resemblance to the areas of the Tabernacle (the tent, the portable Temple) God designed for the Israelites to worship Him, as well as the Temple later built in Jerusalem. We can more accurately imagine how these life forms interact by illustrating them in the same way God designed the Tabernacle and Temple. God gave us these earthly, physical things to help us understand the heavenly, spiritual things.

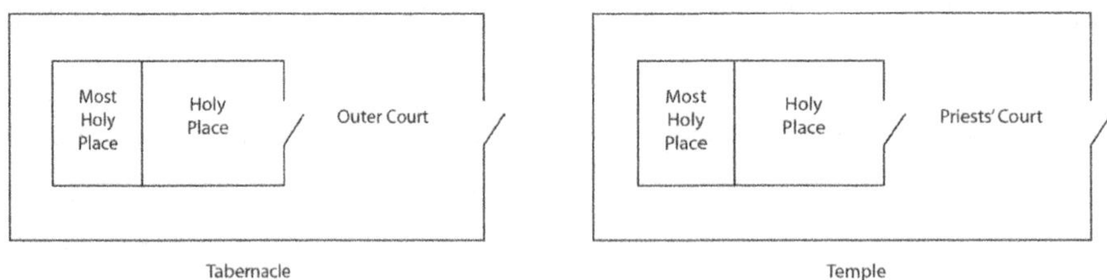

In these designs, the Most Holy Place was closed off even to God's people. As we read earlier, when Jesus died on the cross, the curtain that separated the Most Holy Place from us was torn from top to bottom, and the physical Temple, where physical offerings were made, became obsolete.

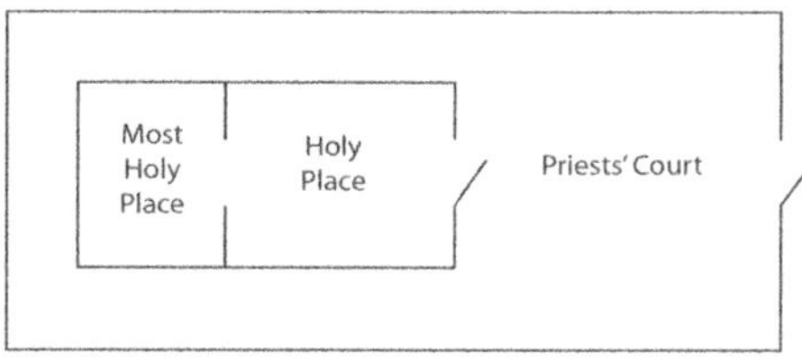

After Jesus' Sacrifice

Since Jesus' sacrifice, the Temple in Jerusalem is no longer needed, because we are now the Temple of God – His Spirit dwells within those of us who are sincere believers. Much like the Temple design, the outer court is our body that all the world can see and that gives an idea of what can be found on the inside. The holy place is our soul in which we make spiritual sacrifices to God. The innermost room is our spirit which communes directly with the Holy Spirit.

1 Corinthians 6:19-20

You should know that your body is a temple for the Holy Spirit that you received from God and that lives in you. You don't own yourselves. God paid a very high price to make you his. So honor God with your body.

When your soul, your will, opens the door to your spirit and allows your spirit to receive the Holy Spirit, your spirit is given new life – it is restored to its original intent/use/function and is holy and righteous before God – you are reborn spiritually. Again, your spirit – which dwells in your most holy place – is the life within you that connects with God directly:

1 Corinthians 6:17

But anyone who is joined with the Lord is one with him in spirit.

You must then allow the Holy Spirit to flow out from your most holy place and work on your soul to change you into the person He wants you to be.

Ephesians 4:23-24

You must be made new in your hearts and in your thinking. Be that new person who was made to be like God, truly good and pleasing to him.

Hebrews 4:12

God's word is alive and working. It is sharper than the sharpest sword and cuts all the way into us. It cuts deep to the place where the soul and the spirit are joined. God's word cuts to the center of our joints and our bones. It judges the thoughts and feelings in our hearts.

The soul is where all of your emotions live – and you have control over those things. You can decide to let the Holy Spirit flow through you by opening the doors to your soul and letting the Spirit of God flow through. It is your will – it is your own power – that allows the doors to open or close. Jesus knocks, but you have to answer. As your soul is renewed and transformed, your body will begin to conform and the fruits of what you do will reflect your inner spirit. God will renew you from the inside out, if you humble yourself and allow Him to do His will.

When you allow the Holy Spirit to work in you, the restoration He performs – His perfecting love – flows through you and out to others. This outflowing of love will attract those who long for God, and it will repel those who deny God.

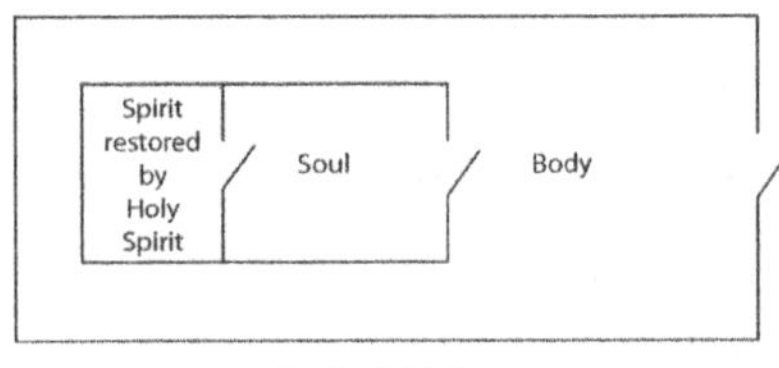

Let the Spirit Flow

Romans 8:13b-14

But if you use the Spirit's help to stop doing the wrong things you do with your body, you will have true life. The true children of God are those who let God's Spirit lead them.

Romans 8:15b-16

The Spirit that we have makes us God's chosen children. And with that Spirit we cry out, "Abba [an Aramaic word that was used by Jewish children as a name for their fathers], Father." And the Spirit himself speaks to our spirits and makes us sure that we are God's children.

Galatians 5:16, 24-25

So, I tell you, live the way the Spirit leads you. Then you will not do the evil things your sinful self wants. . .Those who belong to Christ Jesus have crucified their sinful self. They have given up their old selfish feelings and the evil things they wanted to do. We get our new life from the Spirit, so we should follow the Spirit.

Romans 12:2

Don't change yourselves to be like the people of this world, but let God change you inside with a new way of thinking. Then you will be able to understand and accept what God wants for you. You will be able to know what is good and pleasing to him and what is perfect.

1 Corinthians 2:10-11, 12b, 16b

But God has shown us these things through the Spirit. The Spirit knows all things. The Spirit even knows the deep secrets of God. It is like this: No one knows the thoughts that another person has. Only the person's spirit that lives inside knows those thoughts. It is the same with God. No one knows God's thoughts except God's Spirit. . .We received God's Spirit so that we can know all that God has given us. . .we have been given Christ's way of thinking.

Without God's Holy Spirit, we can have no true understanding of God. Remember the people we discussed in the beginning who would like for us all to believe that the Bible stories aren't real? They can't understand the things of God, because they haven't allowed His Spirit to transform their minds.

1 Corinthians 4:14

People who do not have God's Spirit do not accept the things that come from his Spirit. They think these things are foolish. They cannot understand them, because they can only be understood with the Spirit's help.

All of the details about exactly how the spiritual relationship between the Father, the Son, and the Holy Spirit works are not explained for us in the Bible, and major divisions in God's church have resulted from disagreements over interpretations. We should not allow this to happen. Let's discuss possibilities, but let's remind ourselves of the hard, given facts:

We know that God is the Father, and the Bible tells us to worship Him. We thank Him for sending Jesus and for what Jesus has done for us. When we pray to God, as Jesus showed us to do, we are told to ask things in Jesus' name. We are comforted and guided by the Holy Spirit that has been sent to us as a promise of a better, future life. Jesus will come again to bring all of us who are faithful home to His Father's house. This we know.

John 1:1-5 (Jesus is the Word)

In the beginning, before the earth was made, the Word was there. The Word was with God, and the Word was God. He was there with God in the beginning. Everything was made through him, and nothing was made without him. In him there was life, and that life was light for the people of the world. The light [Jesus] shines in the darkness, and the darkness has not defeated (or, understood) it.

Genesis 1:1-2

In the beginning, when God created the earth and sky, the earth was without life and not yet useful for anything. Deep waters covered the earth, and darkness covered the water. God's Spirit was moving like a storm over the surface of the water.

God's Spirit covered the face of the water and brought earthly life up out of that water, in much the same way that He causes a baby to come up out of a watery womb and be born. God gives us life, but we are not living for Him until we make a decision to do so and are reborn in the spirit through a watery grave.

Galatians 5:25

We get our new life from the Spirit, so we should follow the Spirit.

2 Corinthians 3:17

The Lord is the Spirit, and where the Spirit of the Lord is, there is freedom.

Romans 8:9b

You are ruled by the Spirit, if that Spirit of God really lives in you. But whoever does not have the Spirit of Christ does not belong to Christ.

Isaiah 9:6b

God will give us a son who will be responsible for leading the people. His name will be "Wonderful Counselor, Powerful God, Father Who Lives Forever, Prince of Peace."

John 10:30, 38b (Jesus speaking to the Jewish leaders)

"The Father and I are one. . .understand that the Father is in me and I am in the Father."

Colossians 2:9

I say this because all of God lives in Christ fully, even in his life on earth.

John 1:18

No one has ever seen God. The only Son is the one who has shown us what God is like. He is himself God and is very close to the Father.

Matthew 3:16-17

So Jesus was baptized. As soon as he came up out of the water, the sky opened, and he saw God's Spirit coming down on him like a dove. A voice from heaven said, "This is my Son, the one I love. I am very pleased with him."

Isaiah 45:5a

I am the LORD, the only God. There is no other God except me.

2 Corinthians 13:13

I pray that you will enjoy the grace of the Lord Jesus, the love of God, and the fellowship of the Holy Spirit.

Matthew 28:19

"So go and make followers of all people in the world. Baptize them in the name of the Father and the Son and the Holy Spirit."

Review: God created everything. Jesus was with Him in the beginning. The Spirit of God was present at Creation. They are three in one, one in three.

How did God, Jesus, and the Holy Spirit work together at Passover?

Jesus was on the cross, carrying the weight of all of humankind's sins. We cannot even begin to imagine the tremendous burden of all of those insults against Him that He accepted and absorbed for us. Modern studies have been conducted to record the effects of negative comments vs. positive comments on an individual. We now know that it takes roughly five to seven positive comments to offset one negative comment. In other words, doing something or saying something bad to someone has a much more powerful impact than doing or saying something good.

Jesus, as a man, took on ALL of the insults against God, from Adam and Eve's sin to ours today to those in the future. Additionally, we understand from the Ten Commandments as well as Jesus' teachings that treating another person poorly is also a sin against God. This means that Jesus, like a criminal, accepted the charge as well as the sentencing for committing all the sins directly against God as well as against His creations. He absorbed all of the negativity surrounding the commission of those crimes. That's a LOT of negativity. We know from personal experience how bad it stings emotionally when someone says something negative about us. His flesh suffered cruelly, as any human's flesh would suffer, but how He suffered in His heart (how God suffered) – we cannot imagine.

In His anguish, Jesus cried out a portion of Psalm 22. As He was dying, He did not have the strength to cry out the entire poem, but the Jews watching would have known the rest of the psalm, written by David, in which he foretold how Jesus would go through three stages of feelings. Jesus would first feel forsaken, then He would feel certain that God was with Him, and then He would feel joy at the growth of His family through the goodness of God:

My God, my God, why have you left me?
You seem too far away to save me, too far to hear my cries for help!
My God, I kept calling by day, and I was not silent at night.
But you did not answer me.
God, you are the Holy One.

You sit as King upon the praises of Israel.
Our ancestors trusted you. Yes, they trusted you, and you saved them.
They called to you for help and escaped their enemies.
They trusted you and were not disappointed!
But I feel like a worm, less than human!
People insult me and look down on me.
Everyone who sees me makes fun of me.
They shake their heads and stick out their tongues at me.
They say, "Call to the LORD for help. Maybe he will save you.
If he likes you so much, surely he will rescue you!"

God, the truth is, you are the one who brought me into this world.
You made me feel safe while I was still at my mother's breasts.
You have been my God since the day I was born.
I was thrown into your arms as I came from my mother's womb.
So don't leave me! Trouble is near, and there is no one to help me.
My enemies surround me like angry bulls.
They are like the powerful bulls of Bashan, and they are all around me.
Their mouths are opened wide, like a lion roaring and tearing at its prey.
My strength is gone, like water poured out on the ground.
My bones have separated.
My courage is gone. (Literally, "My heart is melted inside me like wax.")
My mouth (my strength) is as dry as a piece of baked pottery.
My tongue is sticking to the roof of my mouth.
You have left me lying in the dust.
The "dogs" are all around me – a pack of evil people has trapped me.
They have pierced my hands and feet. I can see each one of my bones.
My enemies are looking at me; they just keep staring.
They divide my clothes among themselves, and they throw lots for what I am wearing.
LORD, don't leave me! You are my strength – hurry and help me!
Save me from the sword. Save my precious life from these dogs.
Rescue me from the lion's mouth. Protect me from the horns of the bulls.

I will tell my people about you.

I will praise you in the great assembly.

Praise the LORD, all you who worship him!

Honor him, you descendants of Jacob!

Fear and respect him, all you people of Israel!

He does not ignore those who need help!

He does not hate them.

He does not turn away from them.

He listens when they cry for help.

Lord, because of you I offer praise in the great assembly.

In front of all these worshipers I will do all that I promised.

Poor people, come eat and be satisfied.

(This. . .was. . .a thank offering that would be shared with other people at the Temple.
This was how someone shared their happiness when God blessed them.
[Jesus is the Bread of life that will satisfy us forever.])

You who have come looking for the LORD, praise him!

May your hearts be happy forever.

May those in faraway countries remember the LORD and come back to him.

May those in distant lands worship him, because the LORD is the King.

He rules all nations.

The people have eaten all they wanted and bowed down to worship him.

Yes, everyone will bow down to him –

all who are on the way to the grave, unable to hold on to life.

Our descendants will serve him.

Those who are not yet born will be told about him.

Each generation will tell their children about the good things the Lord has done.

Then Jesus cried out a portion of Psalm 31:

LORD, I come to you for protection.

Don't let me be disappointed.

You always do what is right, so save me.

Listen to me.
Come quickly and save me.
Be my Rock, my place of safety.
Be my fortress and protect me!
Yes, you are my Rock and my protection.
For the good of your name, lead me and guide me.
Save me from the traps my enemy has set.
You are my place of safety.
LORD, you are the God we can trust.
I put my life (Literally, "spirit") in your hands.
Save me!

In the Gospel accounts, these were the last recorded words of Jesus on the cross:

"My God, my God, why have you left me?" - from Psalm 22
"I put my life (spirit) in your hands." - from Psalm 31

Some people read just the first line above and believe that because Jesus said these words, God abandoned Him while He was suffering on the cross. They justify this belief by stating that God cannot be in the presence of sin. We've already shown that God can, in fact, be in the presence of sin – even to the point of having conversations with Satan, so let's address whether God abandoned Jesus at all.

Supposing God abandoned Him, if Jesus did bear all the sins humans ever did or would commit, then God would not be there to witness it. Remember that God, the Greatest Judge, is the one who instituted the sacrifice system to pay for sins. He declared that sincere sacrifices were a sweet-smelling aroma to Him – the sweet smells were not the incense or the sacrifices but the sincerity with which those gifts were offered. God was in the Temple to receive those offerings from His priests. Jesus was THE most perfect – THE sincerest – sacrifice. He is our Great High Priest, and we know that God accepted His offering.

God is omniscient – He is everywhere, all the time. He sometimes allows bad things to happen, but that does not mean He is not there.

Jesus called out to God and knew that God was with Him, ready to accept His physical life as a payment for our sins and ready to receive His Spirit. These verses, assure us that God was there:

John 10:30

"The Father and I are one."

2 Corinthians 5:19a

I mean that God was in Christ, making peace between the world and himself.

God cannot be inconsistent: God, Jesus, and the Holy Spirit act together as one. Jesus, as a man, may have felt abandoned by God in His flesh, but God did not abandon Him while He was on the cross. God accepted the sweet-smelling sacrifice offered by Jesus, the Son of God, on our behalf. Jesus was guilty of nothing. He took the blame and punishment on Himself because He loves us so much. God sent His Son because He loves us so much. The Holy Spirit demonstrates nothing but true love. The purest, most sincere sacrifice God could receive was from Himself. The Spirit was with Jesus the entire time He was on earth as a man, and Jesus sent His Spirit back to God as His fleshly body died on the cross. Jesus, in the flesh, arose and sits now at the right hand of God, while the Holy Spirit came to live in sincere human believers until Jesus comes again.

John 3:16-17

Yes, God loved the world so much that he gave his only Son, so that everyone who believes in him would not be lost but have eternal life. God sent his Son into the world. He did not send him to judge the world guilty, but to save the world through him.

Review: God, Jesus, and the Holy Spirit are completely united in all their work.

I would like to have a symbol of my sincere belief in what God has done

for me through Jesus. As a baptized believer, should I display a cross with or without Jesus on it?

A cross with a figure of Jesus on it is called a crucifix. It is a statue (some are huge, some are tiny) that shows His crucifixion (that is the name for the Roman method of execution used to kill Jesus). Sometimes Jesus is shown alive, sometimes He is shown suffering, sometimes He is shown dead. One reason often given for display of a cross or a crucifix is that it helps us to be mindful of the suffering Jesus endured for us. Remember, there is nothing new in this life. The Bible often compares suffering followed by joy to a mother's experience in giving birth; therefore, Jesus' suffering could be compared to labor and His Resurrection to a new birth. His labor – remember the blood and water that gushed from His side – brought forth a new life for us.

Birth is a grueling, painful, bloody and watery experience, but Jesus knew that this was the price that must be paid to bring a new life for us, His beloved, into existence. In the same way, an expectant mother submits to the pain of childbirth because it is the only way she can fully live life with her new, innocent, beloved person. When the birth is over, and the mother is joyfully holding her new baby, the pain of the birth immediately begins to fade in her memory. A good mother would agree that being with her child – being able to love and be loved by her child – was worth the pain of giving birth to her child.

John 16:21 (Jesus speaking)

"When a woman gives birth to a baby, she has pain, because her time has come. But when her baby is born, she forgets the pain. She forgets because she is so happy that a child has been born into the world."

Jesus did what had to be done in order to gain a life with us. Jesus is no longer in labor – He is no longer on the cross. His blood and water only needed to be poured forth once to give us a new life – a life that will never end. His LOVE for us was the reason for and the whole point of His sacrifice. Through His crucifixion, He is showing His love for each and every one of us. He is showing us how far He is willing to go to give us a new life. God wants us to remember that He loves us more than anything. He loves us so much that He sent His Son to earth as a man to die for us, so that He could give us life again with Him. Jesus instructed us to remember this by celebrating the ritual He began. He said to eat the bread and to drink the fruit of the vine. Remember He loves you.

Hebrews 12:2part

But he accepted the shame of the cross as if it were nothing because of the joy he could see waiting for him.

Romans 8:18

We have sufferings now, but these are nothing compared to the great glory that will be given to us.

Isaiah 42:14part, 16b

"But now I will cry out like a woman giving birth. . .I will do these things for them; I will not abandon my people."

John 19:34

But one of the soldiers stuck his spear into Jesus' side. Immediately blood and water came out.

John 10:10b

"I came to give life – life that is full and good."

Just as it is the love in His heart that is important, it is what's in your heart toward God that is most important. Whatever you decide to display or to wear as a reminder of or as a symbol of your faith, understand that neither the cross nor the crucifix should be worshipped. Only God deserves our worship. Know that in the Old Testament, God specifically said NOT to make any statues or pictures of ANYTHING for the purpose of worship. An idol is an object (or, an image) that people worship, but we know that there is nothing humans can make with their hands that represents God. This was the second rule in God's list of Ten Commandments that He told Moses to tell the people after they left Egypt. God doesn't want ANYTHING to take His place in your heart.

Exodus 20:3

"You must not worship any other gods except me."

Exodus 20:4-5a

"You must not make any idols. Don't make any statues or pictures of anything up in the sky or of anything on the earth or of anything down in the water. Don't worship or serve idols of any kind, because I, the LORD, am your God."

Acts 17:29

"That's right. We all come from God. So we must not think that he is like something people imagine or make. He is not made of gold, silver, or stone."

Isaiah 42:8b

"I will not let statues take the praise that should be mine."

Review: Crosses and crucifixes might be reminders or symbols of your faith, but neither should be used as an object of worship. Remember, too, that Jesus is no longer on the cross, and it isn't possible for us to make something that represents God.

I've seen pictures of Jesus. He's the long-haired guy in sandals, right?

Yes, that is how He is most often shown, but these pictures of Him are just artists' ideas of what He might have looked like in His time on earth. We don't really know for sure what He looked like. Yes, He was a Middle Eastern Jewish man, but He lived 2,000 years ago. At that time, the geographical area east of the Mediterranean was a major cultural crossroads. We do not know how light or dark brown His skin was, how long/short/curly/straight/frizzy/smooth His hair was, how short or tall He was, or what color His eyes were. We do know that His appearance didn't indicate His importance.

God is fond of using people the world views as unlikely to be capable of doing the job He needs done. When He selected young David to be the next king of His people, God sent the prophet Samuel to Bethlehem to anoint him. God told Samuel that one of the eight sons of Jesse would be the new king, but He did not tell him which one. When Samuel saw Jesse's sons, he immediately assumed he knew which one God intended:

1 Samuel 16:6-7

When Jesse and his sons arrived, Samuel saw Eliab and thought, "Surely this is the man who the LORD has chosen." But the LORD said to Samuel, "Eliab is tall and handsome, but don't judge by things like that. God doesn't look at what people see. People judge by what is on the outside, but the LORD looks at the heart. Eliab is not the right man."

The Old Testament book of Isaiah tells us that the man Jesus was not an impressive man in His appearance. He did not look like the great leader or the powerful king (the Savior, the Messiah) that God's people, the Jews, were waiting for – on purpose.

Isaiah 53:2b-3

There was nothing special or impressive about the way he looked, nothing we could see that would cause us to like him. People made fun of him, and even his friends left him. He was a man who suffered a lot of pain and sickness [He carried our sins and sorrows to the cross with Him]. We treated him like someone of no importance, like someone people will not even look at but turn away from in disgust.

God selects the unlikely, so people will understand that God is the power behind the person.

2 Corinthians 4:7

We have this treasure from God, but we are only like clay jars that hold the treasure. This is to show that the amazing power we have is from God, not from us.

As imperfect humans, we are all drawn to physical beauty, but physical beauty dies with the body. Love lives forever, and God wanted people to be drawn to His love, not His looks. A solid relationship is not about appearances – it's about the love each person decides to have and show for the other – it's all about what is in your heart and mind (that is, your soul). The love you have and share is what makes up your inner beauty, and it lasts forever. He has demonstrated a pure and perfect love for us, and He wants the same from us.

Our spirit was forgiven at the cross.
When we accept that, then the Holy Spirit comes to us
and works on purifying us from the inside out.
We must allow His Spirit to work in us.
This is why Jesus said the most important command is:
"Love the Lord your God with all your heart,
all your soul, all your mind, and all your strength."
Mark 12:30

2 Corinthians 4:16

That is why we never give up. Our physical body is becoming older and weaker, but our spirit inside us is made new every day.

God has commanded us to love Him, but it is your choice to obey that command or not. You must understand that He loves you dearly, and He has shown Himself worthy of all your love and respect. God wants His love to fill up your soul until it overflows. He wants you to use your strength, your power, your will, to let that love to flow back to Him and out to others. We are all God's children, and so we are brothers and sisters in Christ. He wants a big family full of love for each other and for their Father.

Our earthly life is a shadow of our future heavenly life. Shadows show very little detail compared to the real object. In our world we generally observe three dimensions of space: an object has length, width (sometimes called depth), and height. Time, which cannot be demonstrated in terms of space, is considered a fourth dimension.

If our shadowy, earthly experience is limited to these dimensions, then we can imagine that in heaven, we will experience many more dimensions. The Bible gives us a little hint of that when describing the love of Jesus for His faithful. Four Dimensions of Christ's Love are mentioned in the New Testament book of Ephesians. It says if we allow Christ into our hearts, and we allow ourselves to be full of love, then we may be able to understand the great love of Christ and just how wide, how long, how high, and how deep His love is.

The Bible tells us His love is wide – it's for everyone and for all time. His love is long – He will go to the ultimate lengths for you. His love is high – as high as the heavens. His love is deep – as deep as the oceans. As extensive as that description is, His love is even greater. We are limited by language and experience, but if we are sincere, God will help us understand His love.

Ephesians 3:18-19

And I pray that you and all God's holy people will have the power to understand the greatness of Christ's love – how wide, how long, how high, and how deep that love is. Christ's love is greater than anyone can ever know, but I pray that you will be able to know that love. Then you can be filled with everything God has for you.

Psalm 103:11,13

His love for his followers is as high above us as heaven is above the earth. . .The LORD is as kind to his followers as a father is to his children.

Review: What Jesus looked like while He was on earth is not important.
His message of love should be our focus.
Allowing His love to work in us should be our goal.

What is our purpose here on earth?

Adam and Eve were put here to be with God. . .to share a life with Him. That is what God wants for us. He plans for us to resume the relationship that Adam and Eve began. He is working toward that by carrying out His plan – the same plan He foretold through the prophets and outlined with the feast days. Our Father wants all of His children to come home to His house. Our job – our goal, our purpose – is to tell everyone about His love and to help as many people as we can understand that God loves us all and wants us all to be with Him. We do this not only by telling others with our words, but also by showing others with our actions. What we say must be backed up by what we do. Our faith must be seen in our words and in our deeds. If we are full of the Spirit, this "work" comes naturally – it's a labor of love.

Colossians 3:23

In all the work you are given, do the best you can. Work as though you are working for the Lord, not any earthly master.

The apostles were given what we now call The Great Commission just before Jesus ascended to heaven. He told them to take His story, His Gospel, to EVERYONE in the whole world. Faithful believers are continuing that work today.

Matthew 28:19-20 (Jesus speaking to His apostles – The Great Commission)

"So go and make followers of all people in the world. Baptize them in the name of the Father and the Son and the Holy Spirit. Teach them to obey everything that I have told you to do. You can be sure that I will be with you always. I will continue with you until the end of time."

When we lovingly spread the news about Jesus, we are priests offering sincere spiritual sacrifices to God, and those sacrifices are a sweet smell to Him, just as the sincerely offered sacrifices in the Temple were. We are now the Temple. God's Spirit lives in us. Spreading the Word is our offering to Him. This is how He uses us to build His church – we help gather as many living stones as we can.

1 Peter 2:5, 9a

You also are like living stones, and God is using you to build a spiritual house. You are to serve God in this house as holy priests, offering him spiritual sacrifices that he will accept because of Jesus Christ. . .But you are his chosen people, the King's priests.

Romans 10:13-15

Yes, "everyone who trusts in the Lord will be saved." But before people can pray to the Lord for help, they must believe in him. And before they can believe in the Lord, they must hear about him. And for anyone to hear about the Lord, someone must tell them. And before anyone can go and tell them, they must be sent. As the Scriptures say, "How wonderful it is to see someone coming to tell good news!"

The Bible tells us it is not our job to decide whether someone is "worthy" to hear about God. We are simply instructed to tell everyone.

Acts 10:28part

But God has shown me that I should not consider anyone unfit. . .

Matthew 5:16

In the same way, you should be a light for other people. Live so that they will see the good things you do and praise your Father in heaven.

The Bible relates spreading the Good News of Jesus to spreading seed. In the days before machines, a farmer would plant a crop by walking around his field with a bag of seed strapped across his shoulder. The farmer would reach into the bag and toss out handfuls of seed all around him. We are told to make sure that the seed we spread is good seed. We can do that by making sure that what we tell others about God is exactly what the Bible says. God will take care of the rest.

1 Corinthians 3:7

So the one who plants is not important, and the one who waters is not important. Only God is important, because he is the one who makes things grow.

Jesus tells us that Satan (through his servants) will come along and spread bad seed in His field, but He will separate the good plants from the bad ones when He comes for His final harvest. This is another of Jesus' parables in which He tells us about how God's plan will work by relating it to something earthly we can all understand.

Matthew 13:30

"Let the weeds and the wheat grow together until the harvest time. At the harvest time I will tell the workers this: 'First, gather the weeds and tie them together to be burned. Then gather the wheat

and bring it to my barn.'"

If you'd like to relate our purpose to another familiar topic, then think of it like sports. We are supposed to recruit people for His team, and God wants EVERYONE on His team. He doesn't want any of His children to be recruited by Satan's team, because that's not His team. How can you recruit for His team? Start with yourself and your family. This is how you can honor and worship Him – this is your purpose.

Jesus has the power of God. And his power has given us everything we need
to live a life devoted to God. . .Because you have these blessings,
do all you can to add to your life these things:
to your faith add goodness; to your goodness add knowledge;
to your knowledge add self-control; to your self-control add patience;
to your patience add devotion to God; to your devotion
add kindness toward your brothers and sisters in Christ,
and to this kindness add love.
If all these things are in you and growing, you will never fail to be useful to God.

2 Peter 1: 3a, 5-8a

God will help you. The Bible heroes, such as Abraham and David, were not people who were smarter or more talented than other people. They were ordinary people who made some of the same mistakes we do. Anything spectacular they did was done with God's help. If you think you aren't talented or smart enough to do His work, you must remember: God chooses the ordinary to do His extraordinary work, so He will receive the honor for what is done. God doesn't want us to worship any of the heroes of the Bible for their great deeds. He wants us to worship Him.

Hebrews 12:1a (about the heroes of the Bible)
We have all these great people around us as examples. Their lives tell us what faith means. So we, too, should run the race that is before us and never quit.

Philippians 3:14

I keep running hard toward the finish line to get the prize that is mine because God has called me through Christ Jesus to life up there in heaven.

If we will submit to what He wants for us like the Bible heroes did, God can accomplish great things through us and bring His plan closer to completion. God wants us to understand that EVERYONE is useful in His eyes. He gives us the stories of these people as examples of what our faith in Him should be like. God will give you everything you need in order to do the job He asks you to do.

Romans 12:2

Don't change yourselves to be like the people of this world, but let God change you inside with a new way of thinking. Then you will be able to understand and accept what God wants for you. You will be able to know what is good and pleasing to him and what is perfect.

Titus 3:14

Our people must learn to use their lives for doing good and helping anyone who has a need. Then they will not have empty lives.

1 Corinthians 1:26-29

Brothers and sisters, God chose you to be his. Think about that! Not many of you were wise in the way the world judges wisdom. Not many of you had great influence, and not many of you came from important families. But God chose the foolish things of the world to shame the wise. He chose the weak things of the world to shame the strong. And God chose what the world thinks is not important – what the world hates and thinks is nothing. He chose these to destroy what the world thinks is important. God did this so that no one can stand before him and boast about anything.

Philippians 2:13

Yes, it is God who is working in you. He helps you want to do what pleases him, and he gives you the power to do it.

Philippians 4:13,19

Christ is the one who gives me the strength I need to do whatever I must do. . .My God will use his glorious riches to give you everything you need. He will do this through Christ Jesus.

Mark 9:23b
". . .All things are possible for the one who believes."

The Jewish nation was given the job of keeping and recording God's instructions for us, but now His chosen people's job is to spread that information to all the world. Who are His chosen people? Whether you are Jew or Gentile does not matter – only God's faithful believers are counted as the children of Abraham, and only they will receive God's promises.

John 11:52
Yes, he would die for the Jewish people. But he would also die for God's other children scattered all over the world. He would die to bring them all together and make them one people.

If you are a faithful believer, you have been adopted into His people and His promise is for you. Start your day with this:

Deuteronomy 6:4-6
"Listen, people of Israel! The LORD is our God. The LORD is the only God. You must love the LORD your God with all your heart, with all your soul, and with all your strength. Always remember these commands that I give you today."

Here is what you should do with those commands:

Deuteronomy 6:7-9
"Be sure to teach them to your children. Talk about these commands when you sit in your house and when you walk on the road. Talk about them when you lie down and when you get up. Tie them on your hands and wear them on your foreheads to help you remember my teachings. Write them on the doorposts of your houses and on your gates."

Here is His promise if you do these things:

Deuteronomy 6:10-11

"The LORD your God made a promise to your ancestors, Abraham, Isaac, and Jacob. He promised to give you this land, and he will give it to you [the New Jerusalem on the new earth when God finishes His plan]. He will give you great and rich cities that you did not build [He is preparing a place for us]. He will give you houses full of good things that you did not put there. He will give you wells that you did not dig. He will give you vineyards and olive trees that you did not plant, and you will have plenty to eat."

Here is what will happen if you don't do these things:

Deuteronomy 6:14-15

"You must not follow the gods of the people who live around you. [Other gods are idols. Anything you put in a place of higher priority than the One True God is an idol.] The LORD your God is always with you, and he hates for his people to worship other gods! So if you follow those other gods, the Lord will become very angry with you. He will destroy you from the face of the earth. [He is going to purify the earth with fire – much like the Jewish people purified their homes by throwing the yeast (sin) into the fire.]"

God has made His promise, and He has made His plan. He is faithful. We are to act as He does and be faithful, too.

Ephesians 5:1-2

You are God's dear children, so try to be like him. Live a life of love. Love others just as Christ loved us. He gave himself for us – a sweet-smelling offering and sacrifice to God.

Ecclesiastes 12:13

Now, what should we learn from everything that is written in this book? The most important thing a person can do is to respect God and obey his commands. . .

Deuteronomy 10:12 part

What does the LORD your God really want from you? The LORD your God wants you to respect him and do what he says. He wants you to love him and to serve the LORD your God with all your heart and with all your soul.

We love Him because we know how much He loves us. There is no risk in this relationship – we can invest in it completely and without fear. He has shown full commitment, and we know He will never leave us. If the relationship ends, it will only be because we have left Him.

Ephesians 2:10b
In Christ Jesus, God made us new people so that we would spend our lives doing the good things he had already planned for us to do.

Galatians 6:9a
We must not get tired of doing good.

Romans 12:21
Don't let evil defeat you, but defeat evil by doing good.

Micah 6:8
Human, the LORD has told you what goodness is. This is what he wants from you: Be fair to other people. Love kindness and loyalty, and humbly obey your God.

Remember, as a sincere believer, you have been given the gift of the Holy Spirit.

Your physical body is a temple of God.

You should live in a way that shows respect to God and thankfulness for this gift.

You can do this by:

- being considerate of His names and only using them in reverent ways.
- being considerate of His other children (whether they are lost or found) and showing them kindness and treating them with dignity (by using good manners).
- being respectful of your body by avoiding behaviors He has spoken against, such as drunkenness and sexual immorality.

1 Corinthians 6:19-20 (*One more time, because this is very important*)

You should know that your body is a temple for the Holy Spirit that you received from God and that lives in you. You don't own yourselves. God paid a very high price to make you his. So honor God with your body.

Review: Everyone's purpose in life is to talk and to live in a way that will help as many people as possible come to know God's love. God will supply the talent you need.

Never before in the history of the world has each individual person had so much access to His Word in such a personal way. God's Message of salvation is being poured out into the world at a rapid pace and, no doubt, it will soon be fully saturated. Jesus' commission to "make followers of all people in the world" gets closer to being fulfilled every day. Do your part to spread the Good News.

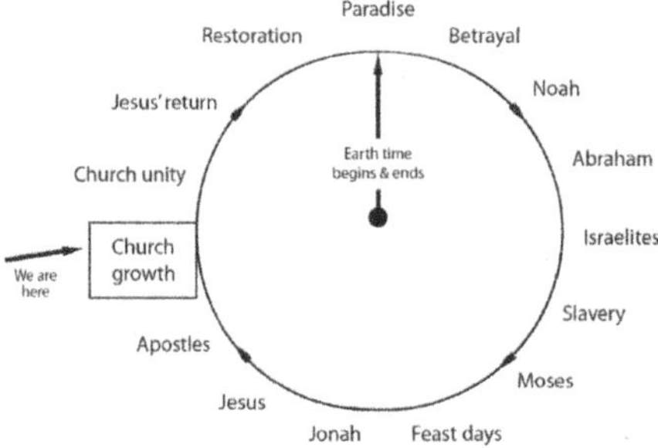

Isn't it politically incorrect to talk about God in public?

If we were to write a list of rules for today's politically correct society, we might include the following: choose your words carefully so as not to offend anyone, don't force people into a group prayer, and don't display pictures about or words from the Bible because some people don't believe what you believe. Some Christians are offended by these new rules, because they believe the rules limit their ability to express their beliefs. While this is true in many instances, we should not let our anger prevent us from our purpose. Perhaps God is at work here – after all, we know He can use anything for His good.

Proverbs 25:15b

Gentle speech is very powerful.

Ephesians 5:1-2a

You are God's dear children, so try to be like him. Live a life of love. Love others just as Christ loved us.

2 John 1:5a-6

We should all love each other. This is not a new command. It is the same command we had from the beginning. And loving means living the way he commanded us to live. And God's command is this: that you live a life of love. You heard this command from the beginning.

We have two important perspectives to consider regarding our communication with others – how we handle relationships with other believers and how we handle relationships with God's lost children – and our success in the former directly impacts our success in the latter. God long ago told His followers to be considerate of everyone in order to more effectively spread the Good News that has been given to them. If we all behave in a considerate manner toward everyone, we will become more united. The more united we become, the more we reflect the true image of God. Both Jesus and Paul set many good examples of this for us.

1 Corinthians 9:22b (Paul talking about his efforts to spread the Gospel of Jesus)

"I have become all things to all people. I did this so that I could save people in any way possible."

God's promise to humans is very user-friendly, but humans have made it complicated.

Instead of strictly using the Bible as a guide, most Christian organizations have a list (and sometimes books) of their own rules and beliefs based on their long-time traditions and/or their particular interpretation of God's Word. Some of these groups fiercely defend their own interpretations/traditions and declare other interpretations/traditions to be wrong. The results have been disastrous: we cannot stand together when the enemy attacks AND we have problems in reaching our goal of recruiting for God's army. Some potential or new recruits are driven away by all of these different opinions – they just don't know where to go for worship or learning, or what to believe when they get there. Some soldiers/members even leave the army/team, because they can't believe that God's army/team would be so divided. We are failing in our duties!

Jeremiah 50:6-7a

"My people have been like lost sheep. Their shepherds led them the wrong way and caused them to wander away into the mountains and hills. They forgot where their resting place was. They were attacked by all who saw them. And their attackers said, 'We were not wrong to attack them because they sinned against the LORD. They should have stayed close to him, their true resting place.'"

This is a time when God's people were living in an unbelieving nation, and God was preparing to send judgment on that nation.

If we show respect for one another as fellow believers and brothers and sisters in Christ, we can strengthen God's house. When our own house is large and well-built, we can more easily bring God's lost sheep home to stay. Right now, our house is fractured and divided, and we are losing people through the cracks. We can't attract people to come live in a house that has cracks (divisions) and crumbling rocks (weak Christians) and weeds (Satan's influence) and cobwebs (spiritual death).

THIS IS VERY IMPORTANT: We need to mend the divisions within God's church so we can more effectively recruit soldiers and deal with attacks from the enemy. If we fail to unite under His banner, He will raise a new army for Himself. God and His plan cannot be stopped.

Isaiah 55:11

". . . my words leave my mouth, and they don't come back without results. My words make the things happen that I want to happen. They succeed in doing what I send them to do."

Recall Gamaliel's advice to the authorities who wanted to stop the apostles from spreading the Good News: "But if it is from God, you will not be able to stop them" (Acts 5:39a).

People can choose to fight Him or to help Him, but they can never do anything that will stop God's progress. He can use the rules of political correctness to help bring His children together, and when He has brought us together, we can do a better job of reaching those who do not know or understand the Promise of God.

What can we do? As believers, we should all carefully pare our beliefs down to the core, removing all of the human-influenced opinions. The seeds are what is needed to grow more fruit, so we should focus on the seed. God's Word is that seed. As the Bible clearly shows – in Jesus' own words – it is when God's followers plant their personal opinions and religious traditions all around His Word so that His Word is hidden that they go wrong. We must get down to the seeds and plant just those seeds in order to do the will of God. We must do away with all of the commandments of men – the rules humans have made about how and when to worship God and what to believe – their traditions. We must narrow our focus to only His Bible.

Mark 7:6-7 (from Isaiah 29:13) (Jesus condemning the religious leaders for holding their own beliefs above God's Word)
Jesus answered, "You are all hypocrites. Isaiah was right when he wrote these words from God about you: 'These people honor me with their words, but I am not really important to them. Their worship of me is worthless. The things they teach are only human rules.'

Mark 7:8-9 (continued from above)
"You have stopped following God's commands, preferring instead the man-made rules you got from others." Then he said, "You show great skill in avoiding the commands of God so that you can follow your own teachings!"

Mark 7:13 (continued)
"So you are teaching that it is not important to do what God said. You think it is more important to follow those traditions you have, which you pass on to others. And you do many things like that."

If our extra teachings or respective interpretations of God's Word are keeping us apart, we must sit down and honestly examine our beliefs. Is our understanding of the Bible and God's plan based on His original Word? If it's based on a faulty translation or a human tradition, then we must examine the facts. If we have a belief that cannot be supported by the original Bible languages, then we cannot insist that it is correct. Doing so creates strife and division.

If all believers focus strictly on His Words, we can stop offending one another's human traditions, understand what He really wants from us, and be in agreement. We can become the united family He wants us to be, and we can stop giving mixed messages to new believers. If we stop giving mixed messages to new believers, God's church will grow exponentially. The bigger God's true church is, the better we can defend ourselves against Satan, and the better our life here on earth will be.

This unity is for all believers – Jew or Gentile. Christ wants us to be one, and it is why He came.

Ephesians 2:14-15

Christ is the reason we are now at peace. He made us Jews and you who are not Jews one people. We were separated by a wall of hate that stood between us, but Christ broke down that wall. By giving his own body, Christ ended the law with its many commands and rules. His purpose was to make the two groups become one in him. By doing this he would make peace.

When God created us in His image, He divided His talents up among us – all of His talents are important. The only true differences between believers are our talents (the gifts He has given us so that we can help one another) and how those talents can be best used to help God's family grow. When we unite, we have more power, because we are using more and more of God's gifts all together. We can each use our different talents and work together to do a better job of reaching more people with His Good News. Growing God's family reduces our chances of offending unbelievers, because there are fewer unbelievers.

Remember, we are weaker when we are divided – and that's just the way Satan would like to keep us. Jesus, the Word that cannot be stopped, prayed for our unity. Let us be faithful servants and do His will.

1 Corinthians 12:7

Something from the Spirit can be seen in each person. The Spirit gives this to each one to help others.

2 Corinthians 3:17, 18b

The Lord is the Spirit and where the Spirit of the Lord is, there is freedom. We all show the Lord's glory, and we are being changed to be like him.

Colossians 2:2-4

I want them to be strengthened and joined together with love and to have the full confidence that comes from understanding. I want them to know completely the secret truth that God has made known. That truth is Christ himself. In him all the treasures of wisdom and knowledge are kept safe. I tell you this so that no one can fool you by telling you ideas that seem good, but are false.

Deuteronomy 4:2 (Moses to God's people)

"You must not add to what I command you. And you must not take anything away. You must obey the commands of the LORD your God that I have given you."

Colossians 2:18b-19

It is so foolish for them to feel such pride, because it is all based on their own human ideas. They don't keep themselves under the control of the head. Christ is the head, and the whole body depends on him. Because of Christ all the parts of the body care for each other and help each other. So the body is made stronger and held together as God causes it to grow.

Ephesians 4:12-13a

Christ gave these gifts to prepare God's holy people for the work of serving, to make the body of Christ stronger. This work must continue until we are all joined together in what we believe and in what we know about the Son of God.

***John 17:21, 23b** (Jesus' prayer for unity of His believers)*

Father, I pray that all who believe in me can be one. You are in me and I am in you. I pray that they can also be one in us. Then the world will believe that you sent me. . . and that you loved them just as you loved me.

Along with honest self-examination, using polite and respectful words toward one another will not only help us join together as believers it will also help us all do a more effective job of reaching God's lost children. Every single human, whether lost or found, is a child of God, and as such, should be respected.

Here is God's promise to His children who had come together to build His house (the Temple) and sincerely honor Him by following His commands – it is the same promise we will receive if we pray for and work toward the unity of His believers, which can only be achieved by adhering to His original Word alone, not His Word adulterated with human words:

2 Chronicles 7:14

And if my people who are called by my name become humble and pray, and look for me, and turn away from their evil ways, then I will hear them from heaven. I will forgive their sin and heal their land.

Review: Believers should use kind words and focus on what we have in common. We must all join together and do what we can to help as many people as we possibly can come to know God and His promise of everlasting life with Him.

What is heaven, exactly?

Three types of heaven are mentioned in the Bible. One heaven houses the birds and clouds, and the next heaven houses the stars and planets. These are simply called "heaven" or "the heavens" in Scripture. A third type of heaven is literally referred to as "the third heaven" by Paul, who equates it with Paradise. We have discussed Paradise before, but we were talking about the Garden of Eden – God's garden – His earthly, physical Paradise.

Genesis 13:10part

At that time the Jordan Valley all the way to Zoar was like the LORD's Garden.

Ezekiel 31:9part

. . .all the trees in Eden, God's garden. . .

The third heaven, Paradise, is the spiritual place above the earth where God lives now.

2 Corinthians 12:2-4
I know a man in Christ who was taken up to the third heaven. This happened 14 years ago. I don't know if the man was in his body or out of his body, but God knows. And I know that this man was taken up to paradise. I don't know if he was in his body or away from his body, but he heard things that he is not able to explain. He heard things that no one is allowed to tell.

Many scholars believe that, in the verses above, Paul is actually writing about himself and the near-death experience he had after being stoned, dragged outside the city gate, and left for dead. He was treated this way for trying to teach others about Jesus.

Acts 14:19 *(Paul was teaching in Lystra, a city in Asia Minor – modern day Turkey)*
Then some Jews came from Antioch and Iconium and persuaded the people to turn against Paul. So they threw stones at him and dragged him out of the town. They thought they had killed him.

The third heaven is God's dwelling place.

Acts 7:49a *(from Isaiah 66:1a)*
'The Lord says, Heaven is my throne, and the earth is where I rest my feet.'

Colossians 3:1
You were raised from [spiritual] death with Christ. So live for what is in heaven [Literally, above], where Christ is sitting at the right hand of God.

Jesus told us that Paradise is the place where the tree of life will be available to us again.

Revelation 2:7b
"To those who win the victory I will give the right to eat the fruit from the tree of life, which is in God's paradise."

Remember, Adam and Eve were removed from the Paradise of Eden so they would not be able to eat from the tree of life and live forever in their sinful state. God has always intended His children to live forever in a wonderful place.

Jesus also spoke of Paradise on the day He died. He was crucified along with two other men who were convicted criminals. As they were all hanging on their crosses, dying, one of the men asked Jesus to remember Him when He came into His kingdom.

Luke 23:43

Then Jesus said to him, "I promise you, today you will be with me in paradise."

Review: Heaven is Paradise. It is where God lives.

Do we go to heaven immediately when we die?

Some people believe that when we die we immediately go to heaven, some people believe we sleep and know no passage of time, and some people believe we experience a waiting period. There is some truth to all of these beliefs, but let's try to understand the whole truth.

We know we are made in the image of God – that our being consists of a body, a soul, and a spirit that are independent and yet intimately connected.

As discussed earlier, our spirits die when we understand sin. When we choose to turn our backs on sin and follow God sincerely, our spirits are born again. Our spiritual death has already been conquered by our spiritual rebirth, or spiritual resurrection. Jesus' work made this possible. When our physical body dies, our spirit returns to heaven (God's presence) immediately.

Luke 23:46a (from Psalm 31:5part - Jesus' last words on the cross)

Jesus shouted, "Father, I put my life in your hands!" (Literally, "I put my spirit in your hands.")

Acts 7:59

As they [the angry Jews] were throwing the stones at him, Stephen was praying. He said, "Lord Jesus, receive my spirit!"

And there is no question that our bodies return to the earth when we die.

Ecclesiastes 3:20

The bodies of people and animals end the same way. They came from the earth, and, in the end, they will go back to the earth.

1 Corinthians 15:50

I tell you this, brothers and sisters: Our bodies of flesh and blood cannot have a part in God's kingdom. Something that will ruin cannot have a part in something that never ruins.

Ecclesiastes 12:7

Your body came from the earth. And when you die, it will return to the earth. But your spirit came from God, and when you die, it will return to him.

1 Corinthians 15:42b-44

The body that is "planted" in the grave will ruin and decay, but it will be raised to a life that cannot be destroyed. When the body is "planted," it is without honor. But when it is raised, it will be great and glorious. When the body is "planted," it is weak. But when it is raised, it will be full of power.
The body that is "planted" is a physical body. When it is raised, it will be a spiritual body.
There is a physical body. So there is also a spiritual body.

Read the last two sentences again. Everything physical has a spiritual counterpart. As complex as some of the earthly, physical things are (like our bodies), their heavenly, spiritual counterparts are infinitely more complex. Earthly things are only shadows of heavenly things. Think about what a shadow is – it's an image of reality that is limited in dimension, color, clarity, reflection, sound, feeling, taste, experience, touch, and even time.

1 Corinthians 15:48-49

All people belong to the earth. They are like that first man of earth [Adam]. But those who belong to heaven are like that man of heaven [Jesus]. We were made like that man of earth, so we will also be made like that man of heaven.

2 Corinthians 5:1

We know that our body – the tent we live in here on earth – will be destroyed. But when that happens, God will have a home for us to live in. It will not be the kind of home people build here. It will be a home in heaven that will continue forever.

It is our bodies that sleep and know no passage of time. Death is a kind of bodily sleep. Remember Jesus' time in the grave. God allowed His body to "rest" for two Sabbaths before being resurrected on the third day. Just as Jesus' body was resurrected, so our bodies will be resurrected when He comes to complete His plan.

So, we understand what happens to our spirit and what happens to our body, but what happens to our soul? Our God-breathed souls are what gives life to our bodies.

Genesis 2:7

*Then the LORD God took dust from the ground and made a man. He breathed the breath of life into the man's nose, and the man became a living thing [Literally, **"nephesh,"** or soul].*

The original words for soul and spirit are not always translated correctly – many Bibles interchange the words, mistakenly interpreting them as referring to the same element of our being. Clarification can be found in an Interlinear Bible which allows you to read the verses in your own language as well as in their original language.

	Body	Soul	Spirit
Hebrew	Geshem	Nephesh	Ruach
Greek	Soma	Psuche	Pneuma

God created your soul with His own breath. Satan cannot snuff it out. Only God can judge the soul and decide whether it merits eternal life with Him or not.

Matthew 10:28

"Don't be afraid of people. They can kill the body, but they cannot kill the soul. The only one you should fear is God, the one who can send the body and the soul to be destroyed in hell."

Revelation 14:13b

. . .there are great blessings for those who belong to the Lord when they die.

1 Peter 1:4

Now we wait to receive the blessings God has for his children. These blessings are kept for you in heaven. They cannot be ruined or be destroyed or lose their beauty.

So, does God judge our soul when our body dies and allow those who are worthy to enter His Paradise immediately, or is there a waiting period?

Remember the criminal on the cross. Jesus said he would be with Him in Paradise that very day.

The apostle Paul evidently believed that his soul would immediately be in the Lord's presence when he died.

Philippians 1:23b

Sometimes I want to leave this life and be with Christ. That would be much better for me.

Paul only tells us about two possibilities: life on earth and life with Christ. He does not mention a waiting time between his death and his reward.

2 Corinthians 5:9

Our only goal is to always please the Lord, whether we are living here in this body or there with him.

The apostle John tells about souls of people who are already in heaven.

Revelation 6:9b-11a (John's vision into heaven)

Then I saw some souls under the altar. They were the souls of those who had been killed because they were faithful to God's message and to the truth they had received. These souls shouted in a loud voice, "Holy and true Lord, how long until you judge the people of the earth and punish them for killing us?" Then each one of them was given a white robe. They were told to wait a short time longer.

These Revelation verses seem a bit strange – like something out of a sci-fi movie. We cannot rely entirely on our own experiences to illustrate heaven in our minds. We need to remember Paul's words. He says repeatedly that being in heaven with Jesus is the best place for us to be, that we will really feel like we are finally where we belong – we will be at home. We just need faith.

2 Corinthians 5:7-8

We live by what we believe will happen, not by what we can see. So I say that we have confidence. And we really want to be away from this body and be at home with the Lord.

The death of our body opens a door for our soul and our spirit to pass through to the better life God has waiting for us.

If the souls of God's true followers are ushered into His presence in heaven immediately when their bodies die, then God must make their souls completely clean. In life, when they sincerely decided to follow God, their sins were removed, and while they were living, the Holy Spirit was working on them from the inside out, continually renewing them.

2 Corinthians 4:16b

Our physical body is becoming older and weaker, but our spirit inside us is made new every day.

Colossians 3:10

Now you are wearing a new life, a life that is new every day. You are growing in your understanding of the one who made you. You are becoming more and more like him.

Romans 12:2

Don't change yourselves to be like the people of this world, but let God change you inside with a new way of thinking. Then you will be able to understand and accept what God wants for you. You will be able to know what is good and pleasing to him and what is perfect.

We are all human, and as such, we continue to sin. Paul shared some rather circular, but accurate, information on how/why a person who professes to follow God continues to sin.

Romans 7:18part, 19part, 22

Yes, I know that. . . nothing good lives in the part of me that is not spiritual. . . I don't do the good that I want to do. I do the evil that I don't want to do. . . In my mind I am happy with God's law. But I see another law working in my body. That law makes war against the law that my mind accepts. That other law working in my body is the law of sin, and that law makes me its prisoner.

We can understand that the spiritual war going on around us is also happening inside of us. We will never be perfected completely as long as we are living this earthly, physical life. God asks us to do our very best. He knows we cannot be perfect on our own – that's why He sent Jesus, and that's why He sends the Holy Spirit.

The physical cannot heal/cure/save the physical. Only the spiritual has true healing power. We struggle with the physical, as Paul related above, because we split time and allow the earthly/physical to lure us some of the time and the heavenly/spiritual to lead us some of the time. When we do this, we are double-minded, and the Bible tells us that those who are double-minded are unstable.

James 4:8b

You are trying to follow God and the world at the same time. Make your thinking pure.

1 John 2:15

Don't love the evil world or the things in it. If you love the world, you do not have the love of the Father in you.

James 1:5-8

Do any of you need wisdom? Ask God for it. He is generous and enjoys giving to everyone. So he will give you wisdom. But when you ask God, you must believe. Don't doubt him. Whoever doubts is like a wave in the sea that is blown up and down by the wind. People like that are thinking two different things at the same time. They can never decide what to do. So they should not think they will receive anything from the Lord.

1 Kings 18:21a (Elijah, the prophet, speaking to the Israelites)

Elijah came to all the people and said, "You must decide what you are going to do. How long will you keep jumping from one side to the other? If the LORD is the true God, follow him. But if Baal [a false god] is the true God, then follow him!"

We must allow the spiritual to flow through us. We have to use our own will, not to save ourselves, but to allow God's Spirit to renew us.

God's Spirit renews us daily, so we can be certain He makes our souls pure before allowing us into heaven.

1 Thessalonians 5:23-24

We pray that God himself, the God of peace, will make you pure – belonging only to him. We pray that your whole self – spirit, soul, and body – will be kept safe and be blameless when our Lord Jesus Christ comes. The one who chose you will do that for you. You can trust him.

Ephesians 5:27

Christ died so that he could give the church to himself like a bride in all her beauty. He died so that the church could be holy and without fault, with no evil or sin or any other thing wrong in it.

Jesus told the story now known as "The Rich Man and Lazarus," so we can know that those who are true to God will pass through to heaven upon their bodily deaths, while those who are not will pass through to a place of torment (a place that doesn't have God). He tells us that the destination of our souls is determined by the actions (fruits) of our living bodies, and that once our bodies have died, we cannot change our destination.

Luke 16:19-31

Jesus said, "There was a rich man who always dressed in the finest clothes. He was so rich that he was able to enjoy all the best things every day. There was also a very poor man named Lazarus. Lazarus' body was covered with sores. He was often put by the rich man's gate. Lazarus wanted only to eat the scraps of food left on the floor under the rich man's table. And the dogs came and licked his sores. Later, Lazarus died. The angels took him and placed him in the arms of Abraham. The rich man also died and was buried. He was sent to the place of death (Literally, "Hades" [the unseen world, a place of torment for the unfaithful dead]) and was in great pain. He saw Abraham far away with Lazarus in his arms. He called, 'Father Abraham, have mercy on me! Send Lazarus to me so that he can dip his finger in water and cool my tongue. I am suffering in this fire!"

"But Abraham said, 'My child, remember when you lived? You had all the good things in life. But Lazarus had nothing but problems. Now he is comforted here, and you are suffering. Also, there is a big pit between you and us. No one can cross over to help you, and no one can come here from there.'

"The rich man said, 'Then please, father Abraham, send Lazarus to my father's house on earth. I have five brothers. He could warn my brothers so that they will not come to this place of pain.'

"But Abraham said, 'They have the Law of Moses and the writings of the prophets to read; let them learn from that.'

"The rich man said, 'No, father Abraham! But if someone came to them from the dead, then they would decide to change their lives.'

"But Abraham said to him, 'If your brothers won't listen to Moses and the prophets, they won't listen to someone who comes back from the dead.'"

Abraham is a living soul in this story. This is one of many verses where God tells us, as He told Moses, that He is the God of the living. All of His faithful followers are alive.

Exodus 3:6a (God speaking to Moses)

I am the God of your ancestors. I am the God of Abraham, the God of Isaac, and the God of Jacob.

Luke 20:35a, 36, 37part, 38

"Some people will be worthy to be raised from death and live again after this life. . .In that life people are like angels and cannot die. They are children of God, because they have been raised from death. Moses clearly showed that people are raised from death. . .he said that the Lord is the 'God of Abraham, the God of Isaac, and the God of Jacob.' So they were not still dead because he is the God only of living people. Yes, to God they are all still living."

Most of us are reasonably comfortable in our earthly bodies – at the very least, we are accustomed to them – but we understand that these, like the Tabernacle, are just temporary dwelling places. When our bodies die, we enter phase two, so to speak. We are closer to our final version. We have completed our earthly life, we move on to our heavenly life, and we know there is a final, perfected life.

Paul and John tell us we will feel at home in heaven. No doubt, we will feel more at home there than we do here because we will be with Him – and since we will be with Him, we will be a better version of ourselves. As we saw from the Revelation verse about the martyrs, we will still know that God's work isn't finished – that we aren't complete. God created us to be physical beings in the beginning, because that is what He wanted us to be. His plan will not be complete until our reborn spirits and cleansed souls are reunited with our resurrected bodies. When God resurrects our bodies, those bodies will be perfected. This perfection will probably not be in the runway model/Hollywood sense you might be imagining. When Jesus was resurrected, He still looked like Himself, and He still had the marks of crucifixion.

John 20:27 (Jesus to Thomas, who had trouble believing that Jesus was alive)

Then he said to Thomas, "Put your finger here. Look at my hands. Put your hand here in my side. Stop doubting and believe."

And so, we can understand that there are two waiting periods: the wait to pass from this earthly life to our heavenly existence and the wait until our physical resurrection, also called the Day of the Lord, when Jesus returns to earth. There is a third waiting period of a different sort during Christ's reign on earth and the subsequent final battle with Satan, which we will discuss later. After that time, humanity will not only be restored to the place God intended for us, but He will also restore that place.

He has told us that He will create a new heaven and a new earth at the end of His plan. God's people will live on this new earth and there will be a place called the New Jerusalem, the Holy City of God. Here is the happy end of God's plan that John described:

Then I saw a new heaven and a new earth. The first heaven and the first earth had disappeared. Now there was no sea. And I saw the holy city, the new Jerusalem, coming down out of heaven from God. It was prepared like a bride dressed for her husband. I heard a loud voice from the throne. It said, "Now God's home is with people. He will live with them. They will be his people. God himself will be with them and will be their God. He will wipe away every tear from their eyes. There will be no more death, sadness, crying, or pain. All the old ways are gone." The one who was sitting on the throne said, "Look, I am making everything new!" Then he said, "Write this, because these words are true and can be trusted."

Revelation 21:1-5

In the Bible, the sea often represents rebellion. The word sea here indicates the widespread resistance to God's ultimate power. He will permanently put an end to rebellion. Those who remain with Him are those who have chosen Him.

We can be certain that because God is all good, and because He only wants good, that everything at the happy end will be good. In the beginning, when He had finished all of Creation (before Satan introduced humans to evil), God said that it was very good. If life in Eden was "very good" even though it was vulnerable to attack, you can be sure that our new earthly home, which can never be attacked, will be very, very good.

How will the resurrection of our bodies happen? When Jesus comes again, the bodies of the faithful believers who have already died will be raised to meet Him first. Then the faithful believers whose bodies are still alive will join them. They will all be perfected in the blink of an eye.

Philippians 3: 20-21

But the government that rules us is in heaven. We are waiting for our Savior, the Lord Jesus Christ, to come from there. He will change our humble bodies and make them like his own glorious body. Christ can do this by his power, with which he is able to rule everything.

Romans 8:11part

God raised Jesus from death. And if God's Spirit lives in you, he will also give life to your bodies that die. . .he will raise you to life through his Spirit living in you.

1 Thessalonians 4:16-17

The Lord himself will come down from heaven with a loud command, and with the voice of the archangel, and with the trumpet call of God. And the people who have died and were in Christ will rise first. After that we who are still alive at that time will be gathered up with those who have died. We will be taken up in the clouds and meet the Lord in the air. And we will be with the Lord forever.

Ephesians 2:6-7

Yes, it is because we are a part of Christ Jesus that God raised us from death and seated us together with him in the heavenly places. God did this so that his kindness to us who belong to Christ Jesus would clearly show for all time to come the amazing richness of his grace.

We cannot know all the details yet, for as Paul also says, "Now I know only a part, but at that time I will know fully" (1 Corinthians 13:12). This is what faith is for – it is for the things we cannot see or fully understand because our bodies and minds have not yet been perfected. We are not mature – we are like children. In the next verse, Paul goes on to say, "So these three things continue: faith, hope, and love. And the greatest of these is love." Love continues forever, because God is love. And He loves you.

Romans 8:38-39

"Yes, I am sure that nothing can separate us from God's love – not death, life, angels, or ruling spirits. I am sure that nothing now, nothing in the future, no powers, nothing above us or nothing below us – nothing in the whole created world – will ever be able to separate us from the love God has shown us in Christ Jesus our Lord."

The book of Revelation tells us that our final version of existence – when we are in our perfected bodies – will be the **nisu'in**, the consummation, of the marriage of Jesus and His bride. The word consummate means "to bring to a state of perfection" and "being of the highest degree." In other words, this is the highest point of the relationship – and it's where we'll stay. Bonus: God doesn't just completely restore us, He adds extra blessings.

Job 42:10b, 12a (After Job's test, in which almost everything he had was taken from him, and he remained true to God)
. . .and the LORD made Job successful again. The LORD gave him twice as much as he had before.
. . .The LORD blessed Job with even more than he had in the beginning [before his test].

Revelation 19:7, 9
Let us rejoice and be happy and give God glory! Give God glory, because the wedding of the Lamb has come. And the Lamb's bride has made herself ready. . .Then the angel said to me, "Write this: Great blessings belong to those who are invited to the wedding meal of the Lamb!" Then the angel said, "These are the true words of God."

Review: God is your Father. He will take care of you. He wants only good for you. And God is really good at giving us good things. Our new life in the presence of God and our new earth will certainly be far, far better than the best place we can imagine, but only God's faithful people will get to enjoy it.

Why can't everyone go to heaven and be with God?

Satan has corrupted this life. As an earthly example, you would never transfer corrupt files to a new computer. If the files fail to be cleaned with the best anti-virus software available, they are left behind to be destroyed with the old computer. In the same way, those who stubbornly refuse to accept God's love and His will for them will be left behind. They will be punished with the old trickster, Satan, and his band of fallen angels in a final, decisive battle. For now, God is recruiting (through us) to build His army — but so is Satan.

Just believing that Jesus is the Son of God is not enough. Jesus tells us clearly that even the demons believe in Him. When Jesus approached two men who were consumed with wickedness, the evil spirits controlling those men shouted out to Jesus, "What do you want with us, Son of God?" (Matthew 8:29part). Because of this verse and others that tell us the fallen angels know and confess that Jesus is the Son of God, we know that we cannot just say, "I believe Jesus is the Son of God," and then return to our previous lives, if we want to go to heaven. It is not enough. Jesus said, "Not everyone who calls me Lord will enter God's kingdom. The only people who will enter are those who do what my Father in heaven wants" (Matthew 7:21). We must be sincerely faithful.

There are only two kinds of people: those who obey and those who do not. To obey, we cannot just acknowledge the Door God has provided to us in Jesus. We have to enter through the Door and walk in the new life He has offered to all of us.

Malachi 3:18b (God defining the only two types of people as far as He is concerned)

You will learn the difference between someone who follows God and someone who does not.

Our chance to go through the door that Christ has provided will end, just like in Noah's day, when God waited for the people to change their hearts while Noah was building the boat. After a certain time (when God decided the boat was ready and the time was right), God closed the door and those who had not listened were left behind with no hope for survival. The same was true in Moses' day when God was preparing the Israelites to leave Egypt. They had to kill the Passover lamb and put its blood on their doorway, then they had to pass through that door and remain inside. Only by submitting to His will did the people avoid the punishment of death coming to those outside the door. They had to obey to live.

Hebrews 10:26-31

If we decide to continue sinning after we have learned the truth, then there is no other sacrifice that will take away sins. If we continue sinning, all that is left for us is a fearful time of waiting for the judgment and the angry fire that will destroy those who live against God. Whoever refused to obey the Law of Moses was found guilty from the testimony given by two or three witnesses. Such people were not forgiven. They were killed. So think how much more punishment people deserve who show their hate for the Son of God – people who show they have no respect for the blood sacrifice that began the new agreement and once made them holy or who insult the Spirit of God's grace. We know that God said, "I will punish people for the wrongs they do; I will repay them." And he also said, "The Lord will judge his people." It is a terrible thing to face punishment from the living God.

In order to truly live, you have to go through the Door that God has provided for you. That Door is Christ. You have to choose to submit to what God wants for your life. You have to let pride go, humble yourself, and obey. No person can close that door and keep you out – Satan cannot close the door and keep you out – God alone has the power to close it, and He alone will decide when the time is right. The door will close when Jesus returns for His bride. Jesus, the Great Shepherd, will sort through us all, ushering the saved ones (sheep) into His house and closing out the unsaved ones (goats) – the stubbornly sinful ones who refused to obey. The unfaithful will be destroyed by fire, much like the yeast (representing sin) was cleaned out of a Jewish home before Passover and traditionally thrown into the fire to be destroyed. The faithful believers will be rewarded with a new earth and a new Jerusalem that God has promised will be a perfect place where we can go in and out of the twelve beautiful, pearly city gates that will never close.

Matthew 25:31-46

"The Son of Man will come again with divine greatness, and all his angels will come with him. He will sit as a king on his great and glorious throne. All the people of the world will be gathered before him. Then he will separate everyone into two groups. It will be like a shepherd separating his sheep from his goats. He will put the sheep on his right and the goats on his left. Then the king will say to the godly people on his right, 'Come, my Father has great blessings for you. The kingdom he promised is now yours. It has been prepared for you since the world was made. It is yours because when I was hungry, you gave me food to eat. When I was thirsty, you gave me something to drink. When I had no place to stay, you welcomed me into your home. When I was without clothes, you gave me something to wear. When I was sick, you cared for me. When I was in prison, you came to visit me.' Then the godly people will answer, 'Lord, when did we see you hungry and give you food? When did we see you thirsty and give you something to drink? When did we see you with no place to stay and welcome you into our home? When did we see you without clothes and give you something to wear? When did we see you sick or in prison and care for

you?' Then the king will answer, 'The truth is, anything you did for any of my people here, you also did for me.' Then the king will say to the evil people on his left, 'Get away from me. God has already decided that you will be punished. Go into the fire that burns forever – the fire that was prepared for the devil and his angels. You must go away because when I was hungry, you gave me nothing to eat. When I was thirsty, you gave me nothing to drink. When I had no place to stay, you did not welcome me into your home. When I was without clothes, you gave me nothing to wear. When I was sick and in prison, you did not care for me.' Then those people will answer, 'Lord, when did we see you hungry or thirsty? When did we see you without a place to stay? Or when did we see you without clothes or sick or in prison? When did we see any of this and not help you?' The king will answer, 'The truth is, anything you refused to do for any of my people here, you refused to do for me.' Then these evil people will go away to be punished forever. But the godly people will go and enjoy eternal life."

Deuteronomy 30:19-20a
"Today I am giving you a choice of two ways. And I ask heaven and earth to be witnesses of your choice. You can choose life or death. The first choice will bring a blessing. The other choice will bring a curse. So choose life! Then you and your children will live. You must love the LORD your God and obey him. Never leave him, because he is your life."

Revelation 21:7-8
"All those who win the victory will receive all this. And I will be their God, and they will be my children. But those who are cowards, those who refuse to believe, those who do terrible things, those who kill, those who sin sexually, those who do evil magic, those who worship idols, and those who tell lies – they will all have a place in the lake of burning sulfur. This is the second death."

Psalm 68:21b
He will punish those who fight against him.

Matthew 7:21
"Not everyone who calls me Lord will enter God's kingdom. The only people who will enter are those who do what my Father in heaven wants."

Galatians 5:1

We have freedom now, because Christ made us free. So stand strong in that freedom. Don't go back into slavery again.

Joshua 24:15part

Today you must decide who you will serve. . .You must choose for yourselves.

If we choose God, and we live our lives according to His will, the rewards will be more wonderful than anything we can imagine. In Revelation, the apostle John describes his vision of the beautiful city of God:

The city was shining with the glory of God. The city had a large, high wall with twelve gates. There were twelve angels at the gates. There were three gates on the east, three gates on the north, three gates on the south, and three gates on the west. The city was built in a square. Its length was equal to its width. The city was made of pure gold, as pure as glass. The foundation stones of the city walls had every kind of expensive jewels in them. The twelve gates were twelve pearls. I did not see a temple in the city. The Lord God All-Powerful and the Lamb were the city's temple. The city did not need the sun or the moon to shine on it. The glory of God gave the city light. The Lamb was the city's lamp. The peoples of the world will walk by the light given by the Lamb. The city's gates will never close on any day, because there is no night there. Nothing unclean will ever enter the city.
No one who does shameful things or tells lies will ever enter the city.
Only those whose names are written in the Lamb's book of life will enter the city.

Revelation 21:11a, 12a, 13, 16a, 18b, 19a, 21a, 22-24a, 25, 27

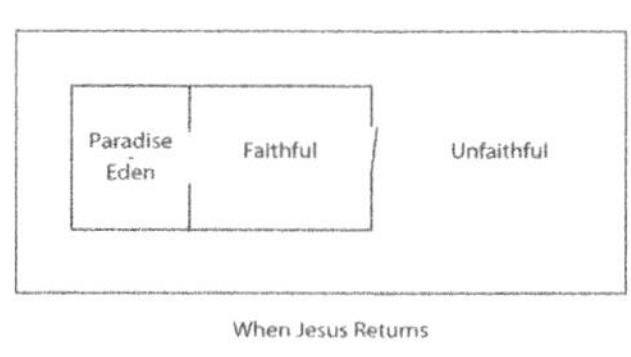

When Jesus Returns

God's Plan Completed

Review: If you choose not to accept God's offer, you will not reach the happy end. Everyone who accepts God's gift (goes through the door that Jesus provided) and does His will wins the prize of a never-ending life with Him.

How can you learn what God's will for you is?

The Jews mistakenly thought they could make themselves holy by following the rules of the Law that said they must wash at certain times and in certain ways, they must eat or not eat certain things at certain times, they must not associate with certain types of people, and so on. These rules concerned things on the outside of their physical body, and many of these rules they made for themselves – they were not in the written Law. When Jesus came, He explained to them that it wasn't what they ate or didn't eat that made them holy. He told them they needed to examine their hearts.

Mark 7:15-16, 20-23

"There is nothing people can put in their mouth that will make them wrong. People are made wrong by what comes from inside them." . . .And Jesus said, "The things that make people wrong are the things that come from the inside. All these bad things begin inside a person, in the mind: bad thoughts, sexual sins, stealing, murder, adultery, greed, doing bad things to people, lying, doing things that are morally wrong, jealousy, insulting people, proud talking, and foolish living. These evil things come from inside a person. And these are the things that make people unacceptable to God."

Know what God says – read His Book for yourself. Jesus has told us the two most important things to do:

1. Love God more than anyone or anything else.
2. Love others like you love yourself.

Jesus set this example for us. He served God first, then others, and then Himself. He told us, "Be like me." You've probably seen the second command expressed in other ways, such as: Treat other people the way you would like to be treated. Sometimes this is called The Golden Rule. The Bible calls it The Royal Law.

James 2:8

One law rules over all other laws. This royal law is found in the Scriptures: "Love your neighbor the same as you love yourself." If you obey this law, you are doing right.

Humility is one of the most important character traits we can develop. Jesus is humble. We should be humble, too. Being humble means that you submit to God's will (what God wants) at all times, just as Jesus did. To submit to God is to allow God to guide you, to correct you, and to teach you. You must use the free will, the power to choose, that God has given you and choose to submit to Him. Sometimes you will do wrong, and God may discipline you in order to help you grow closer to Him. God is like a good gardener and you are like a part of His favorite plant. He will prune you to help you grow. In the same way, a good parent disciplines a child when the child does wrong in order to help the child learn and grow into a better person. God prunes us and disciplines us to help us be more like Him, so be glad when He corrects you. It means He loves you and cares about what you do.

John 15:1-2

Jesus said, "I am the true vine, and my Father is the gardener. He cuts off every branch of mine that does not produce fruit. He also trims every branch that produces fruit to prepare it to produce even more."

Proverbs 3:11-12

My son, don't reject the LORD's discipline, and don't be angry when he corrects you. The LORD corrects the one he loves, just as a father corrects a child he cares about.

Deuteronomy 8:5

You must remember that the LORD your God teaches and corrects you as a father teaches and corrects his son.

Humility is also called meekness. Jesus showed us that meekness is strength under control. Jesus could do anything, but He chose not to show His full strength during His first visit. There was mighty power in His controlled power. By controlling His power (by not using it), He was able to do what He needed to do to save us from being separated from God forever. By not calling His army of angels to save Him from the cruel pain of the cross, He was able to complete His sacrifice. He chose to do this for us because He loves us.

Matthew 26:53
"Surely you know I could ask my Father and he would give me more than twelve armies of angels."

2 Corinthians 12:9part
"My grace is sufficient for you, for my power is made perfect in weakness."

John10:18
"No one takes my life away from me. I give my own life freely."

When it comes to how we act toward God, humility means we understand that He is in charge, and He will have the last say. We do not – we cannot – know everything, but we can humbly accept that He does and that He will take care of His children.

When it comes to how we act toward other people, humility means we should not be puffed up and proud. Treating others well is a part of being humble. We should not think that we are of more value than another person. Like a good father, God loves all His children equally. Jesus treated people, especially people others looked down on, with dignity and respect, and so should we.

Matthew 23:12
People who think they are better than others will be made humble. But people who humble themselves will be made great.

Psalm 37:11
Humble people will get the land God promised, and they will enjoy peace.

Ephesians 5:15a, 16-17
So be very careful how you live. . .I mean that you should use every opportunity you have for doing good, because these are evil times. So don't be foolish with your lives, but learn what the

Lord wants you to do.

Micah 6:8

Human, the LORD has told you what goodness is. This is what he wants from you: Be fair to other people. Love kindness and loyalty, and humbly obey your God.

How you act toward God or toward others is your choice. God has given you the freedom to choose. Controlling yourself, controlling your power, is something like Jesus controlling His power. Control yourself, so you can do the good work of God that He has set before you. You CAN do anything you want. . .but SHOULD you?

1 Corinthians 6:12

"I am allowed to do anything," you say. My answer to this is that not all things are good. Even if it is true that "I am allowed to do anything," I will not let anything control me like a slave.

1 Peter 2:16-17a

Live like free people, but don't use your freedom as an excuse to do evil. Live as those who are serving God. Show respect for all people.

How do you decide if doing something or saying something is good or bad? Sometimes it seems hard to tell. Here's a list of questions you can ask yourself to help you know if something is right or wrong:

- Is what I want to do (or what I have been asked or advised to do) helpful in some way, either to myself or to others? Is it pleasing to God?

- Will it bring me under its power? Will it master me? Will I be able to maintain control over my actions/words? – think addiction, here. You can be addicted to alcohol, food, drugs, shopping, gambling, risky behavior, your phone, the internet – you can even be addicted to feelings, like power, attention, anger, negativity, and much more. Ask yourself honestly, who's in charge? who will be in charge?

- Will it hurt others in any way? Physical harm is sometimes easy to see and identify, but psychological or emotional harm can be difficult to notice and may take years to develop. There is also spiritual harm. Will your actions (or lack of action) create a stumbling block in someone else's journey to a close relationship with God?

- Will it glorify God? Will it further His work? Will it grow His army? Will it bring someone closer to Him?

Proverbs 3:6

With every step you take, think about what he wants, and he will help you go the right way.

1 Corinthians 10:31-32

So if you eat, or if you drink, or if you do anything, do it for the glory of God. Never do anything that might make other people do wrong – Jews, non-Jews, or anyone in God's church.

Romans 14:13b, 19

Let's decide not to do anything that will cause a problem for a brother or sister or hurt their faith. . .So let's try as hard as we can to do what will bring peace. Let's do whatever will help each other grow stronger in faith.

1 Corinthians 6:19-20 (ALL the parts of your body, inside and out)

You should know that your body is a temple for the Holy Spirit that you received from God and that lives in you. You don't own yourselves. God paid a very high price to make you his. So honor God with your body.

When you ask for God's saving grace to come into your life and you allow His Spirit to guide your life, self-control is one of the fruits you will begin to grow. As it grows, self-control will help you avoid doing those things you know you should not do.

Galatians 5:22-23a (These are known as the Fruits of the Spirit)

But the fruit that the Spirit produces in a person's life is love, joy, peace, patience, kindness, good-

ness, faithfulness, gentleness, and self-control.

Zechariah 4:6b

'Your help will not come from your own strength and power. No, your help will come from my Spirit.'

Always let His Spirit lead you. The Bible teaches that whatever is in your heart – the things you care about, think about, work to get, work to keep – is what gives you the will to live. Make sure what's in your heart is good. Stay inside the lines. Live your life inside the frame of God's will – of what He wants for you. Stay in His picture. Don't cross His protective boundary. If you stray from Him, you lose His protection.

Proverbs 4:23

Above all, be careful what you think because your thoughts control your life.

Matthew 6:21

"Your heart will be where your treasure is."

Here are some helpful instructions found in the Bible:

Live in peace with each other. . .warn those who will not work.
Encourage those who are afraid. Help those who are weak.
Be patient with everyone. Be sure that no one pays back wrong for wrong.
But always try to do what is good for each other and for all people.
Always be full of joy.
Never stop praying. Whatever happens, always be thankful.
This is how God wants you to live in Christ Jesus.
Don't stop the work of the Holy Spirit. Don't treat prophecy like something
that is not important. But test everything. Keep what is good,
and stay away from everything that is evil.

1 Thessalonians 5:13b, 14b-22

We can test the prophecies and teachings we hear and read by knowing His Word. Reading the Bible helps us to know what is true and what is false, what is good and what is bad, what we should do and what we should not do. We can choose to build our knowledge of God, and we can choose to use our power for good.

Matthew 7:13 (Jesus speaking)
"You can enter true life only through the narrow gate. The gate to hell is very wide, and there is plenty of room on the road that leads there. Many people go that way."

Proverbs 4:25-27
Keep your eyes on the path, and look straight ahead. Make sure you are going the right way, and nothing will make you fall. Don't go to the right or to the left, and you will stay away from evil.

Philippians 2:3-9
In whatever you do, don't let selfishness or pride be your guide. Be humble, and honor others more than yourselves. Don't be interested only in your own life, but care about the lives of others too. In your life together, think the way Christ Jesus thought. He was like God in every way, but he did not think that his being equal with God was something to use for his own benefit. Instead, he gave up everything, even his place with God. He accepted the role of a servant, appearing in human form. During his life as a man, he humbled himself by being fully obedient to God, even when that caused his death – death on a cross. So God raised him up to the most important place and gave him the name that is greater than any other name.

Matthew 7:24-27
"Whoever hears these teachings of mine and obeys them is like a wise man who built his house on rock. It rained hard, the floods came, and the winds blew and beat against that house. But it did not fall because it was built on rock. Whoever hears these teachings of mine and does not obey them is like a foolish man who built his house on sand. It rained hard, the floods came, and the winds blew and beat against that house. And it fell with a loud crash."

Philippians 4:8
Brothers and sisters, continue to think about what is good and worthy of praise. Think about what

is true and honorable and right and pure and beautiful and respected.

Review: You have the power to choose your behavior.
You have the power to choose to let His Spirit guide you.
Read His Book – He will show you the Way – and choose wisely.
Choose to do God's will: act humbly and love others.

How do you love someone who has done something terrible to you?

Almost all of us care about those who are close to us and who love us, but Jesus tells us that we should also love our enemies. We should love people even if they have done something terrible to us. That sounds illogical on the surface but look at it through His eyes. Humans have sinned against Him over and over, yet He loves us – He forgives us.

Matthew 5:44-47
"But I tell you, love your enemies. Pray for those who treat you badly. If you do this, you will be children who are truly like your Father in heaven. He lets the sun rise for all people, whether they are good or bad. He sends rain to those who do right and to those who do wrong. If you love only those who love you, why should you get a reward for that? Even the tax collectors do that. [Many tax collectors in the Jewish homeland in Jesus' time on earth were dishonest, and all of them were working for the hated Roman occupiers of their land. Tax collectors were generally considered to be bad people.] And if you are nice only to your friends, you are no better than anyone else. Even the people who don't know God are nice to their friends."

When the Bible says we should love our enemies, you can understand that to mean that we must forgive our enemies – we must not hold anger against them. You can forgive people without putting them in your social circle. Remember, God values sincerity. You don't have to force yourself to be friendly with a person when what you really want or need is distance – that would be insincere. **Forgiveness does not mean relationship** – especially if the person who hurt you is not sorry for what they have done. God gave us this example Himself. Jesus died so God could forgive every person's sins, but every person must still admit his/her wrongs and seek a relationship with Him.

This is very important to understand, so let's put it another way to make sure the explanation is clear.

When you forgive those who have wronged you, it doesn't make them right – it just makes you free from their wrongs. They aren't made right until they admit their wrong and accept your forgiveness. In the same way, Jesus forgiving us doesn't make us right – our admission of guilt and acceptance of His forgiveness makes us right.

Leviticus 19:18
Forget about the wrong things people do to you. Don't try to get even. Love your neighbor as yourself. I am the LORD.

Proverbs 24:19
Don't let those who are evil upset you, and don't be jealous of them. They have no hope. Their light will burn out.

Proverbs 25:21-22
If your enemies are hungry, give them something to eat. If they are thirsty, give them some water. This will make them feel the burning pain of shame, and the LORD will reward you for being good to them.

James 2:13
Yes, you must show mercy to others. If you do not show mercy, then God will not show mercy to you when he judges you. But the one who shows mercy can stand without fear before the Judge.

Maybe no one has done anything terrible to you, but there are some people in your life who tempt you to do things that are not pleasing to God. They are people who don't know, don't fully understand, or don't acknowledge the power of God and His Message. If you feel you can do so safely, you should try to share the Good News with them, but do not put yourself at risk spiritually. It can be a dangerous operation to save people who are drowning in sin, because they can pull you under with them. They may not realize they are doing so, but they will try to pull you under in their efforts to raise themselves out of their troubles (or, to make themselves feel better about who they are and what they do). It is much easier for them to pull you down than it is for you to lift them up. The Bible warns us to be very careful in trying to reach these people. If your faith in God is at risk, stay away from them.

1 Corinthians 15:33

Don't be fooled: "Bad friends will ruin good habits."

Proverbs 22:24-25

Don't be friends with people who become angry easily. Don't stay around quick-tempered people. If you do, you may learn to be like them. Then you will have the same problems they do.

Maybe no one is tempting you with wicked ways that separate you from God. Maybe a particular person just "brings you down" when you're around him/her. You should still be very cautious. Listening to too much discouraging talk can be just as hazardous to your faith as actually doing something God does not want you to do. It takes a strong person with strong faith to spend much time talking to a negative person and not become negative themselves. Some people will build you up – they make you feel positive or safe or happy or confident – they fill you up emotionally. Other people will bring you down – they lead you to think or to talk negatively about yourself or others, they make you feel that life is pointless, they rob you of your confidence in yourself – they emotionally drain you. DO NOT listen to or believe ANY of this kind of negative talk. God loves you, He gave you life, and with His help you can do anything.

2 Timothy 2:16 (Words are powerful)

Stay away from people who talk about useless things that are not from God. That kind of talk will lead a person more and more against God.

James 3:9-10 (Words are powerful)

We use our tongues to praise our Lord and Father, but then we curse people who were created in God's likeness. These praises and curses come from the same mouth. My brothers and sisters, this should not happen.

Ephesians 4:29 (Words are powerful)

When you talk, don't say anything bad. But say the good things that people need – whatever will help them grow stronger. Then what you say will be a blessing to those who hear you.

When trying to forgive someone, keep three things in mind. First, the person who wronged you – physically, mentally, or spiritually – was being used by Satan to attack God – s/he was being a servant, or tool, of Satan whether s/he realized it or not.

Ephesians 2:2b

That same spirit [Satan] is now working in those who refuse to obey God.

God has told us very plainly that we are not fighting each other – we are fighting against Satan and his fallen angels who work through people. We must be careful not to allow Satan to work through us.

Ephesians 6:12

Our fight is not against people on earth. We are fighting against the rulers and authorities and the powers of this world's darkness. We are fighting against the spiritual powers of evil in the heavenly places.

We have all done things without realizing the full impact of our actions. Jesus tells us that this is true. While hanging on the cross, He asked God to forgive those who were responsible for His death because they did not understand what they were doing. We should all try to learn from this and be more aware of how our actions affect others.

Luke 23:34a

Jesus said, "Father, forgive them. They don't know what they are doing."

Understand that when people do or say something negative to you, that action or statement is not about YOU – it's about THEM and their relationship with God. You are a Temple of God, so when a person sins against you, s/he is really sinning against Him – s/he is desecrating His Temple. That sin is in His jurisdiction, and

He will judge the sinner. You must release all your anger and hurt to Him and let Him handle it. Pour your heart out to Him – He will understand and guide you down His healing path.

Romans 12:14, 17a, 19part

Wish only good for those who treat you badly. Ask God to bless them, not curse them. If someone does you wrong, don't try to pay them back by hurting them. Wait for God to punish them. . .

Deuteronomy 32:35a

I will punish them for the bad things they did.

The second thing you should remember when trying to forgive someone is that God can make <u>anything</u> work for His good – He can take any evil thing and make something good come from it. We know this is true because of Jesus' crucifixion and what it means for us.

Deuteronomy 31:6

"Be strong and be brave. Don't be afraid of those people because the LORD your God is with you. He will not fail you or leave you."

Thirdly, along with prayer and God's love, distance and time can be powerful parts of the healing process. Do what you can to put yourself in a better place. Try to surround yourself with people who help you rebuild. Pray, pray, pray.

Romans 12:12

Be happy because of the hope you have. Be patient when you have troubles. Pray all the time.

Psalm 138:3

When I called to you for help, you answered me and gave me strength.

Put on the armor God has given you to fight the powers of evil – prepare yourself for spiritual warfare.

Ephesians 6:13

That is why you need to get God's full armor. Then on the day of evil, you will be able to stand strong. And when you have finished the whole fight, you will still be standing.

What is God's armor?

Ephesians 6:14-17

So stand strong with the belt of truth tied around your waist, and on your chest wear the protection of right living. On your feet wear the Good News of peace to help you stand strong. And also use the shield of faith with which you can stop all the burning arrows that come from the Evil One. Accept God's salvation as your helmet. And take the sword of the Spirit – that sword is the teaching of God.

That is the armor, but how do you use it? How is it activated?

Ephesians 6:18

Pray in the Spirit at all times. Pray with all kinds of prayers, and ask for everything you need. To do this you must always be ready. Never give up. Always pray for all of God's people.

We are living in a spiritual war zone. We are in this fight together whether we open our eyes and see it or not. We choose which side we want to join (failing to choose God is still making a choice). We have to come before God and tell Him we want to be on His side. We must show Him that we respect His authority in all things earthly and heavenly. All of us, when we are mature enough to put on armor, must choose a side for ourselves.

Many people don't realize that we are all servants, just as Jesus was when He was here on earth. In His earthly life, Jesus demonstrated that He was a servant of God. As a human, He had the power to choose just as we do. He came before God and submitted to His authority.

Luke 22:42 (Jesus praying just before His arrest and crucifixion)

"Father, if you are willing, please don't make me drink from this cup. (A symbol of suffering. Jesus used the idea of drinking from a cup to mean accepting the suffering he would face in the terrible

events that were soon to come.) But do what you want, not what I want."

We can choose to be servants of the one true God, or we can become servants of Satan. The Bible tells us, and we know from our own experiences, that our choices don't just have an effect on our own lives – they affect those around us as well. Not only that, our influence on others can live on long after our physical body dies. Be careful!

Hebrews 11:4b

God said he was pleased with what Abel offered. And so God called him a good man because he had faith. Abel died, but through his faith he is still speaking.

Deuteronomy 20:8b

'Is there any man here who has lost his courage and is afraid? He should go back home. Then he will not cause the other soldiers to lose their courage too.'

Accept that, in this life, we cannot escape those who do wrong and can harm us. What we can do is recognize it and keep ourselves away from it. Pray for discernment and wisdom.

1 Corinthians 5:10part

You would have to leave the world to get away from all the people who sin. . .

James 1:5

Do any of you need wisdom? Ask God for it. He is generous and enjoys giving to everyone. So he will give you wisdom.

Satan is in the business of demolition. He tears everything down in his misguided effort to build himself up. Don't be like he is. Try to be more like God. Our Creator is in the business of construction. He wants to build people up – to restore them to the elevated position He intended for them at Creation. Be aware of your words and actions and the effect or influence they have on others. Find nice things to say to everyone. Be a person who builds others up. Be a person who makes others feel positive or safe or happy or confident.

Galatians 6:2, 10a

Help each other with your troubles. When you do this, you are obeying the law of Christ. When we have the opportunity to do good to anyone, we should do it.

Jude 22-23

Help those who have doubts. Rescue those who are living in danger of hell's fire. There are others you should treat with mercy, but be very careful that their filthy lives don't rub off on you.

Speech is a special gift from God, and we should be careful when we use it. Words have power, and we can use them as tools to build others up or as weapons to tear others down. In the book of John, Jesus is called The Word. He is The Word of God come down to us from heaven in the form of a man. The words Jesus spoke are called the Words of Life. His Words can lift us up to God – His Words can give us eternal life.

John 1:1, 14a

In the beginning, before the earth was made, the Word was there. The Word was with God, and the Word was God. . .The Word became a man and lived among us.

Psalm 103:6

The LORD does what is fair. He brings justice to all who have been hurt by others.

Review: When trying to forgive someone, pray for God's help.
Ask Him to forgive the person who wronged you. Ask Him to help you forgive.
Know that God can restore everything that has been taken from you by the enemy.
Everything and more.
Healing takes time and sometimes distance.
Surround yourself with people (preferably other true believers) who can help you.
Put on the full armor of God and pray all the time.
Help others when you can.

How do I cope with the trauma of personal illness or the illness or loss of a loved one? If God cares about us, why does He let these things happen?

Specific, personalized treatment is outside the bounds of this book as well as this author's ability, but we've already discussed the most important points you should know and remember in your times of suffering. These are the things you can know for sure:

God never wants anything bad to happen to you.
Right now, we live in a world contaminated by Satan, so bad things will happen.
God can make everything even better than it was before the bad thing happened.
The restoration of your blessings may not happen in this earthly life.
Pain can bring you closer to God, if you allow it.

Concerning your impending death, your loss of a loved one, or your ability to help someone who has lost a loved one, know these things, too:

Death isn't the end – it's a portal to the next phase of life.
Being left behind is likely the worst thing that will ever happen to most of us.

The physical death of someone we deeply love is extremely painful. We often feel that their love flowed through us and powered our days – then s/he is gone, and we are left feeling empty. If the person who left us behind was a believer, we can be certain that the love they had for us did not die, because love never dies. Love is demonstrated through the physical body, but it comes from the will of the soul. Our loved one's soul may have moved through the portal of death to the spiritual world, but it did not die. Their love for us is still there. Trust in God, and you will meet again one day.

1 Corinthians 13:8a

Love will never end.

Psalm 55:22 (This is a long-term promise - it doesn't mean you won't have trouble in this physical life)

Give your worries to the LORD, and he will care for you. He will never let those who are good be defeated.

Matthew 5:4 (Jesus speaking in His Sermon on the Mount - the whole sermon is Matthew Chapters 5-7)

"Great blessings belong to those who are sad now. God will comfort them."

Revelation 21:4a

"He will wipe away every tear from their eyes. There will be no more death, sadness, crying, or pain."

Understand and respect the fact that grieving takes time. It comes in many forms, and everyone grieves differently. Try not to judge others who grieve differently from you. Pray. Ask God to help you work through the healing process. Tell Him you trust Him to make everything right.

When you try to help someone who is grieving the loss of a dearly beloved one, resist the urge to offer unsolicited advice. Try not to say, "S/he is in a better place now." According to a theory developed by psychiatrist Elisabeth Kübler-Ross, there are five stages of grief: Denial, Anger, Bargaining, Depression, and Acceptance. Obviously, each situation is unique, and different people have different experiences – remember the three stages of feelings expressed in Psalm 22 – the psalm Jesus recited a portion of as He suffered on the cross. For some people, stages last longer, stages overlap, different stages are included, and/or stages are skipped. You likely don't know for sure which stage a mourner is in, so be respectful. When someone is in any of the beginning or middle stages of the grieving process, these are not the words they want to hear. These words, while they may be true, are only for mourners who are in the Acceptance stage, which is the very LAST stage.

No words are necessary, just your presence and a warm, comforting hug are more than enough. If you must say something, here are some appropriate things to say:

I love you.
I'm so sorry.
I'm here if you need me.

Only say these things if you are sincere. If you are sincere, you will be there.

Trauma is real. Your feelings are real. Give yourself space to acknowledge your trauma, so you can begin the healing process. Get help from a professional therapist, if you need it. Surround yourself with people who help you move forward.

Review: Be kind to those who are suffering, whether it is you or someone else. Set small goals or help others with small goals. Pray for help for yourself (them). God is sad that you (they) are hurting, and He can make everything better. Surround yourself with people who can help you heal. Be a helper to those who suffer.

Why do believers go to church?

God was not satisfied with His Creation of the world and the first man, Adam, because Adam was alone. Only after God made his wife, Eve, did He declare that everything was "very good." Why does this matter? Because God wasn't satisfied until His people were living in community.

Genesis 2:18

Then the LORD God said, "I see that it is not good for the man to be alone. I will make the companion he needs, one just right for him."

Genesis 1:31

God looked at everything he had made. And he saw that everything was very good. There was evening, and then there was morning. This was the sixth day.

Ecclesiastes 4:9-12

Two people are better than one. When two people work together, they get more work done. If one person falls, the other person can reach out to help. But those who are alone when they fall have no one to help them. If two people sleep together, they will be warm. But a person sleeping alone will not be warm. An enemy might be able to defeat one person, but two people can stand back-to-back to defend each other. And three people are even stronger. They are like a rope that has three parts wrapped together – it is very hard to break.

After Jesus ascended to heaven, His believers worshipped God together, cared for each other, ate together, and lived together. This community was important. Living in a community of believers, your faith can grow stronger because you are bound to others who are faithful. Logic will tell you this. Is it easier to fight off an enemy by yourself or with other good soldiers helping you? Are you more at risk of being tempted by Satan when you are alone or when you are with a group of faithful believers? Why did Satan wait until Eve was alone before he tempted her? There is strength in numbers.

1 John 3:16

This is how we know what real love is: Jesus gave his life for us. So we should give our lives for each other as brothers and sisters.

We are instructed to share the gifts we have been given with others, that we might all benefit together. An example of this that is mentioned in the Bible is the body. Christ is the head and, together, all believers are the body. Each of us is a member of the body of Christ. Our Christian faith is a living faith, and each part of the body gets exercise and grows in strength when given the opportunity to serve, to practice patience, to love, to help, to teach, and to fellowship. We cannot do these things when we are alone.

Colossians 1:18 (about Jesus)

He is the head of the body, which is the church. He is the beginning of everything else. And he is the first among all who will be raised from death. So in everything he is most important.

1 Corinthians 12:27

All of you together are the body of Christ. Each one of you is a part of that body.

Ephesians 4:16b

All the parts of the body are joined and held together, with each part doing its own work. This causes the whole body to grow and to be stronger in love.

1 Corinthians 12:26

If one part of the body suffers, then all the other parts suffer with it. Or if one part is honored, then all the other parts share its honor.

Find your gift – no one is gift-less – and give it your all. Your efforts will be an inspiration to others to do the same. This builds a strong community – it builds strong families. In a community of believers, one person might be gifted at teaching, while another might be gifted with mechanical skills. Someone may have good accounting skills, while another is a great cook. One might be a talented speaker, while others are compassionate listeners. Some are good leaders, and others are willing workers. When these people have a relationship together, and they respect and value each other's gifts, they are able to successfully run a community – for example, a homeless outreach group, a church and its building, a Bible literacy program, and so on. Working together is safer for our faith, and it can help us reach more people who are outside of our community.

1 Corinthians 12:7

Something from the Spirit can be seen in each person. The Spirit gives this to each one to help others.

Ephesians 4:7a, 12

Christ gave each one of us a special gift. . .Christ gave these gifts to prepare God's holy people for the work of serving, to make the body of Christ stronger.

1 Peter 4:10

God has shown you his grace in many different ways. So be good servants and use whatever gift he has given you in a way that will best serve each other.

Romans 12:7-8

Whoever has the gift of serving should serve. Whoever has the gift of teaching should teach. Whoever has the gift of comforting others should do that. Whoever has the gift of giving to help others should give generously. Whoever has the gift of leading should work hard at it. Whoever has the gift of showing kindness to others should do it gladly.

Our purpose is to love one another and to help one another grow closer to God. The New Testament uses the Greek word, **allélón**, meaning "one another," 100 times. When we do something for another believer, we are really doing something for God because His

Spirit is living in that person. When we do something for someone who is not a believer, we are doing something for a lost child of God. Loving or caring for one of His lost children is also doing something for the child's Father. . .any good parent would tell you that is true.

Hebrews 10:24-25a
We should think about each other to see how we can encourage each other to show love and do good works. We must not quit meeting together. . .

1 Thessalonians 5:11a
So encourage each other and help each other grow stronger in faith. . .

We are more than His servants if we do His will. Jesus said we are His friends.

John 15:14-15
You are my friends if you do what I tell you to do. I no longer call you servants, because servants don't know what their master is doing. But now I call you friends, because I have told you everything that my Father told me.

Review: God designed us to live together with other believers.
Our faith lives and grows through contact with others.
Using our gifts to help others is a way to worship Him.
Find your gift and actively pursue the development of it
for the benefit of others.

What is worship?

God invented gift-giving, and we worship God when we are thankful to Him for his many, many gifts (blessings) to us and when we use our gifts to help others. Worship can be formal, such as in a service at a church building, or informal moments scattered throughout the day. We can worship Him by praying and singing alone or with others, by teaching others about God, by sharing a meal (breaking bread) with others, by encouraging someone, by taking part in Communion, by serving others in a physical way, and by going through the day He has given us in a way that is pleasing to Him. When you are thankful for your many blessings, you naturally want others to share in your happiness. Spreading God's love is worship – it is why He created us.

Psalm 68:3b-4a

Let them gather before God and enjoy themselves together. Sing to God! Sing praises to his name!

1 Chronicles 16:23

Let the whole world sing to the LORD! Tell the good news every day about how he saves us.

Psalm 105:1-5a

Give thanks to the LORD and call out to him! Tell the nations what he has done! Sing to him; sing praises to him. Tell about the amazing things he has done. Be proud of his holy name. You followers of the LORD, be happy! Depend on the LORD for strength. Always go to him for help. Remember the amazing things he has done.

Hebrews 13:16

And don't forget to do good and to share what you have with others, because sacrifices like these are very pleasing to God.

James 1:27

The worship that God wants is this: caring for orphans or widows who need help and keeping yourself free from the world's evil influence. This is the kind of worship that God accepts as pure and good.

Romans 12:1

So I beg you, brothers and sisters, because of the great mercy God has shown us, offer your lives as a living sacrifice to him – an offering that is only for God and pleasing to him. Considering what he has done, it is only right that you should worship him in this way.

Revelation 4:11

"Our Lord and God! You are worthy to receive glory and honor and power. You made all things. Everything existed and was made because you wanted it."

Psalm 100:2

Be happy as you serve the LORD! Come before him with happy songs!

Colossians 3:17

Everything you say and everything you do should be done for Jesus your Lord. And in all you do, give thanks to God the Father through Jesus.

Assemblies don't have to take place in an officially recognized church building to be valid. Wherever you choose to gather with other believers is acceptable to God, whether it's in someone's home or at a park or somewhere else that suits the group's needs. Remember, the church is the people, not the building. Notice where the early church was meeting:

Philemon 1:1-2

Greetings from Paul, a prisoner for Jesus Christ, and from Timothy, our brother [in Christ]. To Philemon, our dear friend and worker with us. Also to our sister Apphia, to Archippus, who serves with us in the Lord's army, and to the church that meets in your home.

Acts 20:20 (Paul speaking)

I always did what was best for you. I told you the Good News about Jesus in public before the people and also taught in your homes.

Acts 5:42 (This book is more formally called, "The Acts of the Apostles")

The apostles did not stop teaching the people. They continued to tell the Good News – that Jesus is the Messiah. They did this every day in the Temple area and in people's homes.

The Bible calls Jesus the Living Water, and He calls His believers the salt of the earth.
We can use our talents (salt) to make others thirsty for His Living Water.
This is worship.

Matthew 5:13a
"You are the salt of the earth."

John 7:37-39a (Jesus announced this on the last day of the Feast of Tabernacles, the seventh feast)
The last day of the festival came. It was the most important day. On that day Jesus stood up and said loudly, "Whoever is thirsty may come to me and drink. If anyone believes in me, rivers of living water will flow out from their heart. That is what the Scriptures say." Jesus was talking about the Spirit.

John 4:14
"But anyone who drinks the water I give will never be thirsty again. The water I give people will be like a spring flowing inside them. It will bring them eternal life."

Review: We can worship God throughout each day by salting the earth. We can do that by praying, giving, studying, singing, helping, teaching, and much more. Worship God by making others thirsty for His Living Water.

Why do Christians worship on Sunday mornings and Jews worship on Saturday?

God finished Creation in six days. On the seventh day, He rested from all His work. In the Old Testament, He instructed His people to work for six days and then rest from their work on the seventh day, which is Saturday. They were to keep the seventh day as a Holy Day for the Lord – a Sabbath. Jewish people who are still waiting for the Messiah (as well as some Jews who believe Jesus is the Messiah) continue to observe the Sabbath on Saturday.

Genesis 2:3
God blessed the seventh day and made it a holy day. He made it special because on that day he rested from all the work he did while creating the world.

Leviticus 23:3

"Work for six days, but the seventh day, the Sabbath, will be a special day of rest, a holy meeting. You must not do any work. It is a day of rest to honor the LORD in all your homes."

Christians today celebrate the Sabbath on Sunday because it's the day of the week when Jesus rose from the dead (Feast of First Fruits), it's the day of the week when the Holy Spirit first came to His disciples (Feast of Pentecost), and it's one day of the week that the Bible mentions the first Christians were meeting together and taking up donations. Additionally, during the week of Creation, Day One (Sunday) was the day of the week that God created light, and Jesus is referred to as the Light of the world.

Let's examine these Christian justifications for Sunday Sabbaths more closely.

The Feast of First Fruits is always on a Sunday, the first Sunday after Passover. The original Hebrew text says that the offering of grain is to be made "the morning after the Sabbath."

Leviticus 23:11

The priest will lift the sheaf to show it was offered before the LORD. Then you will be accepted. The priest will present the sheaf on Sunday morning [Hebrew: mimmahorat ha-shabbat] (Literally, "the morning after the Sabbath").

The Feast of First Fruits is always observed on the morning after the weekly Sabbath – it is always observed on Sunday morning. The Feast of First Fruits is not a special Sabbath. Although this feast is used as support for Christian Sunday Sabbaths because it is the date of Jesus' resurrection, the Feast of First Fruits does not necessarily coincide with the date chosen by Christian leaders for Easter. One cannot use this feast as support for weekly Sunday Sabbaths while minimizing its importance as the annual date of His Resurrection. Doing so is hypocritical.

The Feast of Pentecost is always on a Sunday, as well, since it is determined by counting to the day after a week of weeks from the Feast of First Fruits, but God said that Pentecost was a special Sabbath.

Leviticus 23:16, 21

On the Sunday following the seventh week (that is, 50 days later), you will bring a new grain offering to the LORD. On that same day you will call a holy meeting. You must not do any work. This law continues forever in all your homes.

The Jewish people would celebrate the weekly Sabbath on Saturday and the special Sabbath of Pentecost on Sunday. God explained when He gave the Israelites the feasts that any extra Sabbaths the feasts included were to be celebrated in addition to the weekly Sabbath.

Leviticus 23:38

You will celebrate these festivals in addition to remembering the LORD's Sabbath days.

On the weekend of Pentecost, both Saturday and Sunday are Sabbath days. It was the Sunday of Pentecost that Peter and the other apostles preached in the streets to the crowds in Jerusalem.

The example set for us by the early Christians who met together on "the first day of the week" is the most frequently used verse for justification of Sunday Sabbaths.

Acts 20:7-8 (In a page or two, we will examine the translation of "first day of the week")

On Sunday (Literally, "first day of the week,") [which began after nightfall on Saturday] we all met together to eat the Lord's Supper (Literally, "to break bread"). Paul talked to the group. Because he was planning to leave the next day, he continued talking until midnight. We were all together in a room upstairs, and there were many lights in the room.

This indicates that the followers had gathered AFTER the weekly Saturday Sabbath was over – that is, they gathered after nightfall on Saturday (notice all the lights in the room – it was dark outside) to have a meal together (the original Greek says, **klasai arton**, to break bread, and the word for bread here means sustaining food, not unleavened bread, as we learned in our discussion of the Last Supper) and to visit with Paul before he left town. Paul and his companions were travelling around teaching the Good News of

Jesus to groups who were interested in learning, and then making follow-up visits to reinforce the new believers. He was establishing groups of believers (churches) in different areas around the Aegean and Mediterranean Seas. He had been in that town, Troas, for seven days.

Paul talked so late into the night, that one of the people present fell asleep and interrupted Paul's teaching.

Acts 20:9-10

There was a young man named Eutychus sitting in the window. Paul continued talking, and Eutychus became very, very sleepy. Finally, he went to sleep and fell out of the window. He fell to the ground from the third floor. When the people went down and lifted him up, he was dead. Paul went down to where Eutychus was, knelt down beside him, and put his arms around him. He said to the other believers, "Don't worry. He is alive now."

Paul then returned to his teaching.

Acts 20:11-12

Then Paul went upstairs again, broke off some pieces of bread and ate [this occurred after midnight]. He spoke to them a long time. It was early morning when he finished, and then he left. The Lord's followers took Eutychus home alive, and they were all greatly comforted.

Notice, the Bible does not record that he broke the bread, blessed it, and passed it around to the others – it does not say that they reenacted the Last Supper. Also notice that he talked all night and left for a new destination early Sunday morning.

Acts 20:13

We [his fellow travelers] went on ahead of Paul and sailed for the city of Assos, planning to meet him there. This is what he told us to do because he wanted to go by land.

The trip from Troas to Assos on foot was about 20 miles. A person walks at an average rate of about 3 miles per hour, so this was a whole day's journey. Paul clearly made this trip on a Sunday – not something a devout Jewish man in that era would have done on a God-ordained Sabbath day, a holy day, a day of rest. The Jews only approved of very short trips on Sabbath days. They called the approved distance, which was approximately two-thirds of a mile outside of a city gate, a Sabbath Day's Journey. This specific restriction on travel is not in the Bible, but Jews of Paul's day observed many extra teachings instituted by Jewish religious leaders.

As we get to the deeper into the examination of Acts 20:7, let's also look at one more verse about the taking up of a collection that is used to support the Christian Sabbath. We'll put both of the verses here to make it easier:

Acts 20:7a

On Sunday (Literally, "first day of the week,") [which began after nightfall on Saturday] we all met together to eat the Lord's Supper (Literally, "to break bread").

1 Corinthians 16:1-2

Now, about the collection of money for God's people: Do the same as I told the Galatian churches to do. On the first day of every week, each of you should take some of your money and put it in a special place.

In Greek, the phrase "first day of the week" in Acts 20:7 is **mia tōn sabbatōn**, and the "first day of every week" in 1 Corinthians 16:2 is **kata mian sabbatōn**. Translated literally, these two phrases mean "one of the Sabbaths" and "every one of the Sabbaths."

While the English "one" and "first" are similar, "one" expresses an amount and "first" expresses an order. The Greek word for "first" is **prótos**, as we learned in our discussion of the Last Supper. **Prótos** can mean before, first, at the beginning, and in the past – the word "first" doesn't appear in the original phrases. The Greek word for "day," **hémera**, also does not appear in the original phrases. **Sabbatōn** is taken from the Hebrew for Sabbath – the word "week" doesn't appear in the original phrases. The Greeks use the word **ebdomas** when they want to indicate a week. What does all of this mean?

The words "first, day, and week" do not appear in the original Greek verses.

Because of translation situations such as this and others we have discussed, it is important to use multiple sources and pray that God will show you His Truth. We have access to more information now than we ever have before to help us understand. We should always seek the truth, so let's use our resources to reveal His true meaning.

There is a Jewish custom of ushering a holy day in and ushering a holy day out. We have said that the Jews count a day from nightfall to nightfall. Some say the change occurs when the first three stars appear in the night sky, but this custom varies because God did not specify when the exact change occurs in the Bible. A holy day is a day kept to honor God. In a typical Jewish home, preparatory guest accomodations would be made, such as lighting extra candles and preparing a special meal. At the end of the Sabbath, this special meal, called **Melaveh Malkah** (a phrase meaning "escorting the Queen"), and other festivities would usher out the holy day. The Jews treated the Sabbath observance and the traditions it included with respect.

Exodus 20:10a

But the seventh day is a day of rest in honor of the LORD your God.

Exodus 20:11b

An on the seventh day, he rested. In this way the LORD blessed the Sabbath – the day of rest. He made that a very special day.

Isaiah 58:13b

You should call the Sabbath a happy day. You should honor the LORD's special day by not saying and doing things that you do every other day of the week.

The end of the Sabbath, called **Motza'ei Shabbat**, marks the time when normal week-day activities, like handling money, could resume. (The five-day work week is a phenomenon of the 20th century, so the other six days were all alike in Paul's day.) The Jews of Paul's day were accustomed to regularly putting money in the collection box, which was available all the time at the Temple and/or synagogue, but Jews did not typically handle money on the Sabbath. In light of this, Paul is saying that after the Sabbath has ended each week, and normal weekday activities are no longer prohibited, each person should set aside an amount s/he is happy to give. While Paul teaches that it is no longer necessary to be a slave to the Law, he was a Jew, and he showed respect to both Jews and Gentiles in order to grow God's kingdom.

1 Corinthians 9:19-23 (Paul explaining himself)
I am free. I belong to no other person, but I make myself a slave to everyone. I do this to help save as many people as I can. To the Jews I became like a Jew so that I could help save Jews. I myself am not ruled by the law, but to those who are ruled by the law I became like someone who is ruled by the law. I did this to help save those who are ruled by the law. To those who are without the law I became like someone who is without the law. I did this to help save those who are without the law. (But really, I am not without God's law – I am ruled by the law of Christ.) To those who are weak, I became weak so that I could help save them. I have become all things to all people. I did this so that I could save people in any way possible. I do all this to make the Good News known. I do it so that I can share in the blessings of the Good News.

Interestingly, the Complete Jewish Bible translates the phrases **mia tōn sabbatōn** and **kata mian sabbatōn** as follows:

Acts 20:7 (from the Complete Jewish Bible)
*On **Motza'ei Shabbat** [the going out of the Sabbath], when we were gathered to break bread, Sha'ul [Paul] addressed them.*

1 Corinthians 16:2 (from the Complete Jewish Bible)
*Every week, on **Motza'ei Shabbat** [the going out of the Sabbath], each of you should set some money aside, according to his resources, and save it up; so that when I come I won't have to do fundraising.*

Put in perspective, neither of these verses can be used to justify a Sunday Sabbath. Paul is sharing one last meal with other believers before he leaves town in the Acts verse – perhaps they were having the special meal, **Melaveh Malkah**, since it was Saturday evening. The verse, correctly translated, says, "On one of the Sabbaths, we all met together to have a meal." The verse mentions many candles in the room, which is a typical preparation for such a meal. In the Corinthians verse, Paul is advocating that we individually set money aside for God's use at the end of every week after the Sabbath is complete.

Lastly, Jesus calls Himself the Light of the world, and God did command light to shine on the earth on Day One of the week of Creation – but the light God made on Day One was not Jesus. Jesus is as eternal as God and the Holy Spirit – they are all one. Everything God made was made through Jesus. Jesus is the Word God spoke at Creation as His Spirit hovered over the earth.

John 1:1-4

In the beginning, before the earth was made, the Word was there. The Word was with God, and the Word was God. He was there with God in the beginning. Everything was made through him, and nothing was made without him. In him there was life, and that life was light for the people of the world.

The light on Day One was the illumination of God, and it distinguished day from night on earth.

Genesis 1:3-5

Then God said, "Let there be light!" And light began to shine. He saw the light, and he knew that it was good. Then he separated the light from the darkness. God named the light "day," and he named the darkness "night." There was evening, and then there was morning. This was the first day.

John 8:12

Later, Jesus talked to the people again. He said, "I am the light of the world. Whoever follows me will never live in darkness. They will have the light that gives life."

John 9:5

"While I am in the world, I am the light of the world."

We know from multiple examples in the Bible that the glory of God is bright. When Moses came down from the mountain on which God had spoken to him, his face shone from his exposure to God.

Exodus 34:29b-30a

Because he had talked with the Lord, his face was shining, but he did not know it. Aaron and all the people of Israel saw that Moses' face was shining bright.

When Jesus called Paul to be an apostle, He spoke to him from a light that was so bright, Paul was blinded for three days.

Acts 9:3

So Saul [Paul] went to Damascus. When he came near the city, a very bright light from heaven suddenly shined around him.

When we are living on the new earth, we will have no more need of the sun.

Revelation 21:23 *(John describing the revelation he received about the completion of God's plan)*

The city [the New Jerusalem] did not need the sun or the moon to shine on it. The glory of God gave the city light. The Lamb was the city's lamp.

Just as God gave each of us a portion of His talents, He also gave the sun its light.

So, let's review what we've learned about these verses used to support Sunday Sabbaths:

- Jesus arose before dawn following the weekly Saturday Sabbath, after having remained in His grave (at rest) for the special Sabbath on Friday (the first day of the Feast of Unleavened Bread) and the weekly Saturday Sabbath. He rose from the dead on a Sunday, which was the Feast of First Fruits but was not a special Sabbath. Remember, the women who came to work on His body had waited until the Sabbaths were over to come prepare His body for burial.

- Peter preached to the crowd at 9 o'clock in the morning on Pentecost (a Sunday that was a special Sabbath) after he received the Holy Spirit, and he and the other apostles oversaw the baptism of at least 3,000 people on that same day. This is probably the best argument for holding formal services and baptisms on Sundays, but we know about other examples given of teaching and baptism that do not necessarily take place on Sundays.

Acts 5:42

> ***The apostles did not stop teaching the people. They continued to tell the Good News - that Jesus is the Messiah. They did this every day in the Temple area and in people's homes.***

- When the early Christians met together at Troas, we know that Paul pulled an all-nighter teaching a crowd on Saturday night (for Jews, Sunday night) after the Sabbath was over. From our discussion on baptism, we know that Peter taught Cornelius and his friends and baptized them, but we do not know what day of the week that occurred. We know that Paul taught Lydia and her friends and baptized them on the weekly Sabbath (Saturday). We do not know what day of the week Paul and Silas taught and baptized the jailer and his associates, but we do know it was in the middle of the night.

- Paul instructed the believers to set aside what they could give at the end of the work week, after the Sabbath was over and before the new week began.

- Jesus was not made on Day One of Creation. The light on Day One was the glory of God.

We can draw a conclusion that Paul was something of a night owl, and we can understand that preaching/teaching and baptisms are Biblically approved on any day at any time, but we cannot definitively say from any of these verses that God moved the weekly Sabbath from Saturday to Sunday. As Jews, Paul and his companions continued to observe the Saturday Sabbath in order to convince more Jews of the truth of Jesus and treated Sunday like every other weekday, even while they were travelling around spreading the Good News that Jesus had come to save everyone.

Acts 13:14-15

They continued their trip from Perga and went to Antioch, a city near Pisidia. On the Sabbath day they went into the Jewish synagogue and sat down. The Law of Moses and the writings of the prophets were read. Then the leaders of the synagogue sent a message to Paul and Barnabas: "Brothers, if you have something to say that will help the people here, please speak."

Paul made good use of his opportunities to tell the Jewish people that the long-awaited Messiah had come. Not only people of Jewish heritage, but also other people who believed in God were in the synagogue for worship on the weekly Sabbath.

Acts 13:26-27a (Paul in Antioch)

"My brothers, sons in the family of Abraham, and you other people who also worship the true God, listen! The news about this salvation has been sent to us. The Jews living in Jerusalem and their leaders did not realize that Jesus was the Savior. The words the prophets wrote about him were read every Sabbath day, but they did not understand."

Acts 17:17 (Paul in Athens)

In the synagogue he talked with the Jews and with the Greeks who were worshipers of the true God. He also went to the public square every day and talked with everyone who came by.

Acts 17:2 (Paul in Thessalonica)

Paul went into the synagogue to see the Jews as he always did. The next three weeks, on each Sabbath day, he discussed the Scriptures with them.

Acts 18:4 (Paul in Corinth)

Every Sabbath day Paul went to the synagogue and talked with both Jews and Greeks, trying to persuade them to believe in Jesus.

Paul was using the gathering of the Jews on the Saturday Sabbath to try to help them understand that Jesus was part of God's plan, but he understood that all days are the same for spreading the Good News.

Romans 14:5

Some people might believe that one day is more important than another. And others might believe that every day is the same. Everyone should be sure about their beliefs in their own mind.

Paul warns against legalism, though.

Galatians 5:4-5a

If you try to be made right with God through the law, your life with Christ is finished – you have left God's grace. I say this because our hope of being right with God comes through faith.

One final verse used in defense of Sunday Sabbaths is found in the book of Revelation. When John recorded the vision of the future he received, he began describing it by saying:

Revelation 1:10

On the Lord's Day, the Spirit took control of me. I heard a loud voice behind me that sounded like a trumpet.

This phrase, "the Lord's Day," is only used once in the Bible, and there is no clear indication given regarding its meaning in terms of a particular day of the week. Certainly, if John found himself to be under the influence of the Spirit, and the Spirit proceeded to show and tell him what it would be like when Jesus returns (His return is referred to as the Day of the Lord in both Testaments – a similar, but different phrase), John might very well name the day of his vision the Lord's Day.

Nowhere in the Bible did God specifically tell us to change the Sabbath day. He set His feast days and Sabbath days in the beginning and gave them to the Israelites after they left Egypt. They were told to rest on the seventh day of the week and observe it as a holy day. Jesus told us that He would fulfill the Law (and we know He has fulfilled it spiritually), but the Law would not be obsolete until He returns (until He has fulfilled it physically).

Isaiah 66:22a, 23

The LORD says, "I will make a new world – new heavens and a new earth – that will last forever. . . Everyone will come to worship me on every worship day; they will come every Sabbath and every first day of the month [when the new moon has been sighted]. This is what I, the LORD, have said.

Isaiah 40:8

"Grass dies and flowers fall, but the word of our God lasts forever."

Psalms 119:89-90a

LORD, your word continues forever in heaven. You are loyal forever and ever.

Malachi 3:6

"I am the LORD, and I don't change."

In addition to all this Scriptural evidence that God did not change the Sabbath, we also have substantial historical evidence. In AD 274, on December 25th, the Roman emperor Aurelian dedicated a new temple to the Roman sun god, **Sol Invictus** (Latin: unconquered sun), and declared that worship of the Roman sun god was an offically recognized religion. In AD 321, the Roman emperor Constantine issued a mandate that Sundays would be set aside as a national day of rest to honor the Roman sun god. In AD 364, 30 Christian religious leaders met to make decisions about debated church issues. They decided at this meeting to forbid Satuday Sabbath celebrations and support a Sunday Sabbath for Christians.

Review: The apostles were using opportunities on all the days of the week to share the Good News of Jesus.
God never changed His Sabbath day – that was done by people.

Does this mean we should have our day of worship on Saturdays?

Paul preached to the Jews and other believers in the One True God on the Sabbaths while they were gathered in the synagogues for their weekly worship. He also met with other

Gentiles, but he did not instruct them that they should be attending the synagogues for worship. God gave us freedom through Jesus, but we are only free if we accept it. We should worship Him daily in the way we live our lives, and we should take time to rest and celebrate and enjoy His blessings.

Colossians 2:16-17, 18b-19a (The apostle Paul, a Jew, talking to the Gentile Christians)
So don't let anyone make rules for you about eating and drinking or about Jewish customs (festivals, New Moon celebrations, or Sabbath days). In the past these things were like a shadow that showed what was coming. But the new things that were coming are found in Christ. . .Don't listen to them when they say you are wrong because you don't do these things. It is so foolish for them to feel such pride, because it is all based on their own human ideas. They don't keep themselves under the control of the head. Christ is the head, and the whole body depends on him. Because of Christ all the parts of the body care for each other and help each other.

Paul tells the believers not to follow human-made rules and religious ideas.

Colossians 2:22b-23
They are only human commands and teachings. These rules may seem to be wise as part of a made-up religion in which people pretend to be humble and punish their bodies. But they don't help people stop doing the evil that the sinful self wants to do.

In his letter to the believers living in Galatia, Paul explained that there was no need for them to follow Jewish Law. He said that laws were for slaves, but we are free through the saving power of Jesus' blood.

Galatians 4:4-7
But when the right time came, God sent his Son, who was born from a woman and lived under the law. God did this so that he could buy the freedom of those who were under the law. God's purpose was to make us his children. Since you are now God's children, he has sent the Spirit of his Son into your hearts. The Spirit cries out, "Abba, Father." Now you are not slaves like before. You are God's children, and you will receive everything he promised his children.

Galatians 4:10

It worries me that you follow teachings about special days, months, seasons, and years. I fear that my work for you has been wasted.

Paul is frustrated because the Gentile Christians there are trying to follow Jewish rules as they try to understand how to worship God appropriately.

Galatians 3:2

Tell me this one thing: How did you receive the Spirit? Did you receive the Spirit by following the law? No, you received the Spirit because you heard the message about Jesus and believed it. You began your life in Christ with the Spirit. Now do you try to complete it by your own power? That is foolish.

Galatians 5:4 (Again, because this is important)

If you try to be made right with God through the law, your life with Christ is finished – you have left God's grace.

Jewish people are freed not only from sin, but also from the slavery of trying to fulfill all the rules of the Law when they believe that God sent Jesus to set them free. Christians are saved from the slavery of sinful lives when they believe that God sent Jesus to set them free. God promised this to Abraham many years before the Law and many years before Christ.

Galatians 3:9

Abraham believed this, and because he believed, he was blessed. All people who believe are blessed the same as Abraham was. But people who depend on following the law to make them right are under a curse.

The Law, including the Biblical rules about the Sabbath day, that God gave to Moses was made for the Israelites. Let's say that again: **The Law was the covenant between God and the Israelites**. The Law had many requirements, and God's people worshipped Him by performing the requirements of the Law. We know that since Jesus set us ALL free – Gentiles and Jews – we have a new covenant. We now worship God in spirit and in truth, we know that circumcision is in our hearts, and we know that if we are full of the Holy Spirit (if we allow the Spirit to lead us) then we will only do things that are pleasing to God. We are free – free to come in and enjoy looking forward to the promise of eternal life – a gift that is given freely by God, not a gift that we can earn by performing any rituals or practices or regular meetings.

Jesus is the Door, through which we have direct access to God. Accepting Jesus as the Way to eternal life in the presence of God allows the Holy Spirit to enter us and guide us in all that we do. Without Jesus, we cannot access God or the Holy Spirit. So, when someone says, "Jesus is all we need," we can understand that s/he means Jesus is the beginning, the entrance, the Door that leads to our salvation.

1 Timothy 2:5-6a

There is only one God, and there is only one way that people can reach God. That way is through Christ Jesus, who as a man gave himself to pay for everyone to be free.

Go out – physically, not spiritually – to tell those who are on the outside of the Door about Jesus. Spend your life helping others and leading as many people as you can to the Door. Worship together with others in a church building, a home, a prison, an orphanage, a nursing home, or wherever the Spirit leads you.

God allowed the Romans to destroy His Temple, the physical place where His believers came to worship Him, after Jesus had returned to heaven. There are no longer any requirements about coming to a special or appointed place at a specific time or on a specific day to worship Him. Our relationship with God is inside of us and love flows from us out to others and up to Him. His love flows back down to all of us. It's the shape of a cross – the cross that did away with the slavery of the Law and the slavery of sin. It all happened and it all works through the power of love.

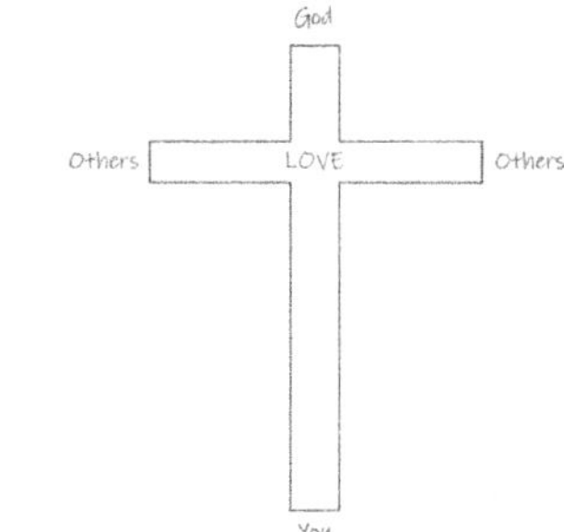

Through His work on the cross Jesus didn't change the Law – He took it from our outside (our bodies) to our inside (our souls).

Matthew 5:17

"Don't think that I have come to destroy the Law of Moses or the teaching of the prophets. I have come not to destroy their teachings but to give full meaning to them [to fulfill them]."

Matthew 5:18

"I assure you that nothing will disappear from the law until heaven and earth are gone. The law will not lose even the smallest letter or the smallest part of a letter until it has all been done."

Matthew 5:19part

"A person should obey every command in the law, even one that does not seem important. . . whoever obeys the law and teaches others to obey it will be great in God's kingdom."

These words of Jesus seem to contradict what we've been discussing, but we must look at the whole context. In the verse above, Jesus was speaking to His disciples about the teachings of some of the Jewish religious leaders who had taken it upon themselves to enforce or relax certain moral (as opposed to ceremonial) parts of the Law according to their own judgment. Jesus is telling His disciples to not only teach the whole truth, but also to live it. Jesus, the Word of God, came to perfect the Law – to take it to the inside. The disciples are to teach the truth of Jesus – to live as He lived, to love as He loved, to lead as He led.

Colossians 3:17a

Everything you say and everything you do should be done for Jesus your Lord.

The moral law of loving God and loving one another that Jesus gave when He was asked about the most important of the Ten Commandments is a summary of the written Law. This summary covers the entire letter of the Law and includes the requirement of sincerity – the circumcision of the heart.

The only ceremonial requirements clearly laid out for us by Jesus are baptism – which can be done in a river, pool, lake, mikveh, baptistry, and so on – and sharing in the Lord's Supper (Communion) – which can be done as a stand-alone ceremony, or as a part of any meal (any breaking of bread) you share with another or several (or many) others.

Matthew 18:20

Yes, if two or three people are together believing in me, I am there with them.

The number of people may have to do with witnessing – remember two witnesses had to see the new moon in order to declare the beginning of the new month. It is perhaps also a rebuttal to a Jewish tradition (a man-made requirement recorded in their extra writings) that there had to be 10 Jewish men present to publicly pray or hold a service.

Review: God does not limit our spreading of the Good News, our worship of Him, to crowds of a certain size or to a certain day(s) of the week.
We can show others the Way, individually or in a group of any number, on any or every day of the week.
He tells us to think about Him and live for Him all the time in everything we do.
Know the Truth, and the Truth will set you free.
Accept the Truth, and you are free indeed.

God wants everyone to be saved and to fully understand the truth.
1 Timothy 2:4

So if the Son makes you free, you are really free.
John 8:36

What should we be doing on a Sabbath?

We have read these directions about Sabbaths:

Genesis 1:31-2:1-3 (the first Sabbath day)

God looked at everything he had made. And he saw that everything was very good. There was evening, and then there was morning. This was the sixth day. So the earth, the sky, and everything in them were finished. God finished the work he was doing, so on the seventh day he rested from his work. God blessed the seventh day and made it a holy day. He made it special because on that day he rested from all the work he did while creating the world.

Exodus 12:16 (God talking about the special Sabbaths during the Feast of Unleavened Bread)

"There will be holy assemblies on the first day and the last day of the festival. You must not do any work on these days. The only work you can do is preparing the food for your meals."

The day of rest, relaxation, and enjoyment of all our work – the Sabbath – is a shadow of the rest, relaxation, and enjoyment we will have when we are fully restored and live our physical lives in the presence of God once again. Remember, God gives us earthly things to help us understand heavenly things.

Hebrews 4:9-10

This shows that the seventh-day rest (Literally, "Sabbath rest," meaning a sharing in the rest God began after he created the world) for God's people is still to come. God rested after he finished his work. So everyone who enters God's place of rest will also have rest from their own work just as God did.

Sabbath rest is a time to enjoy our accomplishments – all the things we have been able to do because God has given us the ability to do them. We should take the time to step back and appreciate all that God has blessed us with, to rest from our labors, and to enjoy fellowship with other believers.

The Jewish authorities (and later, some Christian groups) turned God's command to rest into a burdensome task. They had a long list of activities one could not participate in on a Sabbath (this is legalism). Jesus observed the Sabbath, but He did so in ways that the Jewish leaders did not approve. He was showing them that they had placed their own human commands above God's. He did good works – He healed people – on Sabbath days. He shared God's love with others on Sabbath days. He told the Jews that this day of rest was a gift from God.

Matthew 12:7a, 8 (Jesus explaining approved Sabbath day activities and His authority to do so)
"The Scriptures say, 'I don't want animal sacrifices; I want you to show kindness to people.' The Son of Man is Lord over the Sabbath day."

Mark 2:27
Then Jesus said to the Pharisees, "The Sabbath day was made to help people. People were not made to be ruled by the Sabbath."

The work Jesus did was extraordinary. He carried the burden of all our sins, completely healing all the wounds humans ever did or would create in our relationship with God. When His work was finished – if our calendar is correct – He rested for two Sabbaths (a special Sabbath and a weekly Sabbath) before He arose on the third day.

While we can still accurately follow the moon and lay out monthly calendars based on its phases, our day of the week calculations have become muddled. Over time, calendars have been altered and new calendars have been introduced, sometimes for scientific reasons and sometimes for political reasons. A lunar month is 29.5 days, so there must be a reckoning at some point to "correct" the annual solar calendar – remember, the Hebrew calendar has leap month corrections to keep Passover in the spring. Do not get too caught up in strictly adhering to a specific day for worship, because we have no absolutely certain method for determining exactly what day of the week today is. All the more reason to worship God every day, all the time.

Luke 4:16b-19 (from Isaiah 61:1-2, 58:6)
On the Sabbath day he [Jesus] went to the synagogue [a community building also used for worship] as he always did. He stood up to read. The book of Isaiah the prophet was given to him. He opened the book and found the place where this is written: "The Spirit of the Lord is on me. He has chosen

me to tell good news to the poor. He sent me to tell prisoners that they are free and to tell the blind that they can see again. He sent me to free those who have been treated badly and to announce that the time has come for the Lord to show his kindness."

Because of His work, we now worship God in spirit and in truth, and we can understand the spiritual side of the Sabbath command. The Sabbath is a time to reflect and enjoy, to be satisfied and at peace – not to be worried about breaking any Sabbath laws. The Sabbath is a blessing – not a burden.

Ecclesiastes 9:7-10a

So go and eat your food now and enjoy it. Drink your wine and be happy. It is all right with God if you do these things. Wear nice clothes and make yourself look good. Enjoy life with the wife you love. Enjoy every day of your short life. God has given you this short life on earth – and it is all you have. So enjoy the work you have to do in this life. Every time you find work to do, do it the best you can.

The Sabbath rest isn't about doing or not doing certain things on
a particular day of the week – it's about an attitude.
Work hard, help others, spread the Word, and enjoy your blessings.
Do it and mean it. Sincerely.

Review: Enjoy the good things in your life. Celebrate what
God has given you the ability to do. Look forward to the celebration
we will have when God completes His plan.
Share the Good News with others.

The Bible says only men can teach. Is that true?

In addition to not restricting teaching and worship to a specific day or time, not restricting our public prayer and worship to a certain minimum crowd number, and not restricting where that teaching, worship, or prayer can occur – remember God is consistent, and He has granted us freedom – He also does not limit who can do the teaching.

But wait. Aren't there verses explicitly stating that a woman cannot teach and should be quiet and obedient? Yes, and there is some confusion and serious division among believers because of those verses. In addition, many modern women are so offended by these verses, that it has become a stumbling block for them in the development of their faith. Because we should never allow an inaccurate interpretation to cause a division of God's people or a barrier to someone's faith, we need to examine these verses closely, make sure they are translated correctly, and determine exactly (or, as nearly as we are able) what the author intended. We must always strive to teach the whole truth, because anything less is false doctrine (teaching).

The apostle Paul is the author of all four verses in question. Two of them appear together in a letter he wrote to Timothy, who was guiding the church at Ephesus, and two of them appear together in a letter he wrote to the church at Corinth. Both of these churches were new groups in need of guidance. Let's look at the Timothy verses:

1 Timothy 2:11-12a

A woman should learn while listening quietly and being completely willing to obey. I don't allow a woman to teach a man or tell him what to do.

Without context (the rest of the story – more about Paul's letter, as well as the situation at the church he was writing to Timothy about), this verse makes it seem as though the Bible is teaching that women are less important than men – that women should be subservient to men. Before we analyze it, let's review what we already know about women in the Bible, and then look at a few other examples we haven't already discussed:

One of the very first teachings of the Bible is that both man and woman were created in God's image. Remember, His image consists of the three life forms: Jesus, God, and the Holy Spirit; therefore, each man and each woman consists of three life forms: the body, the soul, and the spirit. Additionally, He has given each man and each woman at least one talent – one gift from Him – that will help further His plan. We are each supposed to use our gift to help others find their own path to God and/or to strengthen others in their journeys. God has given each of us a task and the necessary skills to complete that task.

Genesis 1:27

So God created humans in his own image. He created them to be like himself. He created them male and female.

1 Peter 4:10-11

God has shown you his grace in so many different ways. So be good servants and use whatever gift he has given you in a way that will best serve each other. If your gift is speaking, your words should be like words from God. If your gift is serving, you should serve with the strength that God gives. Then it is God who will be praised in everything through Jesus Christ. Power and glory belong to him forever and ever. Amen.

The Old Testament records how God worked through women with widely different backgrounds to further His Plan. Rahab, a Gentile prostitute, helped the Israelites defeat her own people, and God honored her by including her in Jesus' family line.

Joshua 6:25

Joshua saved Rahab the prostitute, her family, and all those who were with her. Joshua let them live because Rahab helped the spies Joshua had sent out to Jericho. Rahab still lives among the Israelites today.

Joshua had the courage to complete the job God set before him, and he was rewarded for his faith.

Ruth was another Gentile woman God held up as an example for us. Her book tells her story. She, too, was included in Jesus' family line.

Matthew 1:5-6a (part of Jesus' genealogy)

Salmon was the father of Boaz. (His mother was Rahab.) Boaz was the father of Obed. (His mother was Ruth.) Obed was the father of Jesse. Jesse was the father of King David.

Deborah, an Old Testament prophetess, was married, but she was the Judge of Israel – not her husband – and she bravely and faithfully accompanied the army commander, at his request, when he led the Israelites into battle with their enemy.

Judges 4:4

There was a woman prophet named Deborah. She was the wife of a man named Lappidoth. She was judge of Israel at that time.

Judges 4:8 (Comm. Barak's response when Deborah told him God wanted him to raise an army and go fight an enemy)

Then Barak said to Deborah, "I will go and do this if you will go with me. But if you will not go with me, I will not go." "Of course I will go with you," Deborah answered. "But because of your attitude, you will not be honored when Sisera [the enemy commander] is defeated. The LORD will allow a woman to defeat Sisera."

A woman named Jael killed Sisera. The Israelites went on to defeat their king, but Barak's glory was taken from him, because he lacked the courage – the faith – to complete the task God put before him.

Esther, an orphaned young woman, had the courage to save the Jewish nation from slaughter at the risk of her own life and has a book in the Old Testament that is named for her and tells her story. She was rewarded for her bravery and faithfulness in completing the task God gave her.

Esther 4:14 (Esther's elder male cousin encouraging her to speak to the king and save the Jews)

"If you keep quiet now, help and freedom for the Jews will come from another place. But you and your father's family will all die. And who knows, maybe you have been chosen to be the queen for such a time as this."

Esther 8:1 (after she had saved her people)

That same day King Xerxes gave Queen Esther everything that belonged to Haman, the enemy of the Jews.

The book of Proverbs contains the teachings of a woman who was the mother of a king. Her words are in complete harmony with the teachings of Jesus, and her advice is good for us all:

Proverbs 31:1, 8-9

These are the wise sayings that King Lemuel's mother taught him: Speak up for people who cannot speak for themselves. Help people who are in trouble. Stand up for what you know is right, and judge all people fairly. Protect the rights of the poor and those who need help.

In the New Testament, Jesus spent His time on earth setting examples for us to follow. Jesus treated all the women He encountered with dignity. In every single instance recorded, whether the woman was an upstanding citizen or a shunned sinner, Jesus showed respect and consideration. He spoke to women freely in public, He esteemed them as friends, He taught them God's Word, and He used them as positive examples when teaching the right way to live.

Of the 12 men closest to Him, one completely betrayed Him, a number of them deserted Him during His trial and execution, and at least one doubted His Resurrection, but not one woman is recorded as betraying, deserting, or doubting Jesus. Faithful women were the first to be told about His Resurrection, they were the first to speak with Him after His Resurrection, and they were the first to be given the job of telling others about His Resurrection – an empowering and compelling choice by God, since a woman's testimony was not even legal in that day.

Matthew 28:1-2a, 5-7a

The day after the Sabbath day was the first day of the week. That day at dawn Mary Magdalene and the other woman named Mary went to look at the tomb. Suddenly an angel of the Lord came from the sky. . .The angel said to the women, "Don't be afraid. I know you are looking for Jesus, the one who was killed on the cross. But he is not here. He has risen from death, as he said he would. Come and see the place where his body was. And go quickly and tell his followers, 'Jesus has risen from death.'"

Jesus' approaching birth was first told to His mother, His first miracle was at His mother's request, and His last act as a man was to make sure she would be cared for after His death. Mary, evidently a widow by this time, travelled with Jesus as He taught, and she was among the group of faithful women watching as He suffered on the cross.

John 19:25-27

Jesus' mother stood near his cross. Her sister was also standing there with Mary the wife of Clopas, and Mary Magdalene. Jesus saw his mother. He also saw the follower he loved very much [John] standing there. He said to his mother, "Dear woman, here is your son." Then he said to the follower, "Here is your mother." So after that, this follower took Jesus' mother to live in his home.

Jesus treated women as individuals, each having their own value. He demonstrated the loving, respectful leadership a man should have for His family. He led an exemplary, God-pleasing life. He showed without a doubt that every single human being, regardless of sex, nationality, age, or health is one of God's children, and that He loves and values each one of us individually.

Galatians 3:28 (Jesus died for us all, and God's blessings are for us all - Paul wrote this)
Now, in Christ, it doesn't matter if you are a Jew or a Greek, a slave or free, male or female. You are all the same in Christ Jesus.

Romans 2:11 (God's judgment is also for us all - Paul wrote this, too)
God judges everyone the same. It doesn't matter who they are.

Remember, He judges each of us based on whether we followed His teachings and used the talents we've been given – not on what nation we come from, what our financial or social status is, or what sex we are.

Luke 8:1-3
The next day, Jesus traveled through some cities and small towns. Jesus told the people a message from God, The Good News about God's kingdom. The twelve apostles were with him. There were also some women with him. Jesus had healed these women of sicknesses and evil spirits. One of them was Mary, who was called Magdalene. Seven demons had come out of her. Also with these women were Joanna, the wife of Chuza (the manager of Herod's property), Susanna, and many other women. These women used their own money to help Jesus and his apostles.

Think about what these women were chosing to do with their time and money. Do you imagine these women stayed silent about what they had seen and heard firsthand?

At a time when Jesus was building the faith and understanding of His disciples, a Gentile woman came to Him asking for His help. He was slow to agree to help her, but today's reader can see how He might have been stalling purposefully so His disciples would hear her testimony, be ashamed of themselves (be convicted in their hearts), and grow stronger in their faith.

Matthew 15:21-28

> *Jesus went from there to the area of Tyre and Sidon. A Caananite woman from that area came out and began shouting, "Lord, Son of David, please help me! My daughter has a demon inside her, and she is suffering very much."*
>
> *But Jesus did not answer her. So the followers came to him and said, "Tell her to go away. She keeps crying out and will not leave us alone."*
>
> *Jesus answered, "God sent me only to the lost people of Israel."*
>
> *Then the woman came over to Jesus and bowed before him. She said, "Lord, help me!"*
>
> *He answered her with this saying: "It is not right to take the children's bread and give it to the dogs."*
>
> *The woman said, "Yes, Lord, but even the dogs eat the pieces of food that fall from their master's table."*
>
> *Then Jesus answered, "Woman, you have great faith! You will get what you asked for." And right then the woman's daughter was healed.*

Do you imagine this Caananite woman stayed silent about what Jesus had done for her? Do you think His Jewish disciples learned a little something about faith from this encounter with a Gentile woman?

We've discussed how the Jews looked down on the people of Samaria, the country between Galilee and Judea. At one point in His ministry, Jesus traveled to the town of Sychar in Samaria. When He arrived, He went alone to the town well and taught a woman who had an unfavorable reputation (she had been married five times and was living with a sixth man who was not her husband). She believed Jesus and hurried away to tell others about Him. Because of the testimony from this shunned Samaritan woman, people came to see Him.

John 4:42

The people [of Sychar] said to the woman, "First we believed in Jesus because of what you told us. But now we believe because we heard him ourselves. We know now that he really is the one who will save the world."

Summary: Women in the Bible are shown to be children of God who were given gifts by their Father to further His work.
He used women from all walks of life to teach others His truth,
to teach others by their example, to lead His army,
to intervene in government affairs, to financially support His Ministry,
and to show men how they should lead.

Now that we've reviewed the stories of some of the women in the Bible and how they were used to further the kingdom of God, let's return to what Paul was saying and see if we can understand it more clearly.

1 Timothy 2:11-12a

A [or, The] woman should learn while listening quietly [Greek: hésuchia] and being completely willing to obey. I don't allow a [or, the] woman to teach [Greek: didaskein] a man or tell him what to do [Greek: authentein].

We just read a verse above that Paul wrote saying we are all equal in Christ (Galatians 3:28), but in these verses, it seems he is saying that women aren't equal to men. What we need to know is context. Why is Paul saying this in his letter to Timothy?

There is no debate among scholars that Paul is instructing Timothy on how to lead a group of new Christians in the Greek city of Ephesus. Paul is addressing specific concerns of this particular church. We have several points to consider in determining the meaning and purpose of these two sentences.

First, notice that "woman" in these two verses (11-12) and in the remainder of this chapter is singular. In verses 9 and 10, Paul used the plural, "women" in giving general instructions to Christian women regarding how they should present themselves in public. This shift to the singular "woman" indicates that these two verses are directed at the behavior of a particular woman in the Ephesus church. Also notice that the word "man" is singular. This judgment may be referring to a particular situation between a man and a woman that was reported to Paul. Before we pursue this train of thought, let's analyze the other word choices in these two verses in closer detail.

In verse 12, in the original Greek, Paul writes that he does not permit a woman to **didaskein** or **authentein** a man. Scholars debate whether these two words are referring to different activities, or as is often the case with Paul, whether they are two words referencing the same activity. Paul was a well-educated man with extensive language skills (so we should assume he used these words purposefully), and it is reasonable to be of the opinion that Paul followed his usual habit of using two words to refer to the same activity. If so, he used a very common word for teach, **didaskein**, and then emphasized it with the word **authentein**. The word **authentein** is only used this one time in the Bible, so there are no other Scriptures to compare it to in order to confirm the correct meaning. In other Greek writings of that time, **authentein** has a connotation of violence – an idea of domination – of controlling someone against his/her will – even to the point of murder. Paul also used a conjunction between these two words, **oude**, that is typically used to join two negative thoughts under one meaning. In other words, the teaching is joined with the domination in a negative manner. If Paul is saying that a woman should not forcefully or violently exert authority over a man while teaching him, then this statement agrees perfectly with the teachings of Paul/Jesus/the Bible.

As is the case throughout the Bible, just because only one sex is referenced in a directive, doesn't mean that the other sex is exempt. The Ten Commandments are listed in Exodus, as cited earlier, and again in Deuteronomy 5:21. In both cases, in the original Hebrew, the tenth commandment states that a man shall not covet (desire) another man's wife. Now, most reasonable people would understand that this command also applies to the women – that they should not desire another woman's husband. And yet, many assume that Paul's teaching here applies only to women. Paul never advocates anyone domineering over anyone else – ever – not women over men or men over women.

One fact must be perfectly understood: Paul's teachings almost always concern HOW something is done, not WHAT is done.

Let's go back and examine verse 11 now. The truly controversial statement Paul makes in this sentence is not that the woman should be quiet, but that she should LEARN. Paul is advocating the education of a woman – not something that was widely practiced in his day. The admonition to learn quietly and obediently could be a reference to the woman's status as a beginner in understanding the Gospel and the Scriptures. That is, she knows so little of God's truth, it is best if she sits quietly and listens until she understands enough to make intelligent comments/decisions. While this is just a guess, we will see an example of this learning behavior when we discuss sisters Mary and Martha.

Evidence of Paul's meaning is very clear when we examine the vocabulary he chose. The Greek word **hésuchia** refers to the quiet peace a believer finds in God. If he wanted the woman to not talk, he would have indicated that by using the Greek word **siópaó**, meaning, to be silent. As we have seen, looking at the original word choices and their meanings is crucial when trying to understand the truth of the Bible. We should not exclusively depend on a translation to interpret, because important nuances can be lost in translation.

The word **hésuchia** is specifically describing how the woman should learn – in the peace of God as a believer in His ultimate authority in everything. Practicing this would obviously result in quietness and obedience – for anyone, female or male – which Paul confirms by instructing the men in the same way he did this woman. He says the men should be humble and completely willing to obey God in everything. They should, like the woman in these verses, conduct themselves quietly and peacefully – without strife and arguing, without being loud and contentious.

1 Timothy 2:8

I want the men everywhere to pray. Men who lift their hands in prayer must be devoted to God and pleasing to him. They must be men who keep themselves from getting angry and having arguments.

Obviously, God also wants women to pray, to be devoted to Him, and to avoid conflict with others. It is very easy to see that verse 11, while it is apparently directed at one woman, also applies to everyone.

The quietness Paul is seeking among the new Christians, both male and female, is peacefulness and humility, not silence. Again, Paul is emphasizing the MANNER in which something should be done. This is in complete agreement with the teachings of Jesus, whereas the silence and domination of women are not.

Reflecting on verses 9 and 10 again, in which Paul wrote about appropriate dress/hairstyles/jewelry for women (plural), we see that Paul was addressing a particular concern of the church at Ephesus. The problem evidently involved some of the women, but we know from our own experiences that this also applies to both sexes.

1 Timothy 2:9-10

And I want the women to make themselves attractive in the right way. Their clothes should be sensible and appropriate. They should not draw attention to themselves with fancy hairstyles or gold jewelry or pearls or expensive clothes. But they should make themselves attractive by the good things they do. That is more appropriate for women who say they are devoted to God.

Some men and women become overly preoccupied about appearances. When how you look (whether it's clothing or how others perceive you) becomes your most important concern, you have placed that concern above God. Anything you place above God is an idol – a false god – and Satan is the power behind every idol. If the Spirit is alive and working in you, you will be a beautiful person regardless of what you wear or how you fix your hair. You will be beautiful from the inside out, which is the only beauty that lasts.

While it is very clear that verses 9 and 10 are on a different topic from 11-15, some have interpreted verses 9-15 to mean that women should be plain, quiet, and in the background. When people promote this, they are taking Paul's statements out of context. Forcing a woman to be plain, quiet, and in the background, whether you are threatening her or simply convincing her that it's her Biblical duty, is decidely not treating her with love. It is dominating over her. The root of this behavior is pride. Remember the proud

nephilim of Noah's day who built themselves up and dominated over others?

Paul teaches that both men and women should present themselves to others with self-control and moderation of appearance and behavior – humility. No one should be sowing discord or disturbance among the believers – no one should be trying to start arguments – no one should be trying to put themselves first. Everything should be done peacefully.

Romans 12:9-11 (Paul's teaching to the church in Rome)
Your love must be real [sincere]. Hate what is evil. Do only what is good. Love each other in a way that makes you feel close like brothers and sisters. And give each other more honor than you give yourself. As you serve the Lord, work hard and don't be lazy. Be excited about serving him!

Now, let's look deeper at the idea that verses 11 and 12 are about a particular woman and man. Reading all of Chapter 2, you can see that verses 11-15 (the end of the chapter) are diffferent in tone from verses 1-10, but they may be a return to Paul's topic from Chapter 1 of warning about false teachers. In verses 11-15, he seems to be addressing a false teaching believed by a woman. In her misunderstanding, she is exerting a violent (harmful, maybe even murderous) type of authority over someone (in this case, a man – evidently her husband). The situation seems to be private, rather than something occuring in a church meeting.

1 Timothy 2:11-15
*A [or, The] woman should learn while listening quietly and being completely willing to obey. I don't allow a [or, the] woman to teach a man or tell him what to do [**authentein**: exert violent authority over him]. She must listen quietly because Adam was made first. Eve was made later. Also, Adam was not the one who was tricked. It was the woman who was tricked and became a sinner [present perfect tense is used here, (Literally, the woman, having been seduced), so it is referring to the woman who has believed the false teaching and is forcing it on her husband, rather than referring still to Eve]. But [she - singular in the original Greek, and referring to the misled woman] will be saved in [her] work of having children. They [The woman and her husband] will be saved if they continue to live in faith, love, and holiness with sensible behavior.*

Present perfect (continuous) verb tense is used to indicate something that began in the past but is still happening. The woman was misled by a false teaching, and she is continuing in that learned errant behavior.

There were a number of heresies (teachings that don't agree with Scripture – false doctrines) circulating in the time of the early church. We have already discussed legalism (keeping the Law or making new religious laws). There was also an early idea that Jesus was spiritual, but He couldn't possibly be physical. Jesus Himself may have been responding to this false teaching when He shared a meal of fish with His disciples after His resurrection (John Chapter 21) to prove His physical nature. Another teaching, which we will discuss with the next two controversial verses of Paul, is the idea that the freedom Jesus gives us means we can do whatever we like. The false teaching that Paul may have been responding to in the verses above is what we now call Gnosticism, whose believers subscribed to an idea of superior spiritualism. Some followers would try to gain this spiritual high by abstaining from certain foods or activities such as sex. Paul addresses this heresy very directly in his letter to the church at Corinth:

1 Corinthians 7:1-6

Now I will discuss the things you wrote me about. You asked if it is better for a man not to have any sexual relations at all. But sexual sin is a danger, so each man should enjoy his own wife, and each woman should enjoy her own husband. The husband should give his wife what she deserves as his wife. And the wife should give her husband what he deserves as her husband. The wife does not have power over her own body. Her husband has the power over her body. And the husband does not have power over his own body. His wife has the power over his body. Don't refuse to give your bodies to each other. But you might both agree to stay away from sex for awhile so that you can give your time to prayer. Then come together again so that Satan will not be able to tempt you in your weakness. I say this only to give you permission to be separated for a time. It is not a rule.

Paul had two very spiritual experiences that we know of: Jesus spoke to him in a blinding spiritual visitation (Acts 9), and he had a near-death spiritual experience (2 Corinthians 12). Those new Christians who were practicing Gnosticism and wanted to have these types of experiences for themselves believed they could prompt one by doing or not doing certain things. They knew Paul had never married, and perhaps some of them thought they should abstain from marital activities in order to be more like him in the hopes of having a spiritual experience like his. After all, Paul highly recommended his unmarried state:

1 Corinthians 7:7a (This comes at the end of the verses just above - Paul is referring to his celibacy)
I wish everyone could be like me.

1 Corinthians 7:8
Now for those who are not married and for the widows I say this: It is good for you to stay single like me.

However, what Paul is recommending is a life of celibacy – not a circumstance created by refusing relations with your spouse, but a deliberate choice to remain unmarried. Jesus tells us that the ability to sincerely and happily live a celibate life is a gift only given to some. Only those who have been given the gift can decide whether or not they will accept it as a way of life.

Matthew 19:11, 12b (Jesus' response when asked if it was better not to marry at all)
He answered, "This statement is true for some, but not for everyone – only for those who have been given this gift. . .This [gift] is for anyone who is able to accept it."

Paul tells them that although he recommends a celibate life, if a person is already married, s/he should remain married.

1 Corinthians 7:10, 11b, 17, 27a
Now, I have a command for those who are married. Actually, it is not from me; it is what the Lord commanded. A wife should not leave her husband. . .And a husband should not divorce his wife. . . But each one of you should continue to live the way the Lord God has given you to live - the way you were when God chose you. I tell people in all the churches to follow this rule. . .If you have a wife, don't try to get free from her.

If the woman in the Timothy verses was practicing Gnosticism (trying to gain a spiritual experience by withholding sex from her husband), and forcing it on her husband against his will, Paul might very well tell her she needs to learn more about God's truth and to do so humbly and with the peace of God. He might accuse her of violence against her husband, because she is placing a stumbling block in his path that may lead him to sin (sin, of course, leads to death, so this gives Paul a reason to use the particular word **authentein** with its murderous meaning). He might very well defend her husband's rights and say that she had been fooled into believing a false teaching. Paul might also encourage them in sensible behavior and in the saving grace of their marriage.

Summary: In the Timothy verses, Paul is likely addressing a particular situation between a woman and her husband, in which the woman has believed a false teaching and is putting not only her own spiritual life but also her husband's at risk. Paul forbids her behavior.
The core teaching of Paul in these verses applies to both men and women.

****

We will see more examples of Paul correcting false teachings as we examine the other pair of verses used to support the silence of women.

In the verses below, Paul is writing to the church at Corinth. Their assembly meetings were chaotic events. Again, Paul addresses the MANNER of their meeting when he learns (through their letter and through verbal reports) about the problems they are having. He advises that everything the believers do should be peaceful, loving, respectful, and for the benefit of all.

1 Corinthians 14:33
God is not a God of confusion but a God of peace. This is the rule for all the meetings of God's people.

His advice is consistent with his other teachings, consistent with Jesus' teachings, and consistent with the Bible. . .until you get to these two verses:

1 Corinthians 14:34-35

The women should keep quiet in these church meetings. They are not allowed to speak out but should be under authority, as the Law of Moses says. If there is something they want to know, they should ask their own husbands at home. It is shameful for a woman to speak up like that in the church meeting.

Many scholars for many years have expressed concern that these two verses are odd and out of sync with Paul's teachings. Some think perhaps they were inserted in the wrong place, while others contend the verses were added later by someone else. Still others believe the verses are where they are supposed to be but say Paul is quoting from the Corinthians' letter to him in which the men of the church state their opinion. Since we cannot prove either of the first two ideas, let's focus on the third to see if it's a valid argument.

The Corinthians had written to Paul about disagreements/problems the church was having, and Paul had received oral reports from others about the church. What were the problems?

The members were talking/singing/praying/prophesying over one another in assembly rather than taking turns. They were taking each other to civil court to solve differences. The assembly was divided (much like our modern church denominations). They were arguing about which types of meat they were allowed to eat (certain meats were forbidden by the Law). A man of the church had taken his father's wife for himself. At the Lord's Supper, some people were eating without waiting for others, some were eating large amounts of food, and some were unconcerned about the poor in attendance who didn't have enough food. And, of course, the subject of our discussion:

Married women were not respecting their husbands in the church meetings. They were removing their head coverings, which, in that time and culture, meant that they were setting aside all respect for their husbands. They were putting themselves forward as independent people who did not have an obligation to anyone else.

1 Corinthians 11:5a

But every woman who prays or prophesies should have her head covered. If her head is not covered, she brings shame to her head.

These Corinthian women had evidently seized on the teaching that in Christ we are all free. Perhaps they were sick and tired of the cultural female oppression – which has never been ordained by God for His people – imposed on them, but they were taking liberties in their appearance that communicated the wrong message of freedom. The freedom idea was an extreme form of anti-legalism some Gnostics were practicing that eventually became its own belief system. While Paul's responses to this false doctrine are specific to that time and place, his point is timeless and universal and unisex. If you are married, giving others the impression that you aren't married shows an extreme lack of respect for your spouse.

Disrespecting others is the opposite of the teachings of Paul/Jesus/the Bible.

When Paul addresses the various issues this church is facing in his response letter, he quotes the disagreement/problem from the Corinthian letter/verbal report:

1 Corinthians 6:1a
When one of you has something against someone else in your group, why do you go to the judges in the law courts?

1 Corinthians 6:12a
"I am allowed to do anything," you say.

1 Corinthians 7:1b
You asked if it is better for a man not to have any sexual relations at all.

1 Corinthians 8:1a
Now I will write about meat that is sacrificed to idols.

1 Corinthians 11:18-19

First, I hear that when you meet together as a church you are divided. And this is not hard to believe because of your idea that you must have separate groups to show who the real believers are!

1 Corinthians 11:20

When you all come together, it is not really the Lord's Supper you are eating.

1 Corinthians 12:1

Now, brothers and sisters, I want you to understand about spiritual gifts.

For each of their issues, Paul states the problem/disagreement the Corinthians are having, his disapproval of their judgment or lack of it, and his remedy for the situation. Here are verses showing parts of Paul's responses to the group in Corinth regarding some of these problems they reported:

1 Corinthians 6:1b

The way they [unbelievers] think and live is wrong. So why do you let them decide who is right? Why don't you let God's holy people decide who is right?

1 Corinthians 6:12b

My answer to this is that not all things are good. Even if it is true that "I am allowed to do anything," I will not let anything control me like a slave.

1 Corinthians 7:7a

I wish everyone could be like me [and happily live a celibate life].

1 Corinthians 8:4

So this is what I say about eating meat: We know that an idol is really nothing in the world, and we know that there is only one God.

1 Corinthians 1:13a (Some were claiming to follow Peter, Paul, or Apollos, implying their beliefs were superior to others)

Christ cannot be divided into different groups.

1 Corinthians 11:22

You can eat and drink in your own homes. It seems that you think God's church is not important. You embarrass those who are poor. What can I say? Should I praise you? No, I cannot praise you for this.

1 Corinthians 12:5-6 (about spiritual gifts)

There are different ways to serve, but we serve the same Lord. And there are different ways that God works in people, but it is the same God who works in all of us to do everything.

The root of their problems is the same root of all sins: pride.

1 Corinthians 3:3

You are still not following the Spirit. You are jealous of each other, and you are always arguing with each other. This shows that you are still following your own selfish desires. You are acting like ordinary people of the world.

1Corinthians 4:18a, 19b

Some of you are acting so proud. . .I will see if these proud talkers have the power to do anything more than talk.

1 Corinthians 5:1b-2a

People say that a man there has his father's wife. And still you are proud of yourselves!

1 Corinthians 5:6a

Your proud talk is not good.

The people of the church are not showing deference for one another – they are not humble. Paul is speaking against those who are acting in an arrogant and disorderly manner. He tells them that love for God and love for others can remove pride.

1 Corinthians 8:1b-3 (The Corinthian letter writers boasted about the gifts of the Spirit they have been given)

It is certainly true that "we all have knowledge," as you say. But this knowledge only fills people with pride. It is love that helps the church grow stronger. Those who think they know something do not yet know anything as they should. But whoever loves God is known by God.

We should never be proud of the gifts we have been given – we should humbly and lovingly share God's gifts with others.

The Corinthian church's pride problem was so serious that Paul told them:

1 Corinthians 11:17b

Your meetings hurt you more than they help you.

The Corinthian problem Paul quotes in verses 34-35 regarding the silence of women had its roots in prideful, male, Jewish thinking. As discussed earlier, some Jewish believers thought it was important to keep following the Law of Moses as well as their oral traditions (which some wrongly believed were equal to the written Law), even though Jesus had freed them from the Law and the oral tradition was not given by God.

We have seen how Jesus corrected the errant beliefs of the Jews on other occasions. Remember, He told them their idea about how many people must be present to teach or pray publically was wrong.

Matthew 18:20

"Yes, if two or three people are together believeing in me, I am there with them"

He told them their strict rules about approved activities on the Sabbath were incorrect.

Mark 2:27-28

Then Jesus said to the Pharisees, "The Sabbath day was made to help people. People were not made to be ruled by the Sabbath. So the Son of Man is Lord of every day, even the Sabbath."

Jesus also condemned the Jewish authorities for taking the best seats at feasts for themselves, for not caring properly for aging parents and widows (and giving approval to others to do the same), and for reciting long, loud prayers to make themselves look godly. Jesus gave them a scorching condemnation for misinterpreting and misapplying the Law in Matthew, Chapter 23:1-36. These hypocrites, as Jesus called them, wanted the people to honor them with titles showing their authority over others. Jesus' response was very clear:

Matthew 23:8-10 (Note Jesus' comment on equality among His children, regardless of sex)
"But you must not be called 'Teacher.' ***You are all equal as brothers and sisters.*** *You have only one Teacher. And don't call anyone on earth 'Father.' You have one Father. He is in heaven. And you should not be called 'Master.' You have only one Master, the Messiah."*

Let's review the purpose of the Law. In the Law, God set out rules and requirements that defined sin – it showed how people could be sinful. The Law set up the formal sacrifice system designed to teach the people that they could do nothing to remove all their sin without God's help. The Law trapped them in a circle of sin: the people sinned, and the people made offerings, but the offering was never enough. Sacrifices had to be made again and again, because the people continued to sin – we all do, even when we try very hard not to sin. People need to know that they need God to live.

1 Corinthians15:56 (The knowledge of good and evil is what gave birth to sin - the Law identified it)
Death's power to hurt is sin, and the power of sin is the law.

Those Jewish Christians who thought that following the Law was what made them holy (this is legalism) were trying to push new Gentile Christians to be circumcised, or to abstain from certain meats, or to keep the women silent in church assemblies (the first two were a part of the written Law, but the last one was a manmade Jewish tradition – not a command of God and not found in the Old Testament). Paul was against making a list of rules for new believers to follow – and rightly so, as Jesus Himself only put forth two simple commands and declared that they summed up the entire Law.

Galatians 2:16 (Paul, too, corrected errant Jewish thinking)
But we know that no one is made right with God by following the law. It is trusting in Jesus Christ that makes a person right with God. So we have put our faith in Christ Jesus, because we wanted to

be made right with God. And we are right with him because we trusted in Christ – not because we followed the law. I can say this because no one can be made right with God by following the law.

Romans 7:6 (Paul's teaching)

"In the past the law held us as prisoners, but our old selves died, and we were made free from the law. So now we serve God in a new way, not in the old way, with the written rules. Now we serve God in the new way, with the Spirit."

The Law contained many rules about approved/disapproved meat. On the question in this letter regarding meat sacrificed to idols, here is another part of Paul's answer:

1 Corinthians 8:10

You understand that it's all right to eat anything, so you can eat even in an idol's temple.

He taught the same thing to Timothy:

1 Timothy 4:3b-5

And they say that there are some foods that people must not eat. But God made these foods, and those who believe and who understand the truth can eat them with thanks. Everything that God made is good. Nothing he made should be refused if it is accepted with thanks to him. Everything he created is made holy by what he has said and by prayer.

Paul repeatedly tells his audiences that they are free from the obligations set forth in the Law.

Now let's look at the problematic verses again:

1 Corinthians 14:34-35

The women should keep quiet [Greek: ***sigaó****, meaning silent] in these church meetings. They are not allowed to speak out but should be under authority, as the Law of Moses says [the writers are referring to the Jewish oral tradition here]. If there is something they want to know, they should ask their own husbands at home. It is shameful for a woman to speak up like that in the church meeting.*

If you read the whole chapter, you see that verse 34 begins a new topic – today, we would call it a new paragraph. If Paul is quoting the Corinthian letter in verses 34 and 35, then his response to the men who wrote that letter to him – the men who wanted the women to be silent in the same way women had been silenced (by men) in the Temple – is verse 36.

1 Corinthians 14:36 (Paul's response to the men)
God's teaching did not come from you, and you are not the only ones who have received it.

Most widely accepted versions of the Bible translate these as rhetorical questions that more closely follow the original Greek. Here is a very literal translation from the Greek found in an older translation:

From Young's Literal Translation 1898:
From you did the word of God come forth? Or to you alone did it come?

Paul goes on to admonish them further, essentially saying, *"If you are as godly as you imagine yourselves to be, you will know that I speak the truth as given by God. Accept it, or you will be rejected."*

1 Corinthians 14:37-38 (Recall their pride about their various gifts of the Spirit)
If you think you are a prophet or that you have a spiritual gift, you should understand that what I am writing to you is the Lord's command. If you do not accept this, you will not be accepted.

1 Corinthians 14:39-40
So my brothers and sisters, continue to give your attention to prophesying. And don't stop anyone from using the gift of speaking in different languages. But everything should be done in a way that is right and orderly.

Paul's overarching theme is peace. If the brothers and sisters of Christ behave in ways that are peaceful and respectful (ways that demonstrate love for one another), then all will be well.

1 Corinthians 16:14

Do everything in love.

He even dedicates an entire section of his letter to the subject of love – Chapter 13. You may be familiar with this verse:

1 Corinthians 13:13

So these three things continue: faith, hope, and love. And the greatest of these is love.

We have discussed many reasons why love is so important, but do you know why love is greater than faith and greater than hope? Faith and hope have no function once Jesus returns and everything has been perfected. ALL that is left in the end is love.

One would be hard-pressed to argue that Paul sincerely believed and taught what is contained in those two disrespectful verses. He very clearly and repeatedly DOES NOT support Christians following the Law of Moses (whether written or oral), and he very clearly and repeatedly DOES support doing everything in love. The silence and domination of anyone definitely does not show love. Paul wrote 13 of the 27 New Testament books, so there is plenty of Scripture to allow us to get to know him.

Summary: In the Corinthian verses, Paul is quoting the complaint of the men of that church. He follows it with a response clearly informing them that they are wrong.

Philippians 2:2b-3 *(Paul writing to the church at Philippi)*

Agree with each other, and show your love for each other. Be united in your goals and in the way you think. In whatever you do, don't let selfishness or pride be your guide. Be humble, and honor others more than yourselves.

Once again, when addressing the concerns of the various churches he and his helpers established, Paul is most often dealing with the MANNER in which people are conducting themselves – in other words, not so much WHAT they are doing, but HOW they are doing it. . .

And what their love for one another should be accomplishing:

1 Corinthians 14:26b

The purpose of whatever you do should be to help everyone grow stronger in faith.

We help others grow their faith by lovingly sharing our gifts. Taking a closer look at what types of gifts the Corinthians were sharing when they assembled, we find that some were prophesying, some were speaking in foreign languages, some wanted hymns, and so on. Their problem was that everyone was trying to contribute his/her own gift to the assembly in a chaotic, interrupting manner. Paul instructs them to be orderly and take turns:

1 Corinthians 14:31

You can all prophesy one after the other. This way everyone can be taught and encouraged.

We know that women were praying and prophesying in the church meetings, because (as we already discussed) Paul addressed the issue of their personal appearance/conduct while doing so:

1 Corinthians 11:5

But every woman who prays or prophesies should have her head covered. If her head is not covered, she brings shame to her head.

Remember, a wife removing her veil in that day and time was the same as shunning her husband – like a wife today removing her wedding band and acting as though she were single/available.

Paul goes on to explain that the husband and wife are dependent on each other.

1 Corinthians 11:11

But in the Lord the woman needs the man, and the man needs the woman. This is true because woman came from man, but also man is born from woman. Really, everything comes from God.

In the Old Testament, the prophet Joel spoke about women prophets – specifically those who would receive their gift after Jesus' resurrection. Luke quoted Joel in the book of Acts.

Acts 2:17-21 (from Joel 2:28-32)
"After this, I will pour out my Spirit on all kinds of people. Your sons and daughters will prophesy, your old men will have dreams, and your young men will see visions. In those days I will pour out my Spirit even on servants, both men and women. I will work wonders in the sky and on the earth. There will be blood, fire, and thick smoke. The sun will be changed into darkness, and the moon will be as red as blood. Then the great and fearful day of the LORD will come! And everyone who trusts in the LORD will be saved.

So, Paul, Luke, and Joel all tell us that women prophesy. Read what Paul has to say about the gift of prophesy:

1 Corinthians 14:1 (Love doesn't come from the Spirit, it comes from your will - you decide)
Love should be the goal of your life, but you should also want to have the gifts that come from the Spirit. And the gift you should want most is to be able to prophesy.

1 Corinthians 14:3, 4b
But those who prophesy are speaking to people. They help people grow stronger in faith, and they give encouragement and comfort. . .those who prophesy are helping the whole church.

1 Corinthians 14:24a, 25b (Prophesying is preferred over speaking other languages that all might not understand)
But suppose you are all prophesying and someone comes in who does not believe or who is without understanding. Their sin will be shown to them. . .they will bow down and worship God. They will say, "Without a doubt, God is here with you."

He goes on to instruct the believers on HOW they should prophesy in the meeting.

1 Corinthians 14:29, 31
And only two or three prophets should speak. The others should judge what they say. . .You can all prophesy one after the other. This way everyone can be taught and encouraged.

Paul's greatest concern is that everyone should behave in an orderly way – our God is a God of order, and we should try to be like Him.

1 Corinthians 14:40

But everything should be done in a way that is right and orderly.

Matthew 5:48 (Jesus speaking)

What I am saying is that you must be perfect, just as your Father in heaven is perfect.

The Spirit is the Spirit of peace and submission not the Spirit of disorder and pride. The Spirit teaches all of us – men and women alike – to be submissive to and respectful of each other and our talents and roles. We each have a gift. All gifts are important and have value. All of our roles/talents/gifts come from God, they belong to God, and they should be used for His purpose.

What are some of the other talents/gifts the believers were sharing in the early church?

1 Corinthians 12:27-28

All of you together are the body of Christ. Each one of you is a part of that body. And in the church God has given a place first to apostles, second to prophets, and third to teachers. Then God has given a place to those who do miracles, those who have gifts of healing, those who can help others, those who are able to lead, and those who can speak in different kinds of languages.

Romans 12:6-8

We all have different gifts. Each gift came because of the grace God gave us. Whoever has the gift of prophecy should use that gift in a way that fits the kind of faith they have. Whoever has the gift of serving should serve. Whoever has the gift of teaching should teach. Whoever has the gift of comforting others should do that. Whoever has the gift of giving to help others should give generously. Whoever has the gift of leading should work hard at it. Whoever has the gift of showing kindness to others should do it gladly.

Some teach that some of these gifts, the gifts that provide a sign (miraculous gifts), have already ended – that they were only needed to establish the early church. By the time all of the apostles died, the various written letters that make up most of the New Testament were being circulated among the churches – Scripture was complete. They argue that miracles, healing, and speaking in languages unknown to the speaker (such as the apostles were given the ability to do on the day of Pentecost when they received the Holy Spirit) died out with the era of the apostles. When was that? The most recent book of the Bible is Revelation, and it was written by the apostle John in approximately AD 95. About 40 years after the writing of that prophecy, the area of Judea was largely depopulated of Jews in their final confrontation with the Romans. By AD 135, most of the Judean Jews had been killed, displaced, or sold into slavery. Certainly, the church had gained a strong Gentile foothold by then, and perhaps those sign gifts were not as needed as they had been.

However, we have seen repeatedly in our discussion that God doesn't do something without telling us about it first.

Amos 3:7, 8b

When the Lord GOD decides to do something, he will first tell his servants, the prophets. . . When the Lord GOD speaks, a prophet must prophesy.

God did not specifically say that these gifts He has given His children would end when the apostles died. Paul told us the gifts would end when we have complete knowledge because the prophecies are complete.

1 Corinthians 13:8-10

Love will never end. But all those gifts will come to an end - These will all end because this knowledge and these prophecies we have are not complete. But when perfection comes, the things that are not complete will end.

The question then is, when did/will we reach a perfection of knowledge? Some teach that the sign gifts have ceased because we now have all the Scripture we need to understand God's plan. They point to a lack of testimony about certain gifts after the book of Acts (the books of the Bible are not all arranged in chronological order). Paul, who was healing people everywhere in the book of Acts, apparently no longer had the ability to heal later on (after the time period of Acts, Paul mentions fellow workers who were sick but makes no mention of healing them). Others teach that we will not have perfect knowledge until Jesus comes to bring God's plan to perfect completion.

When we look at the signs God sent for His people throughout the Bible, we find that the signs were mostly sent at pivotal moments, such as when God delivered the Israelites from the Egyptians and when Jesus delivered us all from sin and death. These signs were given so that His chosen people (the Jews) would believe Him. The signs for the Jews definitely continued through the day of Pentecost. If these signs were only or mostly for the Jews, the time period of the end of the book of Acts, approximately AD 63, and the destruction of the Temple in AD 70, seems to mark the end of God's signs to the Jews who refused to accept Jesus as the Messiah.

We will see in our discussion of the time of the end that the events leading up to Jesus' return will be signs for everyone. From our discussion of the feasts, we learned that we do not know precisely when Jesus will return, so we do not know precisely when those signs will begin.

Based on the pattern seen in the Bible, it is conservatively safe to believe that these sign gifts might have been paused, but that God can sprinkle them in as He sees fit, unpausing and re-pausing them as often as He needs to for the growth of His kingdom until they begin again in earnest in the time of the end. There are those today who claim to have sign gifts, but some of those people are teaching things that cannot be supported by Scripture. Before there was much written Scripture, God gave directions to the Israelites so they could identify false prophets.

Deuteronomy 18:22a

If a prophet says he is speaking for the LORD, but what he says does not happen, you will know that the LORD did not say it.

Now we have the complete Bible – everything we need to know is in there. You must personally know His book. Jesus warned us to be aware of false prophets as we approach the time of the end. We are called to test what people teach by checking God's Word to make sure what they are teaching is true. If someone gives a sign that is **completely** in agreement with the Bible, then who are we to judge?

Matthew 24:11

"Many false prophets will come and cause many people to believe things that are wrong."

1 John 4:1

My dear friends, many false prophets are in the world now. So don't believe every spirit, but test the spirits to see if they are from God.

Acts 17:11b

They studied the Scriptures every day to make sure that what they heard was really true.

Because God has already revealed everything we need to know, we must beware of anyone who comes along spreading "new" news about God and His plan. Anyone with "new" news about God and His plan is claiming to be a prophet. This is why some teach that the gift of prophecy has been paused. So, let's define prophecy.

The word **prophecy** is a noun. A prophecy is a foretelling of an event. A prophet speaks for God. A prophet speaks prophecies. A prophet tells people about things they do not yet know or understand. **To prophesy** is an infinitive (a verb). Prophets prophesy.

In the Old Testament, some prophecies were about the coming Messiah, some were about a punishment that would be brought on the Israelites for their unfaithfulness in order to teach them, and some were about the time of the end – but the messages delivered by the prophets were all pointed at preparing the people for Jesus and what He would do for them. The whole point of prophecy is, and always has been, Jesus.

All prophecy leads to Jesus.

Revelation 19:10b

Worship God! Because the truth of Jesus is the spirit of prophecy!

Jesus is still working for us – He is preparing our home with him. When we tell others about what Jesus will do for them, we are prophesying to them – we are telling them something they do not yet know or understand. We need to know HOW someone is speaking prophecies before we can judge whether s/he is a true or false prophet. A false prophet spreads "new" news about God's plan, whereas a true prophet spreads the truth of Jesus to those who do not know or understand.

Let's reflect on the women prophets of the Old Testament. Deborah and Huldah are the only two who are explicitly called prophetesses in the Bible, but Jewish tradition says there were seven women prophets: Deborah (a judge of Israel), Miriam (Moses' sister), Huldah (an esteemed advisor to royalty and high priests), Sarah (Abraham's wife), Hannah (mother of the prophet, Samuel), Abigail (who married David before he was king), and Esther (the young woman who saved her people).

Judges 5:7 (Part of the song of victory sung after the defeat of Sisera)

"There were no soldiers in Israel until you came, Deborah, until you came to be a mother to Israel."

Micah 6:4 (Moses, Aaron, and Miriam are siblings)

"I will tell you what I did. I sent Moses, Aaron, and Miriam to you. I brought you from the land of Egypt. I freed you from slavery."

When good King Josiah ordered the Temple to be repaired and a scroll of the Law was found, the high priest Hilkiah took it to Huldah for interpretation. Jeremiah and Zephaniah were also prophets at that time but apparently weren't consulted, even though Jeremiah was Hilkiah's son and Zephaniah was Jeremiah's mentor.

2 Kings 22:14a,15a

So Hilkiah the priest [and some other officials] went to Huldah the woman prophet. . .
Then Huldah said to them, "The LORD, the God of Israel, says. . ."

All of these women (some with documented missteps), whether they are named prophetesses or not, did the jobs God called them to do. Based on the verses we've read, both men and women in the New Testament were clearly given the gift of prophecy – the gift of explaining God's Word to those who do not yet know or understand. Consider these and the warnings about being aware of false prophets and decide for yourself whether the gift of prophecy has been revoked by God.

Now, let's look at some examples of women in the New Testament who were using their spiritual gifts to do the job God has called us all to do – share the truth of Jesus, which is the ultimate point of prophecy.

In Paul's second letter to Timothy, he makes very positive comments about Timothy's faith and the faith of the women who taught him.

2 Timothy 1:5
I remember your true faith. That kind of faith first belonged to your grandmother Lois and to your mother Eunice. I know you now have that same faith.

2 Timothy 3:14-15
But you should continue following the teaching you learned. You know it is true, because you know you can trust those who taught you. You have known the Holy Scriptures since you were a child. These Scriptures are able to make you wise. And that wisdom leads to salvation through faith in Christ Jesus.

We can know Paul did not believe or condone that women should not teach because of these statements as well as his other writings. Paul not only taught women, he also worked with them in the service of Christ and encouraged them to be leaders, as well. Remember that Paul taught and then baptized Lydia and the others who lived with her. Lydia was the head of her household, so Lydia was the leader of the church at her house.

Acts 16:40 (Paul and Silas were arrested for preaching the Gospel and healing a servant girl)
But when Paul and Silas came out of the jail, they went to Lydia's house. They saw some of the

believers there and encouraged them. Then they left.

In the verses below, Paul calls a woman named Phoebe a special servant – a type of servant of the church that is different from the elders. In the original Greek, the word Paul used to describe Phoebe is **diakonon**, from which we derive the modern term deacon, or deaconess.

Paul describes other women as hard workers in the church. Remember, churches weren't buildings then, churches were people. Christians were meeting in homes, for the most part. The work of the church in that day was to spread the Good News – to TEACH. These women were not arranging the flowers, answering the phone, staffing the nursery, or making copies.

Romans 16:(part of 1-12)
*I want you to know that you can trust our sister in Christ, Phoebe. She is a special servant [Greek: **diakonon**] of the church in Chenchrea. I ask you to accept her in the Lord. Accept her the way God's people should. Help her with anything she needs from you. She has helped me very much, and she has helped many others too. Give my greetings to Priscilla and Aquila, who have worked together with me for Christ Jesus. They risked their own lives to save mine. I am thankful to them, and all the non-Jewish churches are thankful to them. Also, give greetings to the church that meets in their house. . .Greetings also to Mary. She worked very hard for you. And greet Andronicus and Junia. . . they were followers of Christ before I was. And they are some of the most important of the ones Christ sent out to do his work. . .Greetings to Tryphaena and Tryphosa, women who work very hard for the Lord. Greetings to my dear friend Persis. She has also worked very hard for the Lord.*

1 Timothy 3:11 (Paul gives the requirements for women who serve the church as special servants)
*In the same way [Greek: **hósautós**], the women [Greek: **gunaikas**] (Probably the women who serve as special servants (see Rom. 16:1). It could be translated, "their wives," meaning the wives of the special servants, although there is no word for "their" in the Greek text.) must have the respect of others. They must not be women who speak evil about other people. They must have self-control and be women who can be trusted in everything.*

Some have interpreted/translated this verse as referring to the requirements for the wives of special servants because the requirements for men who are special servants come immediately before this verse. Again, the Greek words used can help with interpretation. **Hósautós**, here translated as, "In the same way," means "likewise," or "in the same way as," meaning that the requirements have the same spirit of meaning both for men and for women who want to be special servants in the church. **Gunaikas**, can mean wife, or it can simply mean women. As noted in the verse, some Bible translations have "their wives" instead of "the women," but the word "their" isn't found in the Greek text. We can safely assume Paul intends to say women here because of these two facts, and because we just read a verse in which he commends Phoebe – he doesn't mention a husband – and calls her a special servant, a deaconess, of the church.

Some women teachers worked alongside their husbands.

Acts 18:24-26 (Luke tells us about a husband/wife teaching team – Paul also worked with them)
A Jew named Apollos came to Ephesus. Born in the city of Alexandria, he was an educated man who knew the Scriptures well. He had been taught about the Lord and was always excited to talk to people about Jesus. What he taught was right, but the only baptism he knew about was the baptism that John taught. Apollos began to speak very boldly in the synagogue. When Priscilla and Aquila heard him speak, they took him to their home and helped him understand the way of God better.

Notice that they took Apollos into their home – they did not confront him loudly in front of others. They taught him in quietness and peace, just as Paul instructed. Paul, like Jesus, does not want to see discord in the church. Notice also in this text of Acts (written by Luke) as well as in the one above in Romans (written by Paul) that Priscilla's name is mentioned first. Could this be because she is the main teacher with her husband assisting?

In the following verses, Paul earnestly, politely, and respectfully asks two women teachers to agree in quietness and peace.

Philippians 4:2-3
Euodia and Syntyche, you both belong to the Lord, so please agree with each other. For this I make

a special request to my friend who has served with me so faithfully: Help these women. They worked hard with me in telling people the Good News, together with Clement and others who worked with me. Their names are written in the book of life (God's book that contains the names of the people who will be with Him for eternity).

Women, if God has given you a gift of teaching, and if He gives you the opportunity to do it, would you turn Him down? Men, if God has given your wives the gift of teaching and they are called upon to do it, would you tell them to be silent?

Let's set up a possible situation: A woman has a gift for teaching and is inspired to use it. People have witnessed her sharing the Message privately and have invited her to speak publicly at a meeting of believers. Her family and friends support her teaching and see that her efforts are beneficial for increasing the faith of believers and/or adding new believers to God's church. Should this woman decline to speak simply because she is a woman?

If she refuses to teach publicly, is this not the same sin committed by the steward who buried his master's money and didn't allow it to earn interest (to grow)? Jesus told us the talents were taken away from the servant who did not use them. The servants who used their talents were rewarded. When He told this parable, Jesus was expanding on an Old Testament teaching.

Proverbs 11:24-25

Some people give freely and gain more; others refuse to give and end up with less. Give freely, and you will profit. Help others, and you will gain more for yourself.

Matthew 25:29

"Everyone who uses what they have will get more. They will have much more than they need. But people who do not use what they have will have everything taken away from them."

Remember, too: Army commander Barak's glory was taken from him when he lacked the courage to do God's bidding. Esther was rewarded for bravely doing God's work. Joshua was rewarded for his true, faithful testimony.

Jesus taught women. He frequently stayed in the home of two sisters, Mary and Martha.

On one particular visit, Mary was sitting at His feet (the traditional position for learners at that time – generally referring to a student sitting quietly and learning from a teacher) and Martha was tending to household duties. When asked to judge the two women, Jesus praised the learner and admonished the worker, but He did not say that what the worker was doing was wrong. In taking care of her family, her guest, and her home, what she was doing was very right. Jesus was telling her that, at that moment, there was something better she should be spending her time on – learning His Truth directly from Him. Once she understood His Truth, she could teach it to others. This is THE most important work any of us will ever have. This is worship. He did not teach Mary and Martha and tell them to be silent. The Bible repeatedly tells us to share His News.

Luke 10:38-42

While Jesus and his followers were traveling, he went into a town, and a woman named Martha let him stay at her house. She had a sister named Mary. Mary was sitting at Jesus' feet and listening to him teach. But her sister Martha was busy doing all the work that had to be done. Martha went in and said, "Lord, don't you care that my sister has left me to do all the work by myself? Tell her to help me!" But the Lord answered her, "Martha, Martha, you are getting worried and upset about too many things. Only one thing is important. Mary has made the right choice, and it will never be taken away from her."

Summary: Everyone has been given a gift from God to further His plan.
No one should be prevented from sharing his or her gift.
Every gift and every sign can be judged by the Word to test its truth.
God has told us everything we need to know – Scripture is complete.
He doesn't do anything without telling us about it first.

****

Failure to use the gift God has given you to do His work
will result in your glory being taken away from you.
Failure to accept Him by refusing to accept His gift in others
will result in you not being accepted by Him.

****

Now that we've established that we are all supposed to be sharing the Good News by using our gifts for His work and accepting Him by accepting His gifts in/from others, we should acknowledge that men do have an extra leadership role in the family and in the church that was defined from the beginning by God.

Paul encouraged the men to be leaders. He instructed them to lead their families spiritually, to teach others, and to lead the believers by serving as elders and special servants in the church. As the groups of believers grew in size, some organization and leadership became a necessity in making sure that all of God's people were receiving the care they needed (spiritually, financially, physically, etc). Certain men were selected as elders to oversee their own groups. Paul laid out the qualifications for a man to become an elder.

1 Timothy 3:1-7 (These are very similar to the requirements for men who want to be special servants)
It is a true statement that anyone whose goal is to serve as an elder has his heart set on a good work. An elder must be such a good man that no one can rightly criticize him. He must be faithful to his wife. He must have self-control and be wise. He must be respected by others. He must be ready to help people by welcoming them into his home. He must be a good teacher. He must not drink too much, and he must not be someone who likes to fight. He must be gentle and peaceful. He must not be someone who loves money. He must be a good leader of his own family. This means that his children obey him with full respect. If a man does not know how to lead his own family, he will not be able to take care of God's church. An elder must not be a new believer. It might make him too proud of himself. Then he would be condemned for his pride the same as the devil was. An elder must also have the respect of people who are not part of the church. Then he will not be criticized by others and be caught in the devil's trap.

Paul gives the requirements for three positions in the church: elders (men), special servants/deacons (men), and special servants/deaconesses (women). Some interpret the requirements for deaconesses to be not for leadership positions but for deacons' wives. This would be inconsistent, though, because of Paul's repeated statements in the verses listed above and because Paul does not list requirements for elders' wives.

Men are repeatedly instructed to be the head of the family and the head of the church. We see this reflected in God's reference to Himself as male; His creation of Adam first; His selection of Aaron and his sons to be priests; His embodiment as Jesus, the Son of God; and His selection of 12 men to be His disciples. God is not taking responsibility away from women, but He is giving men a huge responsibility.

This idea of leadership, or authority, is a key element in the Bible. Jesus submitted to God by His own choice, Humans must submit to Jesus by their own choice, and a wife must submit to her husband by her own choice. **The idea of submission is only negative in our world because it has been corrupted by Satan.** When we submit to Jesus, He does not rule over us cruelly – He gave His life for those who submit to Him, and He will lift us up to Him. Jesus as a man submitting to God does not make Him inferior to God – they are one and the same. Husbands whose wives willingly submit to them should understand that their wives' submission does not make them inferior – husband and wife are one and the same. Husbands should treat their wives as Christ has treated the believers – husbands should love their wives so much that they would lay down their lives for them – husbands should lift up their wives. Husbands and wives are made to function together as one unit.

Philippians 2:5-11

In your life together, think the way Christ Jesus thought. He was like God in every way, but he did not think that his being equal with God was something to use for his own benefit. Instead, he gave up everything, even his place with God. He accepted the role of a servant, appearing in human form. During his life as a man, he humbled himself by being fully obedient to God, even when that caused his death – death on a cross. So God raised him up to the most important place and gave him the name that is greater than any other name. God did this so that every person will bow down to honor the name of Jesus. Everyone in heaven, on earth, and under the earth will bow. They will all confess, "Jesus Christ is Lord," and this will bring glory to God the Father.

Once again, math can be helpful here. When a man and a woman marry, they are no longer 1 and 1. Furthermore, they are not 2, because, in marriage, they are not added to one another. Nor are they each a part of their union, because they are each still whole. Rather, they become one another – they are each 1 of a set of 1. The only way to get an answer of 1 when combining whole things is to multiply, so the marriage of a man and a woman = 1 x 1. And the spiritual marriage of a man and a woman (a Christian marriage that has the blessing of the Holy Spirit) equals one as well: 1 x 1 x 1 = 1.

Jesus submitted to God's will in His sacrifice, but we know God and Jesus are the same:

John 14:9part, 11a

Anyone who has seen me has seen the Father too. . .Believe me when I say that I am in the Father and the Father is in me.

While God, Jesus, and the Holy Spirit are one, each serves in a specific capacity/role. The same is true in the marriage state. Physically and spiritually, the husband and wife become one, each serving the other. The husband belongs to the wife and the wife belongs to the husband. Each serves a role in the relationship and in the family. The husband's role is to be the head of the household – he is to report to God for his leadership of his family.

Ephesians 5:22-33 (Genesis 2:24)

Wives, be willing to serve your husbands the same as the Lord. A husband is the head of his wife, just as Christ is the head of the church. Christ is the Savior of the church, which is his body. The church serves under Christ, so it is the same with you wives. You should be willing to serve your husbands in everything. Husbands, love your wives the same as Christ loved the church and gave his life for it. He died to make the church holy. He used the telling of the Good News to make the church clean by washing it with water. Christ died so that he could give the church to himself like a bride in all her beauty. He died so that the church could be holy and without fault, with no evil or sin or any other thing wrong in it. And husbands should love their wives like that. They should love their wives as they love their own bodies. The man who loves his wife loves himself, because no one ever hates his own body, but feeds and takes care of it. And that is what Christ does for the church because we are parts of his body. The Scriptures say, "That is why a man will leave his father and mother and join his wife, and the two people will become one." That secret truth is very important – I am talking about Christ and the church. But each one of you must love his wife as he loves himself. And a wife must respect her husband.

Malachi 2:15a

God wants husbands and wives to become one body and one spirit. Why? So that they would have holy children and protect that spiritual unity.

God united with Jesus = Jesus united with God = 1 x 1 = 1
Jesus united with the church = the church united with Jesus = 1 x 1 = 1
Husband united with Wife = Wife united with Husband = 1 x 1 = 1
Believers united with believers = We are all one in Christ

Romans 12:5b ***(The Easy to Read Version uses the word "part," but the Greek uses the word "one")***

In Christ we are all one body. We are [one] body, and each [one] belongs to all the others.

Husbands should be careful to learn how to be good leaders of their households and should always be mindful of improving their leadership skills. Family dynamics change over the years, and leadership skills must evolve with those changes. Husbands cannot lead by pridefully thinking they have all the answers or skills they will ever need, but they should prayerfully and humbly seek the renewal of those gifts from God. Women cannot help by criticizing, but they should positively encourage their husbands and pray for them to become or to remain good leaders as the family changes over time. Both roles are equally important. Women who feel that this role is demeaning should look back to the beginning.

As God completed the various things He created, He declared them to be "good." He said this about the land and seas, the plants and trees, the sun and moon, the birds in the air, the creatures in the sea, and the animals on the land. It was only after He made Adam and saw that Adam was alone that He said something He had made was "not good."

Genesis 2:18 ***(some Bible versions/translations use the word 'helper' or 'helpmeet' instead of 'companion')***

Then the LORD God said, "I see that it is not good for the man to be alone. I will make the companion [ezer] he needs, one just right for him [kenegedo]."

In the original Hebrew, the word translated as helper/helpmeet/companion is **ezer**, which is not a helper in the same way we might think of a helper today. A teacher's aide, for example, is usually someone with no teaching certification who is in the classroom to help the licensed teacher. A sous chef helps the head chef in a fine restaurant. In these situations, there is a clear and established hierarchy – one is the servant helper, the other is the professional. The helper follows the directions of and learns from the professional. The Hebrew **ezer** is an entirely different kind of helper. The **ezer** the Israelites praise and pray for in the verses below is the helper they must have for survival and success.

Exodus 18:4 (The naming of Moses' sons)
*The other son was named Eli'**ezer** [my God helps], because when he was born, Moses said, "The God of my father helped me [**b'ezri**] and saved me from the king of Egypt."*

*Deuteronomy 33:7part (Before Moses died, he prayed for God to be Judah's **ezer**)*
*"LORD, listen to the leader from Judah when he calls for help...Make him strong, and help [**w'ezer**] him defeat his enemies.*

Psalm 33:20
*So we will wait for the LORD. He helps us [**ezre'nu**] and protects us.*

Psalm 70:5 (David praying for God's help)
*I am only a poor, helpless man. God, please hurry to me. You are my helper [**ezri**], the one who can save me. LORD, don't be too late!*

Hosea 13:9 (God allowed the Israelites' destruction because they had turned against Him)
*"Israel, I helped [**b'ezre'ka**] you, but you turned against me. So now I will destroy you."*

The people literally cannot live without this **ezer**, this rescuer, this defender, this ally – and this **ezer** is the same word used to describe the woman's relationship to the man. God resolved to make a customized **ezer** for the man, one with whom he could survive and succeed. In order to do this, God required a very specific sacrifice from Adam. God had made Adam and all the animals from the dust of the ground, but He did not use dust to make Eve.

Genesis 2:7a, 19a

Then the LORD God took dust from the ground and made a man. . .The LORD God used dust from the ground and made every animal in the fields and every bird in the air.

Genesis 2:21-22

So the LORD God caused the man to sleep very deeply. While he was asleep, God took one of the ribs from the man's body. Then he closed the man's skin where the rib had been. The LORD God used the rib from the man to make a woman. Then he brought the woman to the man.

God used the sacrifice from Adam to bless him. Eve was made from Adam's own body, so he would naturally love her, care for her, and respect her as his own body. The two were one. Disrespecting, degrading, or harming her would lead to his own destruction.

Genesis 2:23 (Adam understood this and expressed his joy when God blessed him with Eve, his ally)

And the man said, "Finally! One like me, with bones from my bones and a body from my body. She was taken out of a man, so I will call her 'woman.'"

Adam did not say, "Finally! A woman to serve me – a woman I can rule over." He said, "One LIKE me." Remember, the words **like** and **as** are figures of speech called **similes**. They show how two unlike things are alike. Adam saw that Eve was different but the same. He saw that she would be his partner in life – someone to share the work God had given them. God made Eve as the finishing touch, the crowning jewel, of His entire Creation. She was the final creation – a creation that made everything not just good, but very good.

Genesis 1:31

God looked at everything he had made. And he saw that everything was very good.

Proverbs 12:4a

A good wife is like a crown to her husband. . .

Proverbs 18:22

If you have found a wife, you have found something good. She shows that the LORD is happy with you.

The word **ezer** is a descriptive word that woman shares with God Himself. The one rendering help is in no way subservient to the one being helped – in fact, in the verses referring to God, **ezer** indicates a superiority over the one being helped. However, when God used **ezer** to describe Eve, He followed it with the word **kenegedo**, which means to stand in the presence of an equal. The woman has God-given power of her own, just as the man does, and they stand as equals in the presence of one another.

Matthew 19:4-6 (from Genesis 1 and 2)

Jesus answered, "Surely you have read this in the Scriptures: When God made the world, 'he made people male and female.' And God said, 'That is why a man will leave his father and mother and be joined to his wife. And the two people will become one.' So they are no longer two, but one. God has joined them together, so no one should separate them."

After He made Eve, God was satisfied and rested from His work. Women are made in God's image just as men are, and when a man and a woman marry, they become one. God wants the man to take the firm but kind, loving leadership role that Jesus demonstrated for them, and He wants the woman to submit to her husband just as Jesus submitted to Him. A truly believing husband and wife team, with the leadership of the Spirit, function independently, but also function as one, just as God, Jesus, and the Holy Spirit function independently, but also function as one. Commitment, faithfulness, and unity of purpose are essential, as are peacefulness and humility.

The book of Proverbs contains a poem about the ideal wife. Wives, it's a lofty goal to be the ideal wife described here. Notice, the poem (it has a poem format in Hebrew) does not associate the qualities listed with an actual woman – it is an ideal. No one is perfect, but that does not mean we should not strive to reach lofty goals. Also, notice that she is an independent businesswoman who expertly runs her family, not a silent woman kept at home. Remember, husband and wife function independently, but both function with the same goal in mind. Husbands, if this is the ideal wife, what is the ideal husband? We should all work hard and be the best people we can be.

Proverbs 31:10-31

How hard it is to find the perfect wife. She is worth far more than jewels. Her husband depends on her. He will never be poor. She does good for her husband all her life. She never causes him trouble. She is always gathering wool and flax and enjoys making things with her hands. She is like a ship from a faraway place. She brings home food from everywhere. She wakes up early in the morning, cooks food for her family, and gives the servants their share. She looks at land and buys it. She uses the money she has earned and plants a vineyard. She works very hard. She is strong and able to do all her work. She works late into the night to make sure her business earns a profit. She makes her own thread and weaves her own cloth. She always gives to the poor and helps those who need it. She does not worry about her family when it snows. She has given them all good, warm clothes. She makes sheets and spreads for the beds, and she wears clothes of fine linen. Her husband is a respected member of the city council, where he meets with the other leaders. She makes clothes and belts and sells them to the merchants. She is a strong person, and people respect her. She looks to the future with confidence. She speaks with wisdom and teaches others to be loving and kind. She oversees the care of her house. She is never lazy. Her children say good things about her. Her husband brags about her and says, "There are many good women, but you are the best." Grace and beauty can fool you, but a woman who respects the LORD should be praised. Give her the reward she deserves. Praise her in public for what she has done.

We have discussed a great deal of information in this answer, but this topic is extremely important for all men and women to help everyone understand both their own place and the place of others in God's plan. To summarize, we do know that Paul was addressing a number of serious concerns of the churches in his letters to Timothy and to the church at Corinth. In both cases, and in his letters to other churches, Paul repeatedly calls for peace and humility – submission – among all the believers – male and female – the peace that is found through Jesus (who modeled both our roles) in the presence of God.

Review: Men and women, if you feel called to teach, you should always do so prayerfully. Ask God to give you the knowledge you need.
Ask God to give you the right words to say.
Ask Him to help you do what is pleasing to Him.
Then let His Spirit lead you.

What is prayer, and how do you do it?

Think of prayer as a telephone conversation between you and God. There are many examples of public prayer available, but personal prayer is different. God tells us to go to a quiet, private place and talk to Him freely. He doesn't want us to feel embarrassed the way we might if we thought someone was listening or watching. He wants us to feel free to tell Him anything and everything in our own personal style.

Matthew 6:6

"But when you pray, you should go into your room and close the door. Then pray to your Father. He is there in that private place. He can see what is done in private, and he will reward you."

Jesus gave us a basic outline of prayer, which we now call The Lord's Prayer.

"Our Father in heaven,
we pray that your name will always be kept holy.
We pray that your kingdom will come –
that what you want will be done here on earth, the same as in heaven.
Give us the food we need for today.
Forgive our sins,
just as we have forgiven those who did wrong to us.
Don't let us be tempted,
but save us from the Evil One."

Matthew 6:9b-13

In this prayer, Jesus tells us that when we pray we need to address God and acknowledge His importance, to express our hope that those who are on earth will do what God wants just as those who are in heaven do, to ask for our basic needs to be met, to ask forgiveness for our wrongs (while forgiving those who have wronged God through us), to ask Him to teach us the Way (so that we won't fall for temptations), and to ask for protection from Satan, the Tempter (knowing His Way is our protection).

You can say The Lord's Prayer until you are comfortable saying your own prayer. Keep in mind, though, that God wants you to talk to Him all the time. The Bible encourages us to pray constantly. Praying constantly means that we should keep Him in our thoughts and talk to Him throughout each day as though He were right there with us – of course, we know that He is with us all the time, because His Spirit is living in us.

Romans 12:12

Be happy because of the hope you have. Be patient when you have troubles. Pray all the time.

The Bible also gives examples of different types of prayer. We can say prayers of thanksgiving in which we show God praise and honor for taking care of us and providing what we need. We can say prayers of supplication or petition in which we ask for things such as forgiveness or salvation, spiritual or physical healing, help or protection, knowledge or guidance, or inner or outer peace in our lives. Many, if not most, of your prayers will be (like The Lord's Prayer) some combination of thanksgiving and supplication.

Just start talking to Him. Tell Him about all the things you are thankful for and remember that we are to be thankful for ALL things – even things we think are not so good, because, for His people, God can and does make all things work toward the completion of His plan. Tell Him about all the things you are sorry for and remember that Jesus has saved us from these things. We need only ask His forgiveness, and God freely gives it to us, no strings attached – and since God gives us forgiveness so freely, we must give others forgiveness just as freely. Ask God for what you need and be sure to mention Jesus. Jesus said we are to ask things in His name.

James 5:16b

Anyone who lives the way God wants can pray, and great things will happen.

Psalm 5:1-2

LORD, listen to me and understand what I am trying to say. My God and King, listen to my prayer.

Nehemiah 1:5-6a

"LORD, God of heaven, you are the great and powerful God. You are the God who keeps his agree-

ment of love with people who love you and obey your commands. Please open your eyes and ears and listen to the prayer your servant is praying before you. . ."

John 14:13 (Jesus' directions regarding prayer)

"And if you ask for anything in my name, I will do it for you. Then the Father's glory will be shown through the Son."

John 16:24b

"But ask in my name, and you will receive. And you will have the fullest joy possible."

Psalm 34:4a

I went to the LORD for help, and he listened.

Do not be discouraged if the answer to a prayer is not what you expected. Remember that God, our Father, can see the big picture. We are His children, and He knows what we need. When you reach the end of your prayer, you can finish it by saying, "Amen" – a Hebrew word that means "may it be so."

Philippians 4:6

Don't worry about anything, but pray and ask God for everything you need, always giving thanks for what you have.

1 John 5:14

We can come to God with no doubts. This means that when we ask God for things (and those things agree with what God wants for us), God cares about what we say.

Psalm 19:14

May my words and thoughts please you. LORD, you are my Rock – the one who rescues me.

Review: Prayer is simply talking to God. You can do it anytime, anywhere. Ask in Jesus' name. Be thankful for everything.

How can I be thankful for the bad things?

If life were all good and no bad things ever happened. . .wait, that's the happy end! We live in a fallen world, an imperfect world, where bad things do happen. These bad things are the result of sin. Sin rarely affects just the person who commits it – sin almost always has ramifications for others. Adam and Eve sinned and were removed from their perfect home and sent out into the world where life would be difficult. We are all suffering from the consequences of their sin. We live in this fallen world because they did, and because God has not fully completed His plan yet.

1 Peter 2:11a

Dear friends, you are like visitors and strangers in this world.

John 16:33 (Jesus speaking)

"I have told you these things so that you can have peace in me. In this world you will have troubles. But be brave! I have defeated the world!"

Jesus' sacrifice removed the spiritual consequence of sin – He saved us from a lasting spiritual death, but God has not completed the part of His plan in which He makes our physical lives perfect. That will happen after Jesus comes again. As one bit of proof that the world we live in is imperfect, remember how the Jewish religious leaders received Jesus. If this were God's perfect world, would the religious leaders of His people have rejected Him when He came to visit them? Even today, as followers of and believers in Jesus, we will sometimes be treated badly just for our beliefs. The Bible tells us over and over not to love this world but to love God. This imperfect world will end, and He will give us a wonderful, new, perfect world that will never end.

1 John 2:15, 17

Don't love this evil world or the things in it. If you love the world, you do not have the love of the Father in you. . .The world is passing away, and all the things that people want in the world are passing away. But whoever does what God wants will live forever.

2 Corinthians 5:1a, 2, 4, 5b

We know that our body – the tent we live in here on earth – will be destroyed. . .But now we are tired of this body. We want God to give us our heavenly home. . .While we live in this tent, we have burdens and so we complain. I don't mean that we want to remove this tent, but we want to be clothed with our heavenly home. . .he has given us the Spirit as the first payment to guarantee the life to come.

There is a story in the book of John about a man who was blind from birth. Some of Jesus' disciples thought the man was blind because he or his parents must have sinned. Jesus assured them this was not the case. He told His followers the man was blind so that God's glory could be shown through him, and then Jesus used that blindness to further God's plan. Jesus healed the man, and many people did see God's glory. The man became a follower of Jesus and defended Him in front of the Jewish religious leaders.

John 9:3

Jesus answered, "It was not any sin of this man or his parents that caused him to be blind. He was born blind so that he could be used to show what great things God can do."

The Book of Job in the Old Testament is a deeply thoughtful book that teaches us how to suffer through bad times. In this book, Job is a very successful man who is blessed with many children and possessions. Job worships God faithfully. Satan challenges God by saying that Job will curse Him if his blessings are taken away from him. God allows Satan to take away Job's blessings, but Job's faith remains strong. Job trusts that God has a plan, and that He will follow through with it. After Job's faith is tested and he has proven himself true, God not only restores Job's blessings, He greatly increases them.

Job 23:10

But God knows me. He is testing me and will see that I am as pure as gold.

God isn't out to get you, and He can make the bad things you experience work toward the completion of His plan. Just as He did for the blind man and for Job, God can use the pain and suffering you have to bring you closer to Him. God wants only good for you.

He can restore ALL the blessings that the enemy, Satan, has taken from you and give you more than you ever dreamed.

1 Peter 1:17b

So while you are visiting here on earth, you should live with respect for God.

Jeremiah 17:7 (The prophet Jeremiah quoting God)

"But those who trust in the LORD will be blessed. They know that the LORD will do what he says."

In the Bible, God is often portrayed as a refiner. In a refinery, a product is put through some sort of process – often, more than one process – that will purify it. A product may be washed, dried, boiled, melted, strained, cooled, etc. to remove impurities. God, as our refiner, sometimes allows things to happen that will test our faith in Him. Trials, troubles, tribulation – whatever you call it, we are being refined, we are being purified. If we keep our faith through the process, we become more like the people He wants us to be. If we turn our backs on Him, we distance ourselves from Him and His love. We have a choice in how we respond to our troubles.

Isaiah 48:10

"Look, I will make you pure, but not in the way you make silver pure. I will make you pure by giving you troubles."

1 Peter 1:7

These troubles test your faith and prove that it is pure. And such faith is worth more than gold. Gold can be proved to be pure by fire, but gold will ruin. When your faith is proven to be pure, the result will be praise and glory and honor when Jesus Christ comes.

John 15:2b

"He also trims every branch that produces fruit to prepare it to produce even more."

So, what should we do when something bad happens? Pray. Thank God for everything, and then ask Him for help or healing or whatever is needed. Believe that God can fix it and pray that He is willing to fix it. Remember that only He can see the big picture, and sometimes fixing your problem doesn't fit into His plan in the same way you hope it does. Jesus prayed that God would not require His sacrifice, but that prayer request was not granted. God never wanted the sacrifices, but because He is the fairest of all judges, His judgment of punishment for sin remained – as well as His mercy in accepting one sacrifice, His own sacrifice, for us all. Because Jesus submitted to God's will, He is now exalted above all others and sits at the right hand of God. Trust Him completely.

Job 42:2
"I know you can do everything. You make plans, and nothing can change or stop them."

Romans 5:3b-5a
Why are we happy with troubles? Because we know that these troubles make us more patient. And this patience is proof that we are strong. And this proof gives us hope. And this hope will never disappoint us.

James 1:2-4
My brothers and sisters, you will have many kinds of trouble. But this gives you a reason to be very happy. You know that when your faith is tested, you learn to be patient in suffering. If you let that patience work in you, the end result will be good. You will be mature and complete. You will be all that God wants you to be.

In praying, be careful that you do not limit God's ability in any way. There is no situation so hopeless that God cannot mend it. Know God. Know that there are no limits to His power, His mercy, His goodness, His fairness, His love. Let God be God, and you concentrate on just being His child. Ask Him for what you want and believe that he can grant it – but be content with His answer.

The book of Psalms is a collection of poems/songs. Some of the psalms express praise, some express sorrow, some express faith in God, some express a need for God's help, and some express thankgiving. Because of this, many of the Psalms can help us with prayer. Psalm 103, written by David, is a song of praise to God for His goodness.

Psalm 103

My soul, praise the LORD! Every part of me, praise his holy name!
My soul, praise the LORD and never forget how kind he is!
He forgives all our sins and heals all our sicknesses.
He saves us from the grave, and he gives us love and compassion.
He gives us plenty of good things. He makes us young again,
like an eagle that grows new feathers.
The LORD does what is fair. He brings justice to all who have been hurt by others.
He taught his laws to Moses. He let Israel see the powerful things he can do.
The LORD is kind and merciful. He is patient and full of love.
He does not always criticize. He does not stay angry with us forever.
We sinned against him, but he didn't give us the punishment we deserved.
His love for his followers is as high above us as heaven is above the earth.
And he has taken our sins as far away from us as the east is from the west.
The LORD is as kind to his followers as a father is to his children.
He knows all about us. He knows we are made from dust.
He knows our lives are short, that they are like grass. He knows we are like a little
wildflower that grows so quickly,
but when the hot wind blows, it dies. Soon, you cannot even see where the flower was.
But the LORD has always loved his followers, and he will continue to love
them forever and ever!
He will be good to all their descendants, to those who are faithful to his agreement
and who remember to obey his commands.
The LORD set his throne up in heaven, and he rules over everything.
Angels, praise the LORD! You angels are the powerful soldiers who obey his commands.
You listen to him and obey his commands.
Praise the LORD, all his armies. You are his servants, and you do what he wants.
Everything the LORD has made should praise him throughout the world that he rules!
My soul, praise the LORD!

Here are some encouraging words from one of Jesus' closest friends, Peter:

God's power protects you through your faith, and it keeps you safe until your salvation comes. That salvation is ready to be given to you at the end of time. I know the thought of that is exciting, even if you must suffer through different kinds of troubles for a short time now. These troubles test your faith and prove that it is pure. And such faith is worth more than gold. Gold can be proved to be pure by fire, but gold will ruin. When your faith is proven to be pure, the result will be praise and glory and honor when Jesus Christ comes.

1 Peter 1:5-7

Satan afflicts you in order to demoralize you. He wants you to be depressed. He wants you to lose your faith in God. Remember, his goal is to hurt God, and since he cannot attack God directly, he attempts to accomplish his goal by attacking God's people. As a believer, you are a soldier in His army. Wear the armor God has given you and stand strong. Don't allow your troubles to depress your spirit. As a believer, your spirit communes with God. God knows you are hurting – even if you heal and move past your hurt, God remembers your pain and will restore you. Satan is the enemy, and we should fight against him. We do that by living in a way that shows we are certain God will make everything right.

Focus on God. Focus on happiness. Happiness is a choice. We have the freedom to choose in ALL the affairs of our hearts. We can choose to love or to hate, to be happy or to be sad, to be kind or to be mean, to be grateful or to be resentful. Choose the good.

Choose to be strong in your faith in God's ability to restore.

Philippians 3:12

I don't mean that I am exactly what God wants me to be. I have not yet reached that goal. But I continue trying to reach it and make it mine. That's what Christ Jesus wants me to do. It is the reason he made me his.

Review: God is training us. He refines us to improve us.
He does this by allowing us to be afflicted by Satan.
God wants us to fight Satan by having faith in Him.
This is how we prove ourselves.
This is how we become better soldiers.
Worship Him by trusting Him and by being happy.
Our troubles will make us stronger.

Is giving money at church (or, elsewhere) a way to worship God?

Money is just another one of the gifts we can use to do God's work. Like other gifts, such as time and talents, money can be used in unwise ways. There are ways to use those gifts to serve Him, and we should always work to make sure that God would be pleased with how we use the resources He has given to us. The Bible says not to worry about giving so much that you have nothing left. If you give generously – of your time, your talents, your money – God will give generously to you. He notices when you worship Him by using your resources in a way that pleases Him, and He will reward you for your good works. Your reward may come at a time or in a way that you do not expect, but it will be good.

Matthew 25:29 (Again, because it's important, and it applies to all the gifts God has given us)
"Everyone who uses what they have will get more. They will have much more than they need.
But people who do not use what they have will have everything taken away from them."

Most formal church organizations have a time during their Sunday worship service when an offering of money to support God's work is requested. Offerings may be given electronically, a "plate" may be passed around to the people, or a donation box may be available. The money collected is used for church expenses such as: the building and utilities, office equipment and supplies, children's activities, the minister's salary, and so on. Many church organizations also use a portion of the offering to pay for missionary work. Missionaries are people who visit or move to a place where there aren't many Christians in order to spread the Message about God's love and His plan. They, like Paul and his helpers, generally help get a church started and then move on to another place.

You should only make a donation if: (1) you also pray that the money will be used to do what God would like to have done, and (2) you are giving because deep in your heart, you want to give and help in some way. When you do this, you are a servant of God. You are working for Him. You are worshipping Him.

2 Corinthians 8:12 (This is about sincerity, and it applies to not only money but all gifts)
If you want to give, your gift will be accepted. Your gift will be judged by what you have, not by what you don't have.

When you make an offering or a donation to a church, an organization, or a person, you are simply giving God's money back to Him. You are returning a portion of your blessings in order to share those blessings with someone else. He owns everything, but He is pleased when you have enough love for Him to give "your" possessions to someone else. Giving is different from buying. You cannot buy a place in heaven. You cannot buy forgiveness. You cannot buy God's love. Everything good that you honestly possess was given to you by God. You owe Him everything.

John 3:27
John answered, "A person can receive only what God gives."

Romans 11:35 (from Job 41:11)
"Who has ever given God anything? God owes nothing to anyone."

1 Chronicles 29:14b
All these things come from you. We are only giving back to you things that came from you.

Romans 11:36a
Yes, God made all things. And everything continues through him and for him.

Psalm 24:1
The earth and everything on it belong to the LORD. The world and all its people belong to him.

We are like stewards of an estate. A steward is a person who manages someone else's property or household. Everything on the estate belongs to the master, but the master puts a steward in charge of running the day-to-day operations. A good steward manages the master's estate in a responsible way whether the master is present or not. If the master leaves, the steward will have to give an account for what s/he has done in the master's absence. Jesus told a parable about this that is recorded in Matthew 24:45-51 and Luke 12:42-48. God's estate is heaven and earth and everything in them. He created all life, and all life is given by Him alone. God has put us in charge of the lives He has given us. We are stewards of our own lives (our own talents/gifts) – this is about free will. We are free to do as we like, but there is a right way and a wrong way. In Jesus' parable, He tells us exactly how we should run our lives – how to be good stewards. With the strength of our faith in God, we are to use the talents God has given us to help others develop more of that same faith – we are to increase His investment in us. We are representing Him to others, and we will have to give Him a report when He returns.

Colossians 1:15-16

No one can see God, but the Son is exactly like God. He rules over everything that has been made. Through his power all things were made: things in heaven and on earth, seen and not seen – all spiritual rulers, lords, powers, and authorities. Everything was made through him and for him.

Job 41:11b (God speaking to Job)

"Everything under heaven belongs to me."

Nehemiah 9:6

You are God. LORD, only you are God. You made the sky and the highest heavens and everything in them. You made the earth and everything on it. You made the seas and everything in them. You give life to everything. All the heavenly angels bow down and worship you.

Luke 16:11

"If you cannot be trusted with worldly riches, you will not be trusted with the true riches. And if you cannot be trusted with the things that belong to someone else, you will not be given anything of your own."

Matthew 25:21

"The master answered, 'You did right. You are a good servant who can be trusted. You did well with that small amount of money. So I will let you care for much greater things. Come and share my happiness with me.'"

God has given us life, as well as love, time, skills, education, money and countless other blessings. He has put us in charge of all these things. He has given us free will so that we can decide how to use these blessings. We should always use the power to choose and the blessings that we have been given for God's glory. When we glorify (honor) God, we are like beacons of light in a dark world, showing the lost how to find the way home to Him. This is our purpose.

Philippians 2:15b-16a

But you are living with evil people all around you, who have lost their sense of what is right. Among those people you shine like lights in a dark world, and you offer them the teaching that gives life.

James 1:17a

Everything good comes from God. Every perfect gift is from him. These good gifts come down from the Father. . .

1 Chronicles 28:9part

Serve God with a pure heart. Be happy to serve him, because the LORD knows what is in everyone's heart.

Matthew 6:21, 24b

"Your heart will be where your treasure is. . .You cannot serve God and Money at the same time."

Hebrews 13:5 (from Deuteronomy 31:6)

Keep your lives free from the love of money. And be satisfied with what you have. God has said, "I will never leave you; I will never run away from you."

1 Timothy 6:10a

The love of money causes all kinds of evil.

This verse is often misquoted as, "Money is the root of all evil." Money is a useful tool God has given us, and we should take care to use it responsibly.

The Bible says that God loves a cheerful giver (sincerity is important). It also says that when you give to someone in need, do it quietly and secretly so that the person who receives the gift will thank God and not you. Others might never find out who gave the gift, but God will know what you have done. We can still openly give and receive presents and thank one another, but we need to remember that ALL gifts come from God, and He should be thanked for them all. As a giver, we should be honored to have been chosen by God to deliver the gift. Remember that He blessed you with the gift you are giving.

2 Corinthians 9:7-8

Each one of you should give what you have decided in your heart to give. You should not give if it makes you unhappy or if you feel forced to give. God loves those who are happy to give. And God can give you more blessings than you need, and you will always have plenty of everything. You will have enough to give to every good work.

Matthew 6:2a, 4

"When you give to those who are poor, don't announce that you are giving. . .Your giving should be done in private. Your Father can see what is done in private, and he will reward you."

Review: Giving, like helping and loving others, is a way to worship God. As a steward, you should always keep the Master in mind when you give, because you know that giving is simply giving His blessings back to Him.

What if I forget about God?

Your relationship with God might be like the ocean tide. You might experience high tide when your communication with God is great, and you can really feel His presence in your life. You might experience low tide when your communication with God is poor, and you feel distanced from Him.

God is solid ground – He is holy ground – and He never moves. When we are in a close relationship with Him, we are standing on His holy ground, just as Moses was when he met with God on the mountain top. If our relationship falters, it is because WE have stepped off of His holy ground – WE have left Him.

Acts 7:33 (God answered the cry of His people – they called to Him, and He was there)
"The Lord said to him [Moses], 'Take off your sandals, because the place where you are now standing is holy ground.'"

All relationships require effort. You will have to work to keep your relationship with God healthy and strong. You are in control of how close you feel to God. It is your own forgetfulness and neglect that cause the distance, not God. He is ALWAYS there for you. Talking to God every day will help make your relationship with God a close one. Talk to Him while you walk to the mailbox, while you prepare your food, and while you wait in line. Practice talking to Him at new times, in new places, in new ways until you find a communication comfort zone that keeps you sincerely and intimately connected.

James 4:8a
Come near to God and he will come near to you.

Acts 17:27
"God wanted people to look for him, and perhaps in searching all around for him, they would find him. But he is not far from any of us."

Isaiah 49:15b-16 (God speaking to His people)
"I cannot forget you. I drew a picture of you on my hand. You are always before my eyes."

Isaiah 59:1-2a
Look, the LORD's power is enough to save you. He can hear you when you ask him for help.
It is your sins that separate you from your God.

2 Timothy 2:13a, 19a

If we are not faithful, he will still be faithful. . .God's strong foundation never moves. . .

James 1:17part

God never changes. . .He is always the same.

Malachi 3:6a

"I am the LORD, and I don't change."

Hebrews 13:8

Jesus Christ is the same yesterday, today, and forever.

Acts 3:19

So you must change your hearts and lives. Come back to God, and he will forgive your sins.

Romans 8:38-39

Yes, I am sure that nothing can separate us from God's love – not death, life, angels, or ruling spirits. I am sure that nothing now, nothing in the future, no powers, nothing above us or nothing below us – nothing in the whole created world – will ever be able to separate us from the love God has shown us in Christ Jesus our Lord.

Review: If you are in a relationship with God, you must work to keep that relationship strong. You may pull away from Him from time to time because you are forgetful, but God does not forget you. He loves you more than you can understand. Know Him personally – know He just wants you to return His love.

How can I learn more about God?

Please remember to test what you hear from someone or read somewhere about God. You must check it out for yourself in His Book. In doing this, you can be careful to only believe what His Book says. There are countless other books available, but God has only one Book. It is THE BOOK that tells us what God wants us to know. During His ministry, Jesus told the religious leaders they were too carried away by their own traditions and human-designed beliefs. They had neglected to follow only God's Scriptures. Do not put your faith in the traditions of humans. Other religious books that are often used in worship services and in teaching new believers about a particular church's beliefs were written by humans from their own interpretations and understandings. The Bible is the only Word of God, and it is all we need.

2 Peter 1:20-21

Most important of all, you must understand this: No prophecy in the Scriptures comes from the prophet's own understanding. No prophecy ever came from what some person wanted to say. But people were led by the Holy Spirit and spoke words from God.

2 Timothy 3:16-17

All Scripture is given by God. And all Scripture is useful for teaching and for showing people what is wrong in their lives. It is useful for correcting faults and teaching the right way to live. Using the Scriptures, those who serve God will be prepared and will have everything they need to do every good work.

Mark 7:6-9 (Jesus speaking to the religious leaders) (from Isaiah 29:13)

Jesus answered, "You are all hypocrites. Isaiah was right when he wrote these words from God about you: 'These people honor me with their words, but I am not really important to them. Their worship of me is worthless. The things they teach are only human rules.' You have stopped following God's commands, preferring instead the man-made rules you got from others." Then he said, "You show great skill in avoiding the commands of God so that you can follow your own teachings!"

Isaiah 40:8

"Grass dies and flowers fall, but the word of our God lasts forever."

Psalm 119:160

Every word you say can be trusted. Your laws are fair and will last forever.

Review: Depend only on God's Bible for true instruction.

Are all Bibles the same?

The first major, widely accepted translation of the Bible into English was printed in 1611, and contained 80 books, including the Old and New Testaments and a separate section called the Apocrypha, which contained 14 writings that were considered to be profitable reading but were not considered Scripture. Today, the Protestant Bible has 66 books in it (no Apocrypha), and the Catholic Bible has 73 books (some Apocrypha, which is now called Deuterocanonical). The words Apocrypha and Deuterocanonical both indicate that these writings are secondary to the recognized books of the Bible.

What is a testament? In Biblical terms, each testament records an agreement, or covenant, between God and His people. The Old Testament records the covenant God had with the Israelites (the descendants of Abraham, father (patriarch) of the servant nation), who were later called Jews. This agreement was made between God and His people (through Moses) when He brought them out of Egypt. The old covenant's purpose was to prepare the people for the coming of the Messiah, and the Jewish nation was grown from Abraham to do the job of recording and keeping God's messages to us so that we all might know Him. The old covenant is the foundation of the new covenant – therefore the Old Testament is the foundation of the New Testament. The New Testament records the agreement, or covenant, between God and all people everywhere that began when Jesus was sacrificed. It shows how Jesus fulfilled the Old Testament prophecies that were given about Him. The New Testament, the new covenant, offers the gift of freedom from slavery to make us heirs of His Kingdom.

Covenants and Promises of God

The Old and New Testaments do not only testify about one covenant each. There are a number of covenants, or agreements found in the Bible. Some scholars do not consider all of the following to be covenants, because God did not specifically say He was making an agreement, but one could certainly view all of the following as promises of God.

God-Jesus-Holy Spirit – Humans would be redeemed and restored through the work of each: God would send His Son and accept His payment for the sins of the people, Jesus would obey His Father and complete the sacrifice, and the Holy Spirit would mark and comfort those who are faithful and who believe the promise of redemption and restoration.

Verses testifying about the promise of redemption and restoration make up the whole of the Bible.

God-Adam & Eve – They could live in the Garden of Eden (Paradise) for eternity as long as they didn't eat from the tree of knowledge of good and evil. They were required to show faith in their relationship with God. If they didn't obey, they couldn't stay.

Genesis 2:15-17

The LORD God put the man in the Garden of Eden to work the soil and take care of the garden. The LORD God gave him this command: "You may eat from any tree in the garden [including the tree of life]. But you must not eat from the tree that gives knowledge about good and evil. If you eat fruit from that tree, on that day you will certainly die!"

God-Humans-Satan – God promised that a descendant of Eve (the Messiah) would crush Satan and restore humans to their original place.

Genesis 3.15b

"You will bite her child's foot, but he will crush your head."

God-Noah – God would destroy all flesh that He made, but He would save Noah and his family from harm because Noah was faithful. That was a promise given before the Flood. This is the covenant made after the Flood: God would never again send a flood to destroy life, and the sign of this covenant is a rainbow.

Genesis 6:18a

"I will make a special agreement with you."

Genesis 9:12-13

And God said, "I will give you something to prove that I made this promise to you. It will continue forever to show that I have made an agreement with you and every living thing on earth. I am putting a rainbow in the clouds as proof of the agreement between me and the earth."

God-Abraham – God would make a great nation from him, and God would bless all people through him and his descendants. More specifically, God would send the Messiah through him, and the children of Abraham, whether natural or adopted (all believers), would share that News of salvation with others. God also promised to give the Hebrew nation (and all believers) land.

Genesis 15:18

So on that day the LORD made a promise and an agreement with Abram.

Genesis 17:1-2

When Abram was 99 years old, the LORD appeared to him. He said, "I am God All-Powerful. Obey me and live the right way. If you do this, I will prepare an agreement between us. I will promise to make your people a great nation."

Galatians 3:29

You belong to Christ, so you are Abraham's descendants. You get all of God's blessings because of the promise that God made to Abraham.

The sign of this covenant was the circumcision of all males.
God restates His promises to Abraham in Genesis 22.

God-Moses-the Israelites (the Old Covenant) – After the Israelite nation had grown, and God was ready to set them apart for their special work in His service, He chose Moses to lead them. He promised to show them His power to help them understand the importance of their obedience and service to Him through the Law He gave them when they left Egypt.

Exodus 34:10-11a

Then the Lord said, "I am making this agreement with all of your people. I will do amazing things that have never before been done for any other nation on earth. The people with you will see that I, the LORD, am very great. They will see the wonderful things that I will do for you. Obey what I command you today. . ."

God-David-Jesus – God promises to make David's descendants kings. Jesus is born into the Noah-Abraham-Moses-David family line. Jesus is the eternal king.

2 Samuel 7:11b, 16
I promise that I will make your family a family of kings." (Literally, "make a house for you.") "Your family of kings will continue – you can depend on that! For you, your kingdom will continue forever! Your throne will stand forever!"

2 Samuel 23:5a
"God made my family strong and secure. He made an agreement with me forever."

God-Believers (the New Covenant) – This new agreement replaces the old one given to Moses in the desert. The new covenant begins with the sacrifice of Jesus. Jesus is the One who will fulfill all of the previous covenants.

Jeremiah 31:31b, 32part
"The time is coming when I will make a new agreement with the family of Israel and with the family of Judah. It will not be like the agreement I made with their ancestors. . .when I took them by the hand and brought them out of Egypt. . .they broke that agreement."

Hebrews 13:20part-21part
God is the one who raised from death our Lord Jesus, the Great Shepherd of his sheep. He raised him because Jesus sacrificed his blood to begin the new agreement that never ends.

Luke 22:19-20
Then he took some bread and thanked God for it. He broke off some pieces, gave them to the apostles and said, "This bread is my body that I am giving for you. Eat this to remember me." In the

same way, after supper, Jesus took the cup of wine and said, "This wine represents the new agreement from God to his people. It will begin when my blood is poured out for you."

Review of God's promises:

- God intended for us to live in Paradise for eternity.
- God-Jesus-Holy Spirit will work to restore us and defeat Satan.
- God will preserve the earth until that happens.
- God made a nation to serve Him.
- God set them apart to guide all other nations, just as he set apart a tribe of priests to guide the other tribes of Israel.
- God sent a King from that nation who will rule forever.
- Christ has come, and the new covenant is available to all.
- Jesus will return to complete God's plan.

The covenants are not independent. Each agreement is intimately, elaborately, and inextricably tied to the others. Those who believe that the Old Testament is obsolete are mistaken, as are those who believe the New Testament isn't from God. Every agreement, every book, every word of the Bible is an important part of the whole. This is why God said:

Deuteronomy 4:2a

You must not add to what I command you. And you must not take anything away.

Each of the testaments is made up of individual books that can be grouped together in general topics. The following visual depiction shows how a modern Protestant Bible is divided. Protestants and Catholics agree on the contents of the New Testament, but Catholic Bibles include a few selections from the original Apocrypha in their Old Testament. Protestants and Jews agree that the Apocrypha writings are not Scripture and should not be included in the Old Testament. Jesus did not quote from the Apocrypha, and everything He did quote, He referred to as Scripture or The Word of God. The Jewish Bible, used by Jews who believe Jesus is the Messiah, has the same books as a Protestant Bible, but the Old Testament books are arranged in a different order.

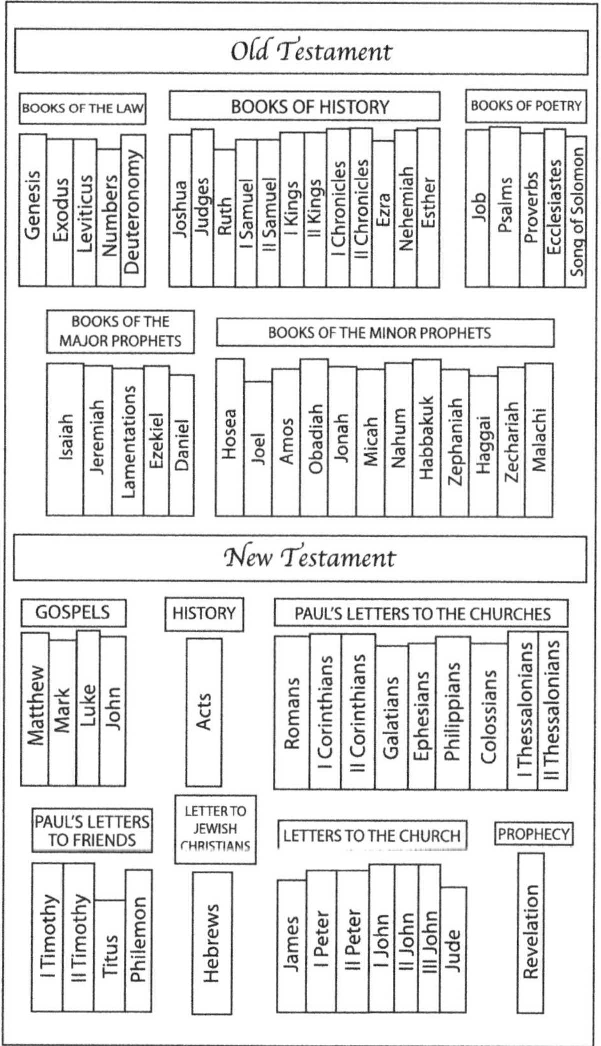

Although the individual books were not originally written this way, all but five of them are divided into chapters (Obadiah, Philemon, 2 John, 3 John, and Jude are very short books, so they don't really need chapters), and each of the chapters is further broken down into verses. These chapters and verses were added because they are very helpful when you are studying the Bible and need to find a particular verse. When you quote something from the Bible, you should state the book, chapter, and verse number of the quotation so that others can find the verse and read it for themselves in its original context.

Here are some common types of Bibles:

Red letter editions have all the words Jesus spoke written in red. Everything else is in black.

Study Bibles have extra information on the bottom or sides of each page to help you understand the verses even better. Remember, many of the explanations are someone's interpretation – check other sources, compare these interpretations to the whole of Scripture to see if they agree, and decide for yourself.

Interlinear Bibles have the Bible text in two languages, English and the original language in which the words were written (Hebrew, Greek, Aramaic).

Parallel Bibles show multiple translations or versions of the Bible side by side.

Dual-Language Bibles are written in two modern languages, such as English and Spanish.

Chronological Bibles have the events recorded in the order they happened to help make the story as a whole easier to follow. Bibles that aren't chronological have the books divided according to literary style, as shown in the chart.

Reference Bibles include maps and other reference material.

One-Year Bibles are formatted to provide a schedule for reading that can be completed in one year.

Bibles for individual use were not printed in earnest until the 1600's when the King James Bible was published. By the 1900's, versions with more modern language styles began to become popular. Today, there are many, many different versions and translations of the

Bible. You can download a free app on your phone or tablet with a particular version. There is also an app called YouVersion that allows you to switch between and to compare many different versions. Some versions of the Bible have a casual, easy-to-read, modern language; some have a more formal language. Here's a list of some Protestant Bible versions that are more modern or conversational in style:

ASV – American Standard Version
ERV – Easy to Read Version
MSG – The Message
NIRV – New International Reader's Version
NAS – New American Standard
NET – New English Translation
ESV – English Standard Version

YLT, Young's Literal Translation, published in 1862, is an extremely literal translation from the Hebrew and Greek. Use it on YouVersion as one of your 'Compare Versions' for insight – it is a valuable study aid. Keep in mind it doesn't rephrase idioms to give them a comparable meaning. For example, in 1 Samuel 24:3, we read that Saul went into a cave to cover his feet. This is a polite way of saying he went in to urinate. The idiom we would use today is he went in to relieve himself. These types of idioms are called euphemisms.

The verses quoted in this book all come from the Easy to Read Version of the Bible on the YouVersion app, with a few exceptions that are noted. The online Interlinear Bible tool at www.Scripture4all.org was used to study the verses in the original Biblical languages and clarify interpretations of specific words. The dictionary tools on www.BibleHub.com were used to look up the definitions of Bible words in their original languages. Bible Hub also has an interlinear tool, a commentary tool, and several other study aids that were used. Other commentaries were found using internet searches. Several Jewish websites were used. Understand that no translation or version of a translation is perfect.

Review: There are many types and versions of the Bible available today.
An app can help you explore these Bibles.

Interlinear Bibles help you better understand what was originally written.

Bible study tools are readily available.

Where should I start reading?

The Gospels, the first four books of the New Testament, would be a great place to start. The books Matthew, Mark, Luke, and John are all about Jesus' time on earth, although John's book tells us more about who Jesus is and less about what Jesus did. The Gospels include Jesus' direct messages to us. His stories, called parables, are in these books as well.

The Acts of the Apostles tells about the earliest days of the church. We have discussed parts of many of the accounts from this book including the report of the apostles receiving the Holy Spirit, the story of Peter and Cornelius, how Paul came to be an apostle of Christ, and the stories of Lydia and the jailer.

Paul's Letter to the Romans (his letter to the believers in Rome) is widely considered to be an excellent guide for all Christians.

The Book of Psalms is a collection. Each Psalm is a song – a poem – written from the author's heart to God. The Psalms give us some examples of how to pray. Many of the Psalms were written by a man named David who served as king of God's people long before Jesus' time. David had many downfalls, but in his heart, he had what God wants. He had a deep desire to please God. Many people can relate well to David because, like many of us, he sometimes couldn't see his own faults.

The Book of Proverbs is a collection of wise sayings that can inspire, teach, and amuse us. It isn't a story or a letter so, like the Book of Psalms, you can start and stop anywhere.

Hebrews Chapter 11 is all about faith and gives an excellent review of the Old Testament heroes.

Isaiah, Daniel, and Revelation (among others) contain information about the time of the end of this world. They also are instructive about how we should behave in the face of adversity that will increase as we near the end. We have been forewarned so that we can be ready.

Once you've gotten acquainted, you can learn a great deal in one year by using a good chronological Bible paired with a study Bible and an Interlinear Bible. When you hear or read something new about God somewhere else, look it up in your Bibles to see if what you have learned is correct.

The people in the Old Testament were told to do this:

Look in the LORD's scroll [Scripture] and read what it says...

Isaiah 34:16a

The believers in the New Testament set an example for us:

They studied the Scriptures every day to make sure that what they heard was really true.

Acts 17:11b

Find it for yourself – then you will know it is true.

John 8:32
"You will know the truth, and the truth will make you free."

Review: Read, read, read. Only then will you know the truth.

Protestant, Catholic, Messianic Jew. . .what's the difference?

The apostles were the very first example of a Jesus-believing group who met together. They were all of Jewish descent, but they were very different types of men with different political, educational, and economic backgrounds. After Jesus ascended, these men He had trained and who had witnessed His Ministry received the Holy Spirit and went about spreading the Good News that we can all be redeemed and have a personal relationship with God. This is what Jesus had told them to do. The groups of people who had heard Jesus' teachings directly from Him and believed, and those who believed what these men taught about Jesus, met together in homes and became what we now call the early church.

In the same way the Levite tribe served as the Israelites' connection to God, the Jewish nation serves as all of humanity's connection to God. Faithful Jewish servants wrote God's words down for us, meaning, the entire Christian Bible was written by Jews. There is widespread speculation that Luke was a Gentile, but when those shallow arguments are thoroughly examined, they quickly evaporate. Read the article by Thomas McCall, "Was Luke a Gentile?" at www.levitt.com/essays/luke.

Many of the early church members were Jewish; although, as shown by the actions of the Jewish religious leaders of Jesus' time, not all Jews believed that Jesus was the Messiah God had promised to send. Many Jewish people today do not believe the Messiah has come – but some people of Jewish descent do (Messianic Jews), and they can provide wonderful insight into understanding the Scriptures from a Jewish point of view. When the Romans conquered Jerusalem about 40 years after Jesus' Ascension (the Jews had rebelled against Roman control of their land one too many times, so the Roman army came to Jerusalem and destroyed the city and the Temple), the believers who survived moved to other places where they continued to share the Good News. Most of the new church members from that point on were not of Jewish descent.

As more people were added to the church, a more organized church structure began to develop. Remember, elders, special stewards (deacons/deaconesses), and travelling missionaries are the only examples of church leadership we can find in the New Testament. (The Old Testament had priests, but since Jesus' sacrifice, we are all priests.) Over time, this human-designed church structure became very intricate, with a hierarchy of priests and bishops, the appointment a pope (a man selected to be the leader of the church on earth), and the establishment of many, many rituals and traditions. This structure evolved and increased and spread its power deeply into world politics over the next 1,500 years. It became known as the Catholic church. The word Catholic comes from the Greek word **katholikos** meaning "throughout the whole," and has also been equated with the Latin word **catholicus** meaning "universal."

In 1517, a Catholic priest/professor named Martin Luther, who was well-versed in the Bible and in all the Catholic church teachings, rejected some of those church teachings. He began to teach people that he rejected certain teachings of the Catholic church because those teachings didn't agree with what the Bible said. The Bible had only been translated into Latin at that point, and only the priests were taught to read it. Martin Luther translated the Bible into the common man's language, so people could read for themselves and decide. This religious revolution was the beginning of Protestantism. The people who believed the teachings of this former Catholic priest became known as Protestants, because they protested against some of the teachings of the Catholic church that they believed didn't agree with the Bible.

Over time, the Protestants divided themselves up into groups based on how they interpreted certain Bible teachings, and they began to call themselves by names that illustrated their interpretations: Lutherans, Baptists, Presbyterians, and Methodists, are a few. Each of these groups is a called a denomination. Today, these denominations and others each have a "head office" that makes important decisions about what the churches in their denomination believe or teach, and many of these head offices publish writings stating those beliefs. Those writings are used as teaching and worship tools in their churches. New denominations are still being formed today, although the idea of non-denominational churches (independent churches without a head office) has also become popular.

Unfortunately, there is one key fact that Christians have tended to ignore. God **never** instructed His church (ALL of His followers) to have divisions. We discussed how Paul objected to the divisions among the Corinthian believers, and below we can read how he begged the church at Ephesus to stay peacefully joined. Most importantly, we know that Jesus Himself prayed to God for the unity of all His believers.

So, as a prisoner for the Lord, I beg you to live the way God's people should live, because he chose you to be his. Always be humble and gentle. Be patient and accept each other with love. You are joined together with peace through the Spirit. Do all you can to continue as you are, letting peace hold you together. There is one body and one Spirit, and God chose you to have one hope. There is one Lord, one faith, and one baptism. There is one God and Father of us all, who rules over everyone. He works through all of us and in all of us.

Ephesians 4:1-6

"I pray not only for these followers but also for those who will believe in me because of their teaching. Father, I pray that all who believe in me can be one. You are in me and I am in you. I pray that they can also be one in us. Then the world will believe that you sent me. I have given them the glory that you gave me. I gave them this glory so that they can be one, just as you and I are one. I will be in them, and you will be in me. So they will be completely one. Then the world will know that you sent me and that you loved them just as you loved me."

John 17:20-23

The word **church** in the Bible comes from the Greek word **ekklésia**, which is a combination of two different words: **ek**, meaning "out from" or "from out of" and the root word **kaleó**, which means "call, invite, or woo" (remember our discussion about marriage). As the church of God, as the body of people who believe in Jesus and the salvation offered through Him, we are "the called out from within" of God. What exactly does that mean? Are we called from inside by the Holy Spirit to change ourselves on the outside? Yes! Are we called out from the safety of God's grace (from inside the Door) – to go out into the world (outside the Door) and bring others home to Him? Yes! Either way you choose to view the meaning, we are "the called out from within." We are the **ekklésia**. We are the church.

Our church groups/buildings should have descriptive names like the ones in the Bible: the church that meets at Lydia's house – Acts Ch. 16, or the church that meets at Priscilla and Aquila's house – Romans Ch. 16. We should have names such as: the Second Avenue Church, the Bedford Town Church, or the Highway 10 Church, etc. Names that tell people where to GO to find a group of believers meeting together, not names that show our divisiveness. Let's pick names of unity for all church groups that honor the ONE TRUE GOD and His Son, Jesus Christ, who died for us all. Let's invest God's money in our own communities and our own people who want to be missionaries and stop sending it to corporate denominational head offices. We are the stewards of our own blessings, and we have to give an account when the Master returns.

You can do good for others and teach others about God anywhere you go. When you do teach others, be sure to only teach what is in the Bible. As believers, we can and should have discussions about possible interpretations of certain Scriptures, but we should not allow those discussions to end in division. Jesus said, "And a family that is divided will not survive" (Mark 3:25). A divided church is exactly what Satan wants. We are weaker when we are divided. We must always remember that we are all different (just like the original 12 disciples), but, as believers, we are all one. Jesus said, "Yes, anyone who does what my Father in heaven wants is my true brother and sister and mother" (Matthew 12:50). What God wants, His will, is for us to be united. We are brothers and sisters in Christ. We are all God's children. We are ONE family.

Isaiah 2:2-4

In the last days the mountain of the LORD's Temple [Mt. Zion] will be the highest of all mountains. It will be raised higher than the hills. There will be a steady stream of people from all nations going there. People from many places will go there and say, "Come, let's go up to the mountain of the LORD, to the Temple of the God of Jacob. Then God will teach us his way of living, and we will follow him." His teaching, the LORD's message, will begin in Jerusalem on Mount Zion and will go out to all the world. Then God will act as judge to end arguments between nations. He will decide what is right for people from many lands. They will stop using their weapons for war. They will hammer their swords into plows and use their spears to make tools for harvesting. All fighting between nations will end. They will never again train for war.

We can have healthy debates about various interpretations, including the ones in this book. These debates should increase our knowledge and tolerance of one another and help us as we try to bring more people to Jesus. Healthy, intelligent debate keeps our tools sharp.

Proverbs 27:17

As one piece of iron sharpens another, so friends keep each other sharp.

Which church building (denomination) you attend is not as important as what is in your heart. Church attendance should not be entirely about what the church body can do for you. Your attendance should also be about what you can do for the church body. Your relationship with other followers should be mutually beneficial – helping and being helped by each other with the gifts you have each been given.

1 Corinthians 11:18

First, I hear that when you meet together as a church you are divided. And this is not hard to believe because of your idea that you must have separate groups to show who the real believers are!

Every person and every church organization has room for improvement. Being humble enough to admit that will help us join forces to do God's work.

Isaiah 2:11

Proud people will stop being proud. They will bow down to the ground with shame, and only the LORD will still stand high.

1 Corinthians 1:10

Brothers and sisters, by the authority of our Lord Jesus Christ, I beg all of you to agree with each other. You should not be divided into different groups. Be completely joined together again with the same kind of thinking and the same purpose.

Romans 15:5b-7

And I pray that God will help you all agree with each other, as Christ Jesus wants. Then you will all be joined together. And all together you will give glory to God the Father of our Lord Jesus Christ. Christ accepted you, so you should accept each other. This will bring honor to God.

He wants His believers to be unified. This is how we honor Him.

John 3:16

Yes, God loved the world so much that he gave his only Son, so that everyone who believes in him would not be lost but have eternal life.

John 17:3 *(Jesus praying to God)*

"And this is eternal life: that people can know you, the only true God, and that they can know Jesus Christ, the one you sent."

We don't have to know any rules, creeds, policies, prayers, etc. to belong to Jesus. His teaching is simply a way of life that puts God first and serves others following the example Jesus gave us. The Word of God has come to you – learn His simple truth.

Review: The important point to remember is that we all worship the One True God, and we all believe that He sent His Son to redeem us and restore us to a close relationship with Him.

We are "the called out from within."
We are the **ekklésia**. We are the church.

Jesus wants us to be one family of believers looking forward to freedom.

This is God's Plan.

****

I want you to know that I am trying very hard to help you. And I am trying to help those in Laodicea and others who have never seen me. I want them to be strengthened and joined together with love and to have the full confidence that comes from understanding. I want them to know completely the secret truth that God has made known. That truth is Christ himself. In him all the treasures of wisdom and knowledge are kept safe.
I tell you this so that no one can fool you by telling you ideas that seem good, but are false.

Colossians 2:1-4

To end my letter I tell you, be strong in the Lord and in his great power. Wear the full armor of God. Wear God's armor so that you can fight against the devil's clever tricks. Our fight is not against people on earth. We are fighting against the rulers and authorities and the powers of this world's darkness. We are fighting against the spiritual powers of evil in the heavenly places. That is why you need to get God's full armor. Then on the day of evil, you will be able to stand strong. And when you have finished the whole fight, you will still be standing. So stand strong with the belt of truth tied around your waist, and on your chest wear the protection of right living. On your feet wear the Good News of peace to help you stand strong. And also use the shield of faith with which you can stop all the burning arrows that come from the Evil One. Accept God's salvation as your helmet. And take the sword of the Spirit – that sword is the teaching of God. Pray in the Spirit at all times. Pray with all kinds of prayers, and ask for everything you need. To do this you must always be ready. Never give up. Always pray for all of God's people.

Ephesians 6:10-18

****

More Q & A's

Does Biblical history agree with secular history?

God shows throughout His Book that there is no point in keeping Bible history separate from secular (non-religious) history, because everything is His Story. This is His world, and He rules over every person and place that has ever been or will ever be.

When we refer to a year that something in history happened, we use BC to mean that the event occurred "Before Christ," and AD to mean that it occurred "Anno Domini," which is Latin for "in the year of our Lord." Some prefer to remove the reference to Christ from the history timeline and use BCE for "Before the Common Era" in place of BC and CE for "Common Era" in place of AD. Many Jewish people use AM, an abbrieviation for the Latin "Anno Mundi," which means "in the year of the world/in the year of man/since Creation," and they count from the beginning of time as recorded in the Bible.

Here is a rough timeline of some well-known secular events and some Biblical events we've discussed listed chronologically in Gentile and Jewish years. The dates of the various Biblical and secular events flow together seamlessly, in part because many secular events are mentioned in the Bible, allowing historians secular timeline validation of Biblical events. Notice that several of the other major world religions were founded thousands of years after Creation.

3761 BC - 1 AM Creation
3300 BC - 600 AM Metalworking and music
3000 BC - 1000 AM Sumerians begin writing on clay tablets
2350 BC - 1656 AM Noah's Flood
2000 BC - 2000 AM Abraham/Stonehenge
1900 BC - 2100 AM Egyptian pyramids
1750 BC - 2240 AM Hammurabi of Babylon writes first legal code
1450 BC - 2650 AM Moses/Exodus
1500 BC - 2500 AM Beginning of Jewish state
1000 BC - 2875 AM King David, golden age of Israelites
930 BC - 2900 AM Israelite nation divides: Israel and Judah
750 BC - 3000 AM Olympics/Rome founded/Jonah
500 BC - 3300 AM Daniel/Siddhartha (Buddha)/Confucius
400 BC - 3400 AM Last Old Testament prophet
300 BC - 3500 AM Alexander the Great
200 BC - 3620 AM Qin Dynasty builds Great Wall of China
63 BC - 3695 AM Rome conquers Israel and Judah
27 BC - 3734 AM Pax Romana (Roman Peace) begins
4 BC - 3760 AM Christ born
30-33 AD - 3790 AM Christ ascends to heaven
70 AD - 3830 AM Rome destroys the Temple
95 AD - 3850 AM John records Revelation
135 AD - 3890 AM End of Jewish state
180 AD - 3940 AM Pax Romana ends
476 AD - 4237 AM Fall of Rome
600 AD - 4360 AM Muhammad founds Islam
1000 AD - 4760 AM Vikings/Middle Ages/Crusades
1500 AD - 5260 AM Exploration/colonization of Americas
1948 AD - 5708 AM State of Israel established
2021 AD - 5781 AM Publication of this book

Dates in this chart are taken from a wide variety of sources (inconsistencies are found in all calendars over time) and are not to be viewed as exact dates. Most historical dates, including the year calculations of AM, BC, and AD were established in the Middle Ages. The intention of the chart is to provide a rough historical structure for our discussion and to illustrate the following:

Some Jews who are still waiting for the Messiah to come (we are all waiting, but we're referring to some of the Jewish people who are still waiting for His first appearance), believe He will come in the year 6000 AM, and begin a sort of Sabbath millennium. The idea is that perhaps each of the days of Creation is represented by (not equal to) a literal 1,000 years of earth time, and His appearance to rescue them from their enemies and restore them to the land promised to Abraham corresponds to a 1,000-year period of rest (Sabbath). What do you think of this? Is there any Biblical basis for this idea? It has some similarities to the 1,000-year reign of Christ foretold in Revelation. How many years from today could this happen? Is your answer based on Biblical years, Hebrew civil calendar years, or our current calculation of a year? Should we become deeply involved with calculations predicting His coming, or is this idea merely interesting in a casual way?

Remember, if we are doing what He has asked us to do, we are already prepared for His arrival. We should continue our work and be happy with the simple knowledge that He is coming soon.

What are the angels doing now?

God uses angels to do His work in a number of ways. They serve Him as worshipers, messengers, guardians, representatives, workers, ministers, and soldiers. Angels are spirits. They and their heavenly home exist in the spiritual world. The Bible only gives us a few glimpses into that spiritual world. According to the books of Daniel and Revelation, God's angels are recorded as having battled Satan and his fallen angels in the past, and they are foretold as having a final battle with them in the future. From these passages, we can conclude that God's angels are still at war today, because Satan and his army are still on the loose. That means there is spiritual warfare happening that we, as humans, cannot ordinarily see, but the Bible tells us about people who were allowed by God to witness some of this spiritual warfare. Although this story found in 2 Kings doesn't specifically mention angels, it does give us a glimpse at a spiritual army of God, and we know from Psalm 103 that His angels are His soldiers, His servants in His army.

Psalm 103:20part, 21part

You angels are the powerful soldiers who obey his commands. . . You are his servants, and you do what he wants.

This story takes place in the days when God was talking to His people through the prophets. Elisha was one of God's prophets. A wicked king did not like Elisha and sent his army out to kill him.

2 Kings 6:14-17

Then the king of Aram sent horses, chariots, and a large army to Dothan [the city where Elisha was]. They arrived at night and surrounded the city. Elisha's servant got up early that morning. When he went outside, he saw an army with horses and chariots all around the city. The servant said to Elisha, "Oh my master, what can we do?"

Elisha said, "Don't be afraid. The army that fights for us is larger than the army that fights for Aram."

Then Elisha prayed and said, "LORD, I ask you, open my servant's eyes so that he can see." [The servant isn't blind. Elisha is asking for the servant to be able to see the spiritual world.]

The LORD opened the eyes of the young man, and the servant saw the mountain was full of horses and chariots of fire. They were all around Elisha.

We should always remember that we have a powerful army on our side when we are fighting evil. God's angels are hard at work for Him.

Be careful that you do not misunderstand the angels' place in God's kingdom. When the apostle John received the message that he recorded in the book of Revelation, he wrote:

> *I am John. I am the one who heard and saw these things. After I heard and saw them, I bowed down to worship at the feet of the angel who showed them to me. But the angel said to me, "Don't worship me! I am a servant like you and your brothers the prophets. I am a servant like all those who obey the words in this book. You should worship God!"*
>
> *Revelation 22:8-9*

Do our pets go to heaven?

Here's what we do know: God obviously cares for His animals. He created them. He instructed Adam to name them. He told us He gave them a living soul. He instructed Noah to take care of them on the Ark. Proverbs 12:10a says, "Good people take good care of their animals." He tells us that animals already exist in some form in the spiritual realm: remember the horses in the army that helped Elisha. And in the book of Isaiah, He describes animals being present at the happy end of our journey.

Isaiah 11:6-8
Then wolves will live at peace with lambs, and leopards will lie down in peace with young goats.

Calves, lions, and bulls will all live together in peace. A little child will lead them. Bears and cattle will eat together in peace, and all their young will lie down together and will not hurt each other. Lions will eat hay like cattle. Even snakes will not hurt people. Babies will be able to play near a cobra's hole and put their hands into the nest of a poisonous snake.

We talked about Easter, but what about Christmas?

Like Lent, Easter, Epiphany, and other religious observances that are familiar today, the Bible does not tell us to celebrate Christmas. Christians didn't begin to celebrate the birth of Christ in earnest until about 300 years after His death and resurrection. Some link the celebration (of the birth of the Son) to the rebirth of the sun near that date in December – that is, the winter solstice, when the hours of daylight begin to increase each day. Others link the celebration to the idea (which we cannot prove) that Creation occurred at the spring equinox, and because the light (or the sun) was created that week, then Jesus must have been conceived that same week many years later – nine months from the spring equinox is roughly December 25th. All of this, of course, is just speculation.

One historical fact we do know is that the Roman emperor Aurelian dedicated a new temple to the Roman god of the sun, Sol Invictus (Latin: "unconquerable sun") on December 25th in the year AD 274. Whether he was attempting to override evolving Christian celebrations on that date, or whether Christian celebrations attempted to override the pagan celebration is an unresolved matter of debate.

We do not know when Jesus was born, though there are many educated guesses that it was on a feast day – none of which are on December 25th. The wise men did not come to the animal stable where He was born. His parents had travelled to Bethlehem for the Roman census and could find no other place in the overcrowded town (or the overcrowded relative's house where they might have otherwise stayed) to spend the night. The wise men (magi, or pagan astrologers/magicians, from the east who were not Jewish, but who knew that the star they saw in the sky indicated that the king of the Jews had been born) were travelling from far away and did not arrive until Jesus was about 1½ years old. By then, He and His parents were living in a house and no longer travelling. We do not know how many wise men came, we only know about the three gifts that were mentioned: gold, frankincense, and myrrh.

At Christmas, we take great joy in giving gifts. This is something God did tell us to do: give to others. He is the inventor of gift-giving, and when we give gifts, we are being His good servants. The givers should be thankful that God has allowed them to serve Him by giving. The receivers of gifts should thank God for His many blessings.

1 Peter 1:18a

You know that in the past the way you were living was useless. It was a way of life you learned from those who lived before you.

What about the other Jewish holidays, like Hanukkah and Purim?

Hanukkah, also called the Feast of Dedication or the Feast of Lights, came about during the approximately 400 years between the writing of the Old and New Testaments. The Jews celebrate it to remember a time when the Temple was rededicated to God after it had been under the control of a foreign army (Syria) and used in unholy ways by them (their leader, Antiochus Epiphanes made unholy sacrifices in the Temple and demanded to be worshipped). One verse in John does mention the feast by name and date (season). It also mentions the fact that Jesus was in the Temple during that time, but it doesn't say that He went to Jerusalem on purpose to celebrate it, and it doesn't mention anything about the celebration.

The Jewish religious leaders approached Him at this time and demanded to know if He was the Messiah – they were very uneasy about this subject due to the remembrance of the false worship surrounding this celebration. When Jesus answered in a way they did not like (He said, "The Father and I are one"), they threatened to kill Him for saying, as Antiochus had, that He should be worshipped. Jesus pointed out that the miracles and wonders He had done (which, of course, Antiochus had not done) proved His identity, but the Jewish leaders did not believe. Jesus went on to point out that the Old Testament says we are all gods, because we are a family with God – we are His children. Jesus demanded to know how it was wrong to refer to Himself as the Son of God if God Himself said we are all gods.

John 10:22, 24part, 25, 33b, 34-37
It was winter, and the time came for the Festival of Dedication at Jerusalem. Jesus was in the Temple area at Solomon's Porch.

"If you are the Messiah, then tell us clearly."

Jesus answered, "I told you already, but you did not believe. I do miracles in my Father's name. These miracles show who I am."

"You are only a man, but you say you are the same as God! That is why we are trying to kill you!"

Jesus answered, "It is written in your law that God said, 'I said you are gods.' [He is quoting Psalm 82:6.] This Scripture called those people gods – the people who received God's message. And Scripture is always true. So why do you accuse me of insulting God for saying, 'I am God's Son'? I am the one God chose and sent into the world. If I don't do what my Father does, then don't believe what I say."

Again, the Bible does not say when or how we should celebrate this time. If God wanted us to mark this occasion, He would have told us.

The Feast of Purim is celebrated by Jews to commemorate a wonderful time in their history when an orphaned young woman was used by God to save His people. The story is told in the Book of Esther. In very short form, an evil man had planned to have his people rise up and kill all the Jews living among them on a certain day. The young woman, who had become queen, convinced the king to allow her people to rise up and defend themselves. He granted the request, and the Jews dominated their enemies.

Esther 9:17-18
This happened on the 13th day of the month Adar. On the 14th day the Jews rested and made that day

a happy day of feasting. The Jews in Susa had met together on the 13th and 14th days of the month of Adar. And then on the 15th day they rested. So they made the 15th day a happy day of feasting.

The events were recorded by the new government official, and he sent letters out to all the Jews of the land:

Esther 9:21

He did this to tell the Jews to celebrate Purim every year on the 14th and 15th days of the month of Adar.

The Bible has no instructions about a feast, offerings, or special meetings regarding this time.

Esther 9:19b (How the Jews celebrated)

On this day they have parties and give presents to one another.

While this was certainly a time for celebration – read the story to understand just how much they had to celebrate, and no doubt they did acknowledge God's hand in their deliverance from their enemies – God Himself did not actually say, "Celebrate these days." Mordecai, a man, did.

Did the dinosaurs all die before God made people? What about evolution?

Some believe God made everything during the event called Creation and that people and dinosaurs lived together on earth for many years. When the Flood of Noah's time happened, the (land) dinosaurs that were not on the Ark died. After the Flood, God did not allow the dinosaurs that were saved with the other animals on the Ark to prosper. Some of these people also believe that the earth is quite young at about 6,000 years old, and that its approximate age is easily calculated by the genealogies given in the Bible alone or combined with and compared to other historical data. As discussed, this agrees with the Jewish beliefs regarding the age of the world. In this scenario, the Ice Age likely occurred when God separated the people at the Tower of Babel (not too long after the Flood, as all that moisture would have been ideal for initiating such a drastic climate change), and the land bridges formed by the ice helped the people to spread to the newly separated (or, separating) continents. The Ice Age may also have inhibited the survival of the dinosaurs that had descended from those saved on the Ark.

Other people, who are also true followers, believe the way the Creation story is told allows for some sort of evolution and modern scientific dating of the earth to be millions or even billions of years old to be true. Some of these people believe the dinosaurs all died out before God made man, perhaps basing that on the idea that if the Bible says a day is like a thousand years, then each of the days of Creation could have been a thousand or more years long. There are two significant arguments against this theory.

First, God defined a day as evening plus morning, and then He said each day of Creation was a day because it had an evening and a morning.

Genesis 1:5

God named the light "day," and he named the darkness "night." There was evening, and then there was morning. This was the first day.

He stated His definition of a day five more times before the end of that chapter. If God is repeating Himself – repeatedly – we should pay close attention. Some will argue that He says later in the Bible that, to Him, a day is like a thousand years. Remember, we have discussed that heavenly, spiritual things are much more multi-dimensional than earthly, physical things. Earthly time is just a simple shadow of heavenly time.

2 Peter 3:8

But don't forget this one thing, dear friends: To the Lord a day is like a thousand years, and a thousand years is like a day.

Psalm 90:4

To you, a thousand years is like yesterday, like a few hours in the night.

Again (because this is important), the verse doesn't say a day IS a thousand years, it says it's LIKE a thousand years. The Psalm verse says a thousand years is LIKE a few hours in the night. LIKE is a **simile** – a word used for comparison – not a word used for literal definition. Similes are a very common figure of speech meant to help the reader understand or imagine something in a new way by comparing it to something different. Example: Her smile is like a ray of sunshine.

It seems clear that His distinct repetition of the definition of a day is meant to literally define a day for our benefit. He doesn't need a thousand years for each part of Creation – He's the same God who is going to send Jesus and round us all up in the blink of an eye.

He also tells us that animals and humans were both created on the sixth day.

Here is a common children's Bible song. It simplifies the descriptions, so the extra information is added in parentheses, but it can be useful to help you remember what God made on each day of Creation. You can easily find it online.

> *Day One, Day One – God made light when there was none.*
> *(made His life, His glory, His love to shine on the dark world)*
> *Day Two, Day Two – God made clouds and skies of blue.*
> *(separated the water above from the water below)*
> *Day Three, Day Three – God made grass and flowers and trees.*
> *(gathered the waters below the sky to make a sea and dry land)*
> *Day Four, Day Four – Sun and moon and stars galore*
> *(made celestial bodies – planets are included here as "lights in the sky")*
> *Day Five, Day Five – God made fish and birds alive.*
> *Sixth Day, Sixth Day – God made animals and man that day.*
> *(and woman)*
> *Day Seven, Day Seven – God rested in His heaven.*

Second, Romans 5:12 says, "Sin came into the world because of what one man [Adam] did. And with sin came death." Death is the judgment (penalty) for sin. Romans 8:20 tells us that we are awaiting a time when all of God's Creation can be completely free from ruin – that is, death, decay, destruction. We are waiting to be restored to the state God created for us in the beginning. Death – spiritual and physical – did not begin until humans sinned. If death did not exist until humans sinned, then the dinosaurs (which God says He created on the same day as humans) could not possibly have died before humans existed. Based solely on these two Biblical facts (definition of a day, and death follows sin), it seems reasonable to believe that the large animals spoken of in the Old Testament were probably dinosaurs. God said the behemoth and the leviathan, both of which He described in detail in the book of Job, were the greatest (strongest, most powerful) creatures He made – animals that only God could defeat (which He may have done with the Ice Age).

Job 40:15-24

"Look at the behemoth. I made the behemoth, and I made you. He eats grass like a cow. But he has great strength in his body. The muscles in his stomach are powerful. His tail stands strong like a cedar tree. His leg muscles are very strong. His bones are as strong as bronze. His legs are like iron bars. The behemoth is the most amazing animal I made, but I can defeat him. He eats the grass that grows on the hills where the wild animals play. He lies under the lotus plants. He hides among the reeds of the swamp. The lotus plants hide him in their shade. He lives under the willow trees that grow near the river. If the river floods, the behemoth will not run away. He is not afraid if the Jordan River splashes on his face. No one can blind his eyes and capture him. No one can catch him in a trap."

Job 41:1- 34

"Can you catch Leviathan with a fishhook? Can you tie his tongue with a rope? Can you put a rope through his nose or a hook through his jaw? Will he beg you to let him go free? Will he speak to you with gentle words? Will he make an agreement with you and promise to serve you forever? Will you play with Leviathan as you would play with a bird? Will you put a rope on him so that your girls can play with him? Will fishermen try to buy him from you? Will they cut him into pieces and sell him to the merchants? Can you throw spears into his skin or head? If you ever lay a hand on Leviathan, you will never do it again! Just think about the battle that would be! Do you think you can defeat him? Well, forget it! There is no hope. Just looking at him will scare you! No one is brave enough to wake him up and make him angry. Well, no one can challenge me either! I owe nothing to anyone. Everything under heaven belongs to me. I will tell you about Leviathan's legs, his strength, and his graceful shape. No one can pierce his skin. It is like armor! No one can force him

to open his jaws. The teeth in his mouth scare people. His back has rows of shields tightly sealed together. They are so close to each other that no air can pass between them. The shields are joined to each other. They hold together so tightly that they cannot be pulled apart. When Leviathan sneezes, it is like lightning flashing out. His eyes shine like the light of dawn. Burning torches come from his mouth. Sparks of fire shoot out. Smoke pours from his nose like burning weeds under a boiling pot. His breath sets coals on fire, and flames shoot from his mouth. His neck is very powerful. People are afraid and run away from him. There is no soft spot in his skin. It is as hard as iron. His heart is like a rock; he has no fear. It is as hard as a millstone. When he gets up, even the strongest people are afraid. They run away when he swings his tail. Swords, spears, and darts only bounce off when they hit him. These weapons don't hurt him at all! He breaks iron as easily as straw. He breaks bronze like rotten wood. Arrows don't make him run away. Rocks thrown at him seem as light as chaff. When a wood club hits him, it feels to him like a piece of straw. He laughs when anyone throws a spear at him. The skin on his belly is like sharp pieces of broken pottery. He leaves tracks in the mud like a threshing board. He stirs up the water like a boiling pot. He makes it bubble like a pot of boiling oil. When he swims, he leaves a sparkling path behind him. He stirs up the water and makes it white with foam. No animal on earth is like him. He is an animal made without fear. He looks down on the proudest of creatures. He is king over all the wild animals."

What about evolution? First, let's be clear about what the word evolution means. Several prominent dictionaries define evolution as a process of gradual change, growth, or development. Believing in evolution does not necessarily mean that you also believe Darwin's theory that humans evolved from monkeys, or that life came from some sort of primordial slime. Let's look at some Biblical examples of evolution:

Because there was no death until Adam and Eve sinned, the humans and all the animals in the Garden of Eden were vegetarian. God very specifically said so.

Genesis 1:29-30
God said, "I am giving you all the grain bearing plants and all the fruit trees. These trees make fruit with seeds in it. This grain and fruit will be your food. And I am giving all the green plants to the animals. These green plants will be their food. Every animal on earth, every bird in the air, and all the little things that crawl on the earth will eat that food." And all these things happened.

Humans and animals evolved into meat eaters after being sent out into the world.

In what other respects have humans changed since leaving Eden?

Noah's three sons were Ham, Shem, and Japheth, and from these three men came all the nations of the world. The ancient nation's names are listed in Genesis, and many of them can be placed on a historical map spreading out from Mt. Ararat in far eastern modern-day Turkey, the place where the Bible says Noah's Ark came to rest after the Flood. After the Tower of Babel incident, when God came down and separated the people and gave them different languages – as a very rough generalization – you might say that Ham's descendants eventually populated Africa, Shem's descendants eventually populated Arabia and Asia, and Japheth's descendants eventually migrated to the north. These migrations took some time, and there was a significant degree of overlap in some areas, but generally speaking, a large, centrally located population of people spread out and settled down in smaller groups.

Most scientists around the world today agree that there is no such thing as race. People are just people. We have nations, as the Bible says, but there are no races. So, why do the people of one nation look different from the people of another nation? Even a very brief study of animal husbandry shows that when smaller population groups are bred together, over time certain characteristics become more emphasized. We can apply this knowledge to inherited human characteristics and see that descendants of a group of similar people become more similar over time in a closed reproduction system. So, we can say with certainty that some evolution (look at the definition again) occurred as the people separated into smaller groups and continued to reproduce.

Additionally, as the people left Babylonia, also called Mesopotamia (literally, the land between two rivers – specifically, the Tigris and Euphrates rivers in present day Iraq, south of Mt. Ararat), where the Tower of Babel was located and traveled to new, more isolated places, they and the animals who also spread over the world may have evolved somewhat in order to adapt to their new climates and geographies.

Does modern science agree with the Bible?

There are scientific facts that cannot be argued today, such as the fact that the earth is suspended in space. Many of these facts support what is found in Scripture. On the subject of astronomy, Job 26:7b tells us that God "hung the earth on nothing." Certainly, it has only been in modern history that we could prove that this was true, although the Scripture was written thousands of years ago. On the subject of health and wellness, as scientific study has revealed more, we can see that many of the Old Testament rules about food and personal hygiene that God gave His people were to protect them from germs and infections that they did not yet know about or understand. On the subject of geography, Psalm 8 mentions paths in the seas, but the Gulf Stream (a warm, strong, swift current) through the Atlantic Ocean was not published on a map until 1769. While He does not cover every scientific fact in His Bible, no scientific facts discovered that weren't mentioned in the Bible have ever disproved the existence of God. Science is based on observation, and Jesus instructs us in Matthew 6:26-30 to observe the things around us, like birds and flowers and grass. Studying the things God created will help us understand God.

We learn new things through science every day, and those facts – ideas that are proven to be true – agree with what God has told us.

Is there life on other planets?

While we have no solid, scientific proof that life doesn't exist on other planets, we also have no solid, scientific proof that life does exist on other planets. The Bible is silent on the subject. All we can do is extrapolate from what we know about God and how He works.

God demands monogamy from us. He does not want to share space in our hearts with other "gods." He loves His people, and He wants to have a close relationship – a marriage – with us.

In the beginning, He created one man and one woman to be together. He said the two become one. True, He did allow polygamy in the Old Testament, but when you read the stories of those people through to the end, you discover that polygamy did not make for happy people. It isn't the ideal situation for the adults or for the children. Monogamy is what He designed, and His design was "very good." Based on this, it seems reasonable to be of the opinion that we are His only people.

Does the Bible contradict itself?

As we have seen, there are some verses that, standing alone, seem to contradict one another – or even themselves. To understand these verses better, consider the speaker, the audience, and the overall topic. Consider whether the verses in question actually contradict one another or simply describe the same event from different perspectives. Consider the various cultures, their customs, and the time in which they lived. Study accurate, time relevant maps on questions of geographical locations. The Old Testament mentions many, many cultures over at least several thousand years and numerous cities and countries. The New Testament covers a much shorter time frame, but it mentions various sects, nations, religions, and legal systems, including Jews from Galilee, Jews from Judea, Romans, Samaritans, Greeks, and more. Use an Interlinear Bible to read the Scripture in the original language it was written and study the various ways a word or phrase might be translated and why. Pray for understanding and have faith that God will reveal His truth to you. Be open to accepting the truth, whether it agrees with your long-held beliefs or not. While God makes what we need to know easy to understand, He has also provided enough information in the Bible to keep scholars busy all of their lives.

Who are the saints?

Some church organizations promote prayers to believers (saints) who are physically dead, but spiritually alive. They argue that the Bible tells us to pray for each other, so we should be able to ask the saints in heaven to pray for us.

James 5:16a

So always tell each other the wrong things you have done. Then pray for each other. Do this so that God can heal you.

According to this teaching, the saints (humans whose bodies have died) who are authorized to offer prayers on a living person's behalf are people whom certain church leaders certify as believers who have physically died but are alive in Christ. This means that those church authorities are deciding whether or not a person has gone to heaven and are telling others that their decision agrees with God's. For example, some advocate prayers to Mother Teresa (known to them now as Saint Teresa of Calcutta), who died in 1997, and was declared a saint in 2016, to help them learn to serve their fellow believers better. In other words, because the church authorities said she is a believer who has gone to heaven (she is spiritually alive), people pray to Saint Teresa (and many other saints) asking her to pray for them.

Internet search: how do the dead become saints

Other people are very much against this practice, calling it a sin to pray to anyone but God.

What does the Bible say?

In the New Testament, the people who believe in Christ are called, as a group, **saints** – the original Greek is always plural. Believers are "the saints." In the original Bible languages, there is no Saint "insert name here" mentioned. There are no Biblical instructions telling us to pray to the dead. The Bible not only tells us it would be useless, but His Word also strictly forbids it.

Ecclesiastes 9:6part

After people are dead. . .they will never again share in what happens on earth.

Deuteronomy 18:11b

And no one should try to talk with someone who has died.

Remember, God is omniscient – He is everywhere all the time and is more than able to hear all of our prayers simultaneously. Also remember, Jesus is our High Priest – the only mediator between God and humans. Pray to God in Jesus' name.

1 Timothy 2:5a

There is only one God, and there is only one way that people can reach God. That way is through Christ Jesus.

This issue has been a serious division point among God's people. One point that God's people are not divided on, however, is that Jesus set an example for us to follow. Jesus clearly tells us to be like Him – to do as He does. His disciples asked Him to teach them how to pray. Jesus did not tell them to pray to anyone except God.

Matthew 6:9part (Jesus teaching the disciples how to pray)

"So this is how you should pray: 'Our Father in heaven, we pray...'"

Luke 11:2a

Jesus said to the followers, "This is how you should pray: 'Father, we pray. . .'"

Luke 22:41-42a

Then Jesus went about 50 steps away from them. He knelt down and prayed, "Father, if you are willing. . ."

If you participate in a religious practice that cannot be fully supported by God's Word, you probably shouldn't be doing it. The second half of the James verse we started this discussion with tells us why:

James 5:16b

Anyone who lives the way God wants can pray, and great things will happen.

Is speaking in tongues a sign of being saved?

When Peter and the other apostles received the Holy Spirit on the day of Pentecost, they went out into the crowded streets of Jerusalem and began to preach the Good News of Jesus. The audience heard the men speaking in their own languages. The miraculous event, which we have already discussed, is recorded in Acts Chapter 2. The apostles did not actually know the languages of all the people present – it was an international crowd. The disciples were speaking in languages they had never studied. God used this miracle to build His church – 3,000 people were added that day. The phrase "speaking in different tongues" is the translation used in some Bibles to describe this sign gift.

Paul, who certainly knew several languages, evidently also had this gift that had been given to the original apostles. He mentions that he might even be able to speak in the language of angels.

1 Corinthians 13:1a

I may speak in different languages, whether human or even of angels.

Because of these two examples, some people today teach that if you can't "speak in tongues," then you haven't received the Spirit – you haven't been saved. Others who want to be saved feel pressured to prove themselves and will babble incoherently in an attempt to please their teachers.

Luke made it very clear that the languages the apostles were speaking on Pentecost were actual languages that someone in the audience could understand. Paul made it clear that incoherent speech is of no benefit to growing the church.

1 Corinthians 14:18-19

I thank God that my gift of speaking in different kinds of languages is greater than any of yours. But in the church meetings I would rather speak five words that I understand than thousands of words in a different language. I would rather speak with my understanding, so that I can teach others.

1 Corinthians 14:23

Suppose the whole church meets together and you all speak in different languages. If some people come in who are without understanding or don't believe, they will say you are crazy.

1 Corinthians 14:6

Brothers and sisters, will it help you if I come to you speaking in different languages? No, it will help you only if I bring you a new truth or some knowledge, prophecy, or teaching.

God is certainly capable of performing a miracle anytime He wants, so we can be sure that it is possible that some people, on some occasions, are given the ability to speak in a language they haven't studied. However, the Bible makes it clear that any gifts that are given are for the purpose of growing God's church – and all gifts should be shared in an orderly, peaceful manner. The whole point of a gift is to teach others the Way.

1 Corinthians 14:9b-11
If you don't speak clearly in a language people know, they cannot understand what you are saying. You will be talking to the air! It is true that there are many different languages in the world, and they all have meaning. But if I don't understand the meaning of what someone is saying, it will just be strange sounds to me, and I will sound just as strange to them.

Once again, Paul is not judging whether people actually have the gift of speaking in different languages, he is concerned with HOW they share that gift. Make sure that when you share your gift, it is truly beneficial for someone. Demanding that others demonstrate a gift that they may not have been given is nothing short of bullying.

1 Corinthians 14:27-28
When you meet together, if anyone speaks to the group in a different language, it should be only two or no more than three people who do this. And they should speak one after the other [not all at once]. And someone else should interpret what they say. But if there is no interpreter then anyone who speaks in a different language should be quiet in the church meeting.

Can I be baptized for someone who has died?

Paul, in his letter to the Corinthians, is actually addressing yet another concern – some in the church are saying there will be no resurrection of the dead.

1 Corinthians 15:12-15a

We tell everyone that Christ was raised from death. So why do some of you say that people will not be raised from death? If no one will ever be raised from death then Christ has never been raised. And if Christ has never been raised, then the message we tell is worth nothing. And your faith is worth nothing. And we will also be guilty of lying about God, because we have told people about him, saying that he raised Christ from death.

There were two main sects of Judaism in Paul's day – the Pharisees and the Sadducees. The Pharisees believed in the spiritual world of resurrections, angels, demons, and so on. The Sadducees did not. Some of these Jews were believers in Christ, and this may have been the root of the problem. Paul, a Pharisee, is arguing the case for the resurrection.

1 Corinthians 15:29

If no one will ever be raised from death, then what will the people do who are baptized for those who have died? If the dead are never raised, then why are people baptized for them?

This phrase has baffled scholars for many years. Paul neither condones nor condemns the practice (whatever it may have been) but uses it to assert that there is no point in doing it if there is no resurrection. While the exact meaning of Paul's words remains unclear, we are going to discuss the most literal and most controversial interpretation.

Paul mentions this baptism casually, which indicates the Corinthians were familiar with it. We're going to assume he is referring to the practice of being baptized as a stand-in for someone who has already died. Obviously, this ritual would be performed by those who believe that baptism is an unnegotiable requirement for getting into heaven, else why would they do it?

Now, we must decide. Is baptism by proxy a Biblically sound belief, or is it based on legalism? Can someone who has never been baptized into Jesus get into heaven?

Suppose someone had accepted Christ, but s/he had not yet been baptized before s/he died. Is this person truly saved? Jesus told the criminal on the cross next to Him that he would be in Paradise that day. Remember, the key feature of all those who please God is a circumcised heart – a sincere love for God.

The following is from the **Group Discussion Guide** about the Q&A **What about all the people who never knew Jesus? Can they be saved?** (p. 452)

Some Biblical legalists argue that you cannot be saved without baptism. Noah was brought out of the water that washed away the sin of the world, so one could argue he was baptized. What about Abraham? There are no floods or seas in his story. Do you believe that Abraham, a man the Bible calls "a friend of God," is saved?

Paul doesn't directly address whether baptism by proxy should be done in his argument supporting resurrection, but he addresses it indirectly elsewhere. Each person must answer for him- or herself – no one can answer for you.

Romans 14:12

So each of us will have to explain to God about the things we do.

This simple sentence written by Paul also answers the question whether it is worthwhile to be baptized for those who have died without accepting Christ as their Lord and Savior.

God obviously overlooks the fact that you haven't been baptized if you die before you are able to complete that ritual, but His leniency in no way lessens the call to be baptized. If you believe, then be baptized without delay.

What are the other names used for the Bible?

Not all of these names are found in the Bible.

Scripture(s), The Holy Scripture(s), The Word, His Word, The Living Word, The Word of God, The Holy Word of God, The Good Book, The Book of Books, Word of Life, The Message, Holy Writ, The Book, The Holy Bible

The Old Testament (and its parts): The Book of the Law, The Pentateuch, Scripture(s), The Holy Scripture(s), The Scroll, The TaNaKh (an acronym for the three sections the Jews have divided the Scriptures into – Torah (Law), Nevi'im (Prophets), and Ketuvim (Writings), The Hebrew Bible

The New Testament: The Gospel(s), The Good News, Salvation, Word of Life, The Message, The Sword of the Spirit

Remember: The words in a Bible are not just words on a page in a book. The Bible is made of Living Words. They are called Living Words because they have the power to save your spiritual life, and they come to us from our living God.

What are the other names used for the church?

Congregation, Body of Christ, Bride of Christ, Bride of the Lamb, Followers, Believers, Christians, Disciples, Brothers and Sisters, Saints, Church of God, Members, Priests, Friends, Ambassadors, Heirs, Lights, Pilgrims, Stewards, Redeemed

What are the other names used for God?

These names are used to express GOD in His fullness as the divine Creator of the universe and everything in it.

YHWH – also called the Tetragrammaton, the 4-letter name of the God of Israel

YAHWEH – Scribes inserted vowels from Adonai/Elohim to make the all-consonant YHWH pronounceable, or to remind Jews to use another name.

I AM – English for YHWH

LORD – English for YAHWEH

GOD – English for Elohim, the plural of El

LORD God – English for YAHWEH Elohim

God Almighty – English for El Shaddai

God Most High – English for El Elyon

Jealous LORD – English for YAHWEH Kanah (jealous and zealous come from the same root word)

These names express the relationship between God and man – He is our Lord and Master, and we are His servants.

Adonai – Hebrew for 'Lord' or 'Master,' which Jews began to use in place of YHWH to avoid breaking the second commandment (misusing the name of God).

Jehovah – a non-Jewish word with origins from the 1200's that combines YHWH and Adonai

Some other names: Eli (Aramaic for God), Abba (Aramaic for 'Father'), Father, Ancient of Days

What are the other names used for Jesus?

Christ, Lord, the Word, Messiah, Master, Yeshua (Hebrew), Rabbi, Son of Man, Son of God, Son of David, Lamb of God, King of kings, Lord of lords, Redeemer, Advocate, Bread of Life, Beloved Son, Bridegroom, Chief Cornerstone, Anointed One, Great High Priest, the Door of the sheep, the Good Shepherd, I AM, Immanuel (Hebrew, meaning God with us), Light of the World, Lion of Judah, Rock, Savior, Son of the Highest, the Resurrection & the Life, the Way, Wonderful, Counselor, the Mighty God, the everlasting Father, Prince of Peace, the True Vine, Branch, Alpha & Omega (Greek for A to Z), the First & the Last, the Beginning & the End, and other descriptive phrases

What are the other names used for the Holy Spirit?

Holy Ghost, Helper, Eternal Spirit, Comforter, Ruach Ha-Kodesh (Hebrew), Spirit of the Lord, Spirit of the Father, Spirit of Christ, Spirit of the Son, Spirit of God, Spirit of life, Spirit of glory, Spirit of truth, Spirit of grace, Spirit of prophecy, Spirit of holiness, Spirit of promise, Spirit of adoption, Spirit of revelation, Spirit of the fear of the LORD, Spirit of wisdom, Spirit of understanding, Spirit of counsel, Spirit of might, Spirit of knowledge

What are the other names used for Satan?

Ruler of demons, god of this world, devil, roaring lion, serpent, dragon, adversary, tempter, Beelzebub (chief of the demons/evil spirits), Belial (leader of those who are wicked, without value, worthless, ruined), wicked one, accuser, crooked serpent, enemy, evil spirit, father of lies, prince of this world, ruler of darkness, old trickster, Abaddon (Hebrew for Destroyer), Apollyon (Greek for Destroyer), angel of the abyss/pit/hell – the place of torment

Satan can alter his appearance, as we learned when he tricked Eve while posed as a snake.

2 Corinthians 11:14b-15a

. . .Satan changes himself to look like an angel of light. So it does not surprise us if Satan's servants make themselves look like servants who work for what is right.

Isaiah 14:12

You were like the morning star, but you have fallen from the sky. In the past, all the nations on earth bowed down before you, but now you have been cut down.

The King James Version of the Bible translated the words "morning star" in Isaiah 14:12 as the proper name, Lucifer, giving rise to the trend of equating Satan and Lucifer. Remember, stars represent angels.

****

Walk in the True Light of Christ

Psalm 1

Great blessings belong to those who don't listen to evil advice, who don't live like sinners, and who don't join those who make fun of God. Instead, they love the LORD's teachings and think about them day and night. So they grow strong, like a tree planted by a stream – a tree that produces fruit when it should and has leaves that never fall. Everything they do is successful. But the wicked are not like that. They are like chaff that the wind blows away. When the time for judgment comes, the wicked will be found guilty. Sinners have no place among those who do what is right. The LORD shows his people how to live, but the wicked have lost their way.

2 Corinthians 6:14-16
You are not the same as those who don't believe. So don't join yourselves to them. Good and evil don't belong together. Light and darkness cannot share the same room. How can there be any unity between Christ and the devil? What does a believer have in common with an unbeliever? God's temple cannot have anything to do with idols, and we are the temple of the living God.

****

What are some common words and phrases you might hear other followers say, and what do they mean?

We are saved by grace through faith – We are **saved** from punishment for our sins and brought back into His presence by God's gift of forgiveness (through Jesus). It is a gift (**grace**) from God. We receive it by believing and trusting (having **faith**) in Him.

Ephesians 2:8
I mean that you have been saved by grace because you believed. You did not save yourselves; it was a gift from God.

State of grace – Those who have accepted God's gift of love and forgiveness are living in a state of grace. God has shown us favor – favor that we cannot earn, favor that we cannot buy, favor that we do not deserve, favor that He does not owe us.

Titus 2:11
That is the way we should live, because God's grace has come. That grace can save everyone.

Romans 3:23-24
All have sinned [all who understand sin – all who know the difference between good and evil] and are not good enough to share God's divine greatness. They are made right with God by his grace. This is a free gift. They are made right with God by being made free from sin through Jesus Christ.

Faith – We have faith when we believe in and trust the things of God that we cannot see or that we cannot fully understand.

Hebrews 11:1, 12:2a
Faith is what makes real the things we hope for. It is proof of what we cannot see. . . We must never stop looking to Jesus. He is the leader of our faith, and he is the one who makes our faith complete.

Walking by faith – While we are living in this earthly life, we cannot actually see or experience the heavenly life that God has waiting for us. We just have to trust that He is who He says He is, and He will keep His promises. If we live our lives trusting Him, we are walking by faith.

2 Corinthians 5:7
We live by what we believe will happen, not by what we can see.

Gospel – The Gospel is the Good News of Jesus – that He died as punishment for our sins, was buried, and arose, thereby conquering both sin and death. Gospel also refers to any one of the first four books of the New Testament which all tell the story of Christ with us and His Message of Salvation from sin.

1 Corinthians 15:1a, 3-6a (Scriptures refers to Old Testament writings)
Now, brothers and sisters, I want you to remember the Good News I told you. . .I gave you the message that I received. I told you the most important truths: that Christ died for our sins, as the Scriptures say; that he was buried and was raised to life on the third day, as the Scriptures say; and that he appeared to Peter and then to the twelve apostles. After that Christ appeared to more than 500 other believers at the same time.

The slavery of sin – Sin becomes a master over us just as the sinful Egyptians became masters over the Israelites. When we are saved, we are freed from the slavery of sin. Like the Israelites were freed from the slavery of labor in Egypt on Passover, we are freed from the slavery of sin by Jesus' sacrifice on Passover.

Galatians 5:1
We have freedom now, because Christ made us free. So stand strong in that freedom. Don't go back into slavery again.

John 8:34
Jesus said, "The truth is, everyone who sins is a slave – a slave to sin."

Original Sin – Some teach that we have inherited the actual sin of Adam and we are sinful from birth. The problem with this view is that it eliminates free will. If we are born sinful, then we have no power to choose. The Bible does not support this view. Others teach that we have inherited the fallen nature of Adam and the tendency to sin; that when we reach an age at which we understand right and wrong, we have a choice. We have free will to choose to love God, and we have the power to flee from Satan. The Bible supports this view. We have inherited the fallen situation and nature of Adam, but God wants us to turn our backs on the devil's temptations and our tendency to sin. Our Father has a much better inheritance for His children, and He wants us to come to Him and claim it. Stand before Him and say that you are His.

1 Corinthians 10:13
The only temptations that you have are the same temptations that all people have. But you can trust God. He will not let you be tempted more than you can bear. But when you are tempted, God will also give you a way to escape that temptation. Then you will be able to endure it.

Consequences of sin – The punishment for sin is a spiritual death – that is a spiritual consequence. It is only through the promise of our Savior that we can have a spiritual rebirth and a new life one day in the presence of God. Although the spiritual consequence can be removed by our faith in Jesus' payment for our sin, there are other, more earthly consequences that cannot always be removed.

When you sin, you will have to deal with the physical, mental, emotional, financial, etc. consequences that occur because of it, and almost always, those consequences affect other people as well. These aftereffects of sin can stay with you and those who have been affected, possibly for generations. Trust that God can and pray that He will make those consequences work for the good for His purpose and plan.

Romans 6:23
When people sin, they earn what sin pays – death. But God gives his people a free gift – eternal life in Christ Jesus our Lord.

Spiritual death – the soul separates from God

Ephesians 2:5
We were spiritually dead because of all we had done against him. But he gave us new life together with Christ. (You have been saved by God's grace.)

Physical death – the soul separates from the body

Matthew 10:28
"Don't be afraid of people. They can kill the body, but they cannot kill the soul. The only one you should fear is God, the one who can send the body and the soul to be destroyed in hell."

Calvary – This is the place where Jesus was crucified. Calvary is also called Golgotha, which means "The Place of the Skull," or just "The Skull." This is the name of the location outside the city walls of Jerusalem where the Romans executed prisoners, frequently by crucifixion. The Romans crucified many, many people.

Mark 15:22
They led Jesus to the place called Golgotha. (Golgotha means "The Place of the Skull.")

Luke 23:33
They were led to a place called "The Skull." There the soldiers nailed Jesus to the cross. They also nailed the criminals to crosses beside Jesus – one on the right and the other on the left.

Hebrews 13:11-12
The high priest carries the blood of animals into the Most Holy Place and offers that blood for sins. But the bodies of those animals are burned outside the camp. So Jesus also suffered outside the city. He died to make his people holy with his own blood.

Repent – When you are sorry for your sins and turn away from them (when you repent), it is the Holy Spirit working in you to circumcise your heart and bring you closer to God. He shows you when you are wrong (listen to His correction), and He helps you turn away from that path of eternal destruction.

Acts 3:19, 26
"So you must change your hearts and lives. Come back to God, and he will forgive your sins. . .God has sent his special servant Jesus. He sent him to you first. He sent him to bless you by causing each of you to turn away from your evil ways."

Isaiah 55:7
Evil people should stop living evil lives. They should stop thinking bad thoughts. They should come to the LORD again, and he will comfort them. They should come to our God because he will freely forgive them.

Luke 13:4-5
"And what about those 18 people who died when the tower of Siloam fell on them? Do you think they were more sinful than everyone else in Jerusalem? They were not. But I tell you if you don't decide now to change your lives, you will all be destroyed too!"

Remission of sins – Remission means forgiveness, pardon, paid in full. When we accept Jesus as our Savior and decide to follow His Way in our hearts, our minds, and our bodies, our sins are forgiven and we have a new relationship with God.

Acts 2:38
Peter said to them, "Change your hearts and lives and be baptized, each one of you, in the name of Jesus Christ. Then God will forgive your sins, and you will receive the gift of the Holy Spirit."

Redeemed/Redemption – rescued/our rescue from the punishment we deserve for our sins against God. We have been redeemed by Jesus. God provided our redemption. Jesus is our Redeemer.

Luke 1:68-70
"Praise to the Lord God of Israel. He has come to help his people and has given them freedom. He has given us a powerful Savior from the family of his servant David. This is what he promised through his holy prophets long ago."

Born again – When we are baptized, we are acting out Jesus' burial and resurrection – we are participating in it. When we come up out of the water, we begin our new life with Jesus leading the way. This is a spiritual rebirth. Our spirits have been born again or born anew. We are made new through Jesus.

John 3:3-4a, 5a
Jesus answered, "I assure you, everyone must be born again. Anyone who is not born again cannot be in God's kingdom." Nicodemus said, "How can a man who is already old be born again?" . . .Jesus answered, "Believe me when I say that everyone must be born from water and the Spirit."

Sanctified – made holy for God's use. We are sanctified by faith.

1 Corinthians 6:11
In the past some of you were like that [sinful]. But you were washed clean, you were made holy, and you were made right with God in the name of the Lord Jesus Christ and by the Spirit of our God.

2 Thessalonians 2:13part
Brothers and sisters, you are people the Lord loves. . .You are saved by the Spirit making you holy and by your faith in the truth.

Colossians 1:22b-23a
He did it [Jesus died] so that he could present you to himself as people who are holy, blameless, and without anything that would make you guilty before him. And that is what will happen if you continue to believe in the Good News you heard.

Justified – made innocent before God. We are justified by faith.

Romans 3:22-24a
God makes people right through their faith in Jesus Christ. He does this for all who believe in Christ. Everyone is the same. All have sinned and are not good enough to share God's divine greatness. They are made right with God by his grace. This is a free gift.

Galatians 3:23-24
Before this faith came, the law held us as prisoners. We had no freedom until God showed us the way of faith that was coming. I mean the law was the guardian in charge of us until Christ came. After he came, we could be made right with God through faith.

Holy – We are made holy when we dedicate our lives to God's service. Because we are imperfect, we have an ongoing need to be sanctified and justified before God. This work is accomplished by the Holy Spirit working within us, which is only possible if we have faith that Jesus was the sacrifice that covered all our sins.

Hebrews 10:14
With one sacrifice Christ made his people perfect forever. They are the ones who are being made holy.

God is Good – When someone says this, you should say, "All the time," because all the time, God is good.

Psalm 34:8
Give the LORD a chance to show you how good he is. Great blessings belong to those who depend on him!

Stewards – A steward is someone who manages another person's household or property for him. During our stay on this earth, we are stewards of the gifts God has given to us. It is our job to use these gifts wisely, so that we will be able to give a good report for ourselves when He returns to take possession once more. He expects us to use our talents (our gifts) to bring more people to Him.

1 Peter 4:10b
So be good servants and use whatever gift he has given you in a way that will best serve each other.

Disciple – A person who follows someone in order to learn from him. Jesus had many disciples.

Matthew 4:19-20
Jesus said to them, "Come, follow me, and I will make you a different kind of fishermen. You will bring in people, not fish." Simon and Andrew immediately left their nets and followed him.

John 13:34
"All people will know that you are my followers if you love each other."

Acts 2:42a
The believers spent their time listening to the teaching of the apostles.

Apostle – Someone who has been sent out to deliver the Good News to people who have not heard. Jesus chose 12 of His disciples to begin the work of spreading His Message in full. They had witnessed His entire ministry. Judas betrayed Jesus and was removed from the group. Later, Jesus called Paul to be an apostle for Him.

Mark 3:14
And he chose twelve men and called them apostles. He wanted these twelve men to be with him, and he wanted to send them to other places to tell people God's message.

Witnesses – Those who saw Jesus and heard His teaching in person and those heroes of the Old Testament who showed us excellent examples of faith in God and His promises are called witnesses. If we testify about Jesus to others, we are also called witnesses. We, like the Bible heroes of old, are not eyewitnesses of Jesus, but we testify by faith in the Message we have heard.

Acts 1:8
"But the Holy Spirit will come on you and give you power. You will be my witnesses. You will tell people everywhere about me – in Jerusalem, in the rest of Judea, in Samaria, and in every part of the world."

Acts 22:15
"You will be his witness to all people. You will tell them what you have seen and heard."

Sojourners – This is what all of us here on earth are in this life. We are just travelers passing through to another place.

1 Chronicles 29:15
We are only strangers traveling through this world like our ancestors. Our time on earth is like a passing shadow, and we cannot stop it.

1 Peter 2:11
Dear friends, you are like visitors and strangers in this world. So I beg you to keep your lives free from the evil things you want to do, those desires that fight against your true selves.

Zion – Can refer to the earthly city of Jerusalem in Israel, the hill in eastern Jerusalem that was the building site of the Temple, the nation of Israel, and/or heaven. Many Jews today still pray facing Jerusalem (specifically, the Temple Mount). Presumably, they are praying for the rebuilding of the Temple so that sacrifices can resume, as well as the coming of the Messiah for the salvation of Israel.

2 Samuel 5:7
But David did take the fort of Zion [from the Jebusites living in Jerusalem]. This fort became the City of David.

Jeremiah 31:6part
'Come, let's go up to Zion to worship the LORD our God!'

Isaiah 46:13b
"I will bring salvation to Zion and to my wonderful Israel."

Psalm 110:2
The LORD will cause your kingdom to grow, beginning at Zion, until you rule the lands of your enemies!

Isaiah 1:27
God is good and does what is right, so he will rescue Zion and the people who come back to him.

Israel's land was ruled by various nations in the years following the Roman destruction of Jerusalem and the Temple in AD 70 and the Jew's removal from that land (the loss of their statehood) in AD 135. When WWI ended in 1918, Britain took control over the area with the permission of the League of Nations (precursor to the UN). After WWII, in 1948, Israel became an independent Jewish state. The Muslim-majority Arab nations in that area felt threatened, and the entire region has continued to be a hotbed of hostility.

Both the Jewish nation and the Muslim nations trace their beginning to Abraham – the Jews through his son, Isaac, and the Muslims through his son, Ishmael. Isaac was Abraham's legitimate heir, born from Abraham's wife, Sarah. Ishmael was born from Sarah's servant woman, Hagar, when Sarah grew tired of waiting for God to fulfill His promise of a child and insisted Abraham father a child through Hagar. After Sarah had Isaac, she banished Hagar and her son.

Fruits of the Spirit – The Holy Spirit is given to us as a guide or counsellor to lead us away from the things that tempt us and to lead us toward the things of God. The acts (the fruits) that come from a person who is led by the Spirit show "love, joy, peace, patience, kindness, goodness, faithfulness, gentleness, and self-control." The true children of God are known by these fruits.

Galatians 5:22-23a
But the fruit that the Spirit produces in a person's life is love, joy, peace, patience, kindness, goodness, faithfulness, gentleness, and self-control.

Spiritual warfare – When we are fighting evil (the bad things that are happening in our lives), the Bible tells us to wear the armor of God. We fight with truth, right living, the Good News, faith, salvation, and the Word. These weapons are activated by prayer. Satan is a spirit, and whether we know it or not, we are either fighting for him or against him. If we are fighting against him, we are fighting for God.

Ephesians 6:11-13a, 14-18
Wear the full armor of God. Wear God's armor so that you can fight against the devil's clever tricks. Our fight is not against people on earth. We are fighting against the rulers and authorities and the powers of this world's darkness. We are fighting against the spiritual powers of evil in the heavenly places. That is why you need to get God's full armor. . .So stand strong with the belt of truth tied around your waist, and on your chest wear the protection of right living. On your feet wear the Good News of peace to help you stand strong. And also use the shield of faith with which you can stop all the burning arrows that come from the Evil One. Accept God's salvation as your helmet. And take the sword of the Spirit – that sword is the teaching of God. Pray in the Spirit at all times. Pray with all kinds of prayers, and ask for everything you need. To do this you must always be ready. Never give up. Always pray for all of God's people.

God does not call the equipped, He equips the called – God gives you what you need to do the job He calls you to do. All you need to bring is faith.

Hebrews 13:20-21part
I pray that the God of peace will give you every good thing you need so that you can do what he wants.

Philippians 4:13
Christ is the one who gives me the strength I need to do whatever I must do.

Don't put God in a box – Don't try to limit what God can do.

Ephesians 3:20
With God's power working in us, he can do much, much more than anything we can ask or think of.

Lord willing – This statement is made to show that we only want to do the things God has in mind for us. We do not want to go against what He wills (what He wants). Another phrase is often tacked onto the end of this. For example, someone might say, "I'll be there – Lord willing, and the creek don't rise." This means: I will be there if God wants me to be there, and if He wants me there, He will prevent major problems that would keep me from attending.

James 4:14a, 15
You don't know what will happen tomorrow. . .So you should say, "If the Lord wants, we will live and do this or that."

Give God the glory – We are to give God credit where credit is due and not take credit for ourselves for good things that are done. ALL good things come from God. He works in us and through us. We are agents representing His goodness.

James 1:17a
Everything good comes from God. Every perfect gift is from him.

Can I get an "Amen!"? – This is said when a person states something that God has done for us and would like for others to share in celebrating His goodness.

1 Chronicles 16:36
Praise the LORD, the God of Israel! He always was and will always be worthy of praise! All the people praised the LORD and said "Amen!"

Hallelujah! or **Allelujah!** – Both of these words mean, Praise the Lord!

Revelation 19:1
After this I heard what sounded like a large crowd of people in heaven. The people were saying, "Hallelujah!"

Jubilee – God told Moses to tell His people that every seventh year was a type of Sabbath year. For six years, the people would plant crops, but on the seventh year, they were to let the land rest. Then, they were to count seven groups of seven years. At the end of that time, on the Day of Atonement, they were to blow a ram's horn throughout the land. Every 50th year would be a Sabbath year called Jubilee (much like the time between the Feast of First Fruits and Pentecost, except instead of counting weeks, they would count years). Jubilee was a year of release for the Israelites – from debt and from slavery – a time when they could regain what God had given them – land and freedom. It was a year of restoration to one's rightful place. Although the year of Jubilee is not officially observed by the Jews today (there is no Temple, there are no religious leaders of the Temple to declare the start of Jubilee, all the tribes of Israel are not on the land God led them to when He brought them out of Egypt, and the calendar has some discrepancies), when Jesus comes again, perhaps it will be when a year of Jubilee would have occurred.

Exodus 23:12a (Seventh day rest)
"Work for six days, but on the seventh day, rest!"

Exodus 23:10-11 (Seventh year rest)
"Plant seeds, harvest your crops, and work the ground for six years. But the seventh year must be a special time of rest for the land. Don't plant anything in your fields. If any crops grow there, allow the poor to have it. And allow the wild animals to eat the food that is left. You should do the same with your vineyards and with your fields of olive trees."

Leviticus 25:10, 12a (Jubilee was to be observed every 50th year - After every seven sets of seven years)
You will make the 50th year a special year. You will announce freedom for everyone living in your country. This time will be called 'Jubilee.' Each of you will go back to your own property. And each of you will go back to your own family. . .That year is Jubilee. It will be a holy time for you.

Fellowship – This refers to time spent with other Christians.

1 Thessalonians 5:11
So encourage each other and help each other grow stronger in faith, just as you are already doing.

Hebrews 10:25
We must not quit meeting together, as some are doing. No, we need to keep on encouraging each other. This becomes more and more important as you see the Day getting closer.

Doctrine of men – the teachings of humans, or human thoughts on a subject. This phrase is used in a negative way to show that a teaching is not a teaching of God.

Matthew 15:1-2a, 3
Then some Pharisees and teachers of the law came to Jesus. They came from Jerusalem and asked him, "Why do your followers not obey the traditions we have from our great leaders who lived long ago?" Jesus answered, "And why do you refuse to obey God's command so that you can follow those traditions you have?"

Mark 7:6b-7 (from Isaiah 29:13)

'These people honor me with their words, but I am not really important to them. Their worship of me is worthless. The things they teach are only human rules.'

2 Timothy 4:3-4
The time will come when people will not listen to the true teaching. But people will find more and more teachers who please them. They will find teachers who say what they want to hear. People will stop listening to the truth. They will begin to follow the teaching in false stories.

1 Timothy 4:16
Be careful in your life and in your teaching. Continue to live and teach rightly. Then you will save yourself and those who listen to your teaching.

Ordinances of the church – An ordinance is a ritual/rite/ceremony that is ordered by Christ in the New Testament. We are to take part in these if we are Christ's followers. The two rites that all Christians agree on are baptism and Communion. Baptism announces a new believer's engagement to Christ, and the partaking of Communion is a remembrance of Jesus' sacrifice (His vows). Believers (the bride of Christ) perform these ordinances while awaiting the arrival of the Groom who will take His bride to her new home. Some Protestant denominations only use the word ordinance, and some use the word ordinance or the word sacrament to mean the same thing. Catholics use the word sacrament, and they observe seven of them. Different denominations of Protestants agree with some of these seven, they just don't call them all sacraments or ordinances.

Acts 2:38
Peter said to them, "Change your hearts and lives and be baptized, each one of you, in the name of Jesus Christ. Then God will forgive your sins, and you will receive the gift of the Holy Spirit."

1 Corinthians 11:23-26
The teaching I gave you is the same that I received from the Lord: On the night when the Lord Jesus was handed over to be killed, he took bread and gave thanks for it. Then he divided the bread and said, "This is my body; it is for you. Eat this to remember me." In the same way, after they ate, Jesus took the cup of wine. He said, "This cup represents the new agreement from God, which begins with my blood sacrifice. When you drink this, do it to remember me." This means that every time you eat this bread and drink this cup, you are telling others about the Lord's death until he comes again.

The Second Coming – when Jesus comes to us again to complete God's plan

1 Thessalonians 4:15-17 (This is the event called the Rapture)
What we tell you now is the Lord's own message. Those of us who are still living when the Lord comes again will join him, but not before those who have already died. The Lord himself will come down from heaven with a loud command, with the voice of the archangel, and with the trumpet call of God. And the people who have died and were in Christ will rise first. After that we who are still alive at that time will be gathered up with those who have died. We will be taken up in the clouds and meet the Lord in the air. And we will be with the Lord forever.

Hebrews 9:28b
And he will come a second time, but not to offer himself for sin. He will come the second time to bring salvation to those

who are waiting for him.

John 14:3
"After I go and prepare a place for you, I will come back. Then I will take you with me, so that you can be where I am."

Mysteries of the Bible – There are some things that we cannot understand because we do not yet know enough. As physical beings, we cannot fully understand the spiritual dimension where God and the angels live now. There are also some things that God has not explained to us. We must respect Him as our Father who knows what is best for His children. We must accept that He is acting in our best interest. Believing in the things we cannot see is faith.

Job 11:7-9
"Do you think you really understand God? Do you completely understand God All-Powerful? That knowledge is higher than the heavens and deeper than the place of death. So what can you do? How can you learn it all? It is greater than the earth and bigger than the seas."

Deuteronomy 29:29
"There are some things that the LORD our God has kept secret. Only he knows these things. But he told us about some things. And these teachings are for us and our descendants forever. And we must obey all the commands in that law."

Proverbs 25:2a
We honor God for the things he keeps secret.

Ecclesiastes 11:5
You don't know where the wind blows. And you don't know how a baby grows in its mother's womb. In the same way, you don't know what God will do – and he makes everything happen.

Daniel 2:47
Then the king said to Daniel, "I know for sure your God is the God over all gods and the Lord over all kings. He tells people about things they cannot know. I know this is true because you were able to tell these secret things to me."

But as the Scriptures say, "No one has ever seen, no one has ever heard,
no one has ever imagined what God has prepared for those who love him."

1 Corinthians 2:9 (from Isaiah 64:4)

In this life, we only see shadows of what is to come.

****

God's Plan
-Simplified

Summary

The things of God that we cannot understand should not worry us. Everything we need to know about God is easy to understand. He did not make it hard for us at all. He is easy to know, easy to love, easy to trust.

We have discussed how God's truths can be found when we study of a variety of subjects including history, astronomy, mathematics, zoology, sociology, and more. We can increase our understanding of the Bible by studying these subjects (especially when the textbooks we use are from authors/publishers who are true believers), but always remember God has given us His Message in a way that requires our spiritual faith, not our worldly intelligence.

1 Corinthians 1:20b-24, 26-31
God has made the wisdom of the world look foolish. This is what God in his wisdom decided: Since the world did not find him through its own wisdom, he used the message that sounds foolish to save those who believe it. The Jews ask for miraculous signs, and the Greeks want wisdom. But this is the message we tell everyone: Christ was killed on a cross. This message is a problem for Jews, and to other people it is nonsense. But Christ is God's power and wisdom to the people God has chosen, both Jews and Greeks. . .

Who is chosen?

Brothers and sisters, God chose you to be his. Think about that! Not many of you were wise in the way the world judges wisdom. Not many of you had great influence, and not many of you came from important families. But God chose the foolish things of the world to shame the wise. He chose the weak things of the world to shame the strong. And God chose what the world thinks is not important – what the world hates and thinks is nothing. He chose these to destroy what the world thinks is important.

Why did God do this?

God did this so that no one can stand before him and boast about anything. It is God who has made you part of Christ Jesus. And Christ has become for us wisdom from God. He is the reason we are right with God and pure enough to be in his presence. Christ is the one who set us free from sin. So, as the Scriptures say, "Whoever boasts should boast only about the Lord."

Your life is all about God and your relationship with Him.

God has given us all free will to come to Him on our own. Having free will means that we have power – the power to choose for ourselves, the power to change our momentum and pursue a better path.

God is our Valentine – He loves us and sends us messages of His love. He is our Sword and Shield – we can use His Word to keep Satan away from us (Satan only has power over us if we let him). He is our Fireman – He will rescue us from the fiery punishment of Satan and his followers. He is our Builder – He is preparing a home for us that is so wonderful we cannot even imagine it. He is our Perfect Father – He loves all His children.

1 John 5:3-5

Loving God means obeying his commands. And God's commands are not too hard for us, because everyone who is a child of God has the power to win against the world. It is our faith that has won the victory against the world. So who wins against the world? Only those who believe that Jesus is the Son of God.

Just love Him. Trust Him completely. Be happy because you know that He has wonderful things in store for you one day. When God completes His plan, everything will be made right, you will know complete joy, and bad things will never again happen to you. Show the joy and love you have with Him to others, so they can know Him, too. Build each other up. Strengthen each other. He is coming soon!

Your faith and love continue because you know what is waiting for you in heaven – the hope you have had since you first heard the true message, the Good News that was told to you. Throughout the world, the Good News is bringing blessings and is spreading. And that's what has been happen-

ing among you since the first time you heard it and understood the truth about God's grace. . .we have continued praying for you. This is what we pray:

> *that God will make you completely sure of what he wants by giving you all the wisdom and spiritual understanding you need; that this will help you live in a way that brings honor to the Lord and pleases him in every way; that your life will produce good works of every kind and that you will grow in your knowledge of God; that God will strengthen you with his own great power so that you will be patient and not give up when troubles come.*

Then you will be happy and give thanks to the Father. He has made you able to have what he has promised to give all his holy people, who live in the light. God made us free from the power of darkness. And he brought us into the kingdom of his dear Son. The Son paid the price to make us free. In him we have forgiveness of our sins.

Colossians 1:5-6, 9b-14

****

The Time of the End

Many are curious to know what the Bible says about the events surrounding Jesus' return. As well they should be. There will be some rough times that precede His second coming. While you can certainly remain faithful through those trials just by always trusting in Him, you may find it reassuring to understand what is happening. Remember, God doesn't do anything without telling us about it first. He wants us to know, and He wants us to understand. He has told us what we need to know so we can be fully prepared.

Amos 3:7
When the Lord GOD decides to do something, he will first tell his servants, the prophets.

The Bible contains three major prophecies about what is to come, as well as several minor ones:

- Daniel not only foretold what would happen over the next several hundred years, he also foretold about the time of the end in his book, Daniel, Chapters 7-12.
- Jesus reiterated and expanded on this prophecy in what is now called His Olivet Discourse – a lesson He taught sitting on the Mount of Olives looking back at Jerusalem. Find it in Matthew 24, Mark 13, and Luke 21.
- John gave us the most information in His book of Revelation, Chapters 4-22, which was recorded after the fall of Jerusalem and the destruction of the Temple.
- Other prophecies are found in Isaiah 13:6-13, 2 Thessalonians 2:1-12, 1 Corinthians 15:50-57, the book of Joel, and Zechariah 14:1-9.

This is not an exhaustive list, meaning it doesn't include every verse that gives information about the time of the end. At this point in our discussion, it should be clear that the Bible is like an intricate, compelling, dynamic tapestry whose verses and stories are threads that are inextricably woven into and around other threads. Reflect on what we've discussed about water, blood, birth, doors, shadows, numbers, etc., and how often these messages appear.

There are some who teach that most of the events mentioned in these prophecies have already happened, and, in a way, they have. God has provided shadows of the future for us all through the Bible. Remember, Abraham preparing to sacrifice his son, Isaac, was a preview of God providing the sacrifice of Jesus. Moses freeing God's people from slavery for the sinful Egyptians was a preview of Jesus freeing God's people from the slavery of sin. The judgment of Noah's day as well as the plagues of Egypt and the Roman conquering of Jerusalem all foreshadow the final judgment against sin, each in its own way.

Babylon, while it was an actual nation in ancient times, has always been and still is symbolic of those who do not follow God. Remember the Tower of Babel when God dispersed humanity for trying to elevate themselves to a higher status in opposition to God? The ancient nation of Babylon also operated in opposition to God, but He used Babylon as a tool to punish His people for their disobedience. After being taken there as a captive of war when he was a teenager, the prophet Daniel spent the rest of his life in Babylon. Among other reasons, Daniel's story is given to us to teach us how we should behave when utterly surrounded by those who are against God.

God wants all of His children, but not all of them will come to Him. Many are turned away by the temptations of Satan, even though all of his temptations are lies.

Matthew 7:13-14 (Jesus speaking)

"You can enter true life only through the narrow gate. The gate to hell is very wide, and there is plenty of room on the road that leads there. Many people go that way. But the gate that opens the way to true life is narrow. And the road that leads there is hard to follow. Only a few people find it."

Nations (groups of people) in the Bible are given the feminine pronoun – they are referred to as female, and those who follow God faithfully are called the Bride of Christ. Those who do not, like Babylon, are called prostitutes – they are not faithful to the One who loves them. They have sold themselves to Satan. Only Jesus can redeem them.

When the time of the end comes, people who are not strong in the faith will be fooled and led astray. As He did with the Egyptians before the Exodus, God will give many opportunities for them to realize the truth, to repent, to humble themselves, and to come back to Him. Just before the Exodus, He sent 10 (a number associated with the Law and testimony that shows completion) terrible troubles on the sinful. At the time of the end, He will send 7 (a number showing perfect completion) troubles – Revelation calls them God's bowls of wrath.

Revelation 16:8-9

The fourth angel poured out his bowl on the sun. The sun was given power to burn the people with fire. The people were burned by the great heat. They cursed the name of God, who had control over these plagues. But they refused to change their hearts and lives and give glory to God.

Acts 3:19-21

So you must change your hearts and live. Come back to God, and he will forgive your sins. Then the Lord will give you times of spiritual rest. He will send you Jesus, the one he chose to be the Messiah. But Jesus must stay in heaven until the time when all things will be made right again. God told about this time when he spoke long ago though his holy prophets.

There will be 7 seals on a scroll (that can only be opened by the Lamb), 7 trumpets (Jesus will return with the blast of the seventh – this is the Day of the Lord), and 7 bowls of wrath. Jesus will return after Satan has infiltrated a leader called the Antichrist who, with the help of a very effective false prophet, gathers the fallen nations of the world together in a great battle against God's people at a place called Armageddon.

Matthew 24:32

"The fig tree teaches us a lesson: When its branches become green and soft, and new leaves begin to grow, then you know that summer is very near. In the same way, when you see all these things happening, you will know that the time is very near, already present."

As seen in the parables we have discussed, those who understand God's Word will recognize the signs of these end times. The events that occur with the opening of the seals and blasts of the trumpets will be those signs. The signs will conclude with the Day of the Lord, which is when Jesus returns and God pours out His bowls of wrath on the earth. God is not willing to tolerate Satan and his followers forever. He is patiently waiting for those He knows will choose Him. Jesus will return, and true justice will be done.

Malachi 3:5a

Then I will bring you to justice. I will be an expert witness and testify about the evil things people do.

Revelation 10:7

"In the days when the seventh angel is ready to blow his trumpet, God's secret plan will be completed - the Good News that God told to his servants, the prophets."

The Old Testament mentions a man named Melchizedek. Unlike others in the Old Testament, neither his parents nor other ancestors are mentioned. Melchizedek serves as an early example of a Christ-like figure, in that he was both a high priest and a king of justice and peace who was sent from God. Since he lived before Aaron and the Levites, he is not listed as being of the lineage of priests (neither was Jesus, since He was born in the tribe of Judah, not Levi), but we know Melchizedek was a legitimate priest, because Abraham gave him a tithe (a portion of his possessions (money, animals, goods) to support his work as a priest of God).

Hebrews 7:2, 16

Then Abraham gave him a tenth of everything he had. The name Melchizedek, king of Salem, has two meanings. First, Melchizedek means "king of justice." And "king of Salem" means "king of peace" . . .He was made a priest, but not because he met the requirement of being born into the right family. He became a priest by the power of a life that will never end.

Psalm 110:4 (about Jesus)

The LORD has made a promise with an oath and will not change his mind: "You are a priest forever – the kind of priest Melchizedek was."

Just as He was the legitimate Passover sacrifice and the legitimate Great High Priest, Jesus Christ is also (He is descended from King David) and will be (He will earn it in battle) the legitimate King of kings. After His Gentile faithful have been taken up to heaven for protection, every sinful nation left will join together and rise up against the faithful remnant of His people Israel – against Him. Jesus will defend His chosen people AND His land. He will arrive at the battle of Armageddon (in Israel) and defeat them all. Rather than arriving in peace on a donkey, as He did in His first visit, He will charge in with wrath on His war-horse and utterly destroy the wicked. In doing so, Jesus will legitimately establish His physical kingdom on earth.

Philippians 2:10-11

God did this [raised Jesus up to the highest place] so that every person will bow down to honor the name of Jesus. Everyone in heaven, on earth, and under the earth will bow. They will all confess, "Jesus Christ is Lord," and this will bring glory to God the Father.

Revelation 5:11-13

Then I looked, and I heard the voices of many angels. The angels were around the throne, the four living beings, and the elders. There were thousands and thousands of angels – 10,000 times 10,000. The angels said in a loud voice, "All power, wealth, wisdom, and strength belong to the Lamb who was killed. He is worthy to receive honor, glory, and praise!" Then I heard every created being that is in heaven and on earth and under the earth and in the sea, everything in all these places, saying, "All praise and honor and glory and power forever and ever to the one who sits on the throne and to the Lamb!" The four living beings said, "Amen!" And the elders bowed down and worshipped.

When you understand the time of the end, you will see references to it throughout the Bible. Once you have read through the Bible, go back and reread Daniel 7-12, the Olivet Discourse, and the book of Revelation. Then, for a very thorough logical and analytical explanation of the time of the end, visit www.revelationlogic.com. There are some people who interpret the time of the end differently, but if any Biblical interpretation does not sensibly flow with the rest of the Bible IN EVERY RESPECT, then you need to look closer. Every word God included in His Book – in His original version, not necessarily a translation – is there for a reason.

God is specific, He is orderly, He follows His plan – He is dependable. And He doesn't do anything without telling us about it first.

Revelation 15:3b-4
"Great and wonderful are the things you do, Lord God All-Powerful. Right and true are your ways, Ruler of the nations. All people will fear you, O Lord. All people will praise your name. Only you are holy. All people will come and worship before you, because it is clear that you do what is right."

For you

Our discussion has not been a full explanation of all things in the Bible, but hopefully it has been enough to help you get started or to make some progress on your journey. I hope it ultimately leads you to discover not only what you believe, but also why you believe it. My prayer is that you develop and maintain a relationship with God that sustains you through all the ups and downs of this temporary, earthly, partial life and carries you through to a permanent, heavenly, full life in His presence.

Let's look back to the very first question:
How can we know for sure that God has a plan?

After everything we have discussed, I hope you are exceedingly confident that God has a plan and that its final fulfillment is coming soon.

God is our Father. We are all rich, because our Father has left us, His children, an inheritance. Our inheritance is a free ticket to a perfect life with Him, but we must each use our own power to claim it. Claim your right as a child of God. Never stop learning His Word – it strengthens your faith. Your child-like faith in our loving Father will take you to the happy end.

Jude 24-25

God is strong and can keep you from falling. He can bring you before his glory without any wrong in you and give you great joy. He is the only God, the one who saves us. To him be glory, greatness, power, and authority through Jesus Christ our Lord for all time past, now, and forever. Amen.

May God bless you, and may He find you always seeking Him.

Semper quaeritis

The simple truths of God:

He has one theme – Love.

He has one desire – Family.

He has one plan – Freedom.

Group Discussion Guide

*Some discussion points assume Biblical knowledge beyond the corresponding section of the book.

Semper quaeritis *Latin for "Always seeking"*

The things of God are so vast and so wonderful, we certainly can never understand them all in this life. God will reveal everything at just the right time. When He does, what are some of the things you hope to discover? What are you looking forward to understanding clearly?

For those who believe, For the unsure, For the disenchanted, For all those who seek God

Do these descriptions sound familiar to you?
Does one of them fit you (now, or in the past)?
Are there other descriptions/situations you've encountered in attending or considering a church group?

Loneliness, confusion, depression, defeat, searching, waiting, and so forth are stressful situations. They are the opposite of peaceful. Do you think God wants you to experience these emotions? Why would He allow you to experience these situations?

2 Corinthians 12:9-10

But the Lord said, "My grace is all you need. Only when you are weak can everything be done completely by my power." So I will gladly boast about my weaknesses. Then Christ's power can stay in me. Yes, I am glad to have weaknesses if they are for Christ. I am glad to be insulted and have hard times. I am glad when I am persecuted and have problems, because it is when I am weak that I am really strong.

Before we begin, what is the framework for this discussion?

Everyone has a unique perspective from which they interpret their world.
What is your perspective? What are other perspectives you have observed?
Does a person's perspective change over time?
What factors can modify a person's perspective?

How can we know for sure that God has a plan?

Without review, what do you know about the Jewish feast days?

Do you view the Old Testament God and the New Testament Jesus this way?
Why or why not?

Do you believe that Satan is actively pursuing the destruction of your faith?
If you do, how has he attacked you?
How has he attacked other people you know?

Do you believe God wants us to be divided?
Are you willing to open your heart and mind in order to join with others who believe?

Where should we begin?

Does a circular timeline make sense to you?
Do you think our individual life timelines are circular? Explain.

Which of the events on the timeline circle are already familiar to you?

Are you curious to know more about any of the events listed?

What's the first step to understanding God?

Do you think the Old Testament stories are just myths – that they aren't true?
Why do you think this?

Were you taught this, or have you studied it yourself?

Have you ever done any research on the subject of Biblical archaeology or Biblical science?

Internet search: proof that the Bible is true
Internet search: Biblical archaeology / Biblical archaeologists
Internet search: does science confirm the Bible

Read what you find but cross-reference the information by checking the facts in the Bible for yourself to make sure the claims are Biblically accurate.

If you searched the above topics, you likely encountered information about or from apologists. What did you learn?

God has created patterns for us. These patterns give us a sense of comfort because the patterns are dependable, even predictable. Discuss some of the patterns of this life in the following categories:

weather
human development
interpersonal human behavior (sociology)
geometric shapes
poetry
laws of science
history
laws of nature
laws of economics
astronomy

Because of these patterns, we can see that nothing is new. In Matthew, Chapter 6, Jesus tells us to study our world to see the beauty, provision, and orderliness of God.

Who is God?

In what ways do you think we are made in the image of God?
The natural gender ratio of humans at birth is 1:1, which is not the case with every creature God made. How might this scientific fact correlate with humans being made in His image? How might this correlate with His plans for us?

What are the similarities between what parents would do today to prepare for a new baby and what God did during Creation?

Are there any humans today who are somehow not a result of God's original Creation?

What do you think of when you hear/read the word Paradise?

We don't live in Eden now. . .what happened?

All sins – lying, cheating, stealing, jealousy, murder, adultery, etc. – boil down to one errant character trait – pride. We think we won't get caught, we justify to ourselves that we deserve it, we think we're better than someone else (we make ourselves the judge), and so on. All of these faulty self-views are rooted in pride.

Can you think of any sin that is not rooted in pride?

Isaiah 2:11-12

Proud people will stop being proud. They will bow down to the ground with shame, and only the LORD will still stand high. The LORD All-Powerful has a special day planned when he will punish the proud and boastful people. They will be brought down.

Is all pride bad, or are there good kinds of pride?

We may refer to an accomplishment using the word pride (I am so proud of you for what you've accomplished! -or- You should be proud, because you worked hard on that project, and you did a good job!) What is the root of good pride? Isn't it really thankfulness to God for the gift (the person who brought you happiness, the talent that enabled you to accomplish something, etc.)?

Is it easy to shift from good pride to bad pride?

As we work to become more like the people God wants us to be, we should turn our backs on negative pride and walk in the opposite direction.

What is the opposite of pride?
If good pride is thankfulness, is that the same thing as humility?

Read the story of the prodigal (wasteful) son in Luke 15:11-32.
If you were the loyal son, would you be jealous?
If you were the prodigal son, would you feel guilty about the blessings your father gave you when you returned?
How could you make peace with your brother? (see humility above)

Did you notice in verse 20 that the father forgave the son even before the son came close enough to apologize? In verse 22, after the son confesses, the father does not even respond directly to him – he is already busy planning a celebration for his son's rebirth! This is God's attitude when we turn toward Him with sincerity in our hearts. We should confess just as the son did, but God's forgiveness rests on us the moment we turn our hearts toward Him.

Was God punishing Adam and Eve by refusing them access to the Tree of Life, or was He showing them mercy?

Where does this leave us?

Everything good in this life comes from God. What are some of the good things you experience?

Everything bad in this life is because of Satan and his lies. What are some of the bad things you experience?

In our court system, can you define what makes a judge good or bad without talking about political differences?

Has God ever made a way for you to escape a situation you knew was not good for you? He has, but did you notice what it was – did you notice it was actually His hand guiding you?

Did God save you from that negativity because He owed you (you earned it by doing something for Him), or because He loves you?

Do you regularly ask God to be near you? In your personal relationship with Him, do you treat Him in a way that would make Him want to be with you – that is, do you treat Him with respect and honor?

Why doesn't God just get rid of Satan?

God is God of everything, but what is everything – the big and the small?

Children have a beautiful sense of wonder as they learn about their world.
Do you still have a sense of wonder?
Take time to see and to be amazed by the incredible things He has made.
What are some things He has made that you cannot explain?
Understand that He is still in complete control of His creations.

Some believe that the verses saying a day is like a thousand years and a thousand years is like a day means that it took God six thousand years instead of six days to complete Creation.

What do you think about this? Is this just a figure of speech to help us understand how God perceives time, or should we take it literally?

If it did take 6,000 years, how does that agree with God saying repeatedly that the cycle of darkness and daylight made one day?

If everything earthly has a heavenly counterpart – if the things of earth are a shadow of the things in heaven, as the Bible says – then there must be some form of time in heaven. What do you think heavenly time is like?

What do you know about God and His numbers? What do some of them mean?

Internet search: Biblical numerology (the study of numbers in the Bible)

Please keep in mind that it was much more modern men who added chapter numbers and verse numbers to the Bible. Those were not included in the original manuscripts. Only give value to the meanings of the numbers God gave us.

Many people are negatively intimidated by math, rather than being positively awed by the beauty and orderliness of God's numbers.

Internet search: *The Most Beautiful Equation in Mathematics* by Keith Devlin

Poetry of words is for those who can appreciate subjectivity.
Poetry of numbers is for those who require exacting objectivity.

God knows us intimately, and He speaks to each of us in ways we can understand.

"Are we there, yet?"
How patient are you? Do you give God time to do His work, or do you grow impatient and take matters into your own hands?
Read the part of the story of Abraham and his wife, Sarah, in Genesis 15-16.
Sarah grew impatient waiting for God, and the results of that were not good.

Should we sit and wait for God? What should we do while we wait? How can we know when the time is right to act?

Have you ever realized that God has been prodding you forward for some time but you didn't notice?

What has God done in His war with Satan?

2 Peter 2:5b

Noah was a man who told people about living right.

Some people call Noah a preacher. Was he a preacher in the same way we think of a preacher today? How did he preach to others – what do we know for sure?

God separated the nations at the Tower of Babel. Read the Q&A, **Did the dinosaurs all die before God made people? What about evolution?** (p. 383) in the **Other Q&A's** at the end of the book to learn about the descendants of Noah's three sons. Does this change your views about the human race?

God desires, above all, faithfulness and commitment. This is the foundation of our relationship with Him. Because He gives us earthly things to explain heavenly things, He has given us the institution of marriage. Faithfulness and commitment are also the foundation of the marriage relationship. When those are broken by one partner, the entire relationship crumbles.

How badly must humans have been behaving for God to decide to destroy His creation? Marriage without reference (or, deference) to God is listed as the number one problem. What are the potential consequences of this sin, then and now?

In light of this, what do you think of the following verse?

Matthew 24:37 (Jesus speaking about His return)

"When the Son of Man comes, it will be the same as what happened during Noah's time. In those days before the flood, people were eating and drinking, marrying and giving their children to be married right up to the day Noah entered the boat."

Have you ever felt like evil was winning a battle? What would you pray if you found yourself in this situation?

If you are sinning and you call out to God for help, does He answer you?

Think about a ladder.
If you were to put all of God's creations on a ladder, with Him above the very top, where are the angels (the fallen and the faithful)? Where is Jesus? Where are humans? Where is Satan? Where are the animals?

Have you ever analyzed Scripture using the original languages? Do you speak more than one language? How difficult is it to translate a sentence? Is the translation always accurate in meaning if you translate literally, that is, translate word for word?

What is figurative language?

Idioms are phrases that simply cannot be translated literally, because each language has its own cultural idioms.

Examples of idioms: raining cats and dogs, go down in flames,
a fish out of water

Euphemisms (a type of idiom) are equally difficult in translation.

Examples of euphemisms: he doesn't have all his oars in the water,
she went to powder her nose, I'm currently between jobs

Literary devices such as similes, metaphors, and personification can also make translation tricky.

Examples we've discussed:
simile – a thousand years is like a day
metaphor – Jesus is light
personification – morning stars sang

Can you name some current or historical pop culture good vs. evil stories? How Biblical are they (intentionally, or not)?

If God is at war, if He is fighting, why do people say God is Love?

When is trust earned in a relationship?
Do you trust someone you just met?
What would make you lose your trust in that person?
How could s/he earn that trust back?

Can you have a true marriage without faithfulness and commitment?

Discuss positive jealousy vs. negative jealousy.

Has God ever lied? Has He ever been unfaithful?

In the Bible, the word 'church' refers to the people, not the building. Would we do better to call our modern churches 'the building where the church meets'?

The Bible tells us there were synagogues in many towns. These were used by the Jewish people as community meeting places – a large building that was convenient for large groups to meet together for a variety of reasons. A similar idea could be seen in small towns on the American frontier – pioneers often initially built one building to serve as the church, school, and/or town hall. The people in the towns were united for worship – an itinerant preacher would come through and believers would participate in the services whenever they were available because it was an opportunity to edify (build up) themselves and one another in their common faith in God. What are the pros and cons of the difference between what we have for worship today vs. the American pioneers?

Internet search: How many hugs a day do you need?

Do you give/get this many? A hug is most often both given and received.

How can we love God if we cannot see or hear Him?

What do you know about long-distance relationships? Are humans good at them? How successful would the relationship be if you had to communicate through a third-party?

If a couple consists of one partner who is committed by choice and another who is only present due to force or guilt, will either of them be happy? Explain.

Think about the word insincerity. A person who is insincere is a dishonest person.

Love is a feeling that we decide we will work to show others by striving to be (among other things) understanding, nonjudgmental, and thoughtful. You will make mistakes, but your heart will be right. It is your decision to commit your heart that makes love true or false. In other words, sincerity is the key.

The Greeks had different words for different types of love:

Agape – unconditional love – God's love for us is unconditional
    God wants us to decide to show Him and each other this same type of love.

Philia – brotherly/friend love – love among equals

Storge – love between parents and children

Eros – romantic love
    Ludus – infatuation – new couples
    Pragma – enduring love – established couples

Can you appreciate how difficult it was for God's people to feel close to Him at this time? Can you empathize with their roller coaster emotions/actions/devotion?

Let's discuss opposites:
God and Satan could be described in this way, but are they opposites in every respect?
God is greater, is He not?

Black and white are often described as opposites, although color is actually defined by the reflection of light. Technically, black is the absence of light, and white is all the colors reflected.

In good vs. evil stories, black has been used to represent evil and white to represent good. Can you think of some examples?

If God is a color, He is white, He is ALL the colors reflected in His light.
If Satan is a color, he is black, he is the absence of light.
When you combine black and white, you get shades of gray.
Jesus doesn't care for those who float around in the gray area.

Revelation 3:15

"I know what you do. You are not hot or cold. I wish that you were hot or cold! But you are only warm – not hot, not cold. So I am ready to spit you out of my mouth."

There seems to be an abundance of talk about the color of human skin these days.
Let's look at that for just a moment, while we're on the subject of color.
All human skin is a version of brown. Think of a paint color swatch showing different shades/tones/tints of brown from very dark to very light. Go to the hardware store, if you need to, and really look at them.

Internet search: color wheel, how to make brown

Your search results should make sense, because humans were created from dust, and dirt comes in all the colors on the color wheel.

Genesis 2:7

Then the LORD God took dust from the ground and made a man. He breathed the breath of life into the man's nose, and the man became a living thing.

1 Corinthians 15:47a, 48a (about our physical bodies)
The first man came from the dust of the earth. . . All people belong to the earth.

How does Jesus fit in as a prophet?

Have you ever looked at someone and thought s/he was a less important person than you are? A handicapped person? An old person? A child? A woman? An uneducated person?

Have you ever looked at someone and thought s/he was a more important person than you are? A very attractive person? A successful person? An educated person? A famous person?

None of these earthly, physical measurements are used by God to determine anyone's worth. Each and every person on earth has the value of being created in God's image, and He is concerned for the eternal welfare of each individual He created.

Do you know any Bible verses by heart? How does it make you feel when you recite a verse from memory?

Have you ever witnessed a child who was excited about his/her approaching birthday? Do you think this resembles the level of anticipation God's faithful people must have felt about the coming Messiah? Do you think their eagerness was heightened because of their oppression by the Romans?

Do your beliefs generally agree with your parents' beliefs? Many Jews today believe what they were taught as children – that the Messiah has not yet come. If a Jew today did hear, understand, and believe the Message of Jesus, s/he would potentially have to leave behind both family and culture in order to follow Him. This would be a very hard thing for anyone to face. Perhaps Jesus was speaking about this when He said:

Luke 14:25-27

Many people were traveling with Jesus. He said to them, "If you come to me but will not leave your family, you cannot be my follower. You must love me more than your father, mother, wife, children, brothers, and sisters – even more than your own life. Whoever will not carry the cross that is given to them when they follow me cannot be my follower."

Look at the helping verb in the last sentence: "Whoever **will** not carry. . ." Some versions say, "Whoever **is** not carrying. . .", or "Whoever **does** not carry. . ." Notice, Jesus did not say, "Whoever **can**not carry. . ." Why?

How can we be with God if we have sin?

Would it be a relief to you if someone told you to stop making your car payments because the debt you owed was paid in full?
How much more of a relief would it be if someone told you your house was paid in full and you owed no more on the mortgage?

When you do something wrong, do you feel badly about what you've done? Do you always try to make it right, or do you sometimes try to justify your actions with excuses?

Suggested reading: Whatever Happened to Justice? by Richard J. Maybury
What is the current basis for law creation in our country?
Can judges today rule in accordance with God's natural laws?
When we are subject to the unjust rules of man, we can then clearly see the superiority of God's rule.

How do you feel about corrupt judges – judges who rule for their biggest donors, or judges who rule in a way they are certain will help them win re-election, or judges who secretly have a stake in a case and rule in their own favor? Can you respect these judges? Can you trust them? People who are present in a judge's courtroom are supposed to call the judge, Your Honor. Are these judges honorable?

The highest religious leaders of Jesus' day were mostly pawns – they were willing to cooperate with the Romans controlling Israel. These men were not the leaders God selected – they were selected by the Romans for their willingness to bow to Caesar. Why would they be willing to do this?

When did God come up with this plan?

What is the difference between a temptation and a test?

A temptation is something placed before you in the hopes that you will fail. Satan places temptations in our path to try to lead us astray. If he can distract us enough, we can get lost forever.

A test is something given to you to measure your mastery, your success. Tests help us measure what we have learned and show us where we must study more. God does test us, by His own actions, or by allowing Satan to act – but He tests us to help us grow stronger – to help us be more like Him. He never seeks our failure.

Read the story of Job. God allowed Satan to take away his blessings, but God knew Job would keep his faith in Him. When Job prevailed, God not only restored, but also rewarded him. How?

> Internet image search: Old Testament family tree
> Internet image search: Table of Nations

How does a person develop a hard heart?
What could Pharaoh have done to stop the punishment?
Why didn't he?
Read the entire story: Exodus 3-14
Did God punish all of the Egyptians? Which ones were spared?
Can God be trusted to judge each person individually?

Do you know someone who is extremely trustworthy? God is infinitely more trustworthy than the most trustworthy human.

How can you earn someone's trust? How can you lose someone's trust?
Do you think God's people lost their trust/faith in Him because He did something to lose it, or because they were tempted away from Him by Satan?

Jesus was not born into the wealthy, aristocratic class. God purposefully (everything God does is in alignment with His purpose) made Jesus not just ordinary, but almost pitiful, especially when you consider His heavenly status. He was a small town, working man until He began to teach. While He taught, He was a homeless wanderer. His earthly parents were not educated or privileged people, but they were honorable and godly.

Leviticus 12: 6-8

"After the time of her purification is finished, the new mother of a baby girl or boy must bring special sacrifices to the Meeting Tent [Tabernacle or Temple]. She must give her sacrifices to the priest at the entrance of the Meeting Tent. She must bring a one-year-old lamb for a burnt offering and a dove or young pigeon for a sin offering. If the woman cannot afford a lamb, she may bring two doves or two young pigeons. One bird will be for a burnt offering and one for a sin offering. The priest will offer them before the LORD. In this way the priest will make her pure, and she will be clean from the blood of childbirth. These are the rules for a woman who gives birth to a baby boy or a baby girl."

Luke 2:22-24 (Their offering showed their poverty)

The time came for Mary and Joseph to do the things the Law of Moses taught about being made pure. They brought Jesus to Jerusalem so that they could present him to the Lord. It is written in the law of the Lord: "When a mother's first baby is a boy, he shall be called 'special for the Lord.'" The law of the Lord also says that people must give a sacrifice: "You must sacrifice two doves or two young pigeons." So Joseph and Mary went to Jerusalem to do this.

Why did God make Jesus such an unremarkable person for His earthly work?

Did you know Moses was not a good speaker? Read Exodus 4:10-16.

Did you know David (who later became king) was just a boy when he killed the giant Goliath? Read 1 Samuel 17:1-54.

There are still only two types of people today.
A person either follows God's Word, or s/he doesn't.

How does Jesus fit into God's debt-forgiveness plan?

The animals that were sacrificed were like blood donors for the people, but it was not a perfect, permanent solution – it was animal blood. Why do you think God allowed this imperfect (and fairly horrifying to our modern sensibilities) system to continue for so long before He sent Jesus?

Do you think God has ever done anything that could be classified as random or chaotic? We cannot know everything, but we can know that God has very good reasons for everything He does.

Internet image search: Jesus' family tree

Go to the Junior Non-Fiction section of your local library and look at the books on ancient Rome (in the 937's of the Dewey Decimal system, so look for JNF 937). Spend 20-30 minutes flipping through some of the books. Junior Non-Fiction books are almost always surprisingly informative and easy to read with lots of pictures – a very learner-friendly experience.

The Romans had built a huge, modern society – the most developed the world had ever seen.

- They built roads all over their empire, making travel easier than it had ever been before.
- There was relative peace throughout vast sections of Europe, Asia, and

Africa.

- The Roman government mostly tolerated other religions.
- Almost everyone spoke Greek.

God waited until this level of human development had occurred, then He used it to spread His Word.

Why is history important? The work of historians and archaeologists gives us a much clearer understanding of what was going on in the Egyptian, Roman, and Jewish worlds. These studies of our past have given us valuable information that supports, enhances, and helps us understand what the Bible tells us.

Have you noticed the doors mentioned in our discussion? Pay attention to them. Notice when they open and close.

What if I was born bad? What if I have done too many bad things? What if I have done things that are too wrong to be forgiven?

What are the worst crimes a person could commit against another person?
Why do we view crimes against children or the mentally/physically challenged as more heinous than crimes against other adults?

If you were the victim of a heinous crime, could you forgive your attacker? Would it be easier if you knew, or if you didn't know, your attacker?

How does God forgive? God created/established the laws of science, and He abides by His own laws. Our life force (soul) is the energy that animates our physical body. The first law of thermodynamics tells us that energy cannot be created or destroyed, but it can be converted/rearranged – it's form can be changed. This law applies here. This law will be followed at the time of the end.

What happened after Jesus died?

Today's calendar and method of distinguishing days, months, and years is very different from the method used in the Bible.

Internet search: Hebrew calendar

Find out what day, month, and year today is according to a calendar that more closely resembles the calendar used in Jesus' time.

As mentioned earlier, God makes extensive use of number patterns. Do you know of anything mentioned in the Bible that comes in the numbers 3, 7, 12, 40? He makes frequent use of other numbers as well.

Have you experienced something that was a surprise to you? Was it a surprise because you truly did not know about it? because you forgot about it? because you didn't believe it would really happen? because you didn't understand what you had been told about it? because you didn't really hear when someone told you about it?
Which of these do you think best explains Jesus' followers' surprise at His resurrection?

If the Holy Spirit comes to live in you, why do people say that a church building is a house of God?

How does Jesus' sacrifice complete Passover?

Read Exodus Chapters 6 -12 to learn all about the plagues of Egypt.
Why do you think the Israelites willingly followed the strange requirements God set for them?

Can you think of any other similarities between Passover and Jesus?

If Jesus had not come, how could you make amends for the hurt you have caused God by acting against Him – by acting on Satan's behalf? A sincere apology is a good start, but how can you pay for your sins? A criminal isn't forgiven by a judge simply because s/he

apologizes sincerely – s/he must still pay for the crime.
If energy cannot be created or destroyed, how can you take the negative energy of your sin and convert it to positive energy?
Do God's work. He can make your negatives work for His positive.

Order and chaos are opposites – part of the binary list that contrasts the characteristics of God and Satan. God's nature is not chaotic; therefore, His behavior is not random. God IS order and purpose. He is the root of order. There is purpose behind everything He does – even if we don't see or understand it.

We can see the war between order and chaos in our world. God established order, and Satan is trying his best to disrupt it. Satan is the root of chaos. What events do you see happening in our current time that show this conflict?

How many signs did God give to show the relationship between Passover and Jesus? Are there enough to believe they couldn't all be coincidences? If you had been a faithful follower of God living in Jesus' time, would you have noticed/heeded the signs, or would you have dismissed them as coincidences?

Remember what happened in the Temple when Jesus died. This is extremely important, and we will revisit the discussion.

What other feasts did God tell the Israelites to celebrate?

Did you know about Passover? What about the other two feasts we discussed?
Did you know that God gave the Israelites seven festivals?

In the verses below the Passover section, find John 19:14-16. Can you sense the corruption of the priests? Can you see that they are what we would call "Yes" men?

After reading this section, you should understand that there are weekly Sabbath days and there are special Sabbath days.

Is God resting on every Sabbath day? This is what Jesus said to the Jews accusing Him of breaking the Sabbath when He healed the man at the pool of Bethsaida on Saturday:

John 5:17

But he said to them, "My Father never stops working, and so I work too."

Does this challenge your view of the Sabbath?

Reread Exodus 12:18-20. Why do you think God repeats Himself so many times regarding the removal of sin (represented by yeast) from His people at this time?

When God speaks, we should always listen. What should we do when He repeats Himself – repeatedly?

The Feasts of Passover and Unleavened Bread are separate but tightly related feasts. The Feast of First Fruits isn't as related to the other two festivals in an earthly way. The feasts all prepare the people for future spiritual events, but the first two also memorialize historical events, while the third is a ceremony/celebration to thank God for His provision. God placed them all very close together on the calendar. Do you think this close and overlapping placement would seem a bit odd without the clarification of Jesus?

Do you acknowledge (celebrate in some way) these feast days? Why or why not?
If you do, do you let all of these important days run together, or do you understand and honor each of them for what they are?

What has happened over the years as believers try to honor Jesus' completion of these three feast days?

Do you celebrate any of these holidays? Did you know they weren't in the Bible?

Should we be celebrating these human-instituted holidays? Why or why not?

Should we judge others who do or do not celebrate them?

How can we attempt to put Jesus' last week onto a calendar?

In Jesus' time, Jews were still routinely traveling from all parts of Judea and Galilee (and other countries) to Jerusalem for worship.

Did you know that to get from His home in Nazareth to the Temple in Jerusalem, Jesus had to travel so far?

Did you realize that Galilean Jews had to travel through a foreign country to get to Jerusalem?

Read the story of The Good Samaritan in Luke 10:25-37. We have adopted the word Samaritan into our vocabulary to mean a person who does good for others. Did you realize the hero of the story, the Samaritan, was called that because he was from Samaria? Did you realize that when Jesus told this story, the Samaritan would have been considered a lesser person, an undesirable, a "bad guy," because of his nationality? Jesus used someone who was looked down upon by both Galilean and Judean Jews to set an example of the kindness we should show for one another. He made His lesson more impactful by saying that the first man who passed by was a priest (someone who was supposed to be the "best" of the Jewish "good guys"), and the second man who passed by was a Temple worker (also a "good guy"). The Samaritan, the true good guy, was someone both the priest and the Temple worker would have viewed as a low-class, no account, unworthy person.

Jesus was admonishing/reproving/scolding the Law expert who asked the questions that prompted this story, because the Law expert's heart was not right with God.

A number of Jesus' stories are like this – not warm and fuzzy, but sharp, pointed, even searing attention-getters for the Jews who were listening to Him. How does this align with the view of Jesus as the loving, forgiving Lord of the New Testament?

Jesus is like the well-respected athletic coach who pushes his players to run faster, jump higher, play better, and achieve their full potential. The players sweat and complain and sometimes think they can't live up to the coach's expectations, but they respect him. They know he coaches hard because he believes in them, he cares about them, and he knows they can achieve great goals – he wants to see them succeed. It's the guidance of coaches like this that stays with players all their lives. It's impactful.

Doesn't the Bible give all the details about that important week?

When a crime has been committed and the investigators and/or detectives begin to question the witnesses, are all of the witnesses going to tell the exact same story? Why?

The point of hearing the story from so many angles is to gather more details. God inspired the Gospel authors to write, but they each do so in their own style, from their own perspective, with their own history coloring what they see and report.

Have you ever noticed a contradiction in your Bible? What did you think about it? What are your thoughts now on Matthew 26:17?

When God gave the Israelites the Passover feast, He told them to explain to their children WHY they were observing the feast. Do you truly know the root of the traditions you celebrate?

Has your view of the term "Last Supper" changed?

Most Christians celebrate Christmas as well as Christmas Eve in some way. It all runs together, doesn't it? With families so spread out these days, "Christmas" tends to extend a number of days both before and after the actual holiday. Use what you know and apply it to the Jewish celebration of Passover and Passover Eve. Add a few more important days to the mix, and you have a week-and-a-half-long holy day season. In the excitement of it all – the food, the extended family visiting, the traveling, the religious observances – you can understand how the days all sort of run together.

Based on what we've just reviewed, what would a calendar showing the last week of Jesus' life probably look like?

What do you think about the proposed calendar?

Has this clarified or confused your thinking about Jesus' last week?

Those who are dismissive of the older, outlandish-sounding stories like Jonah and the Big Fish may also dismiss other details. Remember that the example of Jonah was the ONLY sign Jesus offered to the religious leaders who wanted a sign that He was who He said He was. Don't dismiss what God tells us in His Story – the details are important.
Read Leviticus 13:33-45 concerning the directions for cleansing a contaminated house. Do you think this was a prophecy? God set up rules of operation for our world, and He abides by them.

Challenge: Use a standard wall/desk calendar and try to record the Hebrew calendar on it. Each month try to spot the new moon – take someone with you to look for it so there will be two witnesses. Record when the almanac or your weather app says it should happen as well as when you first spot it. Count from the new moon to the festival of that month. If you start at the new moon before Passover, you are starting at what God said would be the beginning of the religious year. Watch the moon wax full and record the day it is full. Watch the moon wane and become new again. God put the celestial bodies in the sky for us to use to know His appointed times. Get in touch.

Visit The Old Farmer's Almanac website at www.almanac.com and enter your zip code to get a localized monthly moon phase calendar with photos of the moon on each day.

We have said Jesus completed the first four feasts. What was the fourth?

Make a loaf of bread. Understand the good baker's yeast and how it works.
Then mix some flour and water in a small container and leave it sitting in the open air for several days. Watch what happens when the wild, undisciplined yeast spores infect your

dough. This "sourdough starter" can be monitored and trained to be good yeast, but left unchecked, it will spoil.

The good, baker's yeast is the Holy Spirit that can work through us and help us rise to our full potential. The wild, roving yeast is Satan's influence, and, if allowed, it will infiltrate us and lead to our rot and decay.

Do you believe God instituted the feasts as teaching tools about the steps of His plan for redemption, or do you believe He had other reasons for instructing the Israelites to celebrate them?

If you believe the feasts were preparatory for Jesus, are there any details of the first four feasts and Jesus' fulfillment of them that seem unfinished to you?

Now that we know what these feasts are really for, what can we see when we look back to the past?

Did you realize that the old covenant was replaced by the new covenant during the same exact period of time? God is using His appointed times to do the things He said He would do.

The covenant Jesus offered was intended for everyone. All the nations of the world need to call on God. His plan is the only plan that can save us.

What can we do to cultivate the yeast of His Kingdom in others?

What are the fall feasts, and how will we know when these begin to be fulfilled? Some of the Jews who knew the Scriptures didn't recognize Jesus by the feast signs, so how will I?

When you make your Hebrew calendar, will you give more attention now to the Feast of Trumpets (Yom Teruah)? Watch for the new moon, so you can observe the feast on the correct day. If you've been keeping a lunar calendar since the new moon before Passover, you realize what a difficult task this is.

If you've been keeping the Hebrew lunisolar calendar, were you as sure about which day this feast lands on as you were about Passover? If someone asked you a week or so beforehand, "How many days until Yom Teruah?" would you be able to say for sure (without consulting an almanac or other source – which the ancients did not have)? No? So, Yom Teruah is a very important special Sabbath, but you aren't sure what day it is until the day is upon you. Remember this.

In the old days, you would know it as soon as you heard the priests blow their trumpets.

In the future, everyone – faithful and unfaithful – will know when Jesus returns at the blast of the seventh trumpet.

Have you ever observed this special Sabbath? Will you observe it now?

Why does God care about time?

When God explained time, He did not give the days of the week names, and only four of the months have Hebrew names. For the most part, months were called by their order until after the Jews returned from captivity in Babylon. While living there, they adopted Babylonian names for the months and used those in the Bible writings.

Which of the explanations about Jesus' denial of knowing when He would come again do you think is most likely?

In Jesus' day, a couple was engaged for perhaps a year before the marriage was finalized. During the engagement, the groom's task was to prepare a home for his bride. The engagement was much more serious than American engagements today – the couple was essentially married and could only be parted by death or divorce. We can see evidence of this in the following verses:

Matthew 1:18-19

This is how the birth of Jesus the Messiah happened. His mother Mary was engaged to marry Joseph. But before they married, he learned that she was expecting a baby. (She was pregnant by the power of the Holy Spirit.) Mary's husband, Joseph, was a good man. He did not want to cause her public disgrace, so he planned to divorce her secretly.

When Jesus says that He is leaving earth to go and prepare a place for us, He is referring to our marriage contract. When He takes us into His home, our marriage with Him is complete.

These parables don't accurately reflect the stereotype of the loving Jesus with His arms open wide for everyone, do they? Jesus very clearly tells us to be alert to what is happening around us, to be very busy doing His work, and to be prepared for His return so that we can give a good account of our activities. He has high expectations for us. His call is "come as you are," but then it's "get yourself in shape." His work is more of a boot camp than a retirement home.

The calculations of months and years seem messy, but that is only because we are unaccustomed to tracking time on God's three calendars. Let's review:

His holy calendar marks the months since the sacrifice (first, of a lamb, and then, of our Great High Priest) that provided for our salvation from sin.

His civil calendar marks the year changes that are used for calculating Sabbath years, years of Jubilee, and other times of rest, in addition to the years a ruler of the people would serve.

His judicial (prophetic) calendar marks the calculation of time for judgment, as seen in the story of Noah and in the prophecies in Daniel and Revelation about the judgment at the time of the end.

Our current Gregorian calendar, to which we are all so accustomed, and from which we cannot escape and still function in today's world, has absolutely nothing to do with God's calendars. Our modern calendar is Biblically useless.

What follows the Feast of Trumpets?

Look back at the calendar of the Hebrew year. These last three feasts occur in fairly rapid succession. How many days do they encompass?

If God did not intend these feasts to be signs – if He just intended them to mark additional times of worship – would He have placed them so closely together on the calendar?

The Jewish leaders have done the same thing with the fall feasts that Christians have done with the spring feasts – lots of extras have been added. Why have people felt the need to add to what God has given them? Are we saying that God's instructions weren't enough? Does He not know how to mark His own holy days?

Should we be celebrating these appointed times now?

Are you willing to change the human-made customs you follow?

Challenge: Spend the next year acknowledging only what is set out for us in the Bible by God – not the religious festivals and celebrations added later by humans.

Suggestions:
On Passover, come before God and acknowledge all that He has done in instituting and fulfilling that feast. Share a meal with others. During the meal, pass around unleavened bread and fruit of the vine. Be thankful, be grateful, be happy.

During the Feast of Unleavened Bread, think about living under His protection – living free from sin.

On the Feast of First Fruits, remember that Jesus arose, and because He did, you will, too!

Forty days after that, remember that He has ascended to heaven to His Father's house to prepare a place for you, His beloved. (This was not a feast day.)

On Pentecost, acknowledge that the Holy Spirit lives in you, and celebrate all you can do for God with the Spirit's help.

On the Feast of Trumpets, watch for the new moon. Think about how it will be when Jesus returns.

On the Day of Atonement, know that ALL will acknowledge God as the One True God. Read Mark 5:1-20 and note that even the evil spirits recognize Jesus and acknowledge His power.

During the Feast of Booths, think about what your existence will be when God perfects His plan. Understand that He will create a new heaven and a new earth – that earth will be for us.

****

Regularly gather with other believers. Share meals together. Talk about your blessings. Partake of bread and wine in remembrance of what He has done and what He has promised. Be happy we have a God who loves us so much. Invite those who are weak in the faith or who are unsure about God. Remember, Jesus dined casually with many people and used the opportunity to share His love. Showing your love and joy is a very powerful testimony that can help people open the doors to their hearts.

What is God's core message to us in the sacrifice of Jesus?

In the Jewish culture of Jesus' time, families were heavily involved in suggesting potential mates; but, ultimately, the marriage depended upon the willingness of the bride to accept the groom.

Do you understand it is only your own will that can separate you from God?

Were you aware that Jesus' sacrifice represented His vows to you?

He loved you first. He knew you before you were born. He gave you His vows before you knew Him.

1 John 4:19
We love because God first loved us.

Did you know that when He gives you the Holy Spirit, He is essentially giving you an engagement ring with your vows already exchanged? Reread Ephesians 1:1b-14a. All that's left is for Him to take you to your new home. You must remain faithful to Him while you wait.

Does this change how you view Jesus' sacrifice?

What about all the people who never knew Jesus? Can they be saved?

Some Biblical legalists argue that you cannot be saved without baptism. Noah was brought out of the water that washed away the sin of the world, so one could argue he was baptized. What about Abraham? There are no floods or seas in his story. Do you believe that Abraham, a man the Bible calls "a friend of God," is saved?

Even if you were already familiar with the story of Jonah, did you really understand he was sent by God to preach to foreigners? Did you think God only spoke to the Israelites in the time before Jesus?

Do you think the Queen of Sheba spread the knowledge she had gained from King Solomon both on the road and once she arrived back home, or do you think she kept it to herself? Do you think God is capable of finding/inspiring people to spread His Message to everyone?

Has your perspective regarding the Jews being a chosen servant nation changed?

Do you realize the enormity of what the Jews were asked to do? Do you understand that they REALLY stood out from the other nations around them?

Can people who don't believe in God be good people? Can people who don't know about God be good people? What motivates them to be good?

These are very simplified definitions, but it's a starting point:
An atheist doesn't believe there is a God (of any kind).
An agnostic believes that we cannot know whether there is a God (of any kind) or not.

Do you realize how much effect your words can have?
How can you use your words to do God's work?

How can we remember, or honor, what Jesus did for us?

What are your thoughts on Communion after reading this? Does your mind go to a dinner party of friends, family, and new acquaintances and making a toast to the goodness of God in sending His Son as the only true remedy for our relationship problems? Are you toasting Him for His vows to you and your promise of a bright and happy future? – like a wedding toast?

Cheers! This is a joyous occasion!
Each time we have this celebration, we are remembering His promise.
It's a memorial feast.

Who should celebrate Communion?

Do you want people to say they love you, even if they don't? Do you just like to hear the words? Does that truly fill your heart?

How much better do you feel when someone says s/he loves you, and you know s/he really means it? Does that fill your heart more?

Jesus' love, when you understand how sincere He really is, will overflow your heart.

David, although he was still awaiting the Savior, understood the sincere love of God:

Psalm 23

The LORD is my shepherd. I will always have everything I need. He gives me green pastures to lie in. He leads me by calm pools of water. He restores my strength. He leads me on right paths to show that he is good. Even if I walk through a valley as dark as the grave, I will not be afraid of any danger, because you are with me. Your rod and staff comfort me. You prepared a meal for me in front of my enemies. You welcomed me as an honored guest. My cup is full and spilling over. Your goodness and mercy will be with me all my life, and I will live in the LORD's house a long, long time.

What is baptism, exactly? And how can you know that you're ready to be baptized?

God provides us with things in this physical, earthly experience that help us understand spiritual things. Would we be able to fully understand the spiritual circumcision of the heart if God had not given the Jews physical circumcision?

God made apple trees to put forth apples. Somewhere deep in the apple tree's DNA, it knows to only put forth apples – never pears or peaches or plums – only apples. We understand this physical truth. Apple trees produce apples. Plum trees produce plums. Why? Because that's what God wants from them.

God has given us what He calls Fruits of the Spirit – those qualities we exhibit on the outside because of what is on our inside. Sincere followers of God know what type of fruit God wants them to produce. He has used fruit trees to explain what He expects of us.

What are the first two requirements we must meet in order to have a relationship with God?

1. We must hear His message. If we are hearing His message, then someone is teaching us.

2. We must believe His message. If we are to believe His message, we must understand it in our minds and trust it in our hearts.

Do you think infant baptism was instructed by God?
Do you think a 5-year-old can understand what baptism really means?
What about the mentally impaired?

Were you baptized as an infant or young child? What are your feelings about that?

Did you baptize your children as babies or young children? Why did you make that decision?

Reread Paul's statement in Romans 7:9-10a. He was spiritually alive, THEN he heard God's truth, and he understood sin, which caused it to live in him. When sin began to live in him, he died spiritually.

God is infinitely more intelligent and infinitely more compassionate than we are. He made every single one of us – the old, the young, the weak, the strong, and all those in between. He has angels assigned to all the children of the world. Do you trust Him?

Jesus' lessons have multiple applications for our lives. Children are a tremendous blessing to us all because we can understand so much through them – trust, humility, innocence, purity, joy, and more. Many people are dismissive of children, but they are missing out on the most valuable lessons God has for us. Treat all children like the precious gifts that they are and keep those lessons before you always.

Note: Jesus was Jewish. He went to be baptized when He was ready to begin His Ministry of showing/telling people how they could be reconciled to God.

Why should you be baptized? To show that you are ready to begin living for Him – that is, showing/telling people how they can also be reconciled to God.

How do I get baptized?

God knows we understand using water to cleanse our bodies, so He uses water to demonstrate a cleansing of our spirit as well.

What do you know or think about sprinkling/pouring/immersing baptisms?

The Law involved sprinkling to seal the covenant with God.
Jesus' Way (the fulfillment of the Law) involves washing to seal the covenant with God.
Do you believe that Jesus' Way is fuller than the Law?

Can we use superlatives to illustrate the stages of our relationship with God?
The Law – the Old Covenant – preparing for Jesus – made people close to God.
Jesus' New Covenant – makes people closer to God.
Jesus' Return – will make us the closest to God that we can be.

After Jesus' sacrifice, what other sacrifice could we make?
After our baptism into Jesus, what other baptism could we need?
Just as His sacrifice was the ultimate offering, His baptism is the ultimate cleansing.

Internet search: mikveh
Internet search: mikveh near me
If there isn't a mikveh in your city/town, there's likely at least one in the nearest large city.

Did you know before reading this that the Jewish people regularly baptize themselves?

Did you know that John, by ancestry, was a legitimate high priest? He wasn't serving God in the Temple, though. He was serving Him in the wilderness outside of Jerusalem. Remember, the top Temple officials of the day were selected by the Romans for their willingness to cooperate. This and other important information can be found in the writings of Josephus, a Jewish historian who documented information during the intertestamental period (the 400 years between the Old and New Testaments).

God, Jesus, the Holy Spirit. . .which one do we worship?

Looking back at what we've discussed, what are some of the earthly, physical things God has given us to help us understand heavenly, spiritual things?

Science today is often kept very separate from the Bible, even though Jesus instructed us to study the world around us to help us understand God.

How important do you think science is in intimately understanding God's Word?

Remember the patterns discussed in the beginning? We said God has put orderly patterns in:

human development
interpersonal human behavior (sociology)
geometric shapes
poetry
laws of science
history
laws of nature
laws of economics
astronomy

Now that we've come a good distance in our discussion, can you see how much earthly studies have helped us understand God's Word? In addition to the subject list above, we've touched on biology, mathematics, archaeology, languages, anatomy, psychology, and perhaps others.

Education is extremely important, but it should rightly be undertaken with reference and deference to God. Remember the Tower of Babel? The people were prideful regarding their knowledge and abilities. They were taking action on their pride without reference or deference to God.

Everything God does has order and meaning. Do you think He had a purpose for the way He designed the Tabernacle/Temple? Do you think He had a purpose for how He told the Israelites to use the building – how it would function according to His plan?

Do you think He gave the Jewish people the Tabernacle/Temple design to help them understand the "tent" we live in here on earth?

Does the multiplication example, 1 x 1 x 1 = 1 and the Temple design help you understand what Jesus meant when He explained His relationship with God?

John 14:10

"Don't you believe that I am in the Father and the Father is in me? The things I have told you don't come from me. The Father lives in me, and he is doing his own work."

How much clearer is your understanding of body, soul, and spirit now that you've seen it illustrated in its Biblical pattern? Will this help you better understand how God is trying to work in you? Will you be more able to allow His Spirit to flow through your soul and out to your body now that you understand it is your own will that opens and closes the doors? Will the fruits of the Spirit be more visible in your actions now?

How did God, Jesus, and the Holy Spirit work together at Passover?

Do you understand that God was in the Temple to receive the sacrifices made to Him? What would be the point of sincere sacrifices made to God if He were not present to receive them?

Have you ever before read all of Psalm 22? In reference to Jesus' sacrifice?

Were you taught that God left Jesus on the cross because God cannot be in the presence of sin?

If Jesus is the ultimate sacrifice, do you believe that God left Jesus as He hung on the cross? How could He? Based on what you've just read about the Temple design – about the relationship between God, Jesus, and the Holy Spirit – is this even possible?

I would like to have a symbol of my sincere belief in what God has done for me through Jesus. As a baptized believer, should I display a cross with or without Jesus on it?

Have you ever before thought of Jesus' sacrifice as a birth experience? Do you agree with this correlation?

If you display crosses, what is your reason for doing so?
Will your answer be pleasing to God?

Do you know that the Holy Spirit lives in you and is with you wherever you go?

Do you realize that how you choose to live your life is a symbol of your commitment to Him?

I've seen pictures of Jesus. He's the long-haired guy in sandals, right?

Do you have an image in your mind when you think of Jesus? Where did you get this idea of His appearance?

Did you know that the Bible says Jesus was not the most physically attractive guy in the room?

The word command has a rather negative connotation in our world, doesn't it? Perhaps it would be better to think of His command to love Him as a request, understanding that your love is a requirement for the continuation of the relationship. One-sided relationships cannot survive, because the unloving side dies – if we do not love, we die. God is desperately in love with us and desperately wants us to love Him and live. In light of this, does the "command" still have negative connotations?

What is our purpose here on earth?

We are united with God when we set out to do what Jesus did – call others home. We must show AND tell people how to find their way. We are prophets in that we tell people things about the future that they don't already know. We are priests in that we are to act as intermediaries between God and His lost children. We find them, point them in the right direction, and then step out of the way. Jesus is our Prophet and our Great High Priest. Everyone must independently go through Him to have a relationship with God. He is our Intermediary in that it was His sacrifice that allows us to have that relationship. If God has put you here to do a job for Him, will He not also give you what you need to do that job?

In what ways can you help others?

What are some of the things God has asked you to do (by putting them before you)? Has God taken you outside of your comfort zone and tested you in these tasks? Have you become a better helper because of that test?

Do you believe God can do anything? Do you believe He can do it through you?
If you don't believe you are able to accomplish a task with God's help because the task is just too big/difficult, then you are setting God aside – you are putting Him in a box and believing that His power is limited.

Isn't it politically incorrect to talk about God in public?

How many of your religious beliefs have you actually studied in depth on your own?
Do you really know WHY you believe what you believe?

If all believers based ALL of their beliefs solely on solid, Biblically-proven ground, do you think we could eliminate most of the differences we find in our church organizations today? We're talking about beliefs that are in harmony with the whole Bible.

How do you think God views all of our different church organizations?

Do you confuse civil (government) law and moral/holy (God's) law? Think about this carefully. Do you believe something is right or wrong because the government says so, or because God says so?

Likewise, do you confuse church law and God's law? Think about this carefully. Do you believe something is right or wrong because the church organization you attend says so, or because God says so? Are you sure?

If all the people who live on your street or work in your office were faithful followers, how different would your life be?

Spreading the Word of God is and always has been a grassroots effort. What can you do to help? How can you make yourself agreeable to as many people as possible, like Paul did, in order to convince them that Jesus is the only Way?

How do your talents differ from other people you know?

What is heaven, exactly?

Read the rest of Paul's comments in 2 Corinthians 1-10.
Have you, or do you know someone who has, had a near-death experience?
What can you share about it?

Remember that everything earthly is a shadow of something heavenly.
What do you think heaven is like?
Do you think we will sit around on clouds playing harps all day?
Do we become angels?
What do the angels do?

Read Imagine Heaven by John Burke.

Read more about the criminals crucified with Jesus in Luke 23:26-43.
Why was the criminal promised Paradise? Notice Jesus promised the man he would be with Jesus in Paradise that day.
. . .with Jesus. . .in Paradise. . .that day

Do we go to heaven immediately when we die?

God has promised that we will be happy in heaven. What would make you happy? Do you think God is capable of making you happy? Do you think everyone's idea of happiness is the same? Do you think God can make each one of us happy in our own specific way?

Did you know that God's plan includes a new heaven and a new earth?

If you are faithful to God, do you think any part of your experience after death will be scary?

Read Luke 9:28-36. This story is called the Transfiguration because the disciples who were present saw Jesus' appearance transformed during His conversation with Moses and Elijah who are living in heaven.
Read Exodus 34:29-35 about the transfiguration of Moses.
Read Acts 6-7 about the transfiguration of Stephen.

Reread Revelation 14:13b. What do you think He means by "great blessings"?

Reread 1 Peter 1:4. Those blessings are beautiful, and they are waiting for us.

Does this give you comfort? Will it comfort you when your time to pass over comes?

Why can't everyone go to heaven and be with God?

Does it make sense to you that not everyone will be with God? Explain.

Do you look at the Door and understand what is before you? The demons do.
Do you go through the Door? The demons don't.
Why don't the demons go through? Pride.

Just believing that God is who He says is not enough. You have to be sincerely invested in a relationship with Him. What does sincerity mean to you? Do you seek sincerity in your relationships with others?

Do you think we are capable of understanding just how sincere God is?

Although we all still sin, has your wrong-doing decreased as you have learned more about what God wants from you? Apply this question not just to external sin, but also to internal sin – your way of thinking about things. You don't have to understand everything God has told us in His Bible in order to have a sincere relationship, but you do have to allow the Spirit to work on you and improve you from the inside out. How can you do this?

Remember, God only has categories for two kinds of people: those who sincerely obey, and those who do not.

How can you learn what God's will for you is?

How can you have self-confidence and humility at the same time?

American believers live contradictory lives. As Americans, we are told to stand strong and free – to have confidence in ourselves and all that we can accomplish. As believers, we are told to put ourselves last – to think of Jesus and help others first. Let us reconcile these contradictions once and for all. We cannot accomplish anything noble or good without the grace of God. He alone has allowed us to be a part of a country and a time that allows us these freedoms on this fallen earth. When we want to accomplish something good, we should ask God to intervene and help us with our task. When we realize that we have accomplished something good, we must thank God and understand that our success was due to His participation. This is humility. We are strong, but only because God has given us strength. When we realize that it is not through ourselves that we have an effect on the world, we will be humble toward one another.

Many times, it's easy to know right from wrong. Have you ever encountered a situation in which you found it difficult to decide? Was deciding your reaction difficult because you were mixing human ideas of what is right with God's decrees of righteousness? Were you confusing current human laws or standards with God's eternal knowledge?

When you react to something, do you make a conscious effort to let God's fruit of the Spirit show in your reaction? Is your reaction intended to help lead others in the Way?

Do you have self-control? Can you control your ________________?
That was a trick question. Yes, you can control your ________________.
The real question is DO you control your ________________, or does it control you?

Do you take care to not hurt others emotionally? -physically? -spiritually?

Self-control is a life-long pursuit. We do not master it once and move on. We must pray about it and work toward it constantly.
What can we do to make self-control easier to accomplish?

Remember, God has given us power – the power of our self-will. We must use our power for good and submit to His teaching – this is the meekness of Jesus – controlling our power for His greater good. We must allow the Spirit to work in us and heal our physical shortcomings – this is why God sent Him – to give us the help we need to be His faithful people.

How do you love someone who has done something terrible to you?

Have you ever been hurt by someone so badly, that you can hardly find it in yourself to forgive them, much less love them?

Do you understand that forgiveness is a form of love?

Do you understand the difference between being polite to someone (using good manners) and pretending to like someone? Sincerity counts.

If someone who has hurt you badly comes to you and sincerely apologizes, it will soften your heart toward them.

Acknowledge to yourself that healing happens in stages.

Remember our discussion of Jesus' words on the cross. Psalm 22, which He recited a portion of, clearly shows three stages of feelings: Jesus would first feel forsaken, then He would feel certain that God was with Him, and then He would feel joy at the growth of His family through the goodness of God.

Do you know that God made you, so He understands exactly what you are feeling? Accept your feelings as valid and ask God to help you progress through the healing process. Ask Him continually and thank Him for His help.

Forgive others who have taken a wrong turn in their lives and are hurting people. If you get lost on your journey to God, that means that you took one or more wrong turns. While you're off-track, you will hurt yourself and others. You will continue to hurt yourself and others until you get back on the right road. Once you're on the right road, your actions toward others will be helpful to them rather than hurtful.
Can you think of a time when you took a wrong turn? Did the actions you took while off-course affect only yourself?

Most of us who are God-seeking will only veer off the Way a little bit, like veering onto the shoulder of a road. When we make a really wrong turn, we can wind up lost on winding, confusing, side streets. We may need someone to hold up a sign to show us the way back.

Those who are not lost can be sign holders for those who are lost, but they must be careful not to get lost themselves. Sign holders must remember that the lost will not always appreciate the help. Sign holders will be mocked and scorned, but they will be wearing God's armor, so they cannot be truly hurt.

Are you a sign holder for the lost? Have the lost who pass by you turned their backs on you? Do not be dismayed but do move on to a place where your efforts will be useful.

Proverbs 4:25-27

Keep your eyes on the path, and look straight ahead. Make sure you are going the right way, and nothing will make you fall. Don't go to the right or to the left, and you will stay away from evil.

How do I cope with the trauma of personal illness or the illness or loss of a loved one? If God cares about us, why does He let these things happen?

Have you suffered from an illness or accident? What were some of your thoughts and feelings as your body healed?
Have you suffered from the loss of someone very important to you?

Did anyone do anything that was especially helpful or comforting for you during your grieving process? What was it?

Don't judge your feelings. Whatever you are feeling, acknowledge it. Your feelings are real and they are valid.

Journaling can help you get your feelings out and work through them. Your words don't need to be perfect, they just need to be your honest words. No one ever has to see them. You won't be graded. When you have processed and healed, you can shred them.

Being healed doesn't mean you have forgotten what has happened.
You will have scars.
Scars aren't gaping wounds. You can move forward.

Why do believers go to church?

For those of you who meet with other believers:

Do you go to church to worship God?
Do you go to church to be spiritually reinforced?
Do you go to church to spiritually reinforce others?
Do you go to church to learn more about God?

Do you reinforce others outside of the church building?

Do you spiritually feed others who do not attend your church?

For those of you who do not yet meet with other believers:
Why would you attend a church? See the questions above.
We should work to be able to answer yes to all of those questions.

How does a person become a member of God's church?
Where did you learn this? Is it Biblically accurate?

What is worship?

How do you worship God? Make a list of your daily worship activities.
Do you worship at certain times, for example, do you say your prayers every morning?

Can you add something new to your routine?

Should you have a regular worship routine that you follow? Why or why not?

Is your fellowship with other believers enjoyable? Reread Psalm 68:3b-4a.

Do you spend a significant amount of your worship time thinking about, talking about, or making lists of all the blessings God has given you? This is crucial to your own happiness as well as your ability to spread His love to others.

Your whole life should be a living sacrifice to God. Your life isn't about you – it's about Him. You owe Him all the credit for everything good in your life – everything He has given to you that didn't require any effort on your part, as well as everything you have had to work to get. You were able to work for it and be successful because He gave you that ability.

Be happy that He made you! Share your happiness with others.

Why do Christians worship on Sunday mornings, and Jews worship on Saturday?

Why do Christian organizations hold worship services on Sunday mornings? Is this truly Biblical, or is it a tradition of men?

Did you realize that Paul's gathering with the believers on the first day of the week was actually on Saturday night? Did you realize that by Sunday morning, the meeting was over and everyone had gone their separate ways, including Paul, who left town?

Did you realize that God raised Jesus from the dead on a day that specifically was not a Sabbath? Do you think He did this purposefully?

So, Jesus died, rose, and ascended to heaven on days that were not Sabbaths – should we be surprised at this? After all, He was working on those days.

How do you feel about Sunday Sabbaths now?

Should Christians be honoring the Sabbath? If no, why not? If yes, how?
Read Acts Chapter 17 to learn more about what the Apostle Paul was doing. Notice how he finds opportunities to talk to Gentiles, and then he speaks to them politely. (vv.16-34)

Does this mean we should have our day of worship on Saturdays?

When should we worship God?

When should we teach others?

Following Jesus isn't achieved using a to-do list or a calendar – it's a way of life.
It's every breath, every thought, every action, every word.
HE is everything.

Be an opportunist. Take advantage of teaching moments.

How can you teach someone if you haven't had time to prepare your materials? You have to KNOW the Word, and you have to have faith that the Spirit will give you the right words to say to the right person at the right time.

Immerse yourself.

What can you do today to worship Him?

What should we be doing on a Sabbath?

If you observe the Sabbath, do you generally consider it a blessing, or are you frustrated with trying to fulfill a command to rest when you have so much to do?

The Sabbath shouldn't be a religiously legal requirement. God wants you to enjoy your blessings.

He wants you to work hard, and He wants you to sit back and enjoy what you have accomplished with His help.

How can you make your Sabbath time enjoyable?

The Bible says only men can teach. Is that true?

How did you feel about women teaching others about Jesus before you read this section? How do you feel about it now?

Women, what was your honest opinion about Paul before reading this section? How do you feel about him now?

Do you feel differently about women teaching others outside the church building than you do about women teaching others inside the church building? Why?

How should you view your male and female co-workers? Should we all be humble and equally respectful to everyone, regardless of sex, education, nationality, status, or age?

Discuss with your spouse or in a group the symbiotic/interdependent relationship between men and women as it applies to family dynamics, specifically focusing on our dependence upon each other for existence and support.

The ring we wear to symbolize marriage is an accurate representation of the proper relationship. When you look at that circle, there is no line – no separation – no beginning of one and end of the other. What is done for one is done for the other, just as Jesus said that whatever we do for someone else we do for Him.

Can you learn from a man?
Can you learn from a woman?
Can you learn from a child?
Can you learn from an invalid?
Can you learn from an unbeliever?

If you answered no to any of those questions, stop, open your eyes, and try again.
We all have an impact.

What is prayer, and how do you do it?

How do you communicate with God?
Do you use many words? Do you get excited and shout? Do you talk with your hands? Are you on the quiet side and only use a few words? Do you just "think it" instead of "saying it"?

We each have our own style – that's what God wants from you. He made you. He wants to enjoy your personality – the real you – not a formal version of you that is attempting to be more pleasing to Him in a false way.

Sincerity is key.

Have you ever asked for something that God did not grant you? Did you ever reach a point when you understood why the answer was "No"?
Sometimes we are given insight and get that answer – sometimes we aren't.

In spite of the "No" answers you've received, do you still trust that God will do what is best for you in the scope of His plan?
Do you ask for His will to be done, even when you desperately want Him to say "Yes" – just as Jesus did?

How can I be thankful for the bad things?

Do you really know in your heart that God is in control?

Do you understand that He sometimes allows bad things to happen?

Do you have confidence that He will prevail over everything evil in the end?

When the blind man heard what Jesus said about why he was born blind and then He restored his sight, how do you think the man felt about being born blind?

Do you think he would have preferred to have been born with sight and to have skipped the whole healing episode? Do you think he was honored and humbled that God used him as a teaching tool to help others understand the greatness of God?
Read John Chapter 9.

How have you dealt with problems in the past?
Will you deal with problems differently now? If so, how?

There is always room for improvement – we should be constantly growing closer to God. We do that by allowing Him to help us be more and more like Him. How did Jesus deal with Satan? (Matthew 4, Luke 4)

Can you send Satan away from you for good?

Luke 4:13
The devil finished tempting Jesus in every way and went away to wait until a better time.

This is why God gives us armor. We need to have it on at all times.

When bad things happen, what does God require of you?
If you can't be happy in your troubles, can you be thankful because you know what is happening (Satan is interfering, trying to hurt God by hurting you) and you know what to do (put on your armor and pray)?
Can you be thankful for ALL things – good and bad?

When you pray, are there limits to what you can ask?

Is giving money at church (or, elsewhere) a way to worship God?

People veer off the Way when they use money for power. Money, like other blessings, should be used for doing good. Be good stewards of what God has given you. Take care of your family first, then help others who need help.

1 Timothy 5:8

Everyone should take care of all their own people. Most important, they should take care of their own family. If they do not do that, then they do not accept what we believe. They are worse than someone who does not even believe in God.

Carefully and honestly examine how you use the money God has given you.
Where would a dot representing your use be placed on this scale?

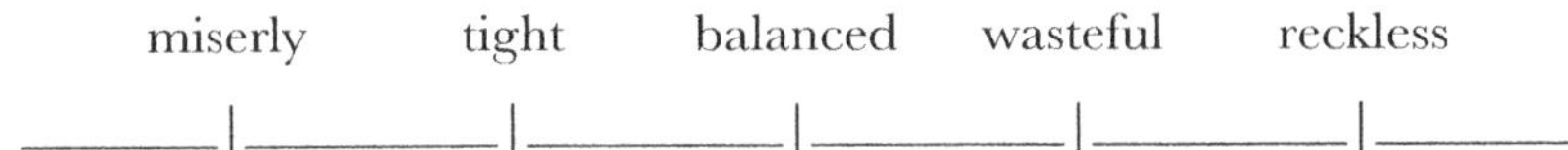

Jesus tells us to use our gifts wisely. Read Matthew 25:14-30 again.

What can you do to use your money more wisely?
You are a steward of all the gifts/blessings He has given to you.

What if I forget about God?

Do you experience high and low tides in your relationship with God?

When you are at low tide, is it because you are talking, but He isn't listening?

God doesn't want stoic, automated updates and requests from you.
He wants all of you – He wants you to sincerely and completely want Him.
He's all in.
You have a choice.
The success or failure of your relationship is up to you.

Do you really want Him to be intimately involved in your life?
Do you believe He cares about all the details of your life? Why or why not?

What did Jesus tell us about the tiny details of our lives?

Luke 12:6-7

"When birds are sold, five small birds cost only two pennies. But God does not forget any of them. Yes, God even knows how many hairs you have on your head. Don't be afraid. You are worth much more than many birds.

He cares. He's paying attention to you. He's waiting for you to speak to Him.

How can I learn more about God?

What is the best way to learn about God?

How often do you read a Bible?
Examine your religious reading material. Is your Bible your first choice when you want to study?

Do you read other books distributed by your church as part of the teachings of that church? Do you value these at the same level as the Bible?

Are all Bibles the same?

Did you know about the Apocrypha? Why do you think both the Jews and the Protestants exclude these books from Scripture?

The Bible printed in 1611 was the King James Bible, so called because it was commissioned by King James I of England. It was translated from the Latin Vulgate, a translation made from the original Hebrew/Greek late in the 4th century. The King James Bible was essentially the only English language Bible widely used for about 300 years. The long list of translations/versions has mostly accumulated over the last 100 years. Some are very literal, some freely paraphrase, and some are in between these extremes.

Have you looked through the Bibles you own to see what kinds you have?

Download an app like YouVersion that lets you read and compare different Bibles. Use it regularly until you've decided which version meets your current needs (your needs may change as your knowledge grows). If you want to be able to take notes in your Bible, you can order a printed one that has space included for that purpose.

Respect the fact that if you aren't reading the Bible in its original languages, you are reading a translation/version. All translations/versions have flaws – some more than others. Certain nuances can be lost when translating a story from one language to another, especially when so much time has passed and so many cultural changes have occurred. Consult an Interlinear Bible when you need clarification.

IMPORTANT: Understand that you can't validly debate your interpretation of a verse or passage until you have studied it for yourself in its original context and form.

Discuss in a group setting why the statement above is so important.
(This is the first step in closing the divisions among God's people.)

Also understand that the best Bible for you is the one you will actually read.
See the suggestion above about the YouVersion app.

Where should I start reading?

Have you read the entire Bible?
What do you most want to read about? – the Creation? – Abraham? – Jesus' life on earth? – the ancient kings of Israel? – poetry?

Set some personal goals and stick to them. If you sincerely want to know God's Word, you will read it.

Be sincerely thankful that today we have such easy access to God's written Word and the wonderful tools we can use to help us better understand it. Never before have we had so much information at our fingertips. God has given us this special opportunity – we are stewards of it – and we must use His gift to increase our Master's house.

Watch on YouTube, or listen to on his podcast, Dr. Tony Evans. His sermons are heavily Bible-based, energetic, enlightening, and encouraging. He preaches in person at Oak Cliff Bible Fellowship in Dallas, Texas.

Protestant, Catholic, Jewish Christians. . .what's the difference?

Did you know there were so many verses about church unity in the Bible?

Do you want to be labeled as a follower of a particular human-made denomination, or do you just want to be known by others as a true follower of Christ?

How many different church buildings are in your town? Are those churches ignoring each other, secretly scornful of each other, or working with each other?

What can we do to begin to work together? How can we break down the barriers between us and strengthen the Lord's army? How can we challenge each other to grow spiritually?

How can we show our united Christian community spirit and bring more followers to Christ, so that they, too, might enter through the Door to everlasting salvation?

Pray for unity – it is God's will, and Jesus told us to pray that God's will be done here on earth.

Matthew 6:9-10

"So this is how you should pray: 'Our Father in heaven, we pray that your name will always be kept holy. We pray that your kingdom will come – that what you want will be done here on earth, the same as in heaven. . .'"

Do you want to continue group discussions?

****

More Q & A's (p.376)

Any of the topics in this section would be a good start for a small group discussion.

****

What are some common words and phrases you might hear other followers say, and what do they mean?

Have you heard others? Have you checked your Bible to make sure they are accurate sayings? There are quite a few **misquotes and errant sayings** that get passed from generation to generation.

Here are some misquotes/errant sayings to get you started:

Money is the root of all evil.
Cleanliness is next to godliness.
God helps those who help themselves.

****

****

The Time of the End (p. 414)

This would be a good topic for a 6- to 12-month regular class study. As a group, read and discuss:

Daniel, Chapters 7-12
The Olivet Discourse in Matthew 24, Mark 13, and Luke 21
Revelation, Chapters 4-22
Isaiah 13:6-13
2 Thessalonians 2:1-12
1 Corinthians 15:50-57
the book of Joel
Zechariah 14:1-9

Again, this is not an exhaustive list of prophecies about the time of the end.

Some will staunchly contend that most of the events described in the above verses have already happened. While the destruction of Jerusalem and the Temple in AD 70 was indeed highly traumatic for many Jews living at that time, that event was a shadow of the destruction that God will pour out on the unbelievers in the time of the end. (John didn't record Revelation until AD 95 – after the destruction of the Temple had happened.) Remember two facts that we have firmly established in our discussion: (1) God gives people many chances to come back to Him, and (2) God always tells us what He will do before He actually does it.

www.RevelationLogic.com

****

Major Takeaways:

Everything spiritual/heavenly/invisible
has a physical/earthly/visible
counterpart to help us understand.

All of the negative energy in this life is because of Satan.
All of the positive energy is because of God.
Literally every good thing you want to do
and actually do with Him in your heart,
honors God.
Do good – daily.

God values sincerity above everything else.
If you do something good, but you didn't truly want to,
it isn't valid and it won't be accepted
because it's counterfeit, fraud, phony, deceitful.

A final request:

If you disagree with anything written in this book, do you honestly know why you disagree? Is it because you were taught something different, or is it because you have studied the Scriptures thoroughly yourself, and you have come to a different conclusion? We should always show respect for others, but healthy, intelligent, respectful debate about interpretations can be a constructive way to grow our faith and sharpen our weapons against Satan. Please don't let our differences divide us in our God-given mission.

References

The verses quoted in this book all come from the Easy to Read Version of the Bible on the YouVersion app, with a few exceptions that are noted. Understand that no translation or version is perfect. The online Interlinear Bible tool at www.Scripture4all.org was used to study the verses in the original Bible languages and to clarify interpretations of specific words and phrases. The dictionary tools found at www.BibleHub.com were used to research the definitions of Bible words in their original languages. BibleHub also has an Interlinear Bible tool, a commentary tool, and several other study aids that were used. Other commentaries were found using internet searches. Several Jewish and Messianic Jewish websites were used. All secular historical information used is readily available on countless websites via internet searches and in a multitude of history books, some of which are available at your local library.

Semper quaeritis

EARTH TIME BEGINS

Loving Paradise in His Presence

Satan's jealous act - The Betrayal - Need for restoration

Noah passes thru door & cleansing water to new life

Abram/Abraham chosen to begin the Israelite nation

Egypt enslaves growing Israelite nation

Moses leads Israelites thru door & cleansing water to new life

Feast days given by God

Jonah, a sign for the Door, passes thru cleansing water to new life

Jesus' First Coming - Door and cleansing water open to all

Apostles begin work to lead all to Door and cleansing water

Unity of church

Jesus' Second Coming - Door closes

Full restoration is accomplished

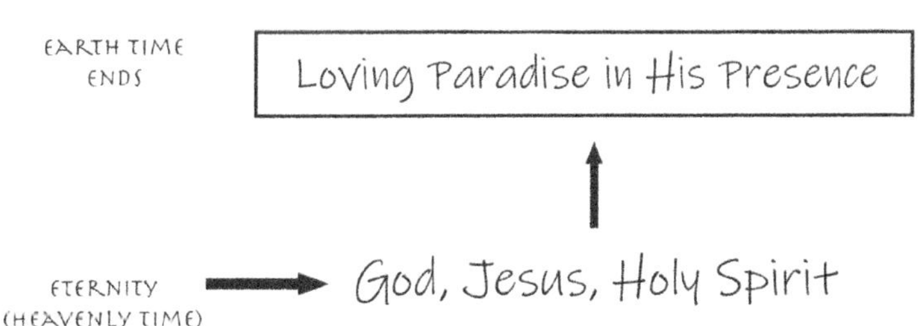

Made in the USA
Coppell, TX
13 January 2024